Human Rights and
U.S. Foreign Policy

Human Rights and U.S. Foreign Policy

Principles and Applications

Edited by

Peter G. Brown
Douglas MacLean
Center for Philosophy and
  Public Policy
University of Maryland

Lexington Books
D.C. Heath and Company
Lexington, Massachusetts
Toronto

Library of Congress Cataloging in Publication Data
Main entry under title:

Human rights and U.S. foreign policy.

   Includes index.
    1. Civil rights—Addresses, essays, lectures. 2. United States—Foreign
relations—1977—Addresses, essays, lectures. 3. Civil rights (International
law)—Addresses, essays, lectures. I. Brown, Peter G. II. MacLean,
Douglas, 1947–
K3240.6.H87   341.48'1   78-24647
ISBN 0-669-02807-X

Published simultaneously in Canada

Printed in the United States of America

International Standard Book Number: 0-669-02807-X

Library of Congress Catalog Card Number: 78-24647

Contents

               Traditions   *J. Bryan Hehir*   121

Chapter 10   **Human Rights and Intervention**   *Mark R. Wicclair*   141

Part IV   *Applications: Information and Interpretation*   159

Chapter 11   **". . . in the National Interest"**   *Peter G. Brown*   161

Chapter 12   **Monitoring Human Rights Violations: How Good
               Is the Information?**   *John Salzberg*   173

Chapter 13   **Human Rights Violations and U.S. Foreign Assis-
               tance: The Latin American Connection**   *William L.
               Wipfler*   183

Part V   *Applications: Problems of Implementing a Human
               Rights Policy*   197

Chapter 14   **Can a Human Rights Policy Be Consistent?**
               Abraham M. Sirkin   199

Chapter 15   **Security Assistance in Perspective**   *Howard M. Fish*   215

Chapter 16   **Human Rights in the Philippines and U.S.
               Responsibility**   *Richard P. Claude*   229

Chapter 17   **Arms Sales and Human Rights: The Case of South
               Korea**   *Jerome A. Cohen*   255

Chapter 18   **Arms Sales and Human Rights: The Case of Iran**
               Richard W. Cottam   281

               Index   303

               About the Contributors   311

               About the Editors   315

List of Figures
and Tables

Figures

Tables

Preface

The project that led to this book was undertaken by the Center for Philosophy and Public Policy. It began by assembling a working group, composed of the authors of the various chapters, who were chosen for their expertise and experience in areas relevant to questions of human rights and foreign policy. Group meetings were held four times in the course of a year, during which each member presented his own views on the issues and submitted them to the scrutiny and vigorous criticism of the other members.

The editors wish to thank the Ford Foundation for support of the research that led to this volume. General support to the Center for Philosophy and Public Policy from the Rockefeller Brothers Fund also contributed to completion of this work.

All the authors gave generously of their time to attend the working group meetings and to write the chapters. The writing often involved significant revision and redirection of the focus of a chapter at the suggestion of the editors. The authors graciously accepted this extra burden for the sake of producing a more unified volume.

Special thanks are due to John Salzberg and to Henry Shue for their roles in helping to organize the working group, and to Elizabeth Cahoon for attending to the details of running it. Louise Collins and Virginia Smith patiently typed the entire final manuscript as well as its several ancestors.

The content of each essay is the sole responsibility of its author. The essays do not necessarily represent the opinions of the project's sponsors, the editors, or the institutions and agencies with which the authors are associated.

December, 1978

Peter G. Brown
Douglas MacLean

Recent Human Rights Provisions in U.S. Law Governing Foreign Policy

A partial text of Section 502B of the Foreign Assistance Act of 1961, as amended, states:

(a) (1) The United States shall, in accordance with its international obligations as set forth in the Charter of the United Nations and in keeping with the constitutional heritage and traditions of the United States, promote and encourage increased respect for human rights and fundamental freedoms through the world without distinction as to race, sex, language, or religion. Accordingly, a principal goal of the foreign policy of the United States shall be to promote the increased observance of internationally recognized human rights by all countries.

(2) Except under circumstances specified in this section, no security assistance may be provided to any country the government of which engages in a consistent pattern of gross violations of internationally recognized human rights. Assistance may not be provided under chapter 5 of this part to a country the government of which engages in a consistent pattern of gross violations of internationally recognized human rights unless the President certifies in writing to the Speaker of the House of Representatives and the chairman of the Committee on Foreign Relations of the Senate that extraordinary circumstances exist warranting provision of such assistance.

(3) In furtherance of paragraphs (1) and (2), the President is directed to formulate and conduct international security assistance programs of the United States in a manner which will promote and advance human rights and avoid identification of the United States, through such programs, with governments which deny to their people internationally recognized human rights and fundamental freedoms, in violation of international law or in contravention of the policy of the United States as expressed in this section or otherwise.

(b) The Secretary of State shall transmit to Congress, as part of the presentation materials for security assistance programs proposed for each fiscal year, a full and complete report, prepared with the assistance of the Coordinator for Human Rights and Humanitarian Affairs, with respect to practices regarding the observance of and respect for internationally recognized human rights in each country proposed as a recipient of security assistance. In determining whether a government falls within the provisions of subsection (a) (3) of this section and in the preparation of any report or statement required under this section, consideration shall be given to—

(1) the relevant findings of appropriate international organizations, including nongovernmental organizations, such as the International Committee of the Red Cross; and

(2) the extent of cooperation by such government in permitting an unimpeded investigation by any such organization of alleged violations of internationally recognized human rights.

(c) (1) Upon the request of the Senate or the House of Representatives by resolution of either such House, or upon the request of the Committee on Foreign Relations of the Senate or the Committee on International Relations of the House of Representatives, the Secretary of State shall, within thirty days after receipt of such request, transmit to both such committees a statement, prepared with the assistance of the Coordinator for Human Rights and Humanitarian Affairs, with respect to the country designated in such request, setting forth—

(A) all the available information about observance of and respect for human rights and fundamental freedom in that country, and a detailed description of practices by the recipient government with respect thereto:

(B) the steps the United States has taken to—

(i) promote respect for and observance of human rights in that country and discourage any practices which are inimical to internationally recognized human rights, and

(ii) publicly or privately call attention to, and disassociate the United States and any security assistance provided for such country from, such practices;

(C) whether, in the opinion of the Secretary of State, notwithstanding any such practices—

(i) extraordinary circumstances exist which necessitate a continuation of security assistance for such country, and, if so, a description of such circumstances and the extent to which such assistance should be continued (subject to such conditions as Congress may impose under this section), and

(ii) on all the facts it is in the national interest of the United States to provide such assistance; and

(D) such other information as such committee or such House may request
. . . .

(d) For the purposes of this section—

(1) the term "gross violations of internationally recognized human rights" includes torture or cruel, inhuman, or degrading treatment or punishment, prolonged detention without charges and trial, and other flagrant denial of the right to life, liberty, or the security of person; and

(2) the term "security assistance" means—

(A) assistance under chapter 2 (military assistance) or part IV (security supporting assistance) or chapter 5 (military education and training) of this subchapter or part VI (assistance to the Middle East) of this Act;

(B) sales of defense articles or services, extensions of credits (including participations in credits), and guaranties of loans under the Arms Export Control Act; or

(C) any license in effect with respect to the export of defense articles or defense services to or for the armed forces, police, intelligence, or other internal security forces of a foreign country under section 38 of the Arms Export Control Act. Security assistance may not be provided to the police, domestic intelligence, or similar law enforcement forces of a country, and licenses may not be issued under the Export Administration Act of 1969 for the export of crime control and detection instruments and equipment to a country, the government of which engages in a consistent pattern of gross violations of internationally recognized human rights unless the President certifies in writing to the Speaker of the House of Representatives and the chairman of the Committee on Foreign Relations of the Senate that extraordinary circumstances exist warranting provision of such assistance and issuance of such licenses.

The full text of Section 116 of the Foreign Assistance Act of 1961, as amended, states:

(a) No assistance may be provided under this part to the government of any country which engages in a consistent pattern of gross violations of internationally recognized human rights, including torture or cruel, inhuman, or degrading treatment or punishment, prolonged detention without charges, or other flagrant denial of the right to life, liberty, and the security of person, unless such assistance will directly benefit the needy people in such country.

(b) In determining whether this standard is being met with regard to funds allocated under this part, the Committee on Foreign Relations of the Senate or the Committee on International Relations of the House of Representatives may require the Administrator primarily responsible for administering part I of this Act to submit in writing information demonstrating that such assistance will directly benefit the needy people in such country, together with a detailed explanation of the assistance to be provided (including the dollar mounts of such assistance) and an explanation of how such assistance will directly benefit the needy people in such country. If either committee or either House of Congress disagrees with the Administrator's justification it may initiate action to terminate assistance to any country by a concurrent resolution under section 617 of this Act.

(c) In determining whether or not a government falls within the provisions of subsection (a), consideration shall be given to the extent of cooperation of such government in permitting an unimpeded investigation of alleged violations of internationally recognized human rights by appropriate international organizations, including the International Committee of the Red Cross, or groups or persons acting under the authority of the United Nations or of the Organization of American States.

(d) The President shall transmit to the Speaker of the House of Representatives and the Committee on Foreign Relations of the Senate, in the annual presentation materials on proposed economic development assistance programs, a full and complete report regarding the steps he has taken to carry out the provisions of this section.

Introduction

The phrase "human rights" has made a remarkably sudden entry into our common political vocabulary. Increasingly, the wrongs and injustices of governments are referred to as violations of human rights, and a concern for promoting respect for human rights is now a highly publicized goal of U.S. foreign policy.

But if we ask what human rights are, or why they should be taken so seriously, we find that these are difficult questions to answer. Moreover, the lack of agreement about these fundamental questions raises other important questions about national policy. What business is it of the United States how other governments treat *their* citizens? Does a foreign policy that demands that other governments measure up to a standard of conduct it establishes make the United States a moral imperialist? Even if moral standards ought to be enforced internationally, how should this goal be integrated into and weighed against other goals of foreign policy?

Some of the essays that follow discuss the philosophical issues, including the moral foundations, that are central to understanding the concept of human rights; others address the problems of promoting human rights, in principle and in practice, as a goal of U.S. foreign policy. In all of the essays, the authors have directed their attention to recent legislation regarding human rights. Thus, the discussions in this volume refer primarily to countries that purchase arms from the United States or receive aid either directly from the United States, or indirectly through multilateral aid institutions to which public U.S. funds contribute. The human rights amendments have been attached to bills controlling arms sales and appropriating or allocating funds. This book does not, therefore, address directly the difficult questions of applying human rights policies to countries like the Soviet Union or South Africa which receive no aid and purchase no arms from the United States. Nor does it discuss some of the most egregious human rights violators, countries like Uganda, with which the United States has no contact through aid and arms sales, and thus no direct influence. Aid recipient and arms purchasing governments that violate human rights pose different complexities because of U.S. involvement in and responsibility for the existence of those regimes. The three case studies in this volume describe some of these complexities.

Human rights concerns became a publicized and prominent part of U.S. foreign policy as the result of a movement begun in Congress in 1973 and aided by the presidential campaign of Jimmy Carter in 1976. These concerns have been reflected specifically in U.S. foreign policy in a number of laws and, more recently, in many speeches by the president and the secretary of state.

That this highly publicized concern should have emerged recently in the United States is the result of a combination of historical factors that brought the abuses of its own and other governments around the world increasingly to

U.S. public attention. As Schneider explains in his essay, the human rights movement was a natural reaction to a series of exposures and revelations. Escalations of U.S. involvement in Vietnam were matched by heightened public concern about U.S. responsibility for causing havoc and suffering there and elsewhere in the world. As intelligence operations aimed at controlling the domestic politics of other countries were exposed, the U.S. public learned that its own CIA had attempted—sometimes successfully—to bring to power some of the world's most repressive governments, occasionally overthrowing popular democracies in order to do so. Finally, the exposures of Watergate and cases of domestic spying revealed the extent to which official respect for human rights and traditional civil liberties, even domestically, had declined in the United States.

This new awareness generated a human rights movement in the United States, and among its leaders one could find many veterans of the civil rights movement and the opposition to the war in Vietnam. With its high moral tone, combined with a growing disrespect for politicians and distrust of American foreign policy, the human rights movement was quick to find expression in Congress. In 1973, the House Subcommittee on International Organizations and Movements began to study the human rights conditions in countries receiving U.S. aid, holding an initial series of fifteen hearings and adopting a report entitled *Human Rights in the World Community: A Call for U.S. Leadership* (issued March 1974). That report called upon the State Department to "respond to human rights practices of nations in an objective manner without regard to whether the government is considered friendly, neutral, or unfriendly" by taking such actions as "private consultation with the government concerned; public intervention in U.N. organs and agencies; withdrawal of military assistance and sales; withdrawal of certain economic assistance programs."

Also in 1973, the Congress began to pass a series of human rights amendments to foreign assistance bills. The first one urged (that is, recommended as "the sense of Congress") that the administration link foreign assistance programs to the level of respect for human rights in the recipient countries. A curious coalition of liberals and conservatives has supported these bills. Some critics of this movement in Congress have charged that "human rights" has merely become the latest banner under which the United States is attempting to make the world conform to its will, or even that it is becoming another theme to use both to cut back on foreign aid programs, which have long been unpopular with the public, and to criticize America's traditional Communist adversaries. Congressman Harkin, however, a liberal leader of this coalition, argues that the aim is simply to institutionalize a legitimate moral objective, so that a concern for human rights will not depend entirely upon the priorities set by any administration. A truly moral goal, Harkin argues, deserves bilateral support.

Human rights advocates, both in the Congress and the administration, agree

that the U.S. commitment to promoting respect for human rights in all countries should be expressed in the rhetoric of foreign policy (see Schneider). The
fact that President Carter and Secretary of State Vance speak out publicly
about the U.S. concern for human rights, and their willingness to discuss the
subject with other heads of state, have important consequences, for good or ill
(see Cottam). Human rights is now a subject that many other governments
cannot avoid, even in their own domestic politics. International groups that
are concerned with human rights have gained wider audiences, and political
opponents of repressive governments are increasingly willing to speak out about
human rights conditions in their own countries, gambling that international
publicity and the importance for their governments of maintaining friendly
relations with the United States have created a climate where it is now safe for
them to express their grievances. Whether they have guessed right in taking
this gamble is often difficult to determine and will depend on the extent to
which the United States will back its rhetoric by using what leverage it has to
bring about changes by other governments (see Cottam and also Harkin). If
the policy merely gives high visibility to human rights, but low priority to
actions that promote them, it may be counterproductive.

Thus, another major focus of concern for human rights in U.S. foreign
policy is the leverage that attaches to large amounts of foreign assistance. A
central issue that divides the advocates of human rights in the Congress from
the Carter administration is whether this leverage should be used at the dis-
cretion of the president and the secretary of state or whether they should be
forced by law to cut foreign assistance to gross violators of human rights.

The Congress has now attached human rights amendments to all its foreign
assistance programs. These amendments define human rights violations in
identical terms. In each case they call for assistance to be withheld, or for a
negative vote on a loan request, "to the government of any country which
engages in a consistent pattern of gross violations of internationally recognized
human rights." The violations "include torture, or cruel, inhuman, or degrading treatment or punishment, prolonged detention without charges, or other
flagrant denial of the right to life, liberty, and the security of person."

The State Department is directed to enforce the human rights provisions
in these new laws and to report to Congress about the human rights conditions
in the countries receiving U.S. aid or buying U.S. arms and about the steps being
taken to improve those conditions where they are bad. The Congress also continues to hold hearings, which help it to evaluate the State Department's judgment. The final policy decisions are complicated by the fact that the human
rights provisions in both the security and the bilateral economic assistance laws
allow for their own respective types of exceptions. Security assistance, which
includes sales of arms as well as grants, may be provided to human rights violators if "extraordinary circumstances exist which necessitate a continuance
of security assistance" and if "on all the facts it is in the national interest of the

United States to provide such assistance." Economic aid may continue to human rights violators if "such assistance will directly benefit the needy people in such country."

Much of the U.S. economic assistance to other countries is administered multilaterally through the International Financial Institutions (IFIs), which include the World Bank, the Inter-American Development Bank, and others. As Harkin explains, the IFIs are heavily supported by congressionally appropriated U.S. funds but are operated with virtually no congressional control beyond initial decisions about level of appropriation. The U.S. directors of the IFIs receive instructions from and report to the White House and the State Department. As of 1977, as a result of a bill that Congressman Harkin coauthored, U.S. directors of the IFIs are instructed to determine their vote on specific loans by the human rights conditions in recipient countries. A stronger bill, that would have given Congress more direct control over IFI loans by adding as a condition of U.S. allocations that specifically named countries would not receive World Bank funds, was opposed by World Bank President Robert McNamara and by President Carter, and was defeated in Congress in 1977. Similar but weaker human rights amendments have been attached to bills appropriating U.S. funds for the International Monetary Fund and for the Export-Import Bank.

Questions of Principle

The new human rights provisions in U.S. laws, and indeed the entire human rights initiative, raise many questions about the principles on which they are based and about the application of these principles. Here, we survey these questions, beginning with the most basic and general of them.

What Are Human Rights? Although the term "human rights" has recently gained wide acceptance and use, it is seldom made clear exactly what these rights are or what it means for something to be a human right. To say that an individual (or a group) has a right to something is to say that he or she has a claim to that thing, and other individuals, groups, or institutions are morally obliged to respect that claim. Moreover, if the claim involves a *right*, and not merely a preference or some other good, the moral weight of that claim cannot normally be overridden by considerations of social welfare. Only extraordinary circumstances can justify ignoring or violating a right, although it is one of the outstanding problems of moral philosophy to characterize those circumstances.

Some of the clearest examples of rights are special rights (so named to distinguish them from human rights), which derive from special circumstances. Thus, if Smith and Jones make an agreement, in which Smith borrows ten dollars from Jones on Tuesday in exchange for a promise to repay Jones on Friday, then Jones has a right to receive ten dollars from Smith on Friday. Jones could tell Smith to forget the debt, but if Jones wants the money, Smith has an obligation to turn it over to him, because of the agreement they made on Tuesday. It won't do for Smith to say on Friday that he wants the money or that he needs it more than Jones, or that he plans to give it instead to a very worthy cause, even if Jones happened to win a lottery on Thursday. Jones has a right to that money, and stronger conditions would be needed to excuse Smith from paying it if Jones asks for it. Certain legal rights are special rights, too, because they derive from specific agreements reached among a country's citizens, or between citizens and the government.

Human rights differ from special rights by not depending on any special circumstances like a specific agreement. But it is precisely this fact about human rights that makes them more difficult to understand and defend, for it is not obvious where we should turn to justify these rights. One view, defended by Bedau, holds that human rights give individuals a veto power over what may be done to them for the sake of the good of society. He argues that an examination of some of the very different lists of human rights that are familiar to us shows nevertheless a continuity in the underlying moral principles the lists are meant to express. They all attempt to guarantee that the institutions governing a society respect and protect the freedom and liberty of all the society's citizens. Bedau identifies four characteristics that are common to all the lists and can serve as criteria for determining when a right is a human right. These are: all persons have them, all persons share them equally, they do not depend on any special status or relations, and they can be claimed from or asserted against the actions of any and all other humans and institutions.

Beitz defends a different view, which holds that human rights express universal requirements of social justice. Principles of justice are derived from the conditions necessary for social institutions to be regarded as morally legitimate. According to Beitz, these principles guarantee individuals within a group the satisfaction of various interests, by structuring the distribution of both the benefits and the burdens of social cooperation. Human rights, therefore, determine which interests deserve satisfaction and which individuals or institutions have the obligation to satisfy those interests.

Still another justification of human rights is defended here by Scanlon. His view is that the defense of something as a right has two components. The first identifies the object of a right as something that is of great value to any individual, with which a government ought to have either no authority to interfere or for which it has the duty to provide assistance. The second component is an empirical claim that unless we take specific measures in our arrangement of social institutions to protect these valuable things, individuals or the government are likely either to violate them or else to fail to provide them. Scanlon's view is designed to allow historical change in what counts as a human right, according

to changing values and to changes in such things as the technologies available
to governments.

It is important to determine which justification of human rights is correct,
because there are substantial disagreements among the different views that are
relevant for determining policy. Perhaps the most important of these disagreements appears in the specific lists of human rights, and their relative priorities,
generated by the different theories.

What Are the Priorities among Human Rights? Human rights are often divided
into three broad categories, a division endorsed by Secretary of State Vance's
definition of human rights. First are personal security rights. These include
the right not to be subjected to torture; to cruel, inhuman, or degrading treatment or punishment; or to arbitrary arrest, imprisonment, or execution. Security rights also include the right not to have one's home invaded and the right
to a fair, prompt, and public trial. These are sometimes called forbearance
rights because, except for the last example (which, in the view of some—for
example, Bedau—fits better in another category), the corresponding duties of
other individuals are duties to refrain from taking certain actions. The government, too, must not interfere, and it may have the further duty to take
necessary steps to prevent common abuses.

The second category of rights are civil and political liberties. These include
the freedoms of thought, religion, speech, the press, and movement. They also
include the freedom to participate in government. Again, except for the last
of these rights, the corresponding duties are primarily of forbearance, although
protecting these freedoms may also require other positive duties of enforcement.

The third category includes economic or welfare rights, the right to fulfill
such vital needs as food, shelter, health care, and education. Depending on
what the correct justification of human rights turns out to be, this category
might be expanded or it might be shrunk or deleted altogether. The corresponding duties involve more positive forms of action, and satisfying all
these rights may be very costly in some societies at some times. On the other
hand, more affluent societies can better afford to fulfill more of people's basic
needs, or fulfill them to a greater degree, than poorer societies. Certain welfare
rights might thus be introduced as human rights at a certain level of development.

The human rights clauses in the new foreign assistance legislation strongly
emphasize personal security rights and give limited attention to civil and
political liberties. No explicit mention is made of economic rights. Is this
emphasis morally justified?

Bedau, agreeing with Justice Brandeis that "the right to be let alone . . .
[is] the right most valued by civilized men," argues that the emphasis on
personal security rights as the proper concern for human rights actions is

justifiable. In the first place, he maintains that people value personal security rights more than economic rights, and that unless personal security rights are assured, civil and political liberties cannot be enjoyed. Moreover, Bedau believes that if people are left alone to manage for themselves, either they can usually fulfill their own economic needs or else they live in societies that simply are unable to fulfill their economic rights. In the latter case, he argues, it would certainly be cruel for the United States to deny assistance to a country if it failed to meet the needs of its citizens because it cannot afford to.

Beitz claims that giving priority to personal security rights is not morally justifiable. He argues that the requirements of social justice show that economic rights are morally as valuable and as basic as human rights that guarantee personal and political freedom, and he is therefore critical of the existing legislation for ignoring economic rights.

Shue focuses on the duties corresponding to various rights. He argues that all rights require both positive and negative duties of others if they are to be enjoyed, and so there is no clear, morally relevant distinction to be drawn between "negative" (that is, personal security) rights and "positive" (that is, economic) rights. He goes on to argue that negative and positive duties are morally indistinguishable. Thus, like Beitz, Shue disagrees with Bedau and is critical of what he takes to be the undefended prejudice of the current laws.

A policy that gave a higher priority to economic rights might have far-reaching consequences. Since we are talking about human rights, which are claims that can be made even against people outside one's own society, the duties to satisfy these rights in some country might fall not only upon *its* own government and people, but upon other governments and individuals as well, including the United States.

What Government Action on Behalf of Human Rights Elsewhere Is Permissible?
Whatever one decides about the nature of and priorities among human rights, a decision to promote any human rights as a goal of our foreign policy raises additional issues. Most opponents of the human rights initiative in Congress argue that the current laws are strategically unwise ways of accomplishing their stated goals, and are morally wrong for being both moralistic and interventionistic.

Regarding the question of strategy, Sirkin maintains that the many goals that the U.S. human rights policy aims to achieve can sometimes conflict with each other, and that these goals can only be served consistently by pragmatic policies. This means that the United States should remain as flexible as possible, making decisions on a case-by-case basis after a careful examination of all the information, rather than tying its hands with laws that let a single standard override all other considerations, goals, and interests. Although the human rights provisions contain clauses providing for the overriding of human rights considerations, Sirkin believes that U.S. human rights objectives would be better served without the mandatory provisions at all. This conclusion is challenged by

MacLean, who suggests that America's overall national interest might best be
served by promoting strict human rights constraints on foreign assistance programs. Strict provisions for using these programs to further human rights goals
might have the additional advantage of being an effective enforcement mechanism of international law on human rights.

One often-heard argument is that the human rights laws impose our values
on other countries, whose different cultures sometimes reflect different moral
standards. Also, by trying to exact a certain standard of conduct from other
governments, we are intervening in matters of domestic concern.

The first part of this argument, which we may call the issue of cultural
relativism, is addressed by two of the chapters in this volume. Scanlon tries to
show that human rights are minimal standards to expect of any government and,
more importantly, that they are neutral among all political ideologies. Thus,
he thinks that the argument from moral relativism, rather than being a tolerant
interpretation of the differeing practices of other cultures, instead masks an
attitude of cultural superiority. Because human rights are such basic values,
if we assume that another culture does not respect them, it can only be because
we assume this other culture simply lacks a full conception of values, not that
it holds different values. This last point is also made by MacLean, who goes on
to claim that arguments about cultural relativism are irrelevant to human rights
policies. The fact is that virtually every nation has endorsed in its own constitution at least the human rights listed in the U.S. foreign assistance laws, and these
same rights are included in the International Covenants currently in force and
thus are part of international law. MacLean argues further that criticizing the
human rights policies as moralistic is not a good reason for abandoning them,
because the reasons that make moralistic behavior objectionable in individuals
do not apply to nations.

The question of interference by one government in the affairs of another
government is a complicated one, and it is discussed in three of the chapters in
this volume. Hehir contrasts two different historical models for thinking about
intervention. In the days of St. Thomas Aquinas (1224-1274) and the *Respublica
Christiana,* when it was widely believed that the world ought to be united under
Christian laws as infallibly interpreted by the Pope, the question of intervention
on behalf of those laws was not an intellectually difficult one. But by the time
of Grotius (1583-1645) the belief in the infallibility of Church doctrine had
eroded, and together with the beginnings of the nation-state, the climate was
one that supported nonintervention as a norm. Although nonintervention continues today to be the norm, the human rights movement is one indication of a
movement toward a more accepting view of certain kinds of intervention.
Hehir's analysis makes clear that the dispute about this depends on the moral
significance of national boundaries for limiting government actions, about
which there is perhaps less agreement today than at other times.

Buergenthal discusses the status in international law of intervention on behalf of human rights. He calls attention to clear precedents for certain forms of intervention that definitely include the steps required in the human rights provisions of the foreign assistance laws. Buergenthal also emphasizes a legal distinction between what is, in commonsense terms, a domestic matter and what is, in legal terms, strictly within domestic jurisdiction and hence a matter of national sovereignty. Some domestic matters, including human rights issues, are by international agreement matters that fall within international jurisdiction and enforcement. This point, according to Buergenthal, is beyond legal dispute.

Wicclair argues that regardless of the status of international law, no sound arguments show that all forms of intervention on behalf of human rights are morally unacceptable. Although all people might agree that they should in general be ruled by their own government and left alone by other governments, none of the moral justifications of this general principle of nonintervention would apply to regimes that violate the human rights of their own population.

Questions of Application

How Should the Exception Clauses Be Interpreted? The decision to provide security assistance or economic aid to a country, and likewise the decision to terminate such aid or sales, is usually made by the executive branch of the government, which can use its power to reward, punish, or threaten governments in a variety of ways. The human rights legislation now directs the executive branch to use this power to promote human rights. Several congressional committees, primarily the House Subcommittee on International Organizations, as Salzberg explains, have taken up the difficult task of gathering information and assessing the human rights conditions in countries that receive U.S. economic aid or security assistance (including arms sales). In addition, the State Department, under the direction of the newly created office of the Assistant Secretary for Human Rights and Humanitarian Affairs, is required to file its own reports to Congress on the human rights conditions in recipient countries. It is useful to compare the State Department reports to the testimony received by the House Subcommittee. As Salzberg indicates, this comparison shows the State Department to be an unwilling critic of recipients of U.S. economic assistance and of purchasers and grantees of military assistance. Most observers agree that the reports by the Department of State are incomplete, less than candid, and biased in favor of nations State considers strategically important.

Once it has been determined that a country has a consistent record of gross violations of human rights, the legislation calls for U.S. aid and arms sales to be cut to that country. These laws, however, allow for two sorts of exceptions, one that applies to security assistance and arms sales and one that applies to the various forms of bilateral and multilateral economic aid. Regarding the first, the Congress asks the State Department to report any "extraordinary circumstances" that would justify continuing to provide the country with security assistance; and a judgment as to whether "on all the facts it is in the national interest of the United States to provide such assistance."

One problem about this process is that the Congress has never made clear what it means by extraordinary circumstances or what should count as being in the national interest. These exceptions clearly provide loopholes that could conceivably be invoked in nearly every instance, since a program of security assistance would never be initiated for a country unless it was thought to be in the national interest, in some sense, to do so. Brown discusses this issue in his chapter and argues that the concept of national interest is too vague to be a significant guide in setting national policy on human rights issues. He defends a principle whereby the government cannot be excused from its duties to protect and promote human rights anywhere in the world unless fulfilling duties correlative to these rights would jeopardize the rights of Americans.

Regarding economic aid, the new laws allow exceptions if it can be shown that ". . . such assistance will directly benefit the needy people in such country." For certain forms of economic assistance this clause is unproblematic. If the United States is engaged in a program to give food to a country whose government violates human rights, and that food is reaching the hungry and starving, it would be cruel and pointless to use this program as a tool for reforming the practices of the government. Similarly, there could be situations where a government must cease to protect some human rights in a time of desperation. In such cases terminating economic aid because of the government's practices might just exacerbate an already bad situation.

But these situations are not typical, and in other instances it is far more difficult to determine whether aid directly benefits the needy. Much of the U.S. bilateral developmental aid, and most of the aid administered through the international financial institutions that the United States heavily supports, goes to build such things as transportation and industrial capacity. While this aid helps a country to develop, quite often the benefits of that development fail to reach the neediest people of the country. The rationale for such programs is that the soundest way to assist an underdeveloped country is by helping it to industrialize, to modernize its technologies, and otherwise to become a participant in the world economy. The benefits of such modernization will then trickle down and eventually make all its citizens better off.

Unfortunately, as Wipfler claims for many Latin American countries, the disparity between rich and poor often grows and the trickle-down of benefits is slow or imperceptible. Harkin even suggests that if economic aid has the effect of increasing the difference in wealth between the rich and the poor, this fact is sufficient to conclude that such aid is not directly benefitting the neediest. Sirkin, however, thinks the issue is not so easily determined. Aid programs aimed exclusively at the needy, which do not help to build a nation's economy, he believes, might be unfair to the future generations of that country's citizens. Such aid could assure that the country will remain relatively poor in the future even though the distribution of the meager resources within the country is more equal.

Wipfler believes that the real reason the United States has been committed to a course of highly centralized industrial development is that the U.S. government, like the international banks, wants to make underdeveloped countries attractive to private investors, thinking that this is the fastest and surest way to develop a country. All too often, however, the attractiveness of a country for investors depends on its having a stable government, and this has often turned out to encourage governmental repression rather than democracy. The cessation of bilateral U.S. and multilateral aid when Salvador Allende was elected President of Chile, and the dramatic increase of international aid and loans when he was overthrown by the brutal Pinochet-led junta, tragically illustrate what banks and industries often determine to be an attractive climate for investors.

Which Special Circumstances Should Be Taken into Account? The rationale for attaching human rights conditions to our foreign assistance and arms sales programs is that these programs give us some leverage and influence over the governments we aid (as well as some responsibility for their practices), and that we ought to use this influence to promote the cause of human rights. Some features of those programs, and of the recipient countries, complicate these attempts.

Fish's description of the U.S. security assistance programs shows some of the reasons why these programs might be ineffective tools for promoting human rights. Because the aid and sales that are approved for any country in a given year are delivered over a period of several years, a large backlog of undelivered orders is built up. With a single exception, Chile, terminations of security assistance because of human rights are terminations of sales and grants only, not of deliveries. So it can be years before the punitive effects of a cut-off are even felt. Moreover, since security assistance is increasingly taking the form of sales and favorable loans or loan guarantees, rather than grants, terminating deliveries of ordered material could lead to default on loans and could result in economic costs to U.S. industries that have begun production on orders received. Other countries can usually find other arms suppliers anyway.

Aspects of some of the particular countries usually singled out for having poor human rights records illustrate other difficulties confronting the human rights movement in its attempt to integrate human rights goals into U.S. foreign policy. The three case studies presented here by Claude, Cohen, and Cottam have several common features. Each country has a depressing human rights record, and each is a major recipient of U.S. foreign aid or security assistance. These three particular countries—the Philippines, South Korea, and Iran— happen to share other important features. In each case the United States has some special responsibility for the existing government, thus raising in especially sharp terms the question of U.S. complicity in human rights violations. Each of these countries is also normally deemed vital to U.S. interests, a fact which has a number of implications for human rights policies. Obviously, the more we need to maintain a friendly alliance with a country, the less likely we will be to use what leverage we may have, even if that government could not maintain power without our aid. But this also means that it is easier, as Sirkin points out, for the United States to make demands upon small, nonstrategically located countries that are not vital to U.S. interests. This has led to the charge that the United States is not applying its human rights policies evenhandedly and is not willing to advance the moral cause of promoting human rights if the United States stands to bear some of the costs.

Claude's discussion of the Philippines shows that if such U.S. military installations as Clark Air Field and Subic Naval Base are taken to have strategic importance, the government of Ferdinand Marcos has considerable leverage over what the United States can demand. Nevertheless, our aid to the Marcos government shows us to be more than an unwilling hostage to blackmail. U.S. narcotics control aid helped to build a modern police force that has oppressed and tortured political dissidents, and security assistance to the Philippines has increased dramatically since Marcos suspended habeas corpus in 1971 and declared martial law the following year. This security assistance has created a backlog of undelivered orders that protects the Marcos regime for several years from the effects of a possible termination of new sales and grants without a termination of deliveries. The United States seems to be rewarding repression in the Philippines while simultaneously attempting to promote human rights.

From 1948, when it helped to create the Republic of Korea, the United States often used its influence to promote democratic government there. Cohen describes how the United States was at first willing to exert some leverage on the authoritarian rule resulting from General Park Chung-Hee's military coup in 1961, and how, until 1965, the United States tried to remain neutral between Park and his political opponents. But then the need for Korean combat assistance in Vietnam led to Washington's embracing Park and supporting him by stepping up its aid to the ROK. After gaining unambiguous support from the United States General Park declared martial law in 1972 and instituted changes that have further eroded the respect for human rights. The government of South Korea is now responsible for widespread arbitrary arrests and torture, restraints on liberties, and a judicial system that can be arbitrarily used for political repression. Yet U.S. military aid to South Korea continues to flow liberally.

Cottam describes a series of events in Iran, which we now know to have been engineered by the CIA, that ousted the liberal but unstable democratic rule of Dr. Mohammed Mossadeq in 1952, in order to bring to power a more stable regime. This was deemed necessary in order to deal seriously with the internal Communist threat and to save Iran from domination by the Soviet Union, with whom it shares 1,200 miles of border. These events led, in 1955 and with American support, to the assumption of dictatorial control of Iran by Mohammed Reza Shah Pahlavi and the formation of SAVAK, an internal security force designed to maintain order. Since then, until quite recently, the government was stable but corrupt, amounting to a dictatorship of the parvenue. Although Iran's great wealth is not equitably distributed, some of it has "trickled down" in a period when Iran's rate of economic growth has been comparable to Japan's. But if economic human rights have been partially served under the Shah, political rights and personal liberties have suffered. SAVAK's suppression of all political dissent in Iran made the Shah's dictatorship a secure one, and curbs on SAVAK's activities, motivated in part by human rights pressures from the United States, have made the Shah's rule insecure again. Although U.S. responsibility for the decline of personal and political liberties in Iran was deep, American military sales to Iran began to increase in the Nixon-Kissinger era and have increased dramatically since then. This has allowed Iran to play a surrogate role for the United States in the Middle East, and it has been economically valuable for helping to offset American oil purchases. The issue of human rights in Iran is one that Americans seem willing to consider only to the extent that they minimize the perceived security threat of the Soviet Union. Complicating these factors is the additional fact that Iran is a close ally of Israel, and thus helps to prevent Arab domination of the Middle East. So although President Carter has said of the Shah that "there is no other leader on earth who is as close a friend and ally," he has also criticized the Shah's human rights record. Cottam suggests, at the end of his chapter, that the criticism, its truth notwithstanding, has forced changes that have seriously threatened the Shah's ability to rule and may have jeopardized valuable U.S. interests in the area. Cottam regards U.S. policy in Iran to be a demonstration of what Sirkin deplores as establishing a foreign policy without paying attention to strategy.

Even among those who agree in their criticisms of the Shah's regime there may be differences of opinion as to where the responsibility lies for the threat to U.S. interests that the current crisis in Iran precipitated. Some might blame the human rights policy, but one could as well criticize America's past involvement in Iran and its unflagging insistence on full support of the Shah. If the Shah is forced from power, this may be another instance of backing the wrong horse in U.S. foreign policy, and a costly one at that.

The essays in this book explore different responses to the moral and political questions that a human rights policy must answer. If public opinion, which may ultimately play a major role in guiding this policy, is to be formed in a responsible way, we must understand what human rights are, how they ought to be weighed against each other and compared to other values, and what obligations and responsibilities they entail, for governments and for individuals. This will include coming to terms with moral and philosophical questions as well as becoming aware of U.S. policies and the circumstances in other countries. This volume is intended to help with both of these tasks.

**Part I
Background: The New Initiative**

1

A New Administration's New Policy: The Rise to Power of Human Rights

Mark L. Schneider

The administration of President Jimmy Carter has achieved global awareness of the centrality of human rights to its declared foreign policy. Yet little attention has been given to the complex set of origins that made the rise to power of human rights almost inevitable. The human rights policy did not materialize unannounced in the American political arena on January 20, 1977. Rather it was an inevitable consequence of a series of massive tremors— domestic and foreign—that shook its own political system over the past decade. Once adopted, its implementation has been far from smooth, yet it has been persistent and it visibly has altered significant aspects of U.S. foreign policy.

Historically, one may find it difficult to understand why the concern for human rights in American foreign policy in 1977 was viewed as a break with the past rather than as a continuation. The United states, from its very beginnings, enveloped itself in moral bindings and asserted its intent to conduct its foreign policies in accord with universal values. However arrogant to others it may have appeared, there was a belief that the New World experiment in government offered a model for all other nations as well. Nevertheless, it is apparent that this moral ideal was balanced and frequently overwhelmed by our pursuit of self-interest, narrowly defined. In minor incursions and major interventions, the United States sent armed forces around the globe 150 times over the past two centuries in pursuit of its foreign policy interests. Yet the concern for human rights was not a hypocritical mask for an underlying realpolitik. This concern, and the pursuit of our own interests, maintained an uneasy state of coexistence. The U.S. Government frequently defended individual freedom, self-determination, and civil liberties in statements condemning violations of human rights by other governments. Pogroms against the Jews, a massacre of Armenians, the denial of freedom to other colonies— all drew sharp public statements from a variety of U.S. presidents.

But if there really was a global concern for liberty reflected in the declarations of Presidents Wilson, Roosevelt, Kennedy, and others, the question remains as to why respect for human rights is both a theme and a specific foreign policy objective of increased priority for the administration of Jimmy Carter.

This essay was begun before the author was appointed to his current position. The views are his own and do not necessarily reflect the views of the Department of State.

3

The answers can be found by examining the dominant domestic and foreign policy events of recent years. In the nation's domestic experience, the civil rights struggle educated vast numbers of Americans, particularly the young, to governmental support of or acquiescence in the denial of basic rights. Segregation's destructive impact on human lives filled millions of television screens in the nation's living rooms for a decade. At the same time, the civil rights movement with its stress on rights and values was visibly transforming our legal and political institutions and, ultimately, human attitudes and behavior.

Then, there was Watergate. It revealed the unfortunate way in which men could use the instruments of power, and it placed in stark outline the question of the adequacy of institutional guarantees against the arbitrary action of governors. Watergate was something done to people by a government out of control. The American public understood fully for the first time in many years that its own government could act arbitrarily and capriciously for self-serving purposes, thereby impinging on the rights of American citizens.

Yet Watergate also yielded a second reaction, a reaction which not only was shared by foreigners, but was magnified abroad. The combination of a free press, an independent judiciary, and an aroused public opinion could combat and halt the excesses of even the most powerful political officials. Watergate was brought to an end without a coup and without violence, thus not only amazing the outside world, but supporting an underlying faith of Americans in the resiliency and strength of their political system. The experience could not help but support the notion that excesses of other governments also could be arrested by effective institutional checks and balances.

The international sphere during the 1960s and early 1970s played the dominant role, however, in raising human rights to its current high profile. Vietnam tore through the entire social, political, and economic fabric of this nation. It was the catalytic event that generated a national receptivity to a higher stress on human rights in foreign policy. To many, Vietnam represented an abdication of moral leadership and a denial of past values. Our perception of the Vietnam conflict included a vague notion that somehow the United States was preventing self-determination for others. We saw our own country intruding in a small land thousands of miles away, involving the United States in a violent and brutal conflict. The nation saw Americans killed, Vietnamese killed, and questions of purpose answered by body counts and predictions of imminent victory. The national interest and national security objectives seemed to have little connection to U.S. support for the Thieu regime or to the bombing of Cambodia. It seemed to represent a course of conduct in total contradiction to the American people's view of themselves. Many Americans felt that their government was expending huge financial and human resources in ways that compounded human suffering and was insensitive to the antidemocratic and repressive nature of the South Vietnamese regime.

Vietnam also posed a challenge to the balance between executive and legislative powers. One has only to recall the first Senate Foreign Relations Committee hearings by Senator J. William Fulbright that began to disclose to the public what was occurring in Indochina. From that moment forward, a sense of alienation from the war began to grow among the American people and clearly within the Congress. Year by year, the Congress went through a struggle over military authorization and foreign assistance bills, which hinged on Vietnam. A growing segment of the Congress began to feel a deep frustration at their inability to bring a halt to American involvement in the war. In that process, one sees the same names then pressing for an end to U.S. involvement who later raised critical questions about the absence of sufficient weight to human rights concerns. In the Senate, these critics included Senators Mansfield, Church, John Sherman Cooper, Clifford Case, Kennedy, Brooke, McGovern, and Hatfield; in the House, Representatives Fraser, Harrington, Abzug, Ryan, and Burton.

The rhetoric was changing in the debate as well. Opponents of the war initially dealt on the same narrow grounds as the war's advocates, examining U.S. involvement in terms of a narrow definition of national interest and national security: Were we overextended? Was the expenditure of resources disproportional to the objectives being pursued?

After Cambodia and Kent State, however, the Vietnam War became almost exclusively a moral, not a military, question for many in the Congress. Speakers on the floor of the House and Senate turned more and more to attacking the Vietnam policy for being in conflict with certain basic moral values.

In the 92nd Congress alone, some 200 amendments to halt or restrict the war were filed. Piece by piece, the goals of these bills became part of the law. But an effort that began in 1968 did not play itself out for five years. And in the Congress each year, the Military Procurement and the Defense Department Appropriations bills and the Foreign Assistance authorizing and appropriating bills became battlefields for the Vietnam debate. In the process, an annual psychological wrenching took place, particularly when final passage was pending. Those bills contained funds for the war along with funds for all defense programs. Each year, how to vote on final passage produced inner-office debate. A handful, but a growing one, in the Senate and the House began to oppose even final passage of these bills.

The debate over Vietnam set in motion three undercurrents whose natural extension included a concern for the way other countries treated their own citizens and explains as well the nearly identical overlap of antiwar and pro-human rights advocates: first, the question of foreign policy in conflict with basic human values; second, the near impossibility in a democractic society of conducting, over a long period of time, a foreign policy against the opposition of a substantial segment of the people, particularly when they hold their views with great passion; third, the willingness of Congress to reassert its role in determining the direction of U.S. foreign policy, and the tendency of Congress to be more responsive to popular opinion than the previous administrations had been. All three of these trends have a direct relationship to the rise to power of human rights issues in this administration's foreign policy.

In addition to Vietnam, a series of linkages with repressive military regimes abroad helped add to a greening of American opinion which made many Americans uneasy about the thrust of U.S. foreign policy. First, there was military support to a Greek junta even as it was suspended by the Council of Europe because of its human rights abuses. Greece's NATO allies adopted a policy of exclusion, all save the United States.

Following Greece came Brazil, where several hearings by Senator Frank Church focused attention on the human rights abuses of the Medici government. In those hearings, the public safety police training programs of the U.S. government also were criticized as tying the U.S. to the abuses of the Brazilian police and military.

In East Timor, the occupation by Indonesian forces and the U.S. refusal to join a clamor of criticism from the United Nations also were the subject of hearings. Then came the coup in Chile and the clear evidence, other issues notwithstanding, that the United States was willing to cut virtually all assistance to a democratically elected government, however inept, because of its ideology, and to provide an excess of support to the military junta that came to power in a coup, no matter how brutal.

The subject of refugees also added impetus to the human rights issue. Hearings of the Senate Refugee Subcommittee, chaired by Senator Edward M. Kennedy, sharply criticized the previous administration for its failure to act with sufficient speed or with adequate resources in Bangladesh, Cyprus, or Vietnam. Hearings on the plight of refugees from the Soviet Union, particularly Soviet Jews, also were held and the administration was criticized for excluding human rights considerations from détente. Each of those events buttressed the belief that a breach had opened between American values and American foreign policy.

If this was the environment that virtually assured a greater concern for human rights as a key plank of the platform of any Democratic standard-bearer, there was a more concrete encouragement in the law as well.

The expansion of involvement in U.S. foreign policy of the Congress, a cyclical performer on the U.S. foreign policy stage, continued in the aftermath of Vietnam. Restrictions on the president's emergency powers, demands that executive agreements be submitted to the Senate for approval, and the War Powers Resolution—all were part of the same movement. The War Powers Resolution, enacted over a presidential veto in 1973, was the most significant step, when Congress tried to restrict the capability of the executive branch to involve the United States in hostilities abroad. It required congressional action, after a brief time period, on any use of U.S. troops abroad. Congress was to be consulted and Congress was to have the final word.

In the human rights area, the same congressional forces who were opposing the war multiplied the legislative conditions on U.S. foreign policy. Perhaps the first broad statement came in 1973, when the Congress accepted an amendment introduced by Senator James Abourezk, which became Section 32 of the Foreign Assistance Act of 1973.[1] That section reads: "It is the sense of Congress that the President should deny any economic or military assistance to the government of any foreign country which practices the internment or imprisonment of that country's citizens for political purposes."

In 1973 Senator Edward M. Kennedy introduced the first amendment related to human rights abuses in Chile.[2] The amendment was only hortatory, however, expressing the sense of the Congress that efforts should be made to enhance respect for human rights in that country.

From that point forward, the action taken by Congress imposed stronger obligations, which were more broadly directed at a variety of human rights and more specifically linked to international obligations and standards.

In 1974, a series of provisions relating to human rights were enacted into law. Congress adopted a provision placing a ceiling on military assistance to South Korea unless that country made "substantial progress in the observance of internationally recognized standards of human rights."[3] The legislation also moved from exhortation with respect to Chile to a cutoff of military assistance and a limitation on economic assistance.[4] It was the same bill that also was amended to include a prohibition on the use of foreign assistance to train or support foreign police or internal intelligence forces.[5] That amendment effectively repealed the public safety program.

In 1974, a more far-reaching provision, but one with less immediate force than the Korea, Chile, or public safety provisions, was enacted. Section 502B affected all security assistance. It applied to any country "which engages in a consistent pattern of gross violations of internationally recognized human rights, including torture or cruel, inhuman, or degrading treatment or punishment, prolonged detention without charges, or other flagrant denial of the right to life, liberty, and the security of the person."[6] However, this provision still merely expressed a "sense of Congress."

In 1974, the human rights issue also extended itself into the area of trade. The Jackson-Vanik amendment[7] was adopted, conditioning the access to trade preferences of "nonmarket economy" countries on their emigration policies. Senator Henry Jackson and Representative Charles Vanik sponsored the provision, which effectively placed human rights conditions on a key component of détente.

The following year, additional human rights provisions were adopted. Section 116,[8] modeled on Section 502B, was enacted, affecting all bilateral economic assistance. It exchanged the hortatory shell around Section 502B for a mandatory provision, stating, "No assistance may be provided under this part to the government of any country which engages in a consistent pattern of gross violations of internationally recognized human rights, including torture or cruel, inhuman, degrading treatment or punishment, prolonged detention without charges, or other flagrant denial of the right to life, liberty, and the security of the person, unless such assistance will directly benefit the needy people in such country." Congress also specified that it could require a report to demonstrate whether the assistance was benefiting the needy and, in the event it disagreed with that report's conclusion, initiate a concurrent resolution to end the program.

This provision was the first across-the-board conditioning of foreign assistance on a country's human rights record. Congress, in enacting the Foreign Assistance Act of 1973, initiated the "New Directions" concept in U.S. bilateral economic assistance, directing that projects shift from large-scale capital transfers toward an emphasis on the crucial areas of food production, nutrition, rural development, population planning, health, education, public administration, and human resource development. These were the areas identified as most directly affecting the lives of the poor. The exception to the human rights provision interfaced significantly with this new thrust in the direction of U.S. foreign assistance policy. It made it likely that much of the aid which otherwise would be barred to violating countries could still continue if it met the criteria of directly benefiting the needy.

In 1975, Congressman Tom Harkin extended the human rights conditions affecting bilateral economic assistance to the Inter-American Development and African Development Banks.[9] That provision directed the secretary of the treasury to instruct the U.S. delegate to those banks to vote against loans to countries which "engage in a consistent pattern of violations. . . ." Once more, a discretionary loophole was provided if the projects were designed to benefit the needy.

The more vigorous course of legislative policy was reaffirmed in 1976 when the original Section 502B was amended from a sense of Congress statement to establish a mandatory cutoff of security assistance for gross violators.[10] In addition, full and complete reports were required on the human rights conditions in countries which are proposed to receive security assistance. The original bill passed by the Congress made the cutoff of such security assistance self-enforcing. That bill was vetoed by Gerald Ford. The revised version maintained the same restriction on assistance to gross violators but its enforcement depended on subsequent congressional action. Instead of an absolute bar in the law to such assistance, unless extraordinary circumstances existed to justify a finding that such aid was in the national interest, the new law simply set forth that concept as a statement of policy.

The Civil Rights movement, Watergate, Vietnam, a revulsion at the support for repressive regimes, and the intervention of Congress to place human rights conditions on important aspects of U.S. foreign policy—these were the forces that propelled human rights into the foreign policy debate in the presidential campaign of 1976.

In the primary campaign, virtually all the Democratic contenders established human rights as a major plank in their foreign policy platforms. Jimmy Carter focused on human rights in many of his foreign policy statements and emphasized that issue in the foreign policy debate with Gerald Ford during the general election campaign. Carter's strong religious background and his living with the civil rights experience of the South made it natural for him to respond to the human rights issue. His campaign was built to a considerable extent on a lack of moral leadership in Washington, and human rights was an effective example.

For Carter, perhaps more than some other Democratic candidates, the human rights issue also carried special benefits. Many commentators, in the aftermath of the convention, asked whether the party activists would do their share in supporting the Democratic nominee. Many of those groups, young people, volunteer organizations, church-affiliated groups, broad-based citizen groups, even some elements of labor such as the UAW, responded to the appeal of the human rights issue. Even the more conservative elements of the labor movement favored the stress on human rights, particularly in dealing with the Soviet Union. Human rights was one factor, clearly not the only or even the major one, but a factor nevertheless, in stirring additional enthusiasm for the party nominee. And during the campaign, it became a recurrent theme in the candidate's attack on the incumbent foreign policy of Gerald Ford and Henry Kissinger.

For all of these reasons, it is not strange that on taking the oath of office on January 20, 1977, President Jimmy Carter pledged, "Because we are free, we can never be indifferent to the fate of freedom elsewhere. Our moral sense dictates a clear-cut preference for those societies which share with us an abiding respect for individual human rights." It can be argued as well that the administration of President Carter was the first in recent years free to raise the banner of human rights. It was the first administration that was both identified clearly with the civil rights movement and unentangled by the Vietnam War. The next step was to carry the human rights banner from the campaign into the administration.

The State Department transition paper prepared for the new Carter administration on human rights stressed a need for greater definition of human rights objectives, additional analyses of responsibilities under new laws, institutional resources to direct the policy, and answers to a set of complex questions. Those questions included how high a priority was to be given human rights, how the human rights objectives would interrelate with other interests, how effective the policy would be and how it would affect other interests and objectives.

By June, a bureaucratic answer was crafted to those questions in a Presidential Review Memorandum on human rights. It was a document reflecting a balancing of the views of different bureaus within the Department of State and different departments as well. Yet, it did set forth firm statements on the implementation of the policy.

The first step taken by the administration was to appoint one of its own, Patricia Derian, a longtime civil rights activist from the South, as the Coordinator

for Human Rights and Humanitarian Affairs. By June, the staff had increased
from an office of two to an office of six, and by December, to an office of
twelve. The administration also supported congressional initiatives to turn the
office into an independent bureau and made the coordinator an assistant
secretary, thereby raising her status somewhat within the Department of
State.

Internally, there were other changes as well. To consider the relationship of human rights objectives to bilateral economic assistance and the U.S.
role in the international financial institutions, a new interagency committee
was established at the direction of the president's national security advisor. The
interagency committee on human rights and foreign assistance was to be chaired
by the secretary of state and have representation from the Defense Department,
the Treasury, and the National Security Council. In time, participants also
frequently included representatives of Commerce, Agriculture, the Overseas
Private Investment Corporation (OPIC), the Export-Import Bank (Ex-Im), and
U.S. executive directors of the World and Inter-American Development Banks.
At the outset, the secretary of state, Cyrus Vance, designated Deputy Secretary
Warren Christopher to chair the activities of this committee. The advisory
committee was responsible for making recommendations on pending loans
within the international development institutions and projects conducted by
the Agency for International Development.

Within the Department of State, the Bureau of Human Rights and Humanitarian Affairs and the Economic Bureau were permanent participants along
with the Policy Planning staff. The regional bureaus also were represented, at
least when countries within their respective areas were being considered. Acting
as a conduit and to a degree screening noncontroversial items, a working group
was established at the staff level with the human rights bureau and the economic
bureau serving as co-chairmen.

By the end of 1978, the U.S. had opposed 52 loans to 16 countries
on human rights grounds. In several other instances, countries were advised
that the human rights concerns of the Carter administration would result in a
negative vote if the particular loan were brought before the bank for consideration. In virtually all of those instances, the country voluntarily withdrew the
loans from consideration, at least for a short period, in hopes of avoiding a
negative statement by the United States, even where the U.S. vote could not
veto the loan approval.

In addition, specific demarches were made in more than two dozen instances
to inform countries that a particular favorable vote was occurring because the
loan itself would serve basic human needs; but the United States viewed specific
practices of the government with concern. In some instances, the demarche
was a warning that potential opposition to loans lay in the future in the absence
of human rights improvements.

Similar actions were taken with regard to the bilateral assistance program.

In some instances, it meant a reduction in the planned budget request for FY '79 and FY '80. In others, it meant the delay or cancellation of specific projects. Again, some decisions were made to move ahead with particular projects in a repressive country where the project was aimed at the needy, but usually with the approval linked to a demarche in which human rights issues were discussed.

The new policy also was extended to the Ex-Im Bank and OPIC. Although not mandated by law initially, both agencies attended the Inter-Agency Committee and advised the Bureau of Human Rights of pending agreements, seeking its advice on human rights issues.

In the area of security assistance, the Department of State established a new interagency committee, the Arms Export Control Board (AECB). The Assistant Secretary for Human Rights and Humanitarian Affairs was designated to sit on that body.

The AECB did not focus on specific cases. Decisions on individual arms transfers, either under the foreign military sales program or as a commercial transaction, were considered by the various bureaus, including the human rights bureau. Where the human rights bureau objected, either other bureaus concurred or the issue would go first to the Under Secretary for Security Assistance and then to the deputy secretary or the secretary for decision.

Once again, as a result of this human rights policy, arms transfer proposals to a dozen countries were altered during both 1977 and 1978. In some instances, they were refused. In other instances, they were sold only after U.S. taxpayer involvement was removed and the transaction became a commercial one. In other instances, particular categories of weapons were refused because they were destined for police forces or because of their potential use against political opposition groups in a particular country by the armed forces.

Beyond the assistance programs, the range of implementing actions included diplomatic dialogue, symbolic acts to identify the United States with the victims of repression, altering the cultural exchange programs to offer political opponents of a repressive regime an opportunity to present their views and to identify the U.S. with those groups, and issuing public statements of criticism. The diplomatic dialogue occurred at all levels, up to and including presidential conversations. Human rights concerns were no longer the unwelcome exception to ambassadorial representations to host governments but, in countries with records of serious abuse of human rights, the standards—still unwelcome—were a high-priority item on the U.S. bilateral agenda. The symbolic actions to emphasize the concern for the victims began with the Carter letter to Sakharov and continued throughout the year with the deputy secretary of state receiving former political prisoners from Chile and Argentina and the Assistant Secretary of State for Human Rights and Humanitarian Affairs personally visiting political prisoners in the Philippines.

A host of administration high officials traveled across the globe on separate missions, including the president, the secretary of state, U.N. Ambassador

Andrew Young, and others. Each time, an emphasis could be found in their speeches and private discussions of human rights issues. A clear example of that occurred in Argentina, where the secretary of state not only visited with the Permanent Assembly on Human Rights in that country but insured that a list of several thousand names of persons allegedly detained or disappeared was turned over to the Argentine government for their response.

These were the major actions taken in the bilateral arena to implement the new policy. In the multilateral theater, the president took the first step in several years to ratify key human rights agreements, signing the American Convention on Human Rights and the International Covenant on Civil and Political Rights and the International Covenant on Economic and Social Rights. Signing these documents was essential to indicate the willingness of the United States to carry out its own international human rights obligations. In addition, in the aftermath of the signing of the American Convention, and following some lobbying, others began to follow suit. After nearly a decade of sitting on the diplomatic shelves, the American Convention suddenly had 19 signatories and 13 ratifiers, and it entered into force.

At the United Nations, the United States also took a more active role in the human rights committee, working for the realization of a U.N. High Commissioner for Human Rights and seeking additional mechanisms to end the use of torture. At UNESCO, the United States worked to achieve establishment of special procedures to permit that agency to receive and act on complaints of human rights violations in the areas under its jurisdiction. Those procedures were adopted early in 1978. And within the United Nations Human Rights Commission the United States sought to break down the North/South and East/West divisions which had stymied that agency's operations in previous years.

These actions and events demonstrate a continuing effort to make concrete the rhetoric of increased concern for human rights in U.S. foreign policy. Nevertheless, as the second year ends, there continue to be calls for more aggressive action as well as complaints that the heavy emphasis on human rights has overshadowed other U.S. interests.

In looking back, it is difficult to define precisely the benefits of the policy. In many instances, U.S. expressions of concern were communicated to a host government and subsequently prisoners were released or changes made in the treatment and processing of political detainees. In many cases, those acts were cosmetic or token, designed to forestall continued U.S. criticism. Perhaps one of the most optimistic statements in support of the value of the policy came not from the government itself but from the International League for Human Rights. The organization, a nongovernmental voluntary organization affiliated with the United Nations, issued a special release on the anniversary of the adoption of the Universal Declaration of Human Rights. It cited as the major positive changes during the course of the previous year in the human rights field the following:

First, within the past year, human rights has for the first time become a subject of national policy debate in many countries. Second, human rights concerns have also been the focus of greater discussion in international organizations such as the United Nations, the Organization of American States and the Belgrade Conference. Third, the world media has focused on international human rights issues to a greater extent than ever before. Fourth, consciousness of human rights among the peoples of the world has increased significantly. Fifth, there has been an easing of repression in a substantial number of cases.

The report went on to say: "A most significant factor has been President Jimmy Carter's affirmation and advocacy of the United States' commitment to the international protection of human rights and United States encouragement of other states to undertake a similar commitment. The United States emphasis on human rights undoubtedly had enormous influence throughout the world."

Whether the human rights policy has been a marginal, complementary, or dominant factor in the positive steps which have been taken is unclear. It is hoped that the International League's assessment is accurate. However, it seems clear, that the rise to power of human rights was a new factor in the thrust and direction of U.S. foreign policy. Equally important, the concentration on human rights issues not only had survived the first two years but it had become a highly visible symbol of the administration's approach to foreign affairs.

Notes

1. Sec. 32, 22 USC 2151 note (Foreign Assistance Act of 1973).
2. Sec. 35, 22 USC 2151 note (Foreign Assistance Act of 1973).
3. Sec. 26, 22 USC 2370 note (Foreign Assistance Act of 1974).
4. Sec. 25, 22 USC 2370 note (Foreign Assistance Act of 1974).
5. Sec. 660, 22 USC 2420 (Foreign Assistance Act of 1961, as amended. Sec. 660 was added by Sec. 30(a) of the Foreign Assistance Act of 1974).
6. Sec. 502B, amending the Foreign Assistance Act of 1961, was added by the Foreign Assistance Act of 1974, Sec. 46, 88 Stat. 1795, amended by the International Security Assistance and Arms Export Control Act of 1976, 90 Stat. 729 at 761.
7. Title IV, 19 USCA 2432 (Supp. 1977) (Trade Act of 1974).
8. 22 USC 2151 note. Sec. 116, amending the Foreign Assistance Act of 1961, was added by Sec. 310 of Pub. L. 94-161 (89 Stat. 849).
9. Sec. 211, Pub. L. 94-302 (May 31, 1976), 22 USCA 283y, 290g-9 (Supp. 1976).
10. 22 USC 2304, as amended by Sec. 301(a) of the International Security Assistance and Arms Export Act of 1976.

2

Human Rights and Foreign Aid: Forging an Unbreakable Link

Tom Harkin

The recent and, I hope, continuing concern for protecting human rights on an international level has its origins in the tragic lessons we learned during the Second World War. Prior to that time the protection of human rights was thought to be a matter to be handled between a state and the people within its territory. The rights of individuals were not thought to be a proper subject of international law.

During the 1930s and 1940s we witnessed one of the most highly developed countries in history descend into barbarism. Out of this experience came the U.N. Charter in 1945, whose preamble recognizes and affirms fundamental human rights, the dignity and worth of the person, and the equal rights of men and women. With this charter, and especially with the Universal Declaration of Human Rights in 1948 and the succeeding U.N. covenants and treaties, human rights has established a foothold in international affairs. Today, finally, I believe it can be said that the rights of individual persons are a primary focus of international law and procedure.

But it is not enough, nor is it acceptable for our country to be concerned with human rights only in international bodies. In all of its own actions, including its domestic as well as its foreign policies, the United States must have as its goal the promotion of respect for basic human rights.

Human rights is a sine qua non of civilization. The other achievements and progress of a culture are meaningless unless the dignity of individual people— their human rights—is protected and affirmed in the daily life of nations.

The past few years have seen the American people, our administration, and the U.S. Congress unite in a basic commitment to promote the protection of human rights by our own and other governments. The American people has expressed its will through public outrage at past abuses of human rights by governments—some of which have sadly involved our own government—and through voting for candidates who are willing to struggle on behalf of human rights. The current administration has made a sincere commitment to promoting human rights and to making this a major concern in conducting foreign policy. And the Congress has enacted some laws and amended others in order to make our commitment to human rights clear and explicit.

In the pages that follow, I would like to discuss the unique and important role the Congress can play in the human rights movement, focusing on some human rights issues it currently faces. Basically, the Congress can take two sorts of action in this area. On the one hand, it can pass resolutions that publicly censure or reprimand governments known to be gross human rights violators, and if U.S. aid goes to one of those governments, Congress can restrict or cut off that aid. In this way, the Congress can play a role in "open diplomacy," which is a proper part of our diplomatic relations with other governments, complementing the open and quiet diplomacy of the administration and the Department of State.

On the other hand, and more importantly, the Congress can institutionalize our concerns for human rights through its capacity to build these concerns into our laws. Thus, the Congress can take steps to assure that promoting human rights will be an enduring goal of ours, and not one that will fade as new administrations come to power and public attention turns elsewhere. By institutionalizing our concern for human rights, I do not mean simply attaching an amendment on an aid bill. Rather, I hope that through our legislation we are beginning to build a body of human rights laws that will become the cornerstone of future laws and will guide future policy. Human rights concerns should affect all of our foreign aid. It is my hope that future generations of policymakers and politicians will come to regard such laws as part of the normal constraints within which they must work, and not as something new and unimportant, which they oppose by reflex and try to circumvent in their actions.

I have sponsored some of these human rights amendments to foreign aid bills that the Congress has passed. But these bills have attracted opposition as well, in the public at large (to judge from some newspaper editorials), in the administration, which would rather pursue our common objective without being constrained by legislative requirements, and within the Congress itself. So in explaining what particular steps we have taken to institutionalize the concern for human rights, I will respond to the criticisms brought against these bills by explaining why we have taken these steps.

The primary purpose of U.S. foreign aid has always been and will continue to be to promote and protect our national interests, which the Department of Defense has identified as including "the physical security of the U.S., its economic well-being, and the preservation of its institutions and values." This is as it should be. Now I believe that adding human rights amendments to foreign aid bills not only poses no conflicts for our national interests, so defined, but may even serve each of those other ends in the long run. The military dictators and others who maintain power through repressive practices while receiving our aid are unpopular rulers. Their governments are inherently unstable, which prevents them from forming the core for any kind of regional security. And whether they contribute anything toward the physical security of the United States is dubious at best. Nor are we serving our long-term economic interests by investing in governments erected on an eroding political, social, and legal foundation. Finally, the absurdity of protecting our values by supporting regimes that openly disregard those rights we take to be universal is quite apparent.

There are basically three kinds of foreign aid to which human rights requirements may be attached: bilateral economic aid, multilateral economic aid, and military or security assistance. If we are to institutionalize our human rights concerns effectively, it is essential to build these concerns into all three kinds of aid. We cannot hope to apply leverage to human rights violators by withholding one kind of aid and increasing another, as we have done in the past. Last year, for example, the United States opposed multilateral loans to South Korea and the Philippines on human rights grounds while stepping up military aid. We denounced apartheid in South Africa but lent the South African government $182.2 million through three federal programs. One of these involved a record-high economic aid package of $464 million from the International Monetary Fund in 1977, of which $107 million comes from the United States. At the same time, South Africa increased its military spending in 1976-77 by $450 million, almost exactly the amount of the IMF assistance.

Let us look briefly at each kind of foreign aid, beginning and focusing especially on the different forms of economic aid.

Bilateral Economic Aid

In 1975, the U.S. Congress adopted Section 116 of the Foreign Assistance Act (FAA), an amendment that I authored, which made the observance of certain basic human rights within the recipient countries a condition for the receipt of U.S. bilateral economic aid. I shall discuss the language of this amendment in some detail, because the list of rights it enumerates is substantially the same as the list that appears in all succeeding human rights amendments. The pertinent part of Section 116 is subparagraph (a), which in its entirety reads:

> No assistance may be provided under this part to the government of
> any country which engages in a consistent pattern of gross violations of
> internationally recognized human rights, including torture or cruel, in
> human, or degrading treatment or punishment, prolonged detention
> without charges, or other flagrant denial of the right to life, liberty
> and the security of person, unless such assistance will directly benefit
> the needy people in such country.

Subparagraph (c) says further that in determining whether or not a government falls within the provisions of subparagraph (a) "consideration will be given to the extent of cooperation of such government in permitting an unimpeded investigation of alleged violations of internationally recognized human rights by appropriate international organizations, including the International Committee of the Red Cross, or groups or persons acting under the authority of the United Nations or of the Organization of American States."

Subparagraph (d) then requires the president to report annually how the provisions of this section are carried out.

Now, this amendment clearly aims to link our direct economic aid to other governments to their level of respect for human rights. One of the arguments against using human rights conditions to restrict or to channel the flow of economic aid is that human rights are vague and nebulous concepts, subject to variation according to the observer. The spectrum of candidates for human rights is certainly broader than those enumerated in the amendment passed by Congress. I believe, in fact, that there are other basic human rights than those listed, some of which are not fully enjoyed even in this country. For example, I believe the right to adequate health care is a human right, but some of our own citizens do not receive adequate health care. But certainly no human rights are more basic than those included in the amendment. The rights of individuals to be free from torture, to be free from arbitrary arrest and detention without due legal process, and to be free from being kidnapped by their government— euphemistically called "disappearing"—these are as fundamental to our values and our belief in the universal equality of all people as any other rights. I do not pretend that the list in Section 116 is a complete list of human rights, but we can all accept the rights on this list, and they can be supported from any observer's point of view.

Moreover, these rights are not local U.S. customs; they are all internationally recognized. Every country with which we have relations has approved at least these rights in various international documents. In fact, violation of these rights as a matter of policy is as abhorrent to the world community today as slavery, and I would like to see such practices as torture and illegal detention—which are very much like slavery—become equally things of the past. I believe the U.S. Congress should use its power, in cooperation with the administration and public support, to lead an international movement that would bring an end to torture by governments.

It has also been argued that if protecting these rights becomes an explicit goal of U.S. foreign policy, then the United States will be interfering in the domestic affairs of other sovereign nations. The first thing to reiterate is that these rights are internationally endorsed, and therefore they ought not to be compromised by any government's domestic policies. In this regard, they are politically neutral. Yet, where a government violates these rights of its own citizens in a gross and systematic way, Section 116 directs the president to terminate economic aid, so the charge of interfering remains.

Let us be realistic. Any U.S. aid (whether military or economic) already "interferes" in the domestic affairs of the recipient country. To think that American aid is politically neutral is naive. Indeed, economic aid may create more wealth in the aggregate, but aggravate economic and political injustice, and some of the most "successful" economic development programs in such countries as the Philippines, South Korea, and Indonesia have been accompanied by both greater economic inequality and increased repression. For such reasons, I believe it is possible to avoid complicity in human rights abuses of other governments only if we pursue economic development with a strong parallel commitment to economic and social justice. While we may not be able to force other governments to embrace human rights principles, we ought not to encourage those governments through economic aid to use secret police, detention without charges, and torture to perpetuate their power.

Finally, I should call attention to the exception clause at the end of subparagraph (a) of Section 116, which says," . . .Unless such assistance will directly benefit the needy people in such country. . . ." Some of my critics in Congress have charged that this amendment is too rigid. They have claimed that aid that genuinely helps people must be terminated if their governments violate human rights. But the clause beginning with "unless" is specifically intended to allow such exceptions. The needy people of a country should not be hurt any more than necessary by the practices of their government. If their rights are being violated, their burden is bad enough already and it should not be compounded by losing aid that really helps them.

A different criticism of this clause in the amendment claims that it creates too large a loophole. These critics claim that broad economic development programs that immediately benefit the rulers and their wealthy supporters in a country could be justified because the benefits will trickle down to the needy. Here I would call attention to the word "directly," which is intended to prohibit such justificiations. When can we say that aid is directly benefiting the poor? Some cases are clearly difficult to assess, but reasonable judgments can be made. One of the most serious problems in underdeveloped countries is not simply the total lack of wealth, but the great disparity between the rich and powerful and the poor and helpless. Whenever our economic aid to such a country does nothing to reduce, and especially in those cases where it aggravates, this inequality, that aid is not directly benefiting the poor. I believe the intent of the amendment, including the exception clause, is clear.

Multilateral Economic Aid

Now I would like to discuss our other form of economic assistance, the multilateral economic aid programs. Economic aid increasingly flows through multilateral institutions, so any successful attempt to pursue our human rights goals must extend to include these important channels for U.S. foreign aid. The Congress has now attached amendments, modeled on Section 116 of the FAA governing bilaterial aid, to the bills authorizing U.S. contributions to the multilateral aid institutions.

The United States cannot control the policies of these multilateral institutions, but the United States does have a director on each of them, and can instruct our directors to use our voice and vote to discourage and disapprove loans and aid to governments that violate human rights. We ought to do at least this much, especially since the United States is a major contributor to these institutions. Human rights amendments have been passed or proposed on bills authorizing U.S. support of the International Financial Institutions (IFIs), the International Monetary Fund (IMF), and the Export-Import Bank (Ex-Im Bank). I shall discuss these individually, since there are important differences between them.

The IFIs include the International Bank for Reconstruction and Development (IBRD—the World Bank); the International Development Association (IDA); the International Finance Corporation (IFC); and the three regional banks—the Inter-American Development Bank (IDB), the African Development Fund (ADF), and the Asian Development Bank (ADB). A decade ago, Congress asked that U.S. foreign aid be channeled increasingly through these banks for the express purpose of removing politics from foreign aid. The fact is that the IFIs have developed policies that clearly show them to have their own political tendencies. In the recent past, these have amounted to rewarding right-wing repressive dictators while withholding funds from Socialist governments. Let me provide a few examples:

> In the three years before President Marcos imposed martial law, aid to the Philippines from the multilateral banks (IBRD, IFC, IDA, ADB) averaged $69 million per year. In the three years after martial law was imposed, that is from 1973 through 1975, aid averaged $210 million per year—a 204 percent increase, compared with the 120 percent increase for East Asia as a whole.

> In Korea during the three years before General Park Chung Hee declared martial law (in 1972) and forced a revision of the constitution to allow him to hold office for life, aid to Korea averaged $105 million per year. In the three years that followed, aid from these institutions averaged $284 million per year—a 170 percent average increase.

> In Chile during the three years before Salvador Allende was overthrown (1971-73), aid from the multilateral banks averaged $6.4 million. In the three years after the military coup, aid from these institutions averaged $77.6 million per year, a 1,112 percent increase, as compared with a 65 percent increase for Latin America as a whole.

As these examples clearly show, the human rights amendments to the multilateral institutions are not injecting politics into the "apolitical" nature of these international banks. I should emphasize that I am not claiming that the IFIs are intentionally advocating some political ideology. But they deal in money, and money is a political commodity. These banks are in the business of lending money to governments in order to aid those countries in development, which will then enable them to repay the loans with interest. Now, what are the social and political consequences of such an economic policy? It turns out that in many countries the loans go to foster an export-based economy. This can mean that a country grows more sugar for export, but no more of the food its citizens need. Or it can mean mining more copper without helping to build a sound economic infrastructure that will help its own citizens. The imports into these countries, which increase the need for export, often consist of things like automobiles and machinery that will not help the poor.

It is also true that many of these countries are ruled by military dictators who have no respect for law, but who gain support and power from IFI loans. For all of these reasons, this is an unacceptable way to use U.S. foreign aid money. The human rights amendment to the IFI Act of 1977 merely seeks to redirect the politics already present in the multilateral banks, to assure that these banks will not—even unintentionally—support regimes that violate *internationally recognized* human rights.

Contrary to the dire predictions of many experts, the International Financial Institutions have adapted well to the human rights language applied to them last October. Section 701 of the IFI Act of 1977 requires the U.S. Executive Director to vote against any assistance to a government that violates basic human rights (as defined in Section116). Although our U.S. Director has subsequently opposed 17 loans on human rights grounds, voting no on 5 and abstaining on 12, all these loans went through because the United States does not have a veto power in these bodies (except for the soft loan window of the IDB). However, several other loans were deferred or withdrawn after the U.S. government indicated its opposition, without seriously affecting the policies of the IFIs. Clearly a first step for human rights, even if it is a small one, has been taken in these institutions.

Section 703 complements Section 701 by requiring the U.S. secretaries of state and treasury to initiate a wide consultation of other bank members to enlist their support—or at least their understanding—of our human rights position. Other industrialized countries were at first skeptical of our motives, but as they begin to understand our policy better and appreciate that our commitment is a moral one, not aimed at pursuing narrow political ends, their support can be counted on. We can best further this understanding of our policy by institutionalizing it and making it explicit, rather than pursuing it solely in the private discussions of quiet diplomacy.

Now let us turn to the IMF, the so-called sister organization of the World Bank. In February of 1978, the House of Representatives attached a human rights amendment to the bill authorizing the U.S. contribution to a $10 billion increase of the IMF funds. This amendment directs the U.S.

representative to the IMF to do everything in his power to guarantee that IMF
transactions do not contribute to the violation of basic human rights or to the
deprivation of basic human needs. Again, the amendment provoked strong
objections, which by then were beginning to appear standard and predictable.
As before, we heard arguments that this institution is different and that the
amendment would politicize a nonpolitical institution.

When Section 116 of the FAA was originally proposed, the argument was
that this is a bad amendment because this case was different: it concerned
economic aid and not security assistance. When it came to the IFI bill, the case
was again different, this time because it concerned multilateral aid and not
bilateral aid. And in this particular case, it was argued that the IMF is different
because it is a *lending* institution, not an institution for *aid*. Its goal is not
economic development, but one of relieving balance of payments problems.
Quite frankly, the relevance of these "uniqueness" arguments escapes me. The
crucial fact about the IMF seems to me to be that it is an institution whose
policies often have a detrimental effect on large numbers of people, and that
it receives U.S. government funding. Human rights is a fundamental part of our
foreign policy, and all forms of U.S. international spending should reflect this.
Moreover, no institution is "unique" enough to be exempt from human rights
considerations. I should also add that, because all money is fungible, it is impossible for the IMF to state that it is not involved in aid.

The claim that the human rights amendment will politicize the IMF fails
again to consider that the rights listed in the amendment are all internationally
recognized. Nevertheless, an understanding of how the IMF operates actually
strengthens the case of those who think it is important that this institution
affirm human rights concerns.

The IMF gains some of its authority precisely because it is an international
institution. IMF loans go primarily to the less-developed countries, but some
are also made to economically troubled industrialized countries, such as Italy
and England. These loans are aimed at reducing balance of payments difficulties,
which have been especially aggravated since the 1973 OPEC price increases. In
order to accomplish its goal, the IMF attaches conditions to its loans—austerity
measures that usually call for reductions of government sponsored social services
in the borrowing countries—which are supposed to reduce inflation and make
their economies sound enough to meet their repayment schedules. Although
the financial experts like to think of these as strictly economic conditions, they
have political consequences by provoking opposition from those who suffer
when social services are cut back. In order to avoid the austerity measures that
stimulate this opposition, hard-pressed governments have been turning instead
to other governments and to private banks for loans, because these lenders are
less able to enforce austerity measures as a condition on a loan. The debts of
these borrowing countries are increasing rapidly, and the possibility of a default
somewhere in the future, which could be very harmful to banks and to the world

economy, is a growing fear of the lending countries and banks. This fear has given rise to a movement to increase IMF funds, to help it reassert its power, and to refuse to make direct loans until the IMF conditions are met. Thus, as reported in *Fortune* magazine (July 1977), "The IMF needs the infusion of cash because the British and Italian loans nearly exhausted its lendable resources. Once it has the new money as an inducement, the Fund hopes to persuade more deficit countries, as one IMF staffer put it, 'to drop their trousers and be examined by the doctor.'"

I am, of course, certainly in favor of stabilizing the world economy and taking the austerity measures necessary to do this. Drastic cutbacks of social services in countries like Italy and England, while unfortunate, will still allow basic needs to be met and human rights to be protected. But when Egypt and Peru recently tried to comply with IMF requirements that they cut back food subsidies and raise food prices, riots broke out in both countries. In Turkey and Portugal, IMF conditions require spending cuts that will increase an already tragic unemployment rate. These austerity steps may only strain already weak democratic structures in these countries. Similar situations exist in Mexico, Pakistan, and Zaire. Austerity measures ought to be imposed in an equitable way, and not in ways that make it more difficult for the poor to feed themselves. Social services ought not be cut back until other measures, such as taxing non-vital imports, have been taken. As Representative Henry Reuss recently put it, "If under the supplementary [Witteveen] facility people on the IMF staff are minded to ratify a country's program, which country's program allows the import without limit of oil for the Mercedes automobiles of the oligarchy, while cutting down on soybeans from the State of Georgia which would give needed protein to everybody, I think our Executive Director should speak up against this."

The governments of hard-pressed countries can expect strong political opposition as a result of complying with IMF requirements. For this reason, it is if anything more appropriate to express human rights concerns in IMF policies, so that governments that must accept IMF austerity conditions will also be prevented from responding to political opposition by resorting to terror. The social costs of economic austerity measures must be borne fairly by a nation's citizens, and the IMF has a responsibility for seeing that they are. It is naive to suppose that the IMF operates in a political and moral vacuum. In fact, even the IMF directors know better. In some confidential minutes of one of their meetings, one member of the IMF staff acknowledged that ". . .there were always important political and social consequences of introducing the kind of stabilization programs that the Fund, on the basis of its long experience, usually recommended."

When the human rights amendment for the Ex-Im Bank was debated in Congress, we heard once more how it was ill-advised, because the Ex-Im Bank is unique. Ex-Im lends money to governments at low interest rates, thereby enabling those governments to buy U.S.-made products. Its goal is to stimulate foreign sales of U.S. products. Once again, we pointed out that this bank is funded by U.S. government money which goes to foreign governments, and once again we pointed out that there is no reason to make this branch of foreign policy exempt from human rights considerations.

Now, even if Congress is successful in drying up U.S. governmental funding for human rights violators, another source exists in the private multinational banks. For example, in 1975 and 1976, when the international community was loudly decrying Chile for human rights violations, private multinational bank lending to Chile increased 500 percent, and soared to over $800 million in 1977. In 1977, when "human rights" became the new watchword for U.S. foreign policy, more American dollars flowed to the Chilean government than ever before. In 1977, private U.S.-based multinational banks provided $514 million in loans and credits to Chile. Since the coup, U.S. banks have lent Chile $927 million.

What has happened in Chile is not atypical. From Brazil, to South Africa, to Indonesia the litany continues. As repressive regimes become more entrenched and financially solvent, thanks to IFI and IMF policies, massive amounts of private capital pour in. To achieve greater "stability," and to entice more investments, regimes frequently become more repressive. If these massive infusions of outside capital significantly aided a country's poor majorities, then the objection to these loans would be weak. But the gap between the rich and poor in these countries is widening.

For these reasons, I have introduced a bill in the House that would require banks to disclose each investment they make in those countries known to be gross violators of human rights. It is important that we have this information. Currently, there are countries in which U.S. corporations and banks are not allowed to make investments for various foreign policy reasons. I do not believe that we should continue to allow private banks flagrantly to thwart U.S. human rights policy goals.

Security Assistance

I shall now discuss, although very briefly, the human rights amendment that has been attached to U.S. military or security assistance. In 1976 the Congress amended Section 502b of the International Security Assistance and Arms Export Control Act. This amendment prohibits military aid and arms sales to any country whose government engages in a consistent pattern of gross violations of internationally recognized human rights.

Attaching human rights conditions to security assistance is natural, since security assistance includes not only weapons but military education and training, and even police equipment—the very tools of repression. Nevertheless,

Section 502b has an exception clause built into it that allows security assistance to go to human rights violators if "extraordinary circumstances" warrant it, or if it is necessary to protect our national interest. Deputy Secretary of State Warren Christopher has acknowledged that "when the human rights performance of the recipient is unsatisfactory, we may continue to provide aid because of our overriding national security interest but not without expressing concern."

Yet Congress did not intend to provide the Pentagon with a loophole large enough to drive a tank through. This exception clause can be exploited, and in FY '79 seven countries known to be egregious violators of human rights— Indonesia, South Korea, the Philippines, Thailand, Haiti, Nicaragua, and Paraguay —are all scheduled to receive security assistance totaling $389.1 million. The reasons for the exceptions are not always clear. The Philippines, for example, as reported by the Department of Defense, "is neither perceived as a threat by other nations in the region nor is it threatened by them." Nevertheless, the Carter administration is requesting $37.7 million in security assistance for the Philippines in FY '79.

I simply fail to see how stopping or reducing our military aid to the Philippines would jeopardize our national interests. In fact, the opposite may be true. Last April's election confirmed that opposition to President Marcos's iron-grip rule on the country is widespread, and if this hatred of the regime develops into a serious political struggle, as well it might, the United States should be at least a neutral party to the conflict.

The Congress must insist that its human rights concerns are applied by the administration equally to all countries. Once a particular government has been identified as a human rights violator, sanctions should apply, and they should not vary from funding mechanism to funding mechanism without a good reason, such as the fact that an overriding national interest is involved. And then this national interest must be clearly established. This is part of what is involved in institutionalizing a concern for human rights. It insists that those who administer foreign policy be held accountable for how they pursue this objective and for the exceptions that must be made.

An Unchanging Commitment

Now that we have discussed these human rights initiatives, we should look at their effects. Of course, the United States is most concerned about long-term trends. Superficial human rights improvements cannot become a subterfuge for frustrating real change. If this were to occur, the cruelest hoax would be played on the oppressed peoples who sincerely believe in our commitment, many thousands of whom have been encouraged by our human rights policy to press their quest for human dignity. At the very least, we must show them that our policy is not merely rhetoric.

Some governments have begun releasing significant numbers of political prisoners and simultaneously curtailing indiscriminate arrests of alleged subversives. Some governments have begun to punish people responsible for torture and have ordered these practices to stop. Moreover, several countries have recently agreed to permit the International Committee of the Red Cross to inspect their jails.

In Latin America, we have seen two states of siege lifted, and some countries are permitting on-site investigations by the Inter-American Commission on Human Rights. Land reform is again being pursued in Latin America, and some African governments, recognizing the enormous gap between rich and poor, are undertaking long-range development programs to provide a better standard of living for their people. A much larger percentage of their resources from the international financial institutions is being redirected toward rural development and agricultural projects which will help the poorest people in a country.

As currently written, the human rights amendments do not preclude the administration from adapting its human rights policy to changing world circumstances. While these amendments are constraining, many State Department officials have indicated that they are not unreasonably so. What they seek to do is "nail down" certain human rights for which the administration's foreign policy must be accountable. With the human rights amendments in front of them, both the Congress and the American people can determine what actions the administration is taking in the area of human rights, and whether the policy is being applied vigorously and fairly.

Undoubtedly, President Carter is a sincere man, deeply committed to human rights. His administration has done more in this area than any other in recent history. But our human rights actions must rest on more than the philosophy of one administration. It must become as institutionalized a foreign policy consideration as national security and economic well-being are now.

To conclude, I can see yet another benefit from institutionalizing human rights goals. According to a 1975 Harris Poll, 63 percent of the American people feel our government has no justification for backing "authoritarian governments that have overthrown democratic governments," and 73 percent oppose U.S. support of a military dictatorship "even if that dictatorship will allow us to set up military bases in that country." The human rights movement can become a legitimizing factor for U.S. policy in general. It can provide a needed sense of purpose and unity for Americans, and perhaps restore some of the dwindling public support for both bilateral and multilateral foreign aid. None of us who are sincerely committed to human rights is a crusader, nor do we desire a holy cause; but if human rights amendments channel U.S. foreign policy into a positive direction, and simultaneously foster a greater acceptance by the American people of our international obligations, then we will be better off as a nation and as a civilization.

**Part II
Principles: The Nature and
Justification of Human Rights**

3 Human Rights and Foreign Assistance Programs

Hugo Adam Bedau

Introduction

During 1976, Congress enacted Public Law 94-329, the International Security Assistance and Arms Export Control Act. Section 502B of Title III constitutes the Human Rights provisions of the Act, key portions of which include the following: "It is the policy of the United States. . .to promote and encourage increased respect for human rights and fundamental freedoms for all without distinction as to race, sex, language, or religion. . .[and] to promote the increased observance of internationally recognized human rights by all countries. . . . No security assistance may be provided to any country the government of which engages in a consistent pattern of gross violations of internationally recognized human rights. . . . The term 'gross violations of internationally recognized human rights' includes torture or cruel, inhuman, or degrading treatment or punishment, prolonged detention without charges and trial, and other flagrant denial of the right to life, liberty, or the security of person. . . ."[1]

This legislation can be viewed as part of what has been called a "human rights offensive" being mounted from Washington in both the legislative and executive branches of the federal government. What began in 1975 as an expression of congressional resentment at the Ford administration's indifference to legislative prerogatives in foreign policy has emerged as a prominent feature of the Carter administration's own outlook on world affairs.[2] The politics of this "offensive" has received considerable attention, as it should.[3] Rather less interest—in fact, hardly any at all—has been shown in some of the underlying assumptions. If the hearings held by Congress[4] and the floor debates prior to the enactment of this legislation[5] are any guide, no systematic and thorough consideration has evern been given to the conceptual and normative issues raised by Section 502B. It is my purpose in the remarks that follow to rectify this omission.

My analysis and defense of Section 502B fall into three parts. First, I shall sketch what it is for something to be a human right, quite apart from whether or not it is recognized in international law. This is a necessary step in the overall argument; it enables us to make explicit some of the important moral considerations that are at stake in the defense of human rights and in the protest of their violation. Next, I shall offer some arguments to show why the human rights cited in Section 502B are more important than others that might have been included, either by way of addition or as substitutes. Finally, I shall try to show the morality of linking these important human rights with our foreign policy and especially our military assistance programs.

The Conception of a Human Right

Section 502B alludes to the violation of "internationally recognized human rights" as the trigger to set in motion a review process that could culminate in termination of foreign assistance. The rights, violation of which are at issue, are "life, liberty, and security of person." One or more of these, it is implied, is always violated where "torture, cruel, inhumane, or degrading treatment or punishment, or prolonged detention without charges and trial" are permitted. There is no doubt that "life, liberty, and security of person" are "internationally recognized human rights,"[6] and that "torture" and the rest violate them.[7] What is not so clear is precisely what it is for something to be a human *right*, as distinct from some other kind of right, and as distinct from universal human *needs*. When positive international law recognizes a human right, what is it that has been embodied in the law? An examination of these questions is essential if we are to understand what is at stake in the defense of human rights and in the protest of their violation.

History shows that human rights are as many and as diverse as the theory of human rights one defends. According to Hobbes, there is only such right: "the right of nature" that each person has to do whatever is necessary to stay alive. Locke defends the familiar trio: "life, liberty, and property." Our own Declaration of Independence specifies a different trio: "life, liberty, and the pursuit of happiness." The French Declaration of Rights of Man cites four: "liberty, property, security, and resistance of oppression." Fifty years ago, the Institute of International Law in its International Declaration of the Rights of Man declared "the equal right to life, liberty and property" to be the foremost among "the rights of man." Thirty years ago, the U.N. Declaration of Human Rights listed more than three dozen human rights, headed by "life, liberty, and security of person." In the most influential philosophical defense of "natural rights" during the past generation, H.L.A. Hart reduces them to one, "the equal right of all men to be free."[8] John Rawls, in his important recent philosophical treatise, *A Theory of Justice,* proposes no list or set of human rights at all.[9] Yet it has been argued, rightly I think, that at the basis of his entire theory lies one such right, the right of all individuals "to equal concern and respect in the design and administration of the political institutions that govern them."[10] This sample from four philosophers and four manifestos spanning four centuries illustrates not only the diversity but also the continuity in substantive natural or human rights. Even apart from further argument, such a record is an adequate basis for claiming that there is considerable philosophical and political agreement on the human rights cited in Section 502B.

What is less clear is whether there is any common denominator for these different rights, something each theorist might grant to be true of all and only the substantive rights his theory contains. Is there a common logic of human rights more or less independent of the substantive content of the rights themselves? In recent years, it has been suggested that a right qualifies as a human right if and only if it has four general characteristics: (1) all and only human persons have such rights; (2) all persons have such rights equally; (3) the rights in question are not derived from any special status or relation of the person, and thus are not contingent for their possession upon any change or loss of such status or relation; and (4) the right can be asserted against or claimed from any and all other human persons and institutions.[11] Whatever else is true of the rights asserted in manifestos and by thinkers from Hobbes to Rawls, including the rights cited in Section 502B, there is no difficulty in holding that they all exhibit these four characteristics.

However, it is still obscure what it is about rights in general and human rights in particular that accounts for their relatively greater importance than many other moral considerations with which they are sometimes in competition. Traditionally, it has been thought that human rights are inalienable, or that they are absolute. Is either of these the feature in question?

To say that a right is *inalienable* is to say that a person who has it cannot voluntarily and irrevocably divest himself of it by gift, sale, or other transfer to another person. It does *not* mean that it is always wrong not to accord such a right, or that it cannot be voluntarily (and to that extent, quite properly) waived or neglected. In particular, the fact that a right is inalienable does not mean that it cannot be *forfeited.* The connection between inalienability and forfeiture is especially illuminating where the morality of slavery is in question. Equal liberty may safely be taken as the paradigm of an inalienable right. If it is inalienable then it becomes conceptually impossible for anyone to become voluntarily another's slave. Hence, either slavery is fundamentally immoral, depending as it does on alienating an inalienable right, or anyone who is rightfully the slave of another must have become so without alienating his liberty. Theorists such as Locke, who believed both in the inalienability of liberty and in the moral tolerability of slavery in some circumstances, resolved this seeming dilemma by introducing the idea of forfeiting a natural and inalienable right. (Forfeiture of rights is as much a part of the general logic of legal rights and special rights as is their waiver, neglect, or violation.) According to Locke, a person forfeits his natural right to life, for example, if he murders another person. Analogously, it could be argued that whenever a person commits a felony, he forfeits his natural rights to life, liberty, or property, depending upon the right violated. Thus, penal servitude need not involve the violation of a right to liberty, nor the denial that this right is inalienable.

Turning to the rights mentioned in Section 502B and the modes of their violation cited there, we can see the irrelevance of appeal to the inalienability of these rights as part of an argument to show the unjustifiability of their violation. Torturers, for example, need not challenge the inalienability of the right of each citizen to bodily security. All that the friends of torture need to insist is that their victims have forfeited the right to bodily security by virtue of the crimes they are believed to have committed. Torturers need not deny that there is a human right of bodily security, or that this right is inalienable. They certainly do not need to advance the bizarre argument that in torturing a person they do no wrong (violate no right of the victim) because that person gave, sold, or otherwise transferred a right to injure himself to his torturer. Consequently, the firm assurance that the right to bodily security is an inalienable human right does not suffice to show that torture violates anyone's rights and is to that extent morally wrong, any more than the alienability of the human right to property or to life suffices to show that fines and taxes (deprivation of property) or the death penalty (deprivation of life) are morally wrong because they violate an inalienable right.[12]

The problem with regarding human rights as *absolute* is quite different. To say that a right is absolute is to say that its scope and exercise are not relative to or contingent upon any other moral considerations in any circumstances. An absolute right, therefore, is something that no competing moral considerations could ever justifiably override or nullify. There are several problems with the idea that human rights are absolute rights. For one thing, it quickly becomes clear that the content of such a right—what it requires and what it forbids—is vague and without any prospect of clarification except arbitrarily. Suppose we assume that the right to life, for example, is an absolute right. Some who hold this view think that induced abortion violates the absolute right to life of a human fetus. Involuntary miscarriage, however, presumably does not. But what about the failure to try to keep persons alive as long as is medically possible, regardless of the costs and regardless of their own settled preferences and convictions? What about death from famine, starvation, and fatal epidemic disease? Do these violate the absolute right to life if, or only if, they are owing to human mismanagement, or if, or only if, however caused, they could have been averted by effective human intervention? I doubt that it is possible to answer such questions except arbitrarily, so long as the right to life is regarded as an absolute right.

There is the further problem that the acknowledgment of even one absolute right tends to lead to the denial that it is an equal right for all persons, and it casts doubt on whether there can be a plurality of absolute rights. These consequences follow because of the way that actions taken by one person in exercise of an absolute right tend to encroach upon or violate what would otherwise be the equally absolute right of another. If free speech, for example, is an absolute right, then presumably those who have this right are within their rights to say what they please when and where they please. But this will surely lead not only to tolerating slander and libel but also to permitting persons to falsely shout "Fire!" in a crowded theater and to incite to riot. Because no society will allow such outrages, the doctrine of absolute rights is certain to encourage the view that there are no natural or human rights at all—as Jeremy Bentham's famous denunciation of the "absolute" Rights of Man of 1789 for its "anarchial fallacies" attests. It is hardly any wonder, therefore, that it is difficult to find a single clear case of a philosophical defense (as distinct from the assertion in a manifesto) of absolute human rights.

An exception can be made, it has been argued, in favor of the right not to be tortured,[13] It does seem that the right to bodily security that torture violates is a right that can be granted and protected without exception or contingency; to grant this right absolutely does not involve infringing upon or violating any right of anyone else. But even here many would not want to go so far. Suppose someone has constructed and cleverly hidden a "doomsday" machine, and set it to go off in a few hours—unless, say, we kill ten perfectly innocent persons whom the mad bomber hates. Would we refuse to torture him, if we could, for the sole purpose of extracting an account of where his infernal machine was located, so that we could try to destroy or disarm it? If we did torture him for this purpose, would we admit that we had violated an absolute right of his? Or would we argue that even though his right was absolute, he had forfeited it by his conduct, which threatened the no less absolute rights of countless others? Or would we argue that the immunity to torture conferred on him by his right to security was outweighed by the competing right to life of innocent persons?

The idea that human rights are inalienable and absolute obscures rather than illuminates the fundamental point vividly illustrated in the anecdote told by Maurice Cranston in his book *What Are Human Rights?* According to the story, a few years ago several men in the Central African Republic had been convicted of theft and duly sentenced to imprisonment. Not content with this punishment, the President of the Republic personally ordered his soldiers to take these prisoners and beat them to death. He is reported to have declared with grim satisfaction, "There will be no more theft in the Central African Republic." Cranston comments, "Even if such methods *did* protect public order...the use of torture at the pleasure of a despot is precisely the kind of thing which declarations of the Rights of Man are meant to outlaw...."[14] Modern thinkers who profess to take rights seriously stress that the essential and underlying feature of a theory of rights is to provide a veto for political action otherwise desirable and justified on the ground of collective preference or social advantage. If someone really has a *right* to something, then it is wrong to withhold it from him on no other ground than that it would be generally advantageous to do so.[15] This is as true whether it is a private individual or a government that does the withholding, and it is especially true where the right in question is a human right. Here we have the decisive and distinctive feature of rights, and it is the feature of paramount relevance to our concern in the present discussion.

What might be said for torture in the hypothetical case of the man with the "doomsday" machine cannot be said on behalf of the use of torture by the regimes that typically employ it. So, if it is granted that what torture violates is a human right to personal and bodily security, then excusing or justifying it on the grounds that it is useful to the preservation of "national security" collapses. It is precisely the point of the very concept of a human right to thwart such reasoning, to smother it in the crib. Once a government acknowledges that its citizens have basic human rights under law, then it can view subsequent charges of torture against these persons in only one of four ways. Either the government must disavow the torture and insist that it was inflicted through an excess of zeal or violence by officers who will be punished; or the government must argue that the torture was undertaken in protection of the conflicting but superior rights of others; or the government must confess that it did authorize the torture and the violation of rights involved, in which case some remedy to the victims is appropriately forthcoming and the highest responsible government officials should resign in disgrace; or the government must deny that the acts in question were acts of torture. What cannot be done with integrity and consistency is for the government to assert that its citizens have a human right of bodily integrity, that the government deliberately tortures some of its citizens, and that no one's rights are violated in such acts.

I have sketched an argument to the effect that although the substantive content of natural and human rights has varied over the centuries, as the writings of philosophers and the texts of manifestos prove, the conceptual nature of what it is to be a human or natural right shows a significant if often hidden continuity. It is true that domestic and international law may incorporate or assert rights quite independently of any moral or philosophical arguments for such rights and indifferent to any conceptual or logical features shared by these rights. Nevertheless, it is my view that the human rights identified in Section 502B are best understood as rights of which the foregoing account is true. To put this another way, when we acknowledge that the rights mentioned by this law as relevant to the arms export policy of the United States are indeed human rights, part of what I mean and what I think others should mean as well is that these rights have the conceptual and normative features identified above. It is *because* they have these features that they are human rights and deserve to be recognized and protected as positive rights of international law.

Priorities among Rights

Section 502B does not explicitly address itself to the violation of all human rights, and this poses a challenge. Even if it is agreed that linking human rights violations to terminating our foreign assistance programs is reasonable, it is still an open question whether the human rights appropriately so linked are all and only those actually incorporated into Section 502B. The Jackson amendment of 1974 to the Trade Act of 1973, for example, favored withdrawal of credits from nonmarket economies that denied their citizens the right to emigrate. Section 502B makes no mention of such a right (and in the hearings it was denied that the right to emigrate was included within the tacit scope of the rights cited in the section).[16] Instead, as we have seen, 502B cites torture as one of several incontestable examples of human rights violation, and it cites as the violated right(s) "the right to life, liberty, or security of person." But why should we choose these human rights as the ones whose violations are to set in motion restrictions on our foreign aid? In order to answer this question we need to look at the full array of basic human rights and determine whether there are priorities among them that Section 502B reflects.

It is possible to arrange human rights by reference to many different considerations, but for our purposes a basic tripartite division will suffice. With this taxonomy, we can sort rights according to whether their chief function is (1) to bar others from interfering with one's conduct, and thus to demark a certain sphere of privacy, liberty, or autonomy; or (2) to entitle the individual to participate in the institutions of self-government, and thus to affect the rules that arise from the rights in (1); or (3) to impose upon the government the responsibility to aid individuals by providing services and facilities beyond those that individuals can provide for themselves. These three categories are not meant to constitute an exclusive division, because there are unavoidable overlaps; but they are meant to be exhaustive.

Rights in the first category can be subdivided into (a) those that bar interference by other persons as such, and (b) those that bar interference by government, and thus by other persons acting in official capacities. The traditional rights of life, liberty, property, and security of person fall mainly into subclass (a), and to protect them the criminal law is erected. Among the rights protected against invasions by government in subclass (b) there are (i) protected liberties, such as the rights of assembly, speech, and the press, and other activities that essentially involve social contact and relationships; and (ii) rights that limit the methods government may use in its presumed defense of the rights of its citizens, including especially the rights in subclass (1) (a) above. These are the rights that are violated by torture and prolonged detention without trial. Habeas corpus and most of the provisions of our Bill of Rights fall into one or the other of these two subcategories of (1) (b).

Rights in the second category include the right to vote and to run for political office, and the other rights specified in the Civil War amendments to our federal Constitution as well as such more recent amendments as the Twenty-fourth and Twenty-sixth. Insofar as the rights of free speech, press, and assembly can be seen as inseparable from the right to participate in the political processes

of self-government, these rights, already located in category (1), also have a
place in category (2).

The third category of rights can be subdivided into three subclasses. One of
them, (a), contains the rights that are the source of the government's responsibility to create institutions to cope with persons who have interfered with the
exercise by others of their rights in categories (1) and (2). The enforcement of
the prohibitions of the criminal law through the design, financing, and administration of the police, the courts, and penal institutions can be viewed as a product
of the rights in this subclass. A second subclass, (b), includes the jury trial,
appellate courts, and other rights of criminal procedure, including habeas corpus.
Even though these are rights to services and facilities and not merely rights to
be let alone, no libertarian defender of the "minimal state" would object to the
rights identified in these two subclasses.[17] Archliberals of this sort would object,
however, to all or most of the rights in the third subclass, (c), the social and
economic or welfare rights that bulk so large in Articles 22 through 30 of the
U.N. Declaration of Human Rights but which were virtually unknown until
quite recently in our own constitutional history.

In summary, then, we have the following structure of rights:

(1) Rights against interference
     (a) by other individuals (life, liberty, property, security of person)
     (b) by government in its protection of the rights of individuals or minorities
          (i)   liberties (assembly, speech, press)
          (ii) limitations against abuse of police power (habeas corpus)
(2) Rights of participation in self-government (voting)
(3) Rights to services and facilities for the
     (a) prevention of interference with the exercise of individual rights (police,
          courts, prisons)
     (b) guarantee of due process
     (c) provision of the social minimum (schools, hospitals, and so on)

Do any of these categories of rights have a preferred status with respect to
the others? If choice must be made among violated rights to be protested, is
there any basis for attempting to terminate some of these violations in precedence to others? I think it can be argued in several different ways that because
the rights in category (1) (a) are our most important rights, the violation by a
government of rights in category (1) (b) (ii) must be the most important to
protest and terminate.

There is, first, what we might call *the argument from indifference to
economic contingencies.* It is not possible to implement social and economic
rights unless a society enjoys a certain level of affluence. Poor societies cannot
provide much in the way of criminal justice (police, courts), social security,
public education, medical care, and so forth. But even the poorest society can

require that its government leave its citizens and residents unmolested, free from torture, lengthy detention, cruel punishments, and other related harms. All that is required is governmental self-restraint. This suggests a criterion: roughly, the more fundamental a right is the less its provision and protection depend upon a society's resources and wealth. This has two important consequences. One is that there is little or no direct economic cost for a government to cease its human rights violations where some rights are concerned, whereas it will cost the government a good deal to cease violation of some other rights. The exercise of habeas corpus puts no strain on tax revenues, whereas it may cost a small fortune to build a new sewage treatment facility as a necessary step in the direction of providing for minimally decent health needs. The other consequence of importance is that by linking termination of foreign assistance to some human rights violations and not to others, as Section 502B does, the direct cost for the terminations is not borne by the poorest and least affluent members of society, as it would be if Section 502B were rewritten to terminate foreign assistance to a nation because its government violates the socioeconomic rights of its people.

A second line of consideration might be called *the argument from the functional interdependence among basic rights.* Persons cannot enjoy rights such as free speech or political participation unless certain of their other rights are relatively secure. So long as due process of law is denied, habeas corpus suspended, or self-incriminating testimony admissible at trial without reservation, the political climate is missing in which persons can take seriously the opportunity to govern themselves. In fact, the degree to which habeas corpus and related rights are denied can serve as a reliable index of the futility of democratic political processes. If persons thus oppressed nevertheless enjoy cradle-to-grave welfare rights, they do so as hostages to fortune and patronized victims of tyranny. It is an insult to one's dignity to have welfare rights at the same time one is subject to arbitrary detention without charge or trial, but the converse is not true. It might be objected that it is no less an insult to one's dignity to be guaranteed scrupulous police protection and an elaborate criminal justice system that incorporates every known safeguard to the rights of the accused when one is also left to starve. The reply is two-fold. A government may in fact be unable to do anything about the starvation of a good portion of its population; but a government is never unable to prohibit (and to that extent, end) the practice of torturing suspects. Second, if the starvation is in fact a result of policy—for example, part of a program of genocide for a certain regional or ethnic minority—then it is of course a more massive violation of fundamental rights than even persistent torture is. In general, then, the governments's responsibility to undertake to feed its own people remains less central than its responsibility not to torture. The people, after all, may be quite able to feed themselves, if only they are allowed to organize to do so. Only in a forcibly collectivized economy or in the face of (natural or man-made) catastrophe will government intervention be a necessary condition of avoiding starvation. What is true of starvation is hardly less true of unemployment and many other human needs at the present time.

The same conclusion can be reached by what might be called *the argument from primary goods.* A primary good is anything whatever that "a rational man wants whatever else he wants."[18] Among the primary social goods are "rights and liberties, opportunities and powers, income and wealth," as well as "a sense of one's own worth."[19] Although all human rights probably qualify as primary social goods, some meet this description more preeminently than others. Whatever else you want, if you are rational, you *don't* want to suffer the abuses of government power that torture and the like involve. You must want to be free of such violence to your body and your spirit. Perhaps one can even argue further that no rational man would trade his independence from governmental interference with his privacy, liberty, and personal security for publicly funded social services. At least, not if the interferences take the form cited in Section 502B: torture, prolonged detection without trial, and so forth. The reason is that every rational man has the prospect, in all but the most extreme circumstances, of being able to manage by his own efforts if simply left alone to do so. Confronted with the choice between governmental aid in the form of social services and governmental interference in the form of torture, a rational man would forego the aid in order to be free of the injury. Every act of torture, cruel and inhumane punishment, or detention without charge or trial directly inhibits freedom and self-respect in ways that failure to provide social services and institutions for self-government do not.

The same conclusion can be reached in yet another way, by what can be called *the argument from analogy to crime.* The violation by government of some human rights is strictly analogous to the commission by a private individual of heinous crimes. Thus, torture and the like have the same effects upon their victims as do the crimes of murder, aggravated assault and battery, and rape: disfigurement, mutilation, maiming, incapacitation, death. The failure to respect other human rights, however, is analogous only to a failure to confer (at worst, a withholding of) certain benefits. Government censorship, exclusion from the political process, or the lack of medical aid amount either to a relatively slight harm or to the failure to provide a service or benefit. Underlying this argument is the principle that, in general, causing someone a personal injury is much worse than failing to confer on someone a personal benefit. At the very worst, an individual incapable of fending for himself will suffer the natural consequences of his circumstances. No one will have undertaken to make him worse off. A person obviously has a more severe complaint against his government for subjecting him to torture than for the failure to undertake to make him better off. It is all the difference between an actively malignant despotism and a passively (or ineptly) benevolent despotism. If one had to choose, one would prefer to be the victim of the latter rather than of the former. John Stuart Mill expressed exactly the point at issue when he said, "A person may possibly not need the benefits of others, but he always needs that they should not do him harm."[20]

Finally, the history of our civilization during the past several centuries shows a progressive development of human rights under domestic law that gives us what we can call *the argument from cultural priority*. Traditional liberal doctrine makes it clear why such a development in the recognition of rights over time is coordinate with a reflective assessment of the relative importance of some rights over others. If a person has his rights of life, liberty, property, and security of person protected against invasion by his neighbors and free of tyrannical government violation as well, then given moderate industry on his part he can fend for himself to secure his other rights to the extent that they matter to him. Thus, in the time of Hobbes and Locke, public health care and old age security were deemed matters of public *charity*, not of individual *right*. As for such rights as voting, they were unequally distributed, being contingent upon property and sex qualifications. Only such rights as habeas corpus and jury trial were part of the law of the land and in theory available to all equally.

There is a lesson in this relevant to the provisions of Section 502B. If the United States is going to link human rights with its foreign policy, the rights in question must be rights that we have already undertaken to recognize in our domestic law. They ought not to be rights that our own government has ignored or violated with impunity until recently. They must not be rights about which there is still ideological or other controversy in our own country. They must be rights rooted in our constitutional history and practiced throughout the land. This is not true of any social or economic rights; it is not even true of political or civil rights, as our history of racism and sexism shows. But it is true of the rights singled out in Section 502B. If Justice Brandeis was correct when he wrote a half century ago that "the right to be let alone . . . [is] the right most valued by civilized men,"[21] we can see why the rights singled out for special attention in Section 502B are not an arbitrary subset of all human rights, but deserve the priority this law would give them.

The overall argument so far gives us a sound basis for several of the steps required to justify the provisions of Section 502B: There are human rights that torture and related activities violate. These rights, asserted or implied by a long tradition of philosophical reflection, are now recognized under international law. Like all rights, these rights express the principle that individual freedom, privacy, and autonomy shall not give way whenever they conflict with collective advantage or administrative convenience and efficiency. Finally, these rights have a preferred status even among human rights. What remains to be examined is the basis for undertaking to link their violations with our foreign policy.

Responding to Violations of Rights

I have assumed from the start that it would be morally unacceptable to have a foreign policy, especially a foreign assistance program, that took no account of the violations of human rights by other countries. It is appropriate here to look more closely at why this is so, because it sheds light on the kind of responses to such violations that are feasible and appropriate. Consider for this purpose a largely hypothetical example. Suppose that in 1930 the government of nation A undertook to provide nonmilitary assistance to the government of nation B in the form of oil, gas, and other petrochemical products. Suppose further that within a couple of years the government of nation B was in the hands of a virulent anti-Semitic faction eager to embark on "the final solution to the Jewish problem." Let us suppose that this involved the construction of extermination camps in which lethal poisons would be used in large quantities, and that these poisons were to be manufactured from the raw materials being supplied by the government of nation A, a portion of which would be diverted to this new purpose. To make the argument simpler, let us assume that the government of nation B could not obtain these products elsewhere as cheaply, as promptly, and in such large supply as they could from the government of nation A. On the facts supposed, is it really conceivable that an adviser to the government of nation A, knowing all the facts, would think it morally permissible to recommend continuation of the foreign assistance? The only ground for such a view would have to be that the government of nation B intended to use these chemicals to violate the human rights only of *its own* nationals.

Under the operative assumptions in the example, there are both of two powerful reasons against continuing the export program. First, those in the government of nation A (and to that extent, its people as well) had become, or were on the verge of becoming, knowing accomplices in a monstrous crime against humanity. Thus, in favor of terminating the assistance there is *the argument from avoiding complicity in wrongdoing.* Second, by threatening to withdraw the aid, or actually terminating it, the government of nation A could exert leverage on the anti-Semitic government to cancel its extermination program, either by way of making it very difficult for them to continue or by making them give it up as the price they must pay in order to continue to receive our assistance (most of which, in the example, is being used for purposes wholly unrelated to their policy of genocide for Jews). This is *the argument from leverage to end wrongdoing.* No matter how politically inexpedient or futile it might turn out to be for our government to terminate its aid, it would be morally untenable for a government to be indifferent to human rights violations consequent to its foreign assistance program merely because the victims of these violations were foreign nationals on foreign territory.

To dispute this claim on moral grounds requires defense of the position that under *no* conditions do the human rights violations by one government, so long as they are perpetrated on its own soil and against its own nationals, establish the immorality of another government's refusal to reduce or terminate its aid and assistance to that country. On the contrary, though a nation's foreign policy by definition begins at the water's edge, it does not follow that its moral responsibilities stop there. So, if what might be called the doctrine of moral indifference in foreign policy matters cannot be seriously defended, then the question becomes one of deciding which human rights, when violated, where and in what ways, and by whom ought to be of concern in foreign policy, and what steps can and should be taken by a government to protest and, if possible, end these violations. The hypothetical example, in other words, suffices to establish the fundamental premise of morality on which any possible argument for Section 502B must ultimately rest.

Beyond both complicity and leverage, there is perhaps a third factor at work in Section 502B, more controversial than the other two. It would be incorrect to ascribe to this factor a large role, but it cannot be wholly neglected. Given that another government has systematically violated the most fundamental human rights of its population, it is extremely difficult for our government both to maintain its alliance (as embodied in the foreign assistance program) with that government, and to take no further notice of these violations beyond, say, an official protest to that nation's ambassador. In effect, Section 502B can be read as a demand that our government go further and inflict a quasi-punitive action—the withdrawal of a service or benefit—on those governments which are convicted by the Congress, as it were, after due investigation, of gross and sustained violations of the human rights of their own people. Of course, our government has no legal or political authority to "punish" another government in this or any other way. Nevertheless, there is a strong analogy at precisely this point between what Section 502B authorizes and the proper moral response to those individuals who violate the basic rights of others. As John Stuart Mill once noted, "To have a right . . . is . . . to have something which society ought to defend me in the possession of."[22] H.L.A. Hart has restated the same point: "There is . . . a special congruity in the use of force or the threat of force to secure. . .what is . . .someone's right. . . ."[23] It is in part in this spirit that we should understand the intended function of Section 502B.

A fully coherent social philosophy addressed to the existence of human rights, their incorporation into positive law, and the empirical fact of their actual or likely violation would also undertake to provide for preventive and remedial steps as well as for the punitive measures to which Mill and Hart alluded. Similarly, on the international scene, Section 502B can be seen as both a partially preventive and as a quasi-punitive step for such violations. Withdrawal of continued arms exports, under the provisions of Section 502B, is not exactly punitive even if it is a negative sanction. Nor is application of the sanction provided by this section wholly preventive, as it might be if the availability of arms and training from the United States under its foreign assistance programs were the only way a government could set about to violate the human rights of its citizens. Nevertheless, Section 502B is a disincentive to such rights violations, and at worst a symbolic gesture expressing the judgment of Congress on the extent and significance of human rights violations in other countries.

Finally, making the criterion for our cutoff of foreign assistance "a consistent pattern of gross violations" of human rights, as Section 502B does, helps to exclude a response both premature and hypocritical. We know that violations of human rights occur in our own country at all levels of government (municipal, state, federal). We also know that it is a rare government official who is willing to acknowledge such acts and defend them for what they are. The very fact that they are concealed, denied, and explained away indicates the guilty conscience with which they are perpetrated in our society. However short we actually fall from the standard of impeccable observance of the rights to "life, liberty, and security of person," they are not subject to "a consistent pattern of gross violations" anywhere in the nation. Our proper embarrassment at their sporadic violation almost everywhere is not a reason for ignoring "a consistent pattern of gross violations" by other governments.

Conclusion

It has been said—properly, I think—that human rights are "the fundamental moral and social values which should be or should continue to be realized in any society fit for intelligent and responsible citizens,"[24] "those minimal things without which it is impossible to develop one's capabilities and to live a life as a human being."[25] If so, then *all* law and policy, foreign no less than domestic, ought to be designed to foster the observance and to discourage the violations of human rights. It is a sobering fact, not to be forgotten, that it is governments rather than individuals that have the greatest capacity for violating human rights. Looked at from the moral point of view, it cannot be right for one nation to allow the people of another nation to become the hostages, captives, slaves, or victims of its own government. Restraints upon governments, or at least disincentives, to prevent and discourage violation of the rights of persons should be a concern of all governments and all peoples. It is on this understanding that Section 502B should be appraised.

Notes

1. See, for the full text, *Congressional Record,* 122:83 (June 2, 1976) at H5129-5130; P.L. 94-329 (1976); and 90 Stat. 748-750.

2. See especially the address by President Carter to the U.N. General Assembly, as reported in *New York Times*, March 18, 1977, p. A10; and the address by Secretary Vance, "Human Rights and Foreign Policy," *Department of State Bulletin*, May 23, 1977, pp. 505-512.

3. See, for example, John Richardson, Jr., "Human Rights Strategy," *Freedom at Issue*, 41 (May-June 1977), 3; Daniel P. Moynihan, "The Politics of Human Rights," *Commentary*, 64:8 (August 1977), pp. 19-26; and the items cited above, note 2.

4. See "International Security Assistance Act of 1976," *Hearings of the Committee on International Relations, on H.P. 11963*, H.R., 94th Congress, 1976. Pages 497-522 are devoted to the Frazier-Solarz amendment, which ultimately became Section 502B of the current law. A few other references to the human rights provisions of this act are scattered throughout the more than 900 pages of the hearing record.

5. See *Congressional Record*, 122:29 (March 3, 1976), H1506-H1580 (especially H1537-H1553); ibid., 122:83 (June 2, 1976), H5122-H5167 (especially H5129-5131); ibid., 122:97 (June 22, 1976), H6415-H6420.

6. See Ian Browlie, ed., *Basic Documents on Human Rights* (Oxford: Clarendon Press, 1971).

7. See Amnesty International, *Report on Torture* (New York: Farrar, Straus and Giroux, 1976).

8. H.L.A. Hart, "Are There Any Natural Rights?" *The Philosophical Review*, 65:2 (April 1955), pp. 175-191, at p. 175.

9. John Rawls, *A Theory of Justice* (Cambridge, Mass.: Harvard University Press, 1971), mentions rights and uses them from one end of his argument to the other, including many central points—for example, in his statement of the principles of justice (pp. 60 ff., 302).

10. Ronald Dworkin, "The Original Position," *University of Chicago Law Review*, 40:3 (Spring 1973), pp. 500-533, at p. 531.

11. Richard A. Wasserstrom, "Rights, Human Rights, and Racial Discrimination," *Journal of Philosophy*, 61:20 (October 29, 1964), pp. 628-640, at pp. 631-632.

12. I have discussed these matters in greater detail elsewhere; see H.A. Bedau, "The Right to Life," *Monist*, 52:4 (October 1968), pp. 550-572.

13. Joel Feinberg, *Social Philosophy* (Englewood Cliffs, N.J.: Prentice-Hall, 1973), p. 87.

14. Maurice Cranston, *What Are Human Rights?* (New York: Taplinger Publishing Co., 1973), pp. 70-71.

15. See Ronald Dworkin, *Taking Rights Seriously* (Cambridge: Harvard University Press, 1978).

16. Remarks of Congressman Don Fraser, in *Hearings*, p. 502.

17. See, for example, Robert Nozick, *Anarchy, State and Utopia* (New York: Basic Books, 1974), especially chapters 3 and 5.

18. Rawls, p. 92.

19. Ibid.

20. John Stuart Mill, *Utilitarianism,* part V, sixth paragraph from the end.

21. *Olmstead* v. *United States,* 277 U.S. 438, 478 (1928).

22. Mill, thirteenth paragraph from the end.

23. Hart, p. 177.

24. Margaret Macdonald, "Natural Rights," *Proceedings of the Aristotelian Society,* 47 (1946-1947), pp. 225-250, at p. 240.

25. Wasserstrom, p. 636.

4 Human Rights and Social Justice

Charles R. Beitz

Among the many questions that might be raised about the American commitment to promote respect for internationally recognized human rights is the question of *scope*: *which* human rights should U.S. policy promote? While philosophers should be able to shed light on this question, it is not only a philosopher's question: the shape of the American human rights policy, its specific goals, its costs, and its main targets, cannot be determined without answering this question.

The scope of a commitment to promote human rights might vary in breadth from a relatively narrow commitment to promote what are usually called rights of the person, to a broader commitment to promote political and/or economic rights as well. A clear statement of the narrow view occurs in the International Security Assistance and Arms Export Act of 1976, and is repeated in more recent legislation concerning foreign economic assistance. These instruments commit the U.S. to oppose "gross violation of internationally recognized human rights," including "torture or cruel, inhuman or degrading treatment or punishment, prolonged detention without charges and trial, and other flagrant denial of the right to life, liberty, or the security of the person. . . ."[1] President Carter used similar language in describing the American commitment to the United Nations, where he identified as "basic human rights" protection against "mistreatment" and "torture or unwarranted deprivation."[2]

What is striking about such language is the narrowness of its interpretation of "internationally recognized human rights." Personal rights are only one part—and, numerically, at least, not the major part—of the rights listed in documents of international law such as the two International Covenants on Human Rights, the European Convention on Human Rights, and the Universal Declaration of 1948. These documents include two further kinds of rights, which I shall call political rights (rights of political participation) and economic rights (rights to such benefits as an adequate job, education, health care, social insurance, and so on). To broaden the scope of the U.S. human rights policy would be to take account of (at least some) political and economic rights as well as of personal rights.

It would be inaccurate to claim that the broader interpretation of "internationally recognized human rights" has gone unremarked by members of the Carter administration. Secretary Vance, in his Law Day speech at the University of Georgia, acknowledged the importance of political and economic rights for a human rights policy, and said that U.S. policy would be formulated with all three types of rights in mind.[3] On the other hand, it is not clear to what extent the secretary's promise is being carried out by various executive and legislative agencies. To date, it seems fair to say, the administration's actions indicate that priority is being given to well-publicized violations of personal rights.[4] That this is consonant with the preponderance of congressional opinion is suggested by the fact that the debate regarding 1977 appropriations for multilateral lending institutions did not produce any broadening of the list of personal rights included in such earlier legislation as the military assistance act cited above.[5]

This position seems anomalous. It runs counter to the broad doctrine of human rights which is represented by the various documents of international law mentioned above. One might well ask, as have many Third World spokespeople, why the scope of the American human rights policy should be restricted to personal rights while benignly neglecting political and economic rights. This is the question I want to address in a preliminary way here.

To some extent the answer to my question might be practical rather than philosophical. For example, one might say that the foreign policy resources available (for example, exhortation, manipulation of aid commitments, and so on) are better adapted, or otherwise more appropriate, to encouraging respect for personal rights than for other kinds of rights. Obviously, practical considerations are important in the human rights debate, but I shall not pursue them here.

The reason that I want to put practical considerations aside is that many people seem to think that personal rights have some claim, *in principle*, to be ranked higher in the scale of foreign policy concerns than political or economic rights. These people contend that there are philosophical rather than practical reasons for concentrating our attention on personal rights. It is this contention that I believe to be false.

My discussion has two parts. In the first, I consider several reasons why one might think that personal rights deserve priority as human rights concerns of foreign policy. While these reasons certainly are not exhaustive, I believe that they include the main considerations that typically move people to be skeptical about any broader view of human rights. The position I shall defend is that none of these considerations shows that personal rights, in general, should have greater emphasis than should economic or political rights in the formation of U.S. foreign policy.

To argue this is not to argue that all internationally recognized human rights should have equal emphasis. My position is the less extreme one that the conventional distinction among personal, economic, and political rights does not provide any significant guidance regarding the scope of a human rights policy. When the policy's scope must, of necessity, be restricted, some other basis than categorical distinctions is required to justify the restrictions. Although I cannot provide such a basis here, I believe that it is possible to outline a more adequate way to approach the issue. In part two, I do so by contrasting two models of human rights, which I call the natural rights model and the social justice model, and suggest that the justification of internationally recognized human rights draws more substantially on considerations of social justice than many human rights theorists have appreciated.

Personal Rights, Human Rights, and Foreign Policy

Personal rights have several features that might move us to accord them priority attention in a human rights policy. For one thing, personal rights seem to be logically different from political and economic rights: personal rights are rights against interference in action while the other rights are rights to be enabled to act. Further, philosophical arguments for personal rights do not seem to require reference to special characteristics of particular societies whereas arguments for political and economic rights seem to require more extensive reference to the empirical circumstances of the societies in which they are claimed. Third, personal rights—especially rights against torture and cruelty—seem more closely linked to individual survival than do political and (most) economic rights. Finally, the world's cultures might seem more fully in agreement on the importance of the human interests protected by personal rights than on the importance of other human interests.

Each of these distinctive features of personal rights gives rise to an argument that personal rights should be the most important human rights concerns of foreign policy, or, at least, that personal rights should survive any limitation of the scope of a human rights foreign policy. While versions of one or more of these arguments seem to be widely accepted, I do not believe that any of them really establishes the conclusion that they are supposed to establish. A more careful look at these four arguments helps to make this point clear.

The first argument is based on differences in *type* of rights. One might say that personal rights are of a different logical type than either political or economic rights. Personal rights (for example, the right not to be tortured, or the right not to be arbitrarily imprisoned) are rights against certain kinds of interference; they secure us against having certain things done to us. But this does not seem to be generally true of political and economic rights. While some political rights are rights against interference (for example, freedoms of religion and thought), others are rights of participation (for example, rights to vote and to hold public office), and still others are rights to institutions which meet certain conditions (for example, the right to a fair trial). Most economic rights are rights to have access to various kinds of benefits (for example, a job or adequate health care). Thus, some political rights, and most economic ones, differ from personal rights in that political and economic rights are rights to be enabled to act, whereas the personal rights are rights not to be interfered with in acting.

It has sometimes been thought that this difference in type supports the view that personal rights are more basic or more important than other kinds of human rights.[6] But it is not obvious why this follows. Perhaps one thinks that human rights are some sort of demythologized natural rights—human rights are metaphysically paler, but at least they retain those central characteristics of inalienability and exceptionlessness which writers like Locke attributed to natural rights. Then one might want to say that political and economic rights aren't human rights at all, since it is hard to imagine many such rights that meet such stringent conditions. As I suggest in the next section, I believe that it is misleading to view human rights on the model of natural rights, and so I think that this approach is inappropriate.[7] But even conceding the immediate point, why should we think that the inalienability and/or exceptionlessness of a right provides a reason for holding the right more important or more basic than the satisfaction of other human interests?

One might respond, to use Cranston's words, that the classical "natural rights" are "rights nobody could find any excuse for not respecting."[8] The suggestion seems to be that the classical natural rights are less subject to controversy than other rights precisely because they admit of no exceptions. Given agreement that a right is a natural right, and hence that it is inalienable and exceptionless, there is no occasion for controversy about its application to particular cases. On the other hand, rights which are *not* exceptionless and inalienable (for example, perhaps, the right to "a decent living") may, for this very reason, arouse disagreement concerning when they apply. For one thing, it may be unclear what conditions justify making an exception. Further, even if it is agreed what is a relevant condition for making an exception, there may be disagreement about whether the condition obtains in a particular case. Because economic and political rights are inherently more controversial than personal rights, one might conclude, they should be regarded as less basic or important for the purposes of foreign policymaking.

This version of the first argument is open to several kinds of attack. It is not obvious, for example, that personal rights are less controversial than other rights. Those who advocate actions offensive to a personal right might simply deny that the right is exceptionless. They might be wrong, but they would at least have demonstrated that the personal right in question is controversial. But surely we would not allow *this* sort of controversiality to defeat the force of a right. It is not controversiality as such, but practical uncertainty about whether a right applies (or may appropriately be claimed) that makes plausible the argument that I have reconstructed. That is, there may be instances in which it is simply unclear whether the conditions which justify exceptions to the right do, in fact, obtain. However, there are two objections even to this (reduced) version of the controversiality claim. First, it is not obvious that all political and economic rights are uncertain in their application. Indeed, one would expect there to be some clear cases of such rights as the right to an adequate diet or the right to freedom of speech. The fact that the application of a right *might* be uncertain does not imply that its application always *is* uncertain. Furthermore, and more fundamentally, the fact that the application of a right is uncertain does not imply that the right is of less intrinsic importance than less troublesome rights. Perhaps it is uncertain under what conditions a promisee can demand that a promise be kept, but this in itself seems irrelevant to the *importance* that should be attached to the satisfaction of the promisee's right that the promise be kept.

A second argument for according greater weight to personal rights might be based on differences in the philosophical foundations of personal vis à vis political or economic rights. One might think that personal, political, and economic rights are supported by different kinds of arguments, and that the differences among these arguments provide grounds for asserting that the various rights have different weights. Let me illustrate. Suppose (as Hart, for example, has suggested in an influential article)[9] that rights can be divided into two classes according to whether or not their philosophical foundation possesses the characteristic of *generality*. "General" rights would be rights which people have as people, regardless of their institutional ties and voluntary undertakings; "special" rights would be all other rights, that is, rights which people come to have in virtue of their institutional memberships (for example, being a citizen of some country) or voluntary actions (for example, being party to a contract). As it happens, Hart says, there is one general right—the equal right of all persons to be free from coercive interference with their actions. He is very clear that this general right is not a right to any particular political or economic benefit. Such rights, on his account, are special rights and arise as consequences of people's participation in schemes of social cooperation for mutual advantage.

While Hart himself does not argue that general rights are weightier than special rights, his account suggests how the distinction between general and special rights might be invoked as part of such an argument. The distinguishing feature of a special right (such as a right to some political or economic benefit) is that it arises among persons who stand in a special relationship with one another constituted by their voluntary undertakings or common citizenship. Special rights are rights against particular persons or groups, namely, those who are parties to the special relationship out of which the right arises. For example, my right to a decent job or to a fair trial is (in Hart's view) a right against those who share membership in our society. If this is true, then it might seem that respect for special rights is the particular concern of those who are parties to the appropriate special relationship whereas general rights are the concern of everyone. If at least some personal rights are derived from the general right of all persons to be free, while political and economic rights are special rights, then the argument I have constructed might be thought to explain why personal rights should have primacy in our foreign policy. To put the argument briefly: violations of *personal* rights are *everyone's* concern because personal rights are possessed by persons *as persons.* But violations of economic and political rights *are not* everyone's concern—they are the concern of the other members of the victim's own society. So, one might conclude, to pay attention to political and economic rights in making foreign policy is to interject oneself where one does not belong, into the private moral affairs of other societies.

The trouble is that this argument is weak in several respects. First, it is not at all obvious that people as people have no right to any political or economic benefits independently of their memberships in particular societies. Indeed, Professor Vlastos has argued that there are *two* rights which meet Hart's test of generality, rights to freedom and to well-being. Vlastos argues that a basic principle of our morality is the belief that everyone has "equal human worth"—that is, that freedom and well-being have the same intrinsic value to everyone, or, that one person's well-being and freedom is as valuable as any other's. From this, Vlastos says it follows that everyone has an equal human right to freedom and well-being, and that we possess these rights simply because we're human—not just because we're parties to any special relationship or members of a particular society.[10]

Even if we concede, as an abstract matter, that economic (and, perhaps, political) rights are special rights, in Hart's sense, it does not follow that such rights arise *within* national communities but not *between* them. In view of the extensive web of economic interdependence characteristic of contemporary international relations, it seems arbitrary to say that the economic cooperation which defines the special relations of members of national societies gives rise to special rights to economic benefits for members of particular societies, but that international economic cooperation does not give rise to similar or analogous rights for members of world society. Perhaps all economic rights *are* special rights: it still needs to be explained why national boundaries should be thought to set the limits within which special rights may arise.[11]

However, I do not want to rest my refutation of the argument on the point that its premise is controversial. Even if Hart is correct in maintaining that political and economic rights are special rights, and if special rights arise only within national communities, it still does not follow that promoting compliance with their requirements is the special business of the parties to the appropriate relationship. Consider a simpler case about interpersonal relations. Suppose that I promise to deliver the finished version of this chapter to the editor by next Friday. The promise would be ill-advised, but if I were incautious enough to make it, I would create a special right for the editor to demand that I do, in fact, deliver the manuscript to him at the appointed time. The right would be the editor's, and the obligation mine; but anyone who was appropriately placed could appropriately urge me to comply. The fact that the right to my compliance is a special right which arises from a special relationship between the editor and myself does not preclude others from taking account of his right to my compliance in determining how to conduct themselves toward me. In other words, one does not have to be a party to the relationship which generates a right in order to be entitled to insist that the right be respected. The point seems to apply as clearly to international relations as to interpersonal relations. Even if political and economic rights are special rather than general rights, this fact in itself provides no reason for weighting them less heavily than personal rights in the formation of foreign policy.

The third argument (perhaps the most straightforward argument considered here) holds that the greater importance of personal rights can be established by considering how a normal individual would evaluate the relative desirability or undesirability of having certain things happen to him/her. It seems plausible, if not self-evidently obvious, that a normal person would prefer hunger to torture, unemployment to cruel, prolonged, and undeserved punishment, or deprivation of the right to vote to deprivation of the right to personal security. After considering several grisly comparisons of this sort, one might conclude that, from the point of view of any normal person, it would worse to be deprived of personal rights than to be deprived of political and economic rights. If so, then it would follow that, from the point of view of any normal person, it would be more important to have secure protection of personal rights than of political and economic ones.

Now, again, I do not want to debate whether this conclusion is true. Perhaps it is possible to imagine cases in which we would think it false. Perhaps, as Isaiah Berlin has written, to offer "safeguards against intervention by the state, to men who are half-naked, illiterate, underfed, and diseased is to mock their condition. . . ."[12] Nevertheless, let us simply assume that the general point as I have formulated it is correct. What I want to say is that it does not obviously follow from this general point that we should give greater weight to deprivations of personal rights than to deprivations of political and economic rights in deciding how American foreign policy should treat some other government. To draw this conclusion would be to commit something like the fallacy of composition, that is, to infer from the fact that something is true of discrete individuals the fact that the same thing is true of groups. Is it worse, all things considered, for a government to torture 100 people than to let 10,000 go without food or medical care? Does it make sense to censure a government for holding political prisoners but not to censure it for pursuing investment and incomes policies that deprive persons of jobs? Certainly any of these prospects would be horrible; my point is just that reflections about discrete individuals do not settle cases involving groups.

Finally, one might argue that personal rights are the only truly universal human rights, and that economic and political rights form a part of human rights doctrine that is the distinctive product of Western moral prejudices. Such a view has been argued by Peter Berger, who claims that political and economic rights "derive from the specifically Western values of liberty and equality," whereas personal rights "pertain to the human condition as such."[13] The basis of such views is not the philosophical position discussed earlier, that the *foundation* of economic and political rights (as "special rights") is different from that of personal (or "general") rights, but rather the sociological observation that different cultures tend to exhibit different moral codes, together with the belief (undefended by Berger) that one should not condemn behavior in another culture that would not be proscribed by the culture's own moral code.

This position is initially attractive, since it takes seriously intercultural disagreements that we all too often ignore. However, on closer inspection, it does not support the conclusion it claims to support, that personal rights are the only universal rights. For one thing, the view involves a rather simple-minded picture of what is going on when a government is accused of a violation of economic or political rights. Berger's image is of a government being accused by meddling foreigners who are insensitive to the nuances of the moral code prevalent in the government's own society. But it is difficult to think of a single real-world case that conforms to this image. Instead, international or foreign interference in support of human rights normally takes place when the society in question is itself divided with respect to the policies its government should pursue. The society's own moral code offers conflicting instructions, and the conflict is reflected in the division among the society's own population. If I am right that this is the more typical case, then relativistic objections to the doctrine of universal human rights lose their force, for international action to support human rights no longer appears to be a form of cultural or intellectual imperialism.

Another difficulty with the fourth argument is that it rests on the very implausible empirical premise that personal rights constitute the least common denominator of the world's moralities, whereas these moralities are divided with regard to economic and political rights. The premise may not be entirely implausible, but it certainly represents a grievous overgeneralization. Can anyone seriously believe that desires for a decent diet, or adequate housing, or minimally satisfying work, are parochial Western concerns? Are these human interests any more "Western" than the interest in not suffering the pains of torture, or the restrictions of prolonged and unjustified confinement? *Perhaps* there is a point at which the human rights of the international declarations diverge from the common core of the world's moral codes, but surely this point does not appear at the dividing line between personal and other human rights.

If these too brief remarks are correct, then the most obvious philosophical arguments for weighting personal rights considerations more heavily than considerations of political and economic rights are invalid. If American foreign policy is to involve a human rights commitment, there are no obvious philosophical reasons for not taking seriously a broader range of human rights than those enumerated in current aid legislation and recent presidential pronouncements.

Of course, to say this is not finally to resolve the issue. All I have done here is to attempt to remove some philosophical reasons for resisting a broadening of the definition of human rights to include some rights which I have called economic and political rights. Nevertheless, it would be unrealistic to think that the human rights concerns of U.S. foreign policy should embrace all of the rights enumerated in such catalogs as the two Covenants or the Universal Declaration. The limited resources available for executing a human rights policy make *some* limitation of the policy's scope inevitable. Also, some rights, like the right against forced marriage, may simply be beyond the reach of the available foreign policy instruments.

In view of these observations, the position I have taken might be reformulated as follows: when choices need to be made among the various rights that might become concerns of foreign policy, it would be philosophically incorrect to make them on the basis of the view that personal rights are inherently more important or more basic than other rights. The conventional division among personal, political, and economic rights presumes a spurious neatness in the philosophical foundations of the array of human rights listed in authoritative international documents. Some other basis is needed for making choices among the rights that foreign policy should take most seriously.

Two Models of Human Rights

Why has there been a persistent tendency among philosophers to assign priority to personal rights when choices among human rights need to be made? This tendency results from thinking about human rights on the model of natural rights, an older variety of rights of which human rights are sometimes thought to be the historical successors. I believe that the natural rights model of human rights is flawed in several respects, and that a different model, the social justice model, is more adequate. In this section, I explore these thoughts.

Offhand, it is not obvious what "models" of human rights are, or why we should take any interest in them. I shall understand a "model" of human rights as a definite characterization of the idea of a human right, together with a conception of the sorts of considerations which justify them. A model of human rights answers two questions: What are human rights? Why do we have them? Although these seem to be distinct questions, in fact they are closely related. Definitions of human rights presuppose that some, but not other, kinds of considerations are relevant as justifying reasons; and conceptions of justification influence judgments about which characteristics human rights do or do not have. If there were available a settled and uncontroversial answer to either question, then the other question might be answered in a straightforward way. However, in cases in which matters of definition and of justification are both controversial, it would be artificial to insist on too great a distinction between these matters. Thus, I shall simply combine correlative definitions and justifications in the two alternative models mentioned, and ask which model provides a better account of the contemporary doctrine of human rights.

Why should we take any interest in these models? The most obvious reason is that the international human rights declarations raise problems of interpretation which must be settled before the rights of the declarations can be implemented. One such problem—which has preoccupied us thus far—is that of priorities. Another is suggested by the frequently noted fact that the declarations seem to address questions of *distribution* (one has claims to what?) without addressing questions of *contribution* (who should satisfy these claims?).

The situation confronting someone who, for practical reasons, must devise responsible solutions to such problems is partly analogous to that confronting a judge in hard cases.[14] A hard case is a case for which legal authority, for example, statute and precedent, does not provide an unambiguous solution. A responsible judge must supply a theory which justifies as much of the documentary authority as possible while settling the troublesome ambiguities regarding the instant case. In other words, the judge must construct a model of the considerations underlying the existing law that permits the hard case to be resolved, as it were, by extrapolation.[15] Such a model is evaluated according to its ability to account for as much existing documentary authority as possible, its theoretical coherence, and its ability to settle hard cases.

The human rights problems mentioned are similar in that the international declarations do not provide unambiguous solutions to them. A model is needed that supplies a coherent justification of as much of the declarations as possible while settling the relevant problems of interpretation. The natural rights and social justice models of human rights are alternative means for accomplishing these ends.

The natural rights model of human rights is more familiar. According to this model, the doctrine of human rights is the historical and philosophical successor of the doctrine of natural rights propounded most influentially in modern times by John Locke.[16] For Locke, natural rights were rights that people might be said to possess in a state of nature devoid of positive institutions:

> The State of Nature has a Law of Nature to govern it, which obliges every one: And Reason, which is that Law, teaches all Mankind, who will but consult it, that being all equal and independent, no one ought to harm another in his Life, Health, Liberty, or Possessions.[17]

Lockean rights express constraints that no one, neither fellow citizens, rulers, nor any other persons, may permissibly infringe. Furthermore, their moral justification is independent of considerations involving positive institutions, and instead involves features possessed by persons regardless of their particular political ties.

Let us look more closely at the main characteristics of natural rights. Natural rights, as rights, typically assert an especially strong kind of claim against others, one which cannot be overridden simply for convenience, or for the sake of custom, or to maximize the social good. While rights in general are not necessarily absolute (in the sense that it is never permissible to override them) they count as especially important reasons for or against particular actions and policies, which only certain special sorts of considerations can justify overriding. Since I am not here concerned with elucidating a general theory of rights, I shall not pursue the difficult problems raised by my claim that rights assert especially strong claims.

In addition to their special weight, *natural* rights assert claims for *immediate* satisfaction; if I have a present right against you in some respect, you have a duty to satisfy my claim *now*. In normal cases, rights express the strongest moral claims one can make, and so, again in normal cases, and absent competing rights, you can have no acceptable excuse for failing to satisfy the claims of right that I press against you. The importance of the immediate satisfaction condition is that it distinguishes natural rights from social goals, even those involving the future satisfaction of rights. On a Lockean view, a claim of natural right is not adequately satisfied by a policy which will increase the chances that the right will be respected in the future but does not require that it be respected in the present. Robert Nozick captures this characteristic of natural rights when he describes rights as "side constraints," that is, as flat prohibitions against treating persons in certain ways.[18]

So far we have been concerned with the characteristics of natural rights as rights. But it must also be asked why certain rights should be called "natural." Richard Wasserstrom's study of the traditional natural rights yields four characteristics that set them off from other rights: natural rights are *universal*, in the sense that everyone has them; they are possessed *equally* by everyone who has them at all; they are possessed by *persons as persons*, without regard to institutional memberships or voluntary undertakings; and they are assertable as claims *against the whole world*, rather than against nameable individuals or subgroups.[19] From a Lockean point of view, these conditions are necessary but not sufficient to qualify a right as a natural right; Locke, like other classical theorists of natural rights, would insist on an additional condition regarding how we come to know that natural rights exist. For example, they can be known by reason, or they can be inferred from the natural law, and/or they are commands of God. Writers like those cited above, who construe human rights on the natural rights model, usually attempt to preserve the first group of features in their doctrines of human rights while dispensing with the second. On this model, human rights are natural rights purged of transcendent metaphysics.

I believe that a good deal of the philosophical insecurity surrounding the subject of human rights results from construing them on the natural rights model. There are two sets of difficulties, one having to do with the appropriateness of the model's characterization of a right, and the other, with the appropriateness of the conditions of "naturalness." Let us begin with the former. Recall that we have said that rights express important moral claims, and that these claims typically demand immediate satisfaction. For the most part, human rights are not embarrassed by the first of these conditions (importance), but there are exceptions such as the (in)famous right to "holidays with pay" recognized by article twenty-four of the Universal Declaration. Of course, there are problems of *relative* importance among human rights, but, for the most part, it does not seem unreasonable to view most of the rights enumerated in the various declarations and covenants as protections of especially important human interests. Human rights, like other rights, give rise to claims that considerations of custom, social utility, and so on do not normally override. The second condition (immediate satisfaction) is more troublesome, because some human rights (for example, the right to "social security") under some circumstances simply cannot be provided immediately, since they may require various economic and social background conditions to be met. In this respect, Feinberg is correct in arguing that some human rights are "rights in an unusual new 'manifesto sense'" which represent social goals rather than claims for immediate satisfaction.[20] The import of designating these goals as "rights" seems to be that, as goals they have special importance for those in a position to promote them: either they should count more heavily than other goals in the formation of policy, or they have objective weight in comparison with the expressed desires of the population involved, or both.

The most pressing problems with the natural rights model of human rights arise with respect to the four conditions of "naturalness" distinguished by Wasserstrom. The difficulty is this: if a right must have all four of the features noted by Wasserstrom in order to qualify as a human right, then there are extremely few human rights. Indeed, it is difficult to find more than a few rights among those listed, for example, in the Universal Declaration, that satisfy all four conditions. Rights of participation, for example, are not *universal* if it is true, as some argue, that politics at low levels of economic development cannot support participatory institutions, or can do so only at unacceptable cost.[21] To choose another type of example, some economic rights, like the right to a satisfying job, may not be possessed by *persons as persons* if the philosophical basis of such claims has to do with the special relations in which people stand as members of a functioning scheme of social cooperation (as, for example, on a Rawlsian view of social justice). For in that case economic rights are assertable only by those who share the special relations which give rise to the rights.[22]

What these examples suggest is that it is extremely difficult to make sense of very many human rights on the natural rights model. But those who are reluctant to give up the natural rights model of human rights might dispute this claim. They might say that the natural rights model has strong independent philosophical support, and if some rights commonly recognized as human rights fail the tests of the model, then so much the worse for these human rights. This view is implied by Hart's argument, noted earlier, that if there are any natural rights, then there is one such right, the equal right of all to be free from deliberate coercion, and that this right specifically does not include rights to economic benefits or to certain means of political participation. On this account, the "rights" enumerated in the human rights manifestos may not be human rights at all, since any such right, to qualify as human, must past the four tests of naturalness listed above. The problem I have identified, natural rights advocates might say, is not so much a problem for the natural rights model as for the human rights manifestos.

This step has an important consequence which must not be overlooked. Since most economic and political rights are excluded from the fold of genuine (that is, natural) human rights, the natural rights approach has the effect of exporting the problem of comparing (genuine) human rights with other moral concerns from the justifying theory of human rights. Furthermore, since this model takes human rights, as rights, to be especially important moral commodities, it resolves the problem of comparison by stipulating that rights should win out over other moral concerns when these conflict. Thus, it is not simply of definitional interest whether or not economic and political rights are *really* human rights; if these supposed rights are not genuine human rights, then the natural rights model holds that their satisfaction must yield to the satisfaction of genuine human rights (personal rights, for the most part) when choices must be made.

If this comparative claim were unproblematic on philosophical grounds, then the natural rights model might be defended against the objection that it does not account for all of the internationally recognized human rights in the way suggested above. However, as I argued in the the previous section, the comparative claim is not unproblematic. Indeed, the most common arguments for according personal rights (and, by extension, "genuine" human rights) priority in cases in which only some rights can be promoted do not seem persuasive. In other words, it is not at all clear that the priority of personal rights follows from their naturalness. Thus, one of the reasons why we need a philosophical theory of human rights—namely, the need to provide a mechanism for making comparisons among human rights when these are unavoidable —is not satisfied by the natural rights model.

There is another problem, more easily formulated. I remarked above that a model of human rights is needed to settle the question of contribution to the satisfaction of human rights claims. Virtually all rights claims involve costs: Who should pay them? This question is not especially problematic for classical doctrines of natural rights because their rights are few and easily satisfied (that is, satisfied at little cost to the satisfier), or because it is usually clear who is responsible when rights are violated. However, when human rights are construed, as they are by the international declarations, to include economic rights the satisfaction of which may be costly, questions of contribution (who pays?)

become more pressing. For example, human beings are supposed to have rights to a decent diet. Whose obligation is it to satisfy these rights, and why? The answer is hardly obvious, yet the question cannot be avoided. The natural rights model, by excluding economic rights from the fold of genuine human rights, simply refuses to answer this question. Again, if there were compelling independent reasons for limiting the range of genuine human rights so as to exclude economic rights, this would be defensible. But these reasons seem to evaporate on investigation. The point remains that the natural rights model does not help to resolve problems about contribution.

By way of summary, let met offer a general hypothesis to account for the difficulties of the natural rights model of human rights. Natural rights are set off from other moral concerns by a least three sets of considerations, regarding their relative importance, their universality, and their justification. Natural rights are conceived as things of great value, possessed by everyone, and justified by considerations that make no essential reference to contingent characteristics of persons (such as their abilities, merit, or group membership) or of social structures (such as their level of development). The human rights of the declarations are supposed to share the first two sets of characteristics—they are very important and everyone has them. From the fact that natural rights and human rights are similar in some respects it has been inferred that they must share the same type of justification.

This is where the problem lies. Guided by the attempt to secure a foundation for human rights that is independent of a person's contingent social relations, the natural rights model leads to a view of rights that guarantees above all else the protection of the person against the onslaught of institutions and other persons. It thus ignores conditions regarding the individual's position in society that are essential in understanding what human interests are most important, all things considered. This is why the natural rights model cannot make sense of most economic and political rights, and why it cannot provide a plausible argument for the greater intrinsic importance of personal rights. The natural rights view of justification is faulty: it is incomplete and partial. As a result, it not only fails to accord with our intuitions about what human interests are important, and with the international declarations; it also does not help settle the problems which originally moved us to look for a model of human rights.[23]

I conclude—admittedly without considering all of the possible defenses of the natural rights model—that we misunderstand the contemporary doctrine of human rights when we think of human rights as demythologized natural rights. Fortunately, another model of human rights is available—I shall call it the social justice model—which, while not without problems of its own, seems more adequately to capture the spirit of the international declarations. The social justice model of human rights has not been the subject of much explicit philosophical discussion, and so we must be content with a very sketchy characterization. Nevertheless, I think this model can be shown to account for a larger range of internationally recognized human rights than the natural rights model and to provide more adequate grounds for comparisons among rights.

According to the social justice model, human rights are entitlements to the satisfaction of various human interests that would be guaranteed to members of a group by principles of social justice appropriate to that group. I understand principles of social justice roughly in Rawls's sense: principles of justice express the conditions under which social institutions may be regarded as morally legitimate, and these conditions, in the first instance, have to do with the manner in which a society's basic institutional structure distributes the benefits and burdens of social cooperation.[24] Thus human rights are rights secured by justice, and the international commitment to implement the human rights of the manifestos is in fact an international commitment to encourage the development of just institutions in every society.

Several features of the social justice model of human rights should be noticed. First, this model is considerably more faithful than the natural rights model to what Feinberg calls the "manifesto sense" of human rights. In the nature of the case, some human rights may simply not be satisfiable immediately. While this fact embarrasses the natural rights model, it does not embarrass the social justice model, since we may (and often do) regard principles of justice as establishing an ideal toward which political and economic change should tend.

Second, because the social justice model recognizes that some rights find their philosophical foundation in certain characteristics of human social cooperation, it can explain the basis of (at least some of) those human rights which do not belong to persons as persons, but rather belong to persons because of the social relations in which they stand. Thus, it seems reasonable to predict that the social justice model will be more able to bring into discussions about human rights considerations about contribution which do not come up on the natural rights view.

Third, the social justice model, because it can provide a foundation for a broader range of human rights, is better equipped to support comparisons among rights. On the natural rights view according to which nonnatural rights are not genuine human rights at all, these comparisons appear as conflicts between human rights and other concerns (perhaps including nonnatural, non-human rights); in this sense, problems of comparison are external to the justifying theory of human rights and the theory itself therefore provides no guidance in reconciling conflicts. On the other hand, the social justice model beings conflicts among human rights into the justifying theory, and supplies a structure within which comparisons can be made. For example, in Rawls's theory, conflicts between rights to liberty and rights to material benefit are reconciled with reference to the philosophical foundation of both types of rights. Thus, he argues that certain liberties may be denied in the short run "if it is necessary to raise the level of civilization so that in due course these freedoms can be enjoyed."[25] While I think that Rawls's brief remarks on this issue suffer from a failure to distinguish different liberties, the general point should be clear: it is possible to address the choices about rights that unavoidable natural facts force upon us only in the context of a theory that draws together the diverse moral considerations that enter into the justification of general principles of social justice.

Finally, the social justice model potentially allows considerations of economic and cultural diversity to play a role in justifying and ranking human rights. Since human rights are conceived as rights guaranteed by the principles of justice appropriate to the social group at issue, the human rights of any particular person depend upon the principles appropriate to his or her social group. If, as on some plausible theories (like Rawls's), the requirements of these principles vary with the level of economic development of the group, the social justice model can explain why it is that some rights (say, the right to an adequate diet) may have greater priority in some circumstances than some other rights (say, the right to free access to higher education).

The drawbacks of the social justice model are obvious. In particular, it suggests that the philosophical foundations of human rights are more complex than is often appreciated. One cannot know which rights specific persons can legitimately claim, nor how these rights should be ranked, without working out a theory of social justice appropriate to the person's social group. And this, we must recognize, is inevitably a difficult task, and one which non-members of the social group are likely to be especially ill-equipped to carry out. Furthermore, the social justice model implies that everyone's complement of rights *sans phrase* may differ, even though everyone's *human* rights are the same. Members of developed societies may, for example, have rights of political participation which support claims for immediate satisfaction, while members of less developed societies may not.

An additional difficulty is that persons may be members of more than one social group to which principles of social justice are appropriate. In particular, if (as I believe it can be shown) all those who participate directly or indirectly in global economic interaction can be said to constitute a social group for the purposes of identifying appropriate principles of justice, there is the problem of deriving human rights from global principles of justice as well as from the principles appropriate to each person's national society. I cannot explore this problem here, and I see no simple way of resolving the conflicts between global and national entitlements that might result.[26]

Nevertheless, I think that the social justice model provides a more appropriate model of human rights than the natural rights model. It more adequately represents human rights, in the words of the Universal Declaration, as "a common standard of achievement for all peoples and all nations." And it makes clear that what is involved in a state's commitment to support and advance human rights in its foreign policy is a commitment to contribute to the development of more just social institutions in the states with which it has relations.

Let me conclude with two caveats. First, my concern here has been to elucidate the doctrine of internationally recognized human rights, and to demonstrate that a commitment to advance these rights by means of foreign policy should be understood more broadly than it is by the current U.S. foreign assistance legislation and by the administration's foreign policy practices. However, I have *not* argued that the United States, or, for that matter, any state, *should* commit itself to the promotion and defense of internationally recognized human rights. I believe that such an argument can be made, but it is not part of my intention to make it here. Second, even if appropriate principles of social justice turn out to underwrite a very broad range of human rights, it would not *immediately* follow that a state committed to promoting human rights in its foreign policy should rush headlong into the role of global moral reformer. The instruments of diplomacy and the resources of states limit what can be expected from foreign policy, and such limitations should be taken into account in fashioning a human rights foreign policy. Furthermore, one would want to consider how the prospects of such a policy might be affected by economic and political forces beyond the control of national foreign policies. Philosophical considerations can help to explicate the logic and scope of our moral commitments; but they cannot make the limitations of practical politics disappear. Whether anything can be said, in general, about the prospects and limitations of state action to enforce human rights in other societies is an important problem in its own right, and I do not mean to prejudge it by anything argued here.

Notes

1. Pub. L. 94-329, *International Security Assistance and Arms Export Control Act of 1976* (June 30, 1976), Sec. 301(a), 90 Stat. 750 [amends Foreign Assistance Act of 1961, Sec. 502B(d)(1)].

2. Jimmy Carter, "Peace, Arms Control, World Economic Progress, Human Rights: Basic Priorities of U.S. Foreign Policy." An address before the United Nations, March 17, 1977, reprinted in United States *Department of State Bulletin,* 76: 1977 (April 11, 1977), p. 332.

3. Cyrus Vance, "Human Rights and Foreign Policy," an address before the University of Georgia Law Day ceremonies, April 30, 1977; reprinted in United States *Department of State Bulletin,* 76: 1978 (May 23, 1977), pp. 505-508.

4. For a discussion, see David Weissbrodt, "Human Rights Legislation and U.S. Foreign Policy," *Georgia Journal of International and Comparative Law,* 7 (1977), 268-270.

5. For the important recent debates in the House, see U.S., Congress, House, debates regarding Conference Committee report on the Omnibus Multilateral Development Institutions Act of 1977 (H.R. 5262), *Congressional*

Record, 123: 144 (September 16, 1977), pp. H9554-H9566; for the Senate debates on the same Conference report, see *Congressional Record,* 123: 128 (July 27, 1977), pp. S12971-S12975.

6. See, for example, Maurice Cranston, *What Are Human Rights?* (New York: Basic Books, 1962), pp. 34-39.

7. For a discussion, see Joel Feinberg, *Social Philosophy* (Englewood Cliffs, N.J.: Prentice-Hall, 1973), pp. 85-88.

8. Cranston, *What Are Human Rights?,* p. 37.

9. H.L.A. Hart, "Are There Any Natural Rights?" *Philosophical Review,* 64: 2 (April 1955), 175.

10. Gregory Vlastos, "Justice and Equality," in R.B. Brandt, ed., *Social Justice* (Englewood Cliffs, N.J.: Prentice-Hall, 1962), pp. 45, 50-52.

11. I have argued that international economic interdependence gives rise to special rights to fair shares of the global product in "Justice and International Relations," *Philosophy & Public Affairs,* 4: 4 (Summer 1975), 360-389.

12. Isaiah Berlin, "Two Concepts of Liberty," in *Four Essays on Liberty* (London: Oxford University Press, 1969), p. 124.

13. Peter L. Berger, "Are Human Rights Universal?" *Commentary,* 64: 3 (September 1977), 62.

14. I say "partly analogous" because there are obvious disanalogies as well. In particular, the international human rights declarations are not "law" in the same sense as are statutes and precedents. This means that whatever human rights claims turn out to be vindicated by a successful model of human rights cannot be represented as having legal validity in the same sense as can claims made under municipal law. However, this partial disanalogy does not undermine the use to which I put the analogy with legal interpretation in the text.

15. This is a very simplified interpretation of Ronald Dworkin, "Hard Cases," *Taking Rights Seriously* (Cambridge: Harvard University Press, 1977), pp. 81-130, esp. pp. 81-90.

16. Much of the literature on human rights takes their identification with natural rights for granted. See, for example, William Frankena, "The Concept of Universal Human Rights," in American Philosophical Association, *Science, Language, and Human Rights* (Philadelphia: University of Pennsylvania Press, 1952), p. 193; Vlastos, "Justice and Equality," p. 36; Richard Wasserstrom, "Rights, Human Rights, and Racial Discrimination," *Journal of Philosophy,* 61: 20 (29 October 1964), p. 628.

17. John Locke, *Two Treatises of Government,* 2nd ed., ed. Peter Laslett (Cambridge: Cambridge University Press, 1967), II, sec. 6, p. 289.

18. Robert Nozick, *Anarchy, State and Utopia* (New York: Basic Books, 1974), pp. 29-33.

19. Wasserstrom, "Rights . . . ," pp. 631-632. These criteria are discussed further in Hugo Bedau's chapter in this book.

20. Feinberg, *Social Philosophy,* p. 95.

21. Such views are common in the history of liberalism. Mill, for example, exempts from the scope of the liberty principle peoples in their "nonage," and Rawls claims that the implementation of some rights may permissibly be delayed when this is necessary to promote the long-term development of just institutions. See, respectively, John Stuart Mill, *On Liberty*, in *Collected Works of John Stuart Mill*, ed. J.M. Robson (Toronto: University of Toronto Press, 1977), vol. 18, p. 224; and John Rawls, *A Theory of Justice* (Cambridge: Harvard University Press, 1971), pp. 152, 543.

22. I do not mean to suggest that economic rights *never* belong to persons as persons, or even that there is a neat partition between economic rights which we have as persons and economic rights which we have as members of particular societies. In an interdependent world, where global trade and investment create something like a global system of social cooperation, economic rights may rest on considerations involving *both* partial and global social relations. But this is not much help to those who would defend economic human rights on the natural rights model, since this model cannot accommodate *any* reference to considerations which dilute the "persons as persons" requirement.

23. For this formulation I am indebted to Douglas MacLean and Peter Brown.

24. See Rawls, *A Theory of Justice,* pp. 7-9.

25. *Ibid.*, p. 152.

26. For a brief discussion, see my "Justice and International Relations," pp. 377-378.

5 Rights in the Light of Duties

Henry Shue

A venerable tradition among theorists of Western Europe and North America attempts to divide rights into positive ones and negative ones.[1] Like many other dichotomies this was at best one of several ways of simplifying a very complex area in order to point out in a preliminary fashion some noteworthy differences, many of which turn out on further examination to be differences only of degree, quite real and worth noticing but not sharp or fundamental, as I will try to show. Unfortunately the supposed significance of the division of rights into positive and negative has become something of an unquestioned dogma among North Atlantic theorists.[2] And in the early days of the United Nations the emphasis upon this dichotomy was one of the influences that led to the later U.S.-advocated splitting of the interrelated rights originally presented together in the Universal Declaration of Human Rights into two separately ratifiable covenants, the International Covenant on Civil and Political Rights and the International Covenant on Economic, Social, and Cultural Rights, as if a nation could provide the one kind of rights without the other.[3] Most nations that have ratified either covenant have had the good sense to ratify both.[4] But even the suggestion that a commitment could be made to take the one set of rights seriously while ignoring the other set is, I will try to establish, misleading in theory and dangerous in practice.

Upon analysis we find that three separable doctrines lie behind this conventional structuring of rights into two clusters, and after a thorough assessment we would find, as I will try to begin to indicate, that each of the three is dubious and that the combination of the three is highly dubious. The three doctrines buried in the conventional view are these:

I. The distinction between negative rights and positive rights is (A) sharp and (B) significant.
II. The distinction between civil and political rights, taken together, and economic, social, and cultural rights, taken together, is (A) sharp and (B) significant.
III. Civil and political rights are negative rights, and economic, social, and cultural rights are positive rights.

It is a pleasure to acknowledge the encouragement received, and harassment suffered, from Douglas MacLean, my colleague at the Center for Philosophy and Public Policy. For the positions I have taken, he can of course not be held responsible.

Thesis I and Thesis II respectively assert the usefulness and importance of each of two distinctions, and Thesis III asserts that the two distinctions happen to overlap.[5] I will sometimes call the situation protrayed by Thesis III the double dichotomy. Sharpness and significance are two different issues, in the cases of each of the first two distinctions. Sharpness is a matter of conceptual usefulness: can the distinction be drawn so that it will clarify, not confuse, discussion? Significance is a matter of moral importance: Who cares? That is, why, provided that the distinction can be drawn sharply, bother to keep drawing it?

Strictly speaking, we could examine five issues: both the sharpness and the significance of each of the first two distinctions and the overall acceptability of the third thesis. Fortunately, we need not grind through a separate assessment of each of the five, since some are dependent upon others. Let me, then, state my own conclusions and indicate the parts of them that I will try to justify here. Concerning (I), I believe that the distinction between negative rights and positive rights can be made reasonably sharp but is of no moral significance anyway. Concerning (II), I think the distinction is arbitrary and therefore of no moral significance. Obviously, then, (III) turns out to be a hopeless quagmire.

I will try to take the bull by the horns (in section 1) and show by means of clear examples how confused Thesis III is. Then, as a partial explanation of that finding, I will consider (in section 2) the weakness of Thesis I: the lack of moral significance in the distinction between negative rights and positive rights. Omitting direct criticism of Thesis II and settling for only this partial critique of the conventional structuring of rights, I will briefly offer (in section 3) a constructive suggestion about a better conceptual framework for thinking about rights.

1. The Dissolution of the Double Dichotomy

Is it true that all civil and political rights are negative, while all economic, social, and cultural rights are positive? Is Thesis III an accurate description of these rights and what the holders of these rights may demand? Before we can usefully consider examples of civil and political rights, and then an example of economic, social, and cultural rights, we need to remind ourselves of the gist of the negative/positive distinction.

The general idea behind the attempt to divide rights into positive and negative is that some rights—namely, the negative ones—impose upon the other people with the duties correlative to those rights only a negative requirement. The fulfillment of a negative right, the doctrine goes, requires only that other people, in effect, do nothing, that is, only that they refrain from interference with the right-holder's enjoyment of the substance of the right. The substance of the right may vary greatly, for example, from keeping things one already has (rights to property) to trying to get things one doesn't have (rights to opportunity). But whatever the substance of the right, the only duties that others are required to perform in order to honor the right consist largely of leaving the possessor of the right alone and not preventing the person from the keeping, the trying to get, or whatever else is that person's project.

Positive rights, then, are rights that are not negative. Positive rights have as their correlative duties, to put it crudely, duties to do something rather than duties to do nothing. Positive rights are more costly to the bearers of the correlative duties, since the bearers will be required, in order to fulfill the positive rights, to expend something: at least energy, effort, or time, if not— Heaven help them—money. Positive rights are viewed as more expensive to duty-bearers and, correspondingly, more valuable to rights-holders, than negative rights are. Negative rights, in Thomas Hobbes's famous and profound image, seem to be only hedges to keep people apart as they each walk or run, as they independently choose, along their own private paths, while positive rights seem to involve—indeed, entangle—people with one another, to a degree that extreme individualists find repugnant. But are civil and political rights actually negative? Unfortunately for defenders of the double dichotomy, even hedges must be planted and maintained, often trimmed and sometimes moved, much of which involves positive action.

If anything is an indisputably central example of "civil and political" rights, the right to a fair trial is. Is the right to a fair trial a negative right? Certainly not. The reason is not the trivial one that this is a right to receive something (namely, a fair trial)—in fact, this right is often called "the right to receive a fair trial." This would be a trivial reason because alternative descriptions that are equally appropriate can be given in negative terms: "the right not to be detained (deprived of property and so forth) without a fair trial." Whether any right is given the name of "a right to receive" something good or the name of "a right not to be" treated badly is liable to be a perfectly trivial matter, and no significant judgments should be based on facts of mere labeling.[6]

What counts is what is involved in actually providing someone with enjoyment of the right to a fair trial (to use the label that is essentially neutral between the positive-sounding "receiving" and the negative-sounding "not depriving"). And what is involved is all sorts of active and expensive undertakings, programs, and institution-building. For a start, if some trials are to have juries, people will have to incur considerable expense to perform their jury duties. Some investors may have to hire someone else to monitor the market, and some real-estate brokers may have to give up the time and energy that would have produced a sale and a commission. Such excuses are sometimes used for evading jury duty, of course, but this simply shifts the burden to those "whose time is less valuable."

Juries are, overall, only a minor part of the story. Consider in the United States the judicial system and its supporting and ancillary institutions—local courts, state courts, and federal courts; courts of first instance, appellate courts,

and supreme courts, not to mention the relevant sections of, for example, the
Law Enforcement Assistance Administration and state and federal departments
of justice. Besides the absence of courtroom intimidation, there must be the
presence of adequate defense counsel, and the latter is an essential part of the
former. And these official institutions by no means explain the extent to which
people actually enjoy the right to a fair trial in this country. If more blacks,
for example, now receive fair trials in the United States than blacks did twenty
years ago, an adequate explanation must include the work of Martin Luther
King, Jr., the NAACP, the ACLU, Amnesty International, hundreds of legal
assistance projects, and thousands of hours of *pro bono* litigation. Even mention of these kinds of organizations and activities does not complete the full
story.[7]

Now obviously everything is indirectly more or less connected to everything else, and it becomes absurd not to draw the line before genuinely tenuous
connections are cited. One can of course distinguish actions needed to bring
it about that other actions do not occur from the nonoccurrence of the other
actions. But to say that the avoidance of race-bias and class-bias is part of the
fulfillment of the right to a fair trial but that the activities of the NAACP and
ACLU, for example, are external and not part of the fulfillment of the right is
to draw an excessively scholastic distinction that might occasionally serve some
useful purpose but is ordinarily highly misleading about the nature of society.
Insistence upon this distinction in this case, for example, creates the false impression that judicial institutions function best when left unmonitored by nongovernmental groups.

To explain why Iran, for example, suffers the systematic brutal repression
of many rights, including rights to fair trial, under martial law with its transfer
of civilian cases to courts martial, it is simply not enough to talk about failures
to refrain on the part of the dictator and his secret police. The unjustifiable
power of the Shah and SAVAK are themselves largely explicable by the absence
of sound national institutions that might have been built but have not yet been,
although the failure to build strong Iranian institutions must be admitted to be
partly because of active foreign, especially American, intervention in matters
within Iranian domestic jurisdiction.[8] Only from an ivory tower could the right
to a fair trial seem to be a negative right, demanding of others only that they
refrain from interfering with well-functioning judicial mechanisms that can be
established by passing a few laws.[9] The need for an end to American attempts
to manipulate Iranian domestic politics to serve American interests is of course
a need for nonintervention, while the need to build a sound system of nonmilitary Iranian courts is a need for positive efforts. But one might well expect
that non-intervention by the United States will occur only as a result of the
building by Iranians themselves of institutions strong enough to resist it, not
by U.S. refraining.

We have, therefore, one clear example of a right that is never listed as "economic, social, and cultural," but always as "civil and political," and is only very misleadingly described as negative. But a doctrine like Thesis III cannot be disproven by a single counter-example—perhaps the right to a fair trial is somehow atypical of the lists of civil and political rights on which it is always found, a defender of the double dichotomy might suggest.

Although the right to a fair trial is so central to the rights ordinarily grouped as civil and political that it is difficult to imagine how it could be treated as atypical, we can very briefly consider another right that undoubtedly belongs on the civil and political list, if such a list is to be used at all: the right not to be tortured. At the superficial level of labeling the usual name is the negative one just used—*not* to be tortured—although security from torture is also naturally included as one of several rights to retain physical integrity or to have physical security. But what does it mean in practice to fulfill people's rights not to be tortured? Is it all negative refraining from the infliction of pain in order to manipulate and so forth, or are positive acts also essential?

In order to establish what a right means, one must consider what is involved in fulfilling it. For a start, the mere reduction of existing torture, which is institutionalized today in dozens of countries, would involve the creation and development of some kinds of institutions that could discover, expose, and stop torture. Since national governments, some of which are the most powerful existing governmental organizations, are themselves sometimes the administrators of the system of torture, the kind of institution that could protect people against torture is by no means clear.[10] In some cases perhaps the building of a more powerful police force that could control the existing secret police might be a possibility. A United Nations High Commissioner for Human Rights has its advocates. Others count on existing nongovernmental organizations like the Campaign for the Abolition of Torture run by Amnesty International. The United States has recently endorsed an International Convention on the Prohibition of Torture. Many think the contemporary tide of torture will not crest until at least the worst of the conditions against which those who later become the victims of torture were initially protesting are improved: given the deprivations, protests will occur, and given the stake of many governments in the deprivations, the protests will be repressed by, among other means, torture.[11]

Whatever exactly it will take even to slow the increase in torture, much less to reduce or to abolish torture, it will take powerful forces, imaginatively designed and courageously maintained. To say in the face of all this that the right not to be tortured is an essentially negative right is either fatuous or extraordinarily scholastic. Of course not being tortured consists in part of not being interfered with in certain painful, coercive ways, but it is crucial also to consider what not being interfered with by torturers actually would consist of. To treat the right not to be tortured as essentially or primarily negative is to create the false impression that a decline in torture would likely be constituted by an increase in refraining from torturing—by an increasing number of cases of self-restraint. On the contrary, any reductions in torture are much more likely to be matters of prevention rather than self-discipline and therefore of powerful positive initiatives organized against torturers. Part of the essential meaning of people's coming to enjoy rights not to be tortured would be their being brought under the protection of such positive forces working contrary to the forces maintaining torture. Describing the right not to be tortured as not including essential positive elements—as being negative—creates false expectations about how torture is likely to be resisted effectively. As often happens, what is misleading in theory is also dangerous in practice.

These two examples of the right to a fair trial and the right not to be tortured are clear indications, I think, of major difficulties in the half of Thesis III that asserts simply that civil and political rights are negative rights. That the other half of Thesis III is incorrect in asserting simply that economic, social, and cultural rights are positive is even clearer and can be indicated by a single example. If any economic, social, and cultural right is a basic right, the right to subsistence is.[12] I take subsistence rights to be rights to the actual use or consumption of unpolluted air, unpolluted water, adequate food, adequate clothing, adequate shelter, and minimal preventive public health care, but we can look merely at adequate food. Quite often poor peasants in poor countries are managing to grow or to purchase adequate food when the national government under which they live introduces a "development plan" for their area that has as its first priority an increase in national aggregates like per capita GNP. It is not at all unusual for diets to decline—temporarily, but long enough for "infant mortality to rise," that is, for children to starve or die of diseases that malnutrition has made them incapable of resisting—as a result of the disruption caused by the transition to the modern economy.[13]

What is needed in order for the subsistence rights of such peasants to be protected is fundamentally that their accustomed patterns of life not be interfered with in disruptive and harmful ways. What is needed is a kind of refraining from harming economic security that is quite analogous to the refraining from harming physical security that is necessary in order not to commit an assault. If it were my contention that what is needed to fulfill subsistence rights is something entirely negative—merely to leave the peasants with adequate diets alone—the proper rejoinder would be that the matter is not so simple. There may be no reason not to develop economically and to modernize, subject to a number of constraints including the constraint that people's diets must not be made worse, at least not so much worse as to drive them below subsistence levels, even "temporarily."

But I am not suggesting that subsistence rights are entirely negative, any more than I was suggesting earlier that rights to a fair trial and rights not to be tortured are entirely positive. The point against Thesis III is that the fulfillment of every right involves essential positive elements *and* essential negative elements, irrespective of which International Covenant the right happens to have been assigned to. Rights cannot be understood without understanding what it means to fulfill them. The actual fulfillment of so-called negative rights essentially includes the building of sound institutions and the mobilization of powerful forces. The fulfillment of so-called positive rights essentially includes the avoidance of deprivations.

This is already enough to call for a reexamination of the conventional North Atlantic way of structuring thought about rights and for the consideration of an alternative conceptual framework, which we will very briefly do in section 3. But first I would like to indicate some still more radical difficulties inherent in the framework presupposed by Thesis III, by looking at Thesis I and specifically at the issue of the moral significance of the distinction between negative rights and positive rights even for any cases that are simple enough to fit into the distinction.

2. The Moral Equivalence of Action and Omission

The point of the previous section is that the negative/positive distinction with regard to rights is inapplicable to the leading case to which defenders of the double dichotomy like to try to apply it: the supposedly parallel distinction between civil and political and economic, social, and cultural, both of which turn out to melt partly into the positive box and partly into the negative box. For all this, however, the negative/positive dichotomy might still turn out to be applicable to, and even highly revealing for, some other cases yet to be identified. That possibility can be undercut, however, if a more profound line of attack upon the distinction is successful. This attack challenges not the applicability but the moral significance of the negative/positive distinction.

The alleged distinction between positive rights and negative rights rests upon a simpler distinction between action and omission. A positive right has correlative duties to act, while a negative right has correlative duties only to omit, or refrain from, actions. The distinction between acting and omitting, or avoiding, action can be made sharp enough, but it is a distinction without a difference unless some moral significance is attached to whether one is duty-bound to act or duty-bound to omit acting.

The defenders of the double dichotomy do of course believe that their division of rights into positive and negative has moral significance. The significance is rarely detailed with precision and undoubtedly varies among the dichotomy's adherents. Among policymakers the usual position is, specifically, that negative rights are morally more binding than positive rights, and often being morally more binding is taken to mean that negative rights ought to be fulfilled immediately, while positive rights may be fulfilled progressively. At best "progressively" means gradually, although it sometimes carries strong hints of "whenever you feel like it," an attitude that erodes what is called a duty into an optional exercise that is far from dutiful.[14]

The usual reasons for supposing that negative rights are morally more binding than positive rights are: (A) that the duties correlative to negative rights are duties to *omit actions* that would result in harm, (B) that the duties correlative to positive rights are duties to *act* so as to eliminate (or prevent) harm, and (C) that duties to omit are morally more binding than duties to act. The previous section took propositions (A) and (B) to be true by definition and raised the question whether many actual cases fall under either definition— whether many concrete rights involve only duties to omit or only duties to act. But since there is no way to be sure that some pure case of a negative right or a positive right will not turn up, however unlikely that may be, we now turn to proposition (C). Thesis I is correct in attributing moral significance to the distinction between negative rights and positive rights only if the underlying distinction between omissions and actions is morally significant, as stated in (C). In short, Thesis I is correct only if assumption (C) is correct.[15] The purpose of this section, then, is to cast doubt upon the correctness of (C), but first it will be useful to consider the sources of the charm of assumption (C).

Why should anyone have thought that duties to omit are morally more binding than duties to act? Judith Lichtenberg, whose forceful counterexample to (C) I will be using shortly, has noticed that two of the features of what one has a moral duty to do, or not to do, that heavily influence one's judgment about how binding one duty is, compared with another, are (1) the respective degrees of *probability* that harm will otherwise result and (2) the respective degrees of *sacrifice* incurred by the duty-bearer.[16] Requiring an omission often has in fact both a *higher probability* that harm can be avoided and a *lower sacrifice* for the duty-bearer than requiring an action has.[17] Consequently it often seems that omissions *as such* are morally more binding than actions *as such*, when it is actually responses that have a higher probability of success at a lower sacrifice that are morally more binding than responses that have a lower probability of success at a higher sacrifice. It simply happens that omissions often score better than actions on these two determinative considerations.

Consider an ordinary case. Does one, other things being equal, have a more binding duty to provide food to a starving child or not to strangle the starving child? It would normally be thought, of course, that one has a far stronger duty not to strangle the child than to provide it with food. This, Lichtenberg's analysis suggests, has been misinterpreted to mean that in general one has morally more binding duties to omit harm (not to strangle) than to act helpfully (provide food). But the important differences between the two cases are that (1) strangling the child is more likely to result in its death than failing to provide it with food, on the (often dubious) assumption that someone else may provide the food and (2) providing the food is taken to involve a greater sacrifice than not strangling the child, which would normally involve no sacrifice at all. For these two reasons it is ordinarily taken to be morally more urgent to prohibit the strangling than to prohibit the failure to provide food.

What count, then, are degree of probability and degree of sacrifice.[18] But since probability and sacrifice often count in favor of requiring an omission (not killing the child) more strongly than an action (providing food to the child), it is easy to receive the mistaken impression that what matters is whether a response is an omission or an action. What does matter is the probability of harm otherwise and the sacrifice in avoiding the harm, irrespective of whether avoidance involves acting or omitting action. This is especially clear in Lichtenberg's case of the stranded person and the sailor, where the probabilities of harm are equal for killing and leaving to die—the harm is certain—and the sacrifices are also equal—no sacrifice is involved either way. With probabilities and sacrifices equal, action and omission are equally compelling:

A person is stranded on a desert island, far from any other land and from human life. The island provides no source of sustenance; and the person's meager provisions are almost gone. Just as he is about to give up hope that he will survive, he sights a vessel heading toward the island. It lands, and a sailor appears and comes ashore. The ship contains plenty of supplies, as well as providing a way back to the human world.

Now consider two possible scenarios that follow. In the first, the sailor won't share his provisions with the stranded man, and won't take him aboard ship. He is ready to leave as he has come. In the second, the sailor attempts to kill the man he finds on the island.

I believe that in these circumstances, the sailor's failure to share his provisions or his ship with the stranded man is morally equivalent to his killing him. . . .

Intuitively, the sailor's refusal to take the stranded man aboard (when he foresees the consequences of refusing and could act with no loss to himself) cries out for an explanation as much as his killing him does. It seems no less plausible that he wants him dead if he leaves him alone than if he kills him. Looked at the other way, the supposition that the sailor kills the stranded man for no reason seems no more absurd than that he leaves him for no reason. . . .

If the very slight chance that another potential rescuer might come along seems to someone to make a significant difference between the cases, we can imagine further that the stranded man is a diabetic suffering from insulin shock, who will die within minutes unless he gets insulin, and that the sailor happens to have insulin aboard. Time lapses between an omission and a harmful consequence suggest the possibility of later interventions. Sometimes the suggestion is warranted, sometimes not.[19]

Although Lichtenberg's example is not described specifically in terms of rights, it is readily adaptable. Naturally the sailor might have duties not to kill the stranded person or duties to rescue him even if the stranded person has no

rights at all, or anyhow no rights with correlative duties that fall upon the
sailor. Duties have many sources other than rights and need not be correlative
to rights at all. But in order to adapt Lichtenberg's example to our question
about negative rights and positive rights we must assume that in this case if the
sailor has a duty not to kill the marooned person, the sailor's duty is correlative to the person's negative right not to be killed, and if the sailor has a duty
to rescue the marooned person, the sailor's duty is correlative to the person's
positive right to receive assistance.

The defender of the double dichotomy, then, would presumably have to
think that the marooned person's negative right not to be killed is morally
more binding upon the sailor than his positive right to be rescued is. The
reason would be that not killing is a mere omission and rescuing is an action.
But in a case like this one, in which the *only* respect in which the respective
requirements of a negative right and a positive right differ is the mere fact that
one involves omitting, or not acting (not killing), and the other involves acting
(rescuing), it is impossible to see any good reason to attach to the distinction
between omission and action the enormous significance that the defender of
the double dichotomy must give it in order to defend the view that the omission could be required when the action was not required. For Lichtenberg's
sailor simply to row away would be as inhuman an act as for him to stab the
stranded person. The bare difference between omission and action would not
support any judgment that the positive right to receive assistance generates a
less compelling duty than the duty generated by the negative right not to be
killed. Thus, although the excerpts from her argument given here hardly do
it justice, I think Lichtenberg is correct that action as such and omission as
such are morally equivalent, or in other words, that assumption (C) is mistaken.
And if (C) is mistaken, the ground has been cut from beneath the portion of
Thesis I that attributes moral significance to the distinction between negative
rights and positive rights.

It might nevertheless sometimes turn out that fulfilling a purely negative
right, if there are any, would involve a higher probability that harm can be
avoided and a lower sacrifice for the duty-bearer than would some alternative,
purely positive right, if there are any of those, and that the negative right ought
therefore to be considered morally more binding. But the determining considerations would be, not the negative/positive distinction, but the degree of
probability, the degree of sacrifice, and probably other morally important
features not mentioned here. The probability and the sacrifice, at least, are
factual questions with answers that will vary from case to case and from time
to time.

It is vital to proceed with extreme caution when moving from artificial
cases like Lichtenberg's designedly pure case to actual cases, because some of
the "impurities" in actual cases may constitute essential disanalogies that
ought to prevent the application of the moral drawn from the pure, artificial

case to the messy, actual case. However, in this instance the artificiality of the counterexample is required by the artificiality of the dichotomies being criticized. My point in this section has been that even if there are negative rights and positive rights, that is, rights respectively with duties exclusively to omit and duties exclusively to act, this difference does not make the one kind of right morally more binding than the other. But I would be the first to admit that discussing negative rights and positive rights is the discussion of artificial fabrications. That was the point of section 1.

3. Similar Rights, Multiple Duties

To some extent the arguments of sections 1 and 2 are pulling in different directions. The conclusion of section 2 is that actions and omissions are morally equivalent and, therefore, that even if negative rights involve only omissions as correlative duties and positive rights involve only actions as correlative duties, negative rights and positive rights are morally equivalent in the sense that we have no good reason to assume that negative rights are morally more binding upon those with the correlative duties than positive rights are. Negative rights and positive rights with the same probabilities of attaining their results and the same sacrifices for the bearers of the correlative duties are equally binding.

But the conclusion of section 1 was that many actual concrete rights are neither exclusively positive nor exclusively negative, but instead involve both essential positive elements and essential negative elements. What, then, is the relevance of the conclusion of section 2? If indeed every right should turn out to involve essential positive and essential negative elements, what are we to say? We could, in effect, throw up our hands and settle for the not very helpful comment that everything is a mixed bag.

Now everything *is* a mixed bag, but I would like to pursue a different method from the confusing double dichotomy of rights for sorting things out a bit more. To help to justify my suggestion, however, it is useful also to have before us now the conclusion of section 2. For my suggestion will involve abandoning the double dichotomy of rights entirely, not only because the negative/positive dichotomy is inapplicable to major specific rights (section 1) but also because the distinction that underlies this dichotomy—action versus omission—is without moral significance in any case (section 2).

Since the artificial conventional dichotomies of rights seem to be in large part a result of the failure to be sufficiently attentive to the correlative duties essential to the fulfillment of rights, a natural suggestion is a shift of focus to the other side of the coin: duties. Instead of the fruitless and confusing attempt to sort rights into those that are and those that are not exclusively, or even dominantly, positive rather than negative, I would suggest that virtually every right be recognized to involve three fundamental kinds of correlative duties:

I.   Duties to *forbear* from depriving right-holders of the substance of their rights.

II. Duties to *protect* right-holders against the deprivation of the substance of their rights.

III. Duties to *aid* right-holders in obtaining or regaining the substance of rights of which they are deprived.[20]

Duties to forbear and duties to protect are together aimed at preventing the violation of rights. They can be described "negatively" as concerned with guaranteeing that potential violators omit, or refrain from, their potential violations or described "positively" as securing and promoting the enjoyment of rights. Certainly duties to protect, in particular, need to be understood to include not only "negative" law enforcement but "positive" designing, building, and maintaining social institutions that increase respect, felt and active, for rights.

Duties to aid are dominantly "positive," that is, they consist of duties to act in ways that may be costly to the duty-bearers and may even involve some sacrifice. How costly is heavily dependent upon the extent to which the first two kinds of duties are fulfilled.

Arthur Danto, in response to an earlier version of this suggestion, has rightly pointed out that there is considerable danger that all the difficulties that haunt the dichotomy of positive rights and negative rights will simply move across the rights/duties line and continue to rattle around in the more spacious trichotomy of forbearance duties, protection duties, and assistance duties.[21] One might suspect that forbearance duties are largely "negative," assistance duties are largely "positive," and protection duties are intermediate, and one might wonder whether the "new" conceptualization, even if marginally more adequate, were not fairly superficial.

Several gains, however, are made by conceptualizing matters in terms of one kind of right with three kinds of correlative duties, instead of two kinds of rights, each with its own distinctive kind of correlative duty. At a theoretical level, the triple-duty conceptualization being recommended has the simple, but very great, virtue of being more accurate. No right can in practice be fulfilled solely by omissions and thereby qualify as a negative right. To take still another example, the right to physical security, that is, the right not to be killed arbitrarily, not to be assaulted, not to be raped, consists in *not* being killed arbitrarily, *not* being assaulted, *not* being raped, and thus in other people's not performing various actions. But their not performing these actions does not consist only of their refraining and restraining themselves. It also must include restraint of potential attackers by the action of third parties like the police and by threats against attackers made credible by well-functioning police and judicial and penal institutions. And this is to say nothing about constructive programs, which would fall under duties to aid and which would enable those who now live in fear for their security to be freed from that fear. To portray all these activities and institutions as somehow basically negative is quite misleading in theory, and may be one factor promoting one-sidedly negative approaches to crime prevention in practice.

Someone might suggest that this insistence upon the mixture of positive and negative elements in what North Atlantic theorists have treated as purely negative is to confuse the right itself with the activities needed to fulfill the right. Insofar as this suggestion is intelligible, it is difficult to see what interest anyone could have in "rights themselves." But the main difficulty with the suggestion is its attempted artificial separation of rights from the correlative duties that fulfill them. An account of the duties correlative to a right is not an account of something additional or supplementary to the right. A right is partly constituted by its correlative duties, and a good account of those duties is an account of what the holder of that right has a right to.

At a practical level, the recognition that every right involves three kinds of duties, not all of which necessarily must be borne by all the same people, has two strong advantages. First, it makes it more difficult totally to dismiss some kinds of rights, especially some economic rights, as necessarily involving duties so much more expensive than the duties correlative to other rights that these rights must all be restricted to the twilight status of "manifesto rights" or even denied the status of being rights at all.[22] For example, it will often be said that if there were a universal right to adequate food, the correlative duties would involve providing food to hundreds of thousands of people around the globe, which would cost billions of dollars and which therefore is clearly too much for others to bear. Hence, the argument goes, there must not be any such right. This might be called denial by contraposition: if there were such a right, the correlative duties would be very expensive; there can be no such expensive duties; and if there are no such duties, there is no such right.

Now this argument does at least appreciate the tightness of the connection between rights and correlative duties, but that is all that can be said for it. The implicit assumption that mere adequate nutrition for everyone is possible only by means of impoverishment for those currently well-off, is in fact false.[23] But even if it were true—even if the cost of fulfilling the duties to aid correlative to rights to adequate food were somehow prohibitive—the right to food would continue to be genuine, and at least the duties to forbear from depriving people of food and the duties to protect people against such deprivations would still have force.

In other words, if one thinks of an economic right as involving only correlative duties to aid and one believes those duties to aid to be too onerous, it is relatively easy to convince oneself that the right must somehow not be genuine. But the recognition of the tripartite duties correlative to every right makes it more difficult entirely to dismiss any right simply because one correlative duty— the duty to aid—seems, or is, impossible or burdensome to fulfill. The duties to

prevent deprivation of food—by, for example, constraining corporate investment schemes and government development schemes from making people's
diets worse—remain, and they are clearly not too much to ask. Thus, the
right can be acknowledged and the duties to forbear and to protect can be
performed, while the question of duties to aid continues to be investigated.

The second practical advantage of the recognition of the multiplicity
of duties correlative to every right is the resulting possibility of recognizing
that not all the kinds of duties fall equally upon everyone who shares in at
least one kind of them. Duties to forbear must be universal, otherwise a
person with a right to something would be secure in the enjoyment of the
right only if, and only until, he or she happened to cross the path of one of
the people with no duty to forbear in this case.

But duties to aid certainly are not necessarily universal. This is an important point, because it means that even in the case of a right that is universal—
a right that everyone has—some of the correlative duties may not be universal—
not everyone need have all the duties. It is conceivable, for example, that
duties to aid fall only upon the affluent and not upon other poor people who
are but marginally better off, or only upon those whose failures to perform
their duties resulted in the deprivation, or only upon fellow citizens and not
upon the rest of the world, and so forth. The question of how to allot duties
to aid fairly—fair to duty-bearers and fair to right-holders—is indeed extremely
difficult to settle. But not everything about the fulfillment of a particular
right depends upon arriving at a reasonable settlement of the assignment of
its correlative duties to aid. A right has not been fully honored until all three
kinds of duties have been assigned and carried out, but this is no reason to
fail meanwhile to honor each right as fully as possible, even if only partially.
Indeed, the more fully duties to forbear and to protect are honored, the less
need there will be to implement duties to aid.

For these reasons, among others, I believe that what is becoming the
standard explicit list of rights in laws governing U.S. foreign policy, most
notably Sections 116 and 502B of the Foreign Assistance Act, is too short
and restrictive. At a minimum, the most basic and least costly economic
rights—rights to subsistence—ought also to be given weight in decisions about
which regimes are to receive the material and moral support implicit in economic and military sales and grants.[24]

Notes

1. Good recent formulations of essentially the traditional view include
the chapter by Bedau in this volume and A.I. Melden, *Rights and Persons*
(Oxford: Basil Blackwell, 1977). Another critique of the traditional view,
as well as other alternative suggestions, are in the chapter by Charles Beitz.

2. See, for example, Maurice Cranston, *What Are Human Rights?* (New York: Taplinger Publishing Co., 1973).

3. See Louis B. Sohn, "A Short History of United Nations Documents on Human Rights," in *The United Nations and Human Rights,* Commission to Study the Organization of Peace, 18th Report (Dobbs Ferry, N.Y.: Oceana Publications, 1968), pp. 101-169, esp. 105-106.

4. United Nations, *Multilateral Treaties in Respect of Which the Secretary-General Performs Depositary Functions,* List of Signatures, Ratifications, Accessions, etc. as at 31 December 1977, ST/LEG/SER. D/11, pp. 99-106.

5. By "overlap" I do not of course mean that the two distinctions are coextensive. There are no implications that all negative rights are civil and political or that all positive rights are economic, social, and cultural.

6. Compare Richard P. Claude, "Comparative Rights Research: Some Intersections between Law and the Social Sciences," in *Comparative Human Rights,* ed. Richard P. Claude (Baltimore: Johns Hopkins University Press, 1976), esp. table 3 on pp. 392-393.

7. It should not be assumed that the right to a fair trial is now secure for all Americans. This right is not guaranteed for many, especially the nonwhite poor, and large expenditures of funds and much creative construction of better institutions, governmental and nongovernmental, will be necessary before this right is secure for the currently deprived segments of the population.

8. For a disturbing account of U.S. interference with the development of sound civil and political institutions in Iran, see the chapter by Cottam. Also see William J. Butler and Georges Levasseur, *Human Rights and the Legal System in Iran* (Geneva: International Commission of Jurists, 1976). For a denial that violations of human rights in Iran are on the whole very important, see Alvin J. Cottrell and James E. Dougherty, *Iran's Quest for Security: U.S. Arms Transfers and the Nuclear Option* (Cambridge, Mass.: Institute for Foreign Policy Analysis, Inc., 1977), pp. 51-56.

9. Compare the gross oversimplifications about the fulfillment of civil and political rights in Cranston, esp. chapter VIII.

10. For information on the extent and features of contemporary torture, see Amnesty International, *Report on Torture* (New York: Farrar, Straus and Giroux, 1975). For a preliminary conceptual framework for assessing torture and further references, see Henry Shue, "Torture," *Philosophy & Public Affairs,* 7: 2 (Winter 1978), 124-143; also see William Twining and Barrie Paskins, "Torture and Philosophy," *Aristotelian Society,* Supplementary Volume LII (1978), 143-194.

11. For the statement of U.S. policy on an international agreement to outlaw torture, see Secretary of State Cyrus Vance, "Building a Healthy Global Community," speech before the United Nations General Assembly September 29, 1978, (Washington: Department of State, Bureau of Public Affairs, Office of Public Communication), p. 6. For an attempt to set institutions of torture in

a broader context, see Malise Ruthven, *Torture: The Grand Conspiracy* (London: Weidenfeld and Nicolson, 1978), especially pp. 281-298. For a clear account of the dynamics by which economic deprivation can stimulate political protests that must be repressed by terroristic torture if the economic policies are to be maintained, see Richard R. Fagen, "The Carter Administration and Latin America: Business as Usual?" *Foreign Affairs,* 57:3 (America and the World 1978), pp. 663-669.

12. For arguments intended to establish that no right is more fundamental than the right to subsistence, see Henry Shue, *Basic Rights: A Philosophical Perspective on Some Foreign Policy Choices,* forthcoming, chapters I and III.

13. See, for example, Shelton Davis, *Victims of the Miracle: Development and the Indians of Brazil* (New York: Cambridge University Press, 1977). For another instance, see Economic and Social Council (CEPCIES), "Report on Chile," March 25, 1976 (Washington: Organization of American States, 1976).

14. For an example of the "whenever you feel like it" approach to economic and social rights, see the official position of the U.S. Department of State on the terms of any Senate ratification of the *International Covenant on Economic, Social and Cultural Rights* in Senate, 95th Cong., 2d Sess., *Message from the President of the United States Transmitting Four Treaties Pertaining to Human Rights,* pp. v, viii-ix (Star Print 1978).

15. Since assumption (C) concerns all duties, many of which are not grounded in rights, (C) is of course much broader than Thesis I.

16. Judith Lichtenberg, "On Being Obligated to Give Aid: Moral and Political Arguments," Diss., City University of New York 1978, Chap. V. Also see Onora O'Neill, "Lifeboat Earth," in *World Hunger and Moral Obligation,* ed. William Aiken and Hugh LaFollette (Englewood Cliffs, N.J.: Prentice-Hall, Inc., 1977), pp. 148-164.

17. Strictly speaking, Lichtenberg suggests, if I understand her, that one should focus on the probability that the response (action or omission) *prohibited* would have resulted in harm. Thus, to require an action is to prohibit an omission, and the extent to which the action is morally binding is dependent upon the probability that the omission, if allowed, would have resulted in harm. I will not pursue the reasons for this suggestion and will, insofar as possible, ignore here the complexity it introduces into the analysis.

18. At least probability and sacrifice, *among other things,* count more than the action/omission distinction. For the provocative suggestion that the principle of moral priority for omission over action is what could be expected to result from a compromise between the powerful wealthy and the powerless poor, as well as additional analysis, see Gilbert Harman, "Moral Relativism Defended," *Philosophical Review,* 84:1 (January 1975), 3-22. Also compare Rousseau's account of the origin of the social contract in the *Second Discourse.*

19. Lichtenberg, chapter IV.

20. For a fuller explanation and complementary arguments, see Shue,

Chapter II. I of course nowhere have a negative existential proof that there is no right that lacks one of these three kinds of duties. I await a good non-artificial example of such an exceptional right.

21. Personal correspondence, April 1978.

22. For the attempt to create an intermediate category of "manifesto rights," see Joel Feinberg, *Social Philosophy* (Englewood Cliffs, N.J.: Prentice-Hall, 1973), pp. 63-64, 67, 94-95.

23. Of the many relevant sources for this judgment, see Wassily Leontief and others, *The Future of the World Economy,* A United Nations Study (New York: Oxford University Press, 1977); Bruce Russett, "The Marginal Utility of Income Transfers to the Third World," *International Organization,* 32:4 (Autumn 1978), 913-928; and Susan George, *How the Other Half Dies: The Real Reasons for World Hunger* (Montclair, N.J.: Allanheld, Osmun and Co., 1977).

24. Thus the implications for policy of my position are in conflict with those of the position taken in the chapter by Bedau. In Winter 1979 the Department of State suffers internal contradiction over which rights deserve priority in U.S. foreign policy. The Bureau of Human Rights is to be commended for a small step in the right direction in the form of the inclusion in its reports on human rights violations of scores on the Physical Quality of Life Index (PQLI), which is one measure of, roughly, the fulfillment of subsistence rights. See Senate Comm. on Foreign Relations and House Comm. on Foreign Affairs, 96th Cong., 1st Sess., *Report on Human Rights Practices in Countries Receiving U.S. Aid by the Department of State* (Joint Comm. Print 1979), Appendix II, pp. 666-673. The Bureau of Legal Advisers, in contrast, continues to resist the need to take subsistence rights seriously. See reference cited in note 14 above.

For a brief critique of the usefulness of the PQLI in measuring fulfill-ment of economic rights, see Stanley J. Heginbotham, "Measuring Social and Economic Human Rights Conditions," in *Human Rights Conditions in Selected Countries and the U.S. Response,* Subcomm. on International Organizations, House Comm. on Foreign Affairs, 95th Cong., 2d Sess. (Comm. Print 1978), pp. 359-372. For a comprehensive discussion of the PQLI, see Morris D. Morris, *Measuring the Condition of the World's Poor: The Physical Quality of Life Index* (New York: Pergamon Press for the Overseas Development Council, 1979).

Human Rights as a Neutral Concern

Thomas M. Scanlon

The thesis that human rights should be an important determinant of foreign policy derives support from certain ideas about what human rights are like. These include the following. Human rights, it is held, are a particularly important class of moral considerations. Their gross and systematic violation represents not just the failure to meet some ideal but rather a case of falling below *minimum* standards required of political institutions. Second, human rights are of *broad application*. They apply not only to countries that have recognized these rights in their legal institutions, and not merely to countries that are "like us" in their political traditions or in their economic development, but to virtually all countries. Human rights are not controversial in the way that other political and economic issues are. This is not to say that everyone respects them or that there is full agreement about what they entail. But the central human rights are recognized, for example, in the constitutions of countries whose political principles are otherwise quite divergent. This normal acceptance, and the fact that violations of human rights are not confined to governments of any particular ideological stripe but occur both on the left and on the right, lend support to the idea that concern for human rights is a ground for action that is neutral with respect to the main political and economic divisions in the world. Thus, whatever our other political commitments may be, we have reason to be opposed to violations of human rights whether they are carried out by regimes of the right or of the left; whether these regimes are parlimentary democracies, military dictatorships, or monarchies. In addition to having this *ideological neutrality*, it is often held, or at least thought, that human rights are *practically separable* from partisan political issues. Thus, in particular, to advocate a cessation of human rights violations in a country does not involve advocating a change in regime. One can oppose what the government is going without opposing the government, or supporting the opposition.

The first of these ideas—the minimal character of human rights—is important to the positive case for making human rights a determinant of foreign policy. The others—broad applicability, ideological neutrality, and practical separability—are important in overcoming natural objections to giving human rights such a role. These objections turn, for example, on the assertion that human rights are ideal considerations that one cannot hope to see realized, or on the assertion that they are applicable only to countries like our own, or that they are parochial concerns peculiar to our political tradition, not shared by others, or on the assertion that to combat human rights violations in other countries represents an unwarranted intrusion into their domestic affairs, an attempt to impose on them our conception of the government they should have.

In the following brief discussion I will examine some of these claims, specifically, the claims that human rights are ideologically neutral and practically separable from partisan political disputes. I will also consider, on the other side, the charge that it is intrusive to bring pressure on other countries to end human rights violations when these countries may have different political traditions from ours and may not share these values. First, however, I want to say something about what I take rights to be and what kind of foundation I see them as having.

1. It sometimes seems that to invoke a right, particularly one in our familiar pantheon of civil and political liberties, is to appeal to a discrete moral principle whose validity can be apprehended just by thinking about it, without recourse to complicated reasoning or to the calculation of the costs and benefits flowing from a given course of action. But this impression fades when we discover that it is extremely difficult even to give a coherent statement of any of our familiar rights. For example, while we feel that we know what religious persecution is, and that it violates a right, it is not easy to state what this right is. Freedom of religion is violated when there is an established religion; that is, when everyone is required by law to observe the dictates of a particular faith or when membership in a particular religion is made a condition for the possession of other political and legal rights. Freedom of religion is also violated when particular religions are forbidden to hold ceremonies and gatherings or when the publication and dissemination of their tracts and religious materials are proscribed. At least freedom of religion is infringed when these things are done *for certain reasons*—roughly speaking, for reasons concerned with the religious views involved. Not just any restriction on the practice of one's religion infringes freedom of religion. Religion is not a heading under which everything becomes legally permitted. It is compatible with freedom of religion to outlaw the torture of animals in religious rituals, though it would not be so compatible to outlaw it in Baptist rites but allow it for Episcopalians.

What lies behind the claim that the complex of elements I have briefly described here represents a *right*? This claim is supported, first, by the idea that religious belief is important, and important in a particular way. Its primary importance is seen to rest in the value for an individual of remaining true to his or her conscience (and in fact the right in question is often referred to as "freedom of conscience"). The interest in bringing other people's actions into conformity with one's own religious beliefs is seen as having lesser value. But a second element in the case for the right of religious freedom is the belief, drawn from historical experience, that the tendency to look down on other religious groups, to try to drive them out or to force them to convert, is strong and pervasive. Experience strongly suggests that when governments have the power to act in the ways forbidden by the right as described above they will frequently use this power, at great cost to those who find themselves in the minority. Finally, a third element in the case for the right of freedom of religion is the belief that a pluralistic society incorporating the form of religious toleration that this right describes is both possible and desirable. The belief that this is so—that the losses involved in tolerating other beliefs are outweighed by the gains in social harmony, decreased risk of persecution, and so on—depends on the particular view of the importance of religion mentioned above.

I believe that other rights have this same structure.[1] That is to say, first, that to assert a right is not merely to assert the value of some goal or the great disvalue of having a certain harm befall one. Rather, it is either to deny that governments or individuals have the authority to act in certain ways, or to assert that they have an affirmative duty to act in certain other ways, for example, to render assistance of a specified kind. Often, the assertions emodied in rights involve complexes of these positive and negative elements. The backing for a right lies in an empirical judgment that the restrictions on authority or assignments of affirmative permission or duty that the right embodies are both necessary and efficacious. They are necessary because, given the nature of social life and political institutions of the type we are familiar with, when the restrictions or requirements that the right embodies are absent, governments and individuals can be expected to behave in ways that lead to intolerable results. They are efficacious in that recognition of the right will provide a significant degree of protection against these results at tolerable cost. Rights do not promise to bring the millennium, and not just any way of improving things gives rise to a right. Rather, rights arise as responses to specific serious threats and generally, though not always, embody specific strategies for dealing with these threats.

The empirical judgments on which rights are based presuppose certain background conditions. The claim that a right is necessary is not a claim about what would happen in a "state of nature" but rather a claim about what we expect to happen in societies of the kind we are familiar with in the absence of a right of the kind in question. The threats that rights are supposed to help meet are generally ones that arise because of the distribution of power and the patterns of motivation typically found in such societies. These conditions are not universal, though in the case of most rights commonly listed as "human rights" they are sufficiently widespread to be considered universal for all practical purposes.

The judgment that a right is efficacious also depends on a view of "how things work." Religious freedom depends on the belief that people can and will develop the patterns of motivation necessary to make a pluralistic society work. Similarly, a belief in the right to due process depends on the belief in the possibility of an independent judiciary or, minimally, on the belief that the need to defend a charge publicly and with reference to a known law serves as a significant, though far from infallible, check on the arbitrary use of power. Commonly claimed rights vary in the degree to which they involve specific institutional strategies of this kind. What are sometimes called welfare or humanitarian rights differ from traditional civil or personal rights in this respect. For example, when people speak of "the right to a decent diet," they are not just saying that it is a very bad thing for people to be without adequate food. They are also, I believe, expressing the judgment that political institutions must take responsibility in this area: institutions that do not take reasonable steps to avert starvation for their citizens (and, one might add, for others) are not meeting minimum conditions of legitimacy. It is this connection with institutional authority and responsibility that makes it appropriate to speak here of a *right*. What differentiates this claim of a right from the rights embodied in our Constitution, however, is in part that it does not focus on any particular institutional mechanisms that would count as "reasonable" protections against the threat in question.

Even among traditional civil rights, and among those commonly called "rights of the person," there are some involving only minimal commitment to institutional mechanisms. Thus, for example, the right against torture, or cruel and unusual punishment, has less such commitment than the right to due process or various political rights. This lack of dependence makes these rights the most clearly exportable, since it frees them from the limitation of being applicable only where the relevant institutional mechanisms can be expected to work.

Even those human rights involving the least commitment to specific institutional remedies retain a political character that differentiates them from mere goals. To condemn torture as a gross violation of human rights is not simply to deplore pain, suffering, cruelty, and degradation. These things are great evils, but the condemnation of torture involves the invocation of a human right because torture is an evil to which political authorities are particularly prone. Torture, as a violation of a human right, is a political act—political in being carried out by agents of the state and political in its aims, which are typically to crush opposition through the spread of fear. The recognition of a human right against the use of torture reflects the judgment that the temptation to rule in this manner is a recurrent threat and that the power to use torture is a power whose real potential for misuse is so clear as to render it indefensible.[2]

I believe that the view of rights just sketched supports the claims, mentioned at the outset, that human rights are minimal requirements on social and political institutions and that they have broad application. These rights embody fixed points in our judgment of what tolerable institutions must be like. While not literally universal in application, they apply very broadly. In particular, they are not limited to those countries in which they are generally recognized or where they are embodied in law. If they were so limited then much of their critical point would be lost. To hold that there is a certain right is to hold that when people complain of being treated in this way their complaints are justified, whether the perpetrators grant this or not.

2. I turn now to the question of acting in defense of human rights. The moral case for such action is an instance of the general case for aiding a victim of wrongful harm and for doing what one can to stop, or at least not to aid, the person who is wrongfully harming him. Given the minimal character of human rights, gross violations of these rights represent particularly strong instances of the moral requirement to aid a victim and not aid his aggressor. Of course there is also a presupposition against interfering in the affairs of another country, which applies in these cases as well. But this presupposition can be overridden. To argue by analogy, there is a generally strong presupposition against interference in the affairs of another family, but this presupposition does not preclude intervening to protect a battered wife. Now it may seem that there is a clear disanalogy here. No one would suggest that the wife's only recourse is to her husband as protector, but it is more plausible to claim that the political institutions of a country are singled out as the source of protection for citizens. Intervention gains plausibility in the domestic case because here the state stands as an authority outside the family with a duty to protect all of its citizens, including battered wives. But in the international case, while multinational bodies exist, their claim to have this kind of special responsibility and authority is a matter of dispute. Other states and private citizens, on the other hand, have the status of neighbors, on a par with one or another of the disputes.

I do not accept this response. Even in the domestic case, private parties with no special authority can be justified in bringing pressure to bear to protect the wife and even, I think, in intervening physically to protect her if all else fails. People who know well what is going on but do nothing are justly criticized for failure to aid. And the duties of third parties are not limited to cases of physical cruelty. The person who grossly neglects his family is appropriately subject to social pressure as well as to the force of law. I don't know exactly what kinds of pressure third parties are entitled or required to use in such cases, but surely they are required at least not to make things worse. The neighbor who gets a man into debt by selling him expensive cars and hunting rifles when he knows that the man's family is already suffering is clearly morally blameworthy. This suggests that, if the analogy I have been working with holds at all, humanitarian rights too can give rise to moral requirements on third parties.

3. I should say clearly that this analogy has its problems. One of these is simply the fact of scale: attempts by one state to affect the internal affairs of another are fraught with incomparably greater dangers than are analogous interventions between individuals. But the main argument that I want to consider against

acting to defend human rights is quite different. This argument, which I have often heard, holds that while human rights have a special place in "our" moral and political tradition they are not universally shared. Many countries have different notions of political morality, and it is therefore inappropriate for us to bring pressure to bear on them to conform to our conception of human rights. To do so is a kind of moral imperialism.

I believe this argument to be seriously mistaken. It puts itself forward as a kind of enlightened and tolerant relativism, but this masks what is in fact an attitude of moral and cultural superiority. Like many forms of relativism, this argument rests on the attribution to "them" of a unanimity that does not in fact exist. "They" are said to be different from us and to live by different rules. Such stereotypes are seldom accurate, and the attribution of unanimity is particularly implausible in the case of human rights violations. These actions have victims who generally resent what is done to them and who would rarely concede that, because such behavior is common in their country, their tormentors are acting quite properly. But even if the victims did take the view that they have no rights against what is done to them, would this settle the issue? Couldn't they be wrong in thinking this? Isn't this what we would say in the case of the battered wife who protests that of course her husband beats her every week, that's what any woman has to expect? (Does our reaction here depend on what we assume to be the customs of the surrounding society? Do we feel differently if we suppose ourselves to be considering a foreign culture in which wife beating is much more common than here and people expect it?) The question here is the following: Which is the more objectionable form of cultural superiority, to refuse to aid a victim on the ground that "they live like that—they don't recognize rights as we know them," or to attempt to protect the defenseless even when they themselves feel that suffering is their lot and they have no basis to complain of it?

I admit that we may answer this question differently in different cases. We may feel differently, for example, if the victims are in fact recent perpetrators, and show every intention of becoming perpetrators again when they have the chance. Perhaps we are moved here by retributionist sentiments. But I believe that an important variable is the kind and degree of intervention that would be required to achieve a significant effect. It is one thing to bring diplomatic pressure to bear, to decline to make military assistance agreement, or to use economic pressure in order to bring about an end to a specific series of acts. It would be something else to continue to exert such pressure over a long period of time in order to bring about a general change in people's outlook and in the operation of their political institutions. Such action might in some cases be justified, but it raises obvious and severe problems. I believe that appeals to cultural differences have their main force not by way of a relativism of values but rather through the fact that such differences may greatly increase the scale of any intervention that could hope to be successful, and decrease the chances that any intervention would actually succeed. If people are very different from us in their attitude toward human rights, this doesn't make what they do *right*, but it may mean that there is little we can do about it short of remaking their whole society, and this may be something we are neither required nor even able to do.

I believe that this problem can be a genuine one. Nonetheless, it does not seem to be an important factor in the cases we have actually considered. Despite some mention of the problem of the parochiality of rights in our discussions, none of these cases seems to be an example of a society marked by a complete lack of concern for rights, where implanting such concern would be a major exercise in cultural change.

4. This brings me to my last question, that of separability. As I mentioned earlier, I think that some support for human rights as a foreign policy objective is aided by the belief that one can oppose human rights violations in a country without taking a stand on domestic political questions such as the question of who is to rule. Thus, support for steps to halt torture or religious discrimination in foreign countries draws its particular strength not only from our strong feelings of revulsion at these practices but also from the view that they are discrete evils whose persistence is separable from that of the prevailing government, whose policies we may or may not agree with but which we would not think it proper for us to attempt directly to alter.

Perhaps no one holds this view. It once played a role in my thinking about human rights, at least, but I now think it mistaken. In those cases in which they raise the most serious problems, the practices just mentioned are engaged in because they are seen as serving important political purposes. These perceptions can, of course, be incorrect, but I see no reason to think that they generally are. A regime may have good reasons to believe that it can remain in power only by quelling opposition through terror, or only by exploiting and catering to religious differences in the country. When such beliefs are correct, ending human rights violations will involve, as a consequence, bringing down the regime. But even though they are practically linked, these two events remain intellectually separable, and the doctrine of separability may persist in a revised form. The fall of the government may be only an unintended consequence of our action, the purpose of which was merely to bring an end to violations of human rights. This distinction may be important; perhaps such an action is less of an objectionable intrusion than an action whose purpose is to bring about a change in government.

This may seem more plausible if it is put in the following way. It is intrusive in an objectionable sense to attempt to bring about a change in government in another country to suit one's own interests. But, as argued above, human rights violations may be a serious enough matter to justify, indeed even to require, outsiders to do what they can to protect and aid the victims. And this

may be true even if the result of this aid is internal political change. The force
of this argument may lead us to reverse our original question: When a regime
engages in serious violations of basic human rights is it even permissible to
refrain from taking action on the ground that any successful defense of human
rights would lead to undesirable political change?

If by "undesirable" we mean unfavorable to our own country's interests,
it seems that the answer to this question will generally be "no," unless the
unfavorable results are of major proportions. There is a limit to the sacrifices
one is required to make to aid innocent victims, but it is surely corrupt to stand
by while someone is beaten up because the aggressor is a customer of yours and
you want to keep his business.

Suppose, alternatively, that the undesirable consequences of a change in
government would accrue to the people whose government is engaging in human
rights violations. It seems that this is, for most people, a more difficult case.
Most people are reluctant to take steps to oppose human rights violations when
they see the regime in question as basically a good one, but unstable, and likely
to be replaced by one that would be much worse from the point of view of most
people in the country. Their view seems to be that in situations of political
instability a decision whether to bring pressure to end human rights violations
has to be made on the basis of a full assessment of the political situation in the
country in question. Human rights are one important element in this assessment,
but not the only consideration.

This position strikes me as too lenient. While I would not take the extreme
position that human rights may never be violated no matter what the consequences, I do want to say that the situations in which their violation could be
justified would have to be very extreme indeed. To make my position clearer
let me consider a particular problem of separability. It is sometimes asserted
that many countries face a choice between adherence to human rights and economic development. The belief that there is such a conflict seems to represent a
common ground between people who take it as a justification for suspension of
human rights and others who take it as part of a case against economic development for these countries. I say "economic development" here, though of course
what is at issue is a particular path of economic development pursued at a particular rate. The two groups just mentioned may be divided over whether what
conflicts with human rights is the only path of economic development possible
for these countries or whether it is just the particular path favored by outside
financial interests.

If this conflict, in either form, is a real one for a society, then a successful
defense of human rights there would not only affect the stability of a particular
government but also affect and perhaps settle an important question of national
policy. This problem might be brought within the account of rights offered
earlier in this chapter in the following way. I have said that to claim that there
is a right of a particular sort one must, among other things, claim that a society

recognizing such a right is feasible—that the right avoids the harms to which it is addressed at tolerable cost. But what costs are "tolerable"? In particular, what sacrifices in economic progress are an acceptable price to pay for the benefits of a society in which civil liberties are observed? Surely, it may be said, different societies may legitimately give different answers to this question, and also to the related question of which forms of development are to be preferred. Isn't it therefore inappropriate for us, as outsiders, to impose our judgment of these matters on another society? Aren't these questions ones that each society is best left to answer for itself?

But here it is important to ask what one means by "letting a society decide for itself." How does a conflict between human rights and the pursuit of economic development (or some other social policy) arise? Most often it arises because there is considerable opposition to the policy in question and human rights must be violated to prevent this opposition from becoming politically effective. In such a situation there is likely to be no consensus on the question of the relative value to be attached to the success of this policy and to human rights. In deciding whether to act in support of human rights in such a society, then, there is no way to escape the need for an independent judgment of the case for these rights in comparison to the competing goals. This judgment should take into account special features of the society—its particular needs, level of development, and so on—which determine the options open to it and affect their desirability. The need for a judgment cannot, however, be finessed by appealing to a supposed consensus in the society in question.

I might summarize this argument by saying that the goal of "letting a society decide for itself" counts more in favor of support for human rights than in favor of a policy of careful neutrality. I believe this to be generally true, particularly in those contemporary cases cited as examples of the conflict between human rights and economic development. But this belief does depend on some conception of the process through which a social decision would be reached in the absence of human rights violations: it depends on the claim that this process could be called one through which the society decides for itself. Perhaps one can imagine cases where this claim would be hard to make; for example, cases where the goal in question is not economic development but political democratization, and the method of decision that will operate if human rights are not violated will allow the traditional oligarchy to preserve its power.[3] But such examples are special in that the goal that is at stake is itself a matter of human rights. The question then becomes whether some human rights may be violated in order that other rights can be secured. Surely this question can *sometimes* be answered positively; it depends on the rights at issue and on the nature of the violations.

I have discussed the practical inseparability of human rights from internal political issues as a problem affecting the arguments for and against action by outsiders in defense of human rights. But this inseparability is an important fact to recognize for another reason as well: it indicates what one is up against in fighting human rights violations. If these violations represent not isolated outbreaks of cruelty and prejudice but, rather, strategic moves in an earnest political struggle, then they will not easily be given up. Moral suasion and the pressure of world opinion, or even the canceling of a few contracts, cannot be expected to carry much weight against considerations of political survival. Those who are serious about human rights must be prepared for a long, hard fight.

Notes

1. Here I outline a view of rights presented at greater length in my paper "Rights, Goals and Fairness," in S. Hampshire, ed., *Public and Private Morality* (Cambridge, Eng.: Cambridge University Press, 1978).

2. See Henry Shue, "Torture," *Philosophy & Public Affairs* 7 (Winter 1978).

3. For a good discussion of this problem see part III of Charles Beitz, *Political Theory and International Relations* (unpublished doctoral dissertation, Princeton University, 1977).

7

Constraints, Goals, and Moralism in Foreign Policy

Douglas MacLean

The common fate of ideals that reach Washington these days, it seems to me, is not death by corruption but rather death by sophistication. The affairs of government, we are told, should be handled discreetly, by experts. "[F]oreign policy is not a matter of objectives, it is a matter of strategy."[1] Even our most basic values should not rigidly constrain the experts who play the games of global strategy as they administer our foreign policy. According to former secretary of state Henry Kissinger, human rights should not be a "vocal objective" of foreign policy.[2] This is the view I wish to challenge.

The human rights movement began in the U.S. Congress in 1973, several years before Jimmy Carter was elected president and announced that human rights would be a major concern of his administration. It comes as no shock to learn that, in the early days, congressional attempts to use the human rights issue in order to exert some control over U.S. foreign policy were vigorously opposed by the Ford-Kissinger administration. What is more surprising is that every human rights bill brought before the Congress since President Carter took office has been just as vigorously opposed by his administration, and for remarkably similar reasons.

The Congress has been rather explicit in its human rights legislation. Section 502B of the Foreign Assistance Act, for example, says that "a principal goal of the foreign policy of the United States shall be to promote the increased observance of internationally recognized human rights by all countries." This act goes on to order that security assistance not be provided to countries whose governments violate these rights. It also orders the president to

> formulate and conduct international security assistance programs of the United States in a manner which will promote and advance human rights and avoid identification of the United States, through such programs, with governments which deny to their people internationally recognized human rights and fundamental freedoms, . . .

The Congress has clearly expressed its concern for both practices that violate human rights in other countries and American responsibility for and complicity in those practices.

Many people have read and criticized earlier drafts of this paper. I am especially indebted to Susan Wolf and to my colleagues Peter G. Brown and Henry Shue.

93

Henry Kissinger consistently doubted whether such human rights legislation was an appropriate expression of either concern. Acknowledging that "it is our obligation as the world's leading democracy to dedicate ourselves to assuring freedom for the human spirit," he went on to warn:

> But responsibility compels also a recognition of our limits. Our alliances . . . serve the cause of peace by strengthening regional and world security. If well conceived, they are not favors to others but a recognition of common interest. They should be withdrawn when those interests change; they should not, as a general rule, be used as levers to extort a standard of conduct or to punish acts with which we do not agree.[3]

Apparently, Dr. Kissinger did not think that promoting human rights should be a principal goal of foreign policy. He certainly did not think that Congress had any business passing laws that would firmly constrain U.S. involvement with governments that violate human rights:

> We have generally opposed attempts to deal with sensitive international human rights issues through legislation, not because of the moral view expressed, which we share, but because legislation is almost always too inflexible, too public, and too heavyhanded a means to accomplish what it seeks.[4]

I would like to address both the criticism that the existing human rights amendments are too inflexible and the criticism that promoting respect for human rights ought not be a principal goal of U.S. foreign policy. These are the most frequent criticisms brought against the current administration's human rights policy and against the human rights legislation. They are also heard more and more frequently as the costs of a serious human rights policy become more obvious. Sometimes the criticisms are run together. Thus, any attempts to include the promotion of human rights and the removal of American responsibility for their violations as goals of foreign policy are thought to make policy too inflexible. These attempts are derided for being moralistic. Although this criticism sometimes merely expresses a belief that morality may have its place, but not in the real world, the warning against moralism in foreign policy is an old one,[5] and I shall consider it in some detail below. But the criticisms can be separated, and they must be if we are to understand how even the Carter administration can oppose human rights laws. Although it professes its concern for human rights, this administration opposes legislation it feels will "tie its hands." There is no inconsistency here, for President Carter himself has usually spoken only about the goal of promoting respect for human rights; he has never been very explicit about how this should be done. Typical of his state-

ments on this subject is the following excerpt from one of his campaign
speeches.

> Ours is a great and powerful nation, committed to certain enduring
> ideals, and those ideals must be reflected in our foreign policy. . . . If
> other nations want our friendship and support, they must understand
> that we want to see basic human rights respected.[6]

In what can be considered a gloss on this statement, a State Department
official, sounding not unlike former Secretary Kissinger, explains that

> quite frankly, to grasp the meaning of this nation's time-honored
> [human rights] principles is not to understand the hard choices that
> must be made when applying them . . . . [T]he *why* and the *what*
> are easy. It is the *how* that complicates the pursuit of a human rights
> policy.[7]

The first thing to notice about such statements is how promoting respect
for human rights in other countries is assumed to be the only goal of a foreign
policy that takes human rights seriously. Removing or reducing America's
complicity in moral wrongdoings, the closely related goal mentioned in the
legislation, is somehow lost sight of. Otherwise, the *how* becomes rather easy
in many cases; only the *whether* remains difficult. By focusing exclusively on
only the one goal, the concerns of the human rights movement are inaccurately
represented. And the growing chorus, critical of enforcing the strong human
rights provisions in foreign assistance legislation, tells us to leave this task to the
experts. They can decide how best to realize this end on a case-by-case basis,
unhampered by rigid principles.

If the position of these critics were simply that all that matters is the end
result, and not the means of achieving it, the discussion could end right here.
This view is obviously morally unacceptable and requires no further discussion.
However, the criticism might instead be intended to claim only that human
rights amendments are ineffective or self-defeating ways of achieving the goal
of promoting respect for human rights in other countries. A "dirty hands"
argument might further be invoked, to the effect that the goal of avoiding
complicity in the wrongdoing of other governments is a moral luxury that it
would be wrong to indulge. A challenge to such a position should ideally
show both that it is not wrong to avoid complicity and that the human rights
amendments do not interfere with the goal of promoting respect for human
rights. This is what I shall argue presently. The challenge need not be a proof—
mine is not—but only an argument that makes clear that the burden of justification falls on the side of the critics, and that the burden amounts to more
than the familiar appeals to the complexity of foreign relations.

Obeying Constraints

At least part of the justification of the human rights provisions is an appeal to the goal of removing U.S. responsibility for the human rights abuses of other governments. Our government is a moral agent which, like all moral agents, is bound by some moral requirements. There are constraints on the way a government can conduct its foreign policy. This simply means that a government is not allowed to do whatever it wants, disregarding the effects of its actions on people outside its borders.

The reasons for acknowledging limits on a government's actions are similar to the justifications offered for laws of war; without saying very much about national goals or the reasons for existing policies, we can still determine limits on how to attain those goals. We can even acknowledge that our policymakers ought to view the world of nations as a highly competitive arena in which the different parties pursue the goals of their own national security and domestic economic prosperity, realizing that this struggle consists to some considerable degree in gaining a relative advantage over others. Still, large numbers of people are affected by what our government does, and this fact places limits on what our policies can be. We cannot appropriate land or people as suits us. The justification for this does not have to be based on any agreement or contract that exists between our government and the other peoples of the world. In order to argue that certain values must be respected universally by our own government's activities, it is sufficient to appeal to the agreement that exists between *us* and our government. That agreement presupposes a consensus among our own citizens about certain ideals, such as that all people are equal and that every human being is entitled to certain liberties. Our government must respect such ideals, because its authority is granted partly for that purpose. Even though it is true that our government does not assume nearly the same responsibilities to foreign peoples as it does to its own citizens, certain ways of treating any human being are nevertheless inconsistent with our own ideals. Although it is fashionable to speak about universal human rights, for the purposes of justifying moral constraints on our own government's policies, we can instead appeal to the rights of U.S. citizens to have certain ideals respected and even affirmed by their government. We are not, for the moment, taking this to mean that our government must promote those ideals abroad, only that it is bound to respect them and not to violate them in its actions and policies where it represents the nation.

Thus, to say that moral ideals place constraints on how our government can act means at least that some of the moral beliefs that are basic to our justification of our own political institutions, in particular those that establish rights and liberties extending to all people, must be applied consistently to all of our government's activities. It has not been given the authority, under normal circumstances, to act otherwise. If these ideals define the rules of legitimate governmental activity, I can see no reason not to embody them in laws and make them public. The question of strategy does not even arise here, for the goal we are now considering is that of prohibiting the U.S. government from engaging in morally unacceptable activities. Our Bill of Rights is a public and inflexible document that aims in part to constrain the activities of the government that affect our fellow citizens. The human rights laws simply function in a similar way to protect all people from our government's activities, where we believe all people equally deserve and need protection. Enforceable laws alone can achieve this goal. To argue that the experts who administer foreign policy should police themselves as they see fit is to demand more trust from our citizens than it is reasonable for them to give.

Consider some hypothetical examples. Suppose we have an embassy in a country that practices apartheid, and that the embassy employs local citizens. It would be wrong to let racist laws affect our government's hiring practices, even if we make no attempt to alter apartheid in that country. This is because racist practices are fundamentally at odds with our most basic views, and our government must be responsible for not allowing them to govern its own behavior. This is not to deny that forcing such consistency in our own practices might create difficulties, but these would be difficulties it would be seriously wrong not to face. If, to imagine another example, some country prohibited the parctice of Christianity, our government would still be bound in principle—and should be bound in practice—to insist that our diplomats stationed there be free to practice any religion. It would be convenient to make sure that we sent non-Christian representatives of our government there, but we would presumably be prohibited by our own principles from doing this as a matter of policy. That would constitute unfair religious discrimination in our government's hiring practices. Our government might have no obligation, however, to promote religious liberty in that other country, under their government, or even to demand such liberty for our own citizens who happened to be there voluntarily, in some private capacity.

These are relatively easy cases that show how constraints are applied to our government's actions. The constraints are based upon beliefs about values that we take to be universal, but it is not because they are universally believed that certain values impose constraints that are binding in the ways just described. Rather, it is because our belief that they are universal means that we must *apply* them universally to all people. Whatever authority or power our government has is legitimate only because it embodies and protects these values, enforcing them in our own society, including the government's own practices. This is how the universality applies: it governs all of our practices and extends to protect all people who are affected by them or by their consequences. That means we have no reason to restrict the application of these values to our citizens, even though there might be reasons to restrict them to our own practices and activities. Thus, we do not have to claim that these values ought to govern the practices of others, but only that they limit the effects on others that are permitted by our own practices.

Consider now the more difficult cases that involve the relationship between our government and other governments that violate human rights. Should our relations with that government be constrained by our judgments of *its* actions? Certainly where we are responsible for having brought repressive regimes to power, we share complicity in their wrongdoings. Some of these cases, where our aid is necessary for their remaining in power, are morally equivalent to cases where we ourselves are the proximate causes of human rights violations. No doubt awareness of U.S. complicity in such cases is one of the principal explanations for the current popularity of the human rights movement. There can also be no doubt that the human rights amendments mean to address such cases.

The central issue in this part of my argument is complicity, and it is important to realize how complicity extends to less obvious cases. Complicity in the wrongdoings of governments that receive aid or buy weapons from the United States is in fact difficult to avoid. Where we give security assistance, even though we specify that it cannot be used for any internal police activities, we aid police functions nevertheless, by easing the burden and the cost that the other government must assume for security against its outside enemies. Without necessarily intending it initially, we enable it to carry on its domestic practices and we help to protect it while it does, even after these practices come to our attention. Security assistance is in this way fungible. Similarly, economic and developmental aid associates us with the governments of recipient nations and can contribute to the cost of repressive practices by freeing funds that are then channeled into police activities.

It is not impossible, perhaps, to aid the citizens of the country without associating ourselves so closely with its government. Some economic aid, for instance, administered through multilateral or nongovernmental channels, might go directly to the intended recipients, but that is certainly not the way all or even most of our foreign aid programs work. More importantly, however, that is not even the way we want our foreign aid to work, because it would defeat some of the purposes of such programs, which are not meant simply to achieve humanitarian goals, but to make closer ties between governments or otherwise to further our own ends and create relationships advantageous to us.

A further effect of our bilateral foreign assistance programs is to give tacit approval and support to the recipient government, which is usually not offset even when the assistance is accompanied by denunciations of the government's policies. In the minds of most people, I think, the effects of our aid in linking us to a government are stronger than are our speeches aimed at dissociating ourselves from its policies. This, too, is complicity. However, this raises another issue, about the proper response to charges of complicity.

It is argued that maintaining our foreign assistance programs gives us leverage for continuing to affect the policies of other governments. If we terminate those programs because of moral constraints on our own actions, thereby keeping our hands clean, we lose our leverage and our ability to help people who are suffering under repressive regimes. This argument has been made recently about countries where we have terminated assistance, especially Chile.[8] It is claimed to be important to maintain our involvement in those countries if we have any hope of making things better, and it is wrong to ignore this fact by placing moral constraints on our own actions and policies, because by working within rigid constraints we bring about worse consequences than by ignoring constraints. In such cases, different moral goals conflict with one another.

Where we are responsible for a repressive regime's very existence, this pragmatic argument is thinly disguised hypocrisy, but it is a serious question whether one ought to act on principle when one is aware that the consequences of such a policy are worse than they would be if the principles were ignored. The best response to this dilemma attempts to avoid it. Where a regime *needs* our aid, we have leverage, and by constraining our own programs for giving aid, in order to remove our own complicity in wrongdoings, we use that leverage in the most effective way. If another government is not dependent on our aid, then we have little leverage, if any at all, and thus we have no justification for supporting them and accepting some of the responsibility for their wrongs. Some people will argue that in diplomatic forums leverage does not work in this straightforward way, and that we must maintain our complicity while working for gradual change. At this point, however, the burden of proof is with the advocates of this view to show that loosening the moral constraints on our own policies is the only effective way of decreasing the suffering in the world because of another government's violating human rights. Even then, it remains to be shown that relaxing the moral constraints would be the right thing to do.

A parallel response can be made about arms sales, except that here the costs of constraining our activities can be significantly higher. How should we respond to the threat of higher costs? Moral rules are not absolutely binding, and they can bend in the face of extraordinary circumstances. Yet when a plea is made to sell helicopters to Argentina or sophisticated airplanes to Iran, in spite of the dismal human rights records in those countries, the economic issues are sometimes the only ones cited. All too often the moral issues are ignored, as if any economic cost were enough to set aside all other values. Strong human rights amendments—public and inflexible rules (but with their permissible exceptions explicitly included, as they now are)—may at least be able to remedy this inexcusable blindness.

Do the constraints imposed by the human rights amendments generally threaten other (and perhaps nonmoral) national interest? Of course there will be costs in some cases, but I believe the human rights amendments can in general be defended strictly on grounds of prudence. A tacit agreement between us and our government justifies but also limits governmental authority, giving to the government the responsibility for protecting human rights domestically. Many of these rights are ways of constraining social interference, including that of the government itself, in the lives of individuals. These rights express a moral ideal, that individuals should be allowed to exercise as much autonomy as is possible and reasonable in pursuing their own lives. Our rights are not merely ways of protecting us from harm, for we would want to be able to claim our rights even if those in power were completely benevolent. This view about the importance of rights may not be universally shared, but perhaps it is not necessary to appeal to this moral ideal in order to justify the practice of constraining governmental authority. That practice may be seen instead as the condition necessary to secure full support for a government, without which it might not have any authority at all. Thus, one important reason for protecting human rights is to promote the social stability that results when a government operates with general approval and support.

Now a government that prohibits all dissent, that arrests and tortures its opposition, secures its authority in a way that is not naturally stable and self-reinforcing. It is unreasonable to think that such practices are based ultimately on principle; they are instead deemed necessary for maintaining control. They are bound to be unpopular practices which are resorted to anyway because the use of force and terror are needed to secure authority for an unpopular government. If the government had popular support, it could allow dissent and would not have to engage in practices that make itself vulnerable to worldwide criticism. Whatever stability these practices gain for a regime is linked to the practices and the fear they generate. They must continue to be employed successfully. As the regime becomes less popular among its own people, the chances increase that it will be overthrown whenever this becomes possible. These regimes may become increasingly dependent on outside aid to finance the unpopular programs aimed at suppressing their own citizens. We ally ourselves with such governments, therefore, at some risk and perhaps at some cost; for if they lose control we stand to lose whatever advantage we sought to gain by allying ourselves with them in the first place.

The conclusion to draw from these considerations is that if we want to use our foreign assistance programs to gain influence in the countries we aid, it is prudent to ally ourselves with popular regimes wherever this is possible. Realistically, however, such reasoning carries limited weight because the argument has a limited application. A tyrannical regime, especially with outside aid, may be able to tolerate the costs of oppression and unpopularity for a long time, long enough, for instance, to serve our ends. Furthermore, the argument assumes that popular regimes are likely not to violate (what we take to be) human rights because they do not have to. Although the argument gives reasons for thinking that this is generally true, exceptions can and do occur. This only shows that agents are not always prudent, or else that morality and prudence can conflict.

The "experts" who oppose the human rights amendment may pick up on this "realistic" suggestion to argue the merits of making decisions on a case-by-case basis. Nevertheless, recent cases can be cited (for example, Cambodia, Vietnam, Greece) where U.S. attempts to gain influence by supporting repressive regimes have backfired.[9] We have shown a disturbing tendency in our pragmatic foreign policy to back the wrong horse, and when some current crises are resolved, they are likely to show that we have made the wrong bets again in Nicaragua and Iran.

Promoting Other Goals

Turning now to consider the other, more publicized goal of the human rights movement, promoting respect for human rights by *other* governments, we confront a different set of objections. Some charge that this goal itself is indefensible, accusing the human rights movement of being moralistic or morally imperialistic for imposing American values abroad; others criticize the human rights amendments for being too rigid, and thus counterproductive to realizing their goal. The first criticism questions the appropriateness of the goal itself, while the second questions only the means chosen to realize it.

The criticism that our human rights policy is moralistic, and therefore bad, is a philosophically interesting one. It appeals to the logic or structure of our concept of morality to, an asymmetry that exists between our duties not to interfere and our duties to give more positive forms of aid. When we think of a person's moral relationship to other persons, anyway, this is clearly true. We have strong duties not to harm others by our actions, duties to avoid causing suffering. These are not, however, unqualified duties to reduce the harm and suffering in the world, for that way of putting it is indifferent between avoiding harming others and taking more positive action to reduce suffering. If we were indifferent to this distinction, a commitment to being moral would be intolerable for normal people. The possibilities for doing something to reduce suffering in the world are nearly always available to most people, just as the possibilities for causing suffering are. If positive duties to aid and negative duties not to harm bind us equally to act upon these possibilities, our whole lives would have to be devoted to meeting these duties and fulfilling our obligations. Morality would engulf us. It would not be *wrong* of somebody, a saint, perhaps, always to feel duty-bound in this way, however unnatural such an attitude might be. But it would be wrong of any moral theory to require this of everyone.[10] It is important for sainthood to be above and beyond the call of duty, regardless of how real saints might actually feel.

We reasonably insist that stronger conditions must be met to justify imposing positive duties than to justify imposing negative ones; the consequences

of inaction have to be greater before a reason to act becomes a duty to act.
The duty to promote human rights is a positive duty, whereas the duty to constrain our own actions, in order not to be responsible for violating the human
rights of people anywhere in the world, is a negative duty.

If we recognize an asymmetry between duties not to harm and duties to
give aid, which is not a difference in consequences, we are forced to admit that
in general the consequences of an act (or of inaction) cannot alone tell us our
duties. A mere weighing of consequences cannot account for important moral
differences that are the result of the various ways an agent can be related to a
state of affairs and its consequences.[11]

To account for these other differences, some philosophers have sought to
determine the moral value of an act by looking to the nature of the action
itself, or at any rate the reasons for doing an act. These philosophers have then
required the moral principles to be incorporated into those reasons. Thus,
duties are determined by the principles guiding the action, not by the consequences resulting from the action, and realizing and obeying these principles
itself becomes a goal—or *the* goal—of moral activity.

To show that consequences are not all that matter, however, is not to show
that consequences do not matter at all. Not only are the consequences of
actions morally important, it is also difficult or impossible to see why, ultimately, the truth of a moral principle, rather than an agent's interests, must always
be the reason for acting.[12] We do not ordinarily believe that a person's actions
must be motivated by impartial and objective moral principles as a necessary
condition for his or her act to be right, or even virtuous. A person is not morally
worse who does not formulate moral principles whenever he or she acts, but
instead responds to natural desires and simply does what is right. We can hold
people responsible for acting on moral principle or including the dictates of
moral principles among their intentions when following their natural inclinations would cause unnecessary harm or unfair treatment of others. These
situations, however, constitute only a part of any person's moral life, and in
other situations it is both right and natural to act on other motives and to pursue other values. Morality, after all, is meant to serve people and their interests,
not the reverse.

Although this latter attitude toward moral principles—we can call it a
minimalist attitude—is not universally shared, it is a coherent view and it demands a response. The minimalist view holds that people are required to follow
or promote moral principles consciously only when they are otherwise likely to
do something wrong. It recognizes only the ways that morality constrains what
a person can permissibly do. It is also part of this minimalist account that
cultivating further moral attitudes to make moral principles, or principles that
promote morality, into goals is not necessary for an individual to lead a morally
good life. The critics of the human rights movement, then, simply apply a
minimalist attitude to the activities of nations. They argue that stronger moral

attitudes, which require placing human rights concerns among the principal
goals of foreign policy, cannot be justified and might, by frustrating our other
goals, have bad consequences.

Thus, critics of the human rights movement are reacting to what they take
to be moral excess. The new legislation appears to them to be morally zealous,
designed to make the United States become not just a moral nation but a moral
crusader.

Some people do tend to act in the morally extreme ways that go beyond
minimalist attitudes. While we are reluctant to criticize them, a minimalist
would regard such people as moralistic, which is to deprecate this tendency. To
be moralistic is to be more than a very moral person, it is to make morality into
a cause in an objectionable way. Although moralism usually applies to the
practice of trying to make other people moral, there is also another sense in
which a person can be moralistic. We sometimes think a person is moralistic
who is unusually conscious about following moral principles in his or her own
actions. We must not confuse this person with a person who is unusually moral,
who could not harm a flea. A moralistic person makes morality itself a goal;
he or she lets moral principles override even laudable natural tendencies. Thus,
moralism in a person can be directed toward others, or it can be directed toward
oneself. A moralistic person, especially when the moralism is self-directed, is
mildly obsessive, and even though he or she may be harmless (though perhaps
a bit cold or calculating), we do not normally think moralism is a good thing.

The human rights movement appears to its critics to be moralistic in both
of the ways just described. It embodies self-directed moralism by making moral
principles explicit goals of policy, in order to meet our own moral constraints,
and it embodies crusading moralism by including in those goals the promotion
of our moral values in other countries.

We have now isolated the issues that must be confronted in defending the
strong human rights legislation against its critics. What are a government's
positive duties? Do moralistic policies ask too much of nations in the same way
and for the same reasons as they ask too much of individuals? I shall begin by
responding to the charge of self-directed moralism.

We have so far been treating governments as like persons because they
are agents, their actions affect people, and they can be held responsible. It is
also important to realize the morally relevant ways in which governments, and
nations, are not like people. Governments do not possess all the properties
of persons that are relevant to morality, the properties that are necessary in
order fully to understand the moral life of persons. What is missing in governments is a similar psychology, and perhaps any psychology at all. Persons have
inner lives and natural drives, which are entirely absent in governments, and
some moral concepts address the psychological aspects of persons but do not
apply to governments. A government can do wrong, but it cannot be incon-
tinent. Governments cannot have honest or open characters, which persons

often have. And although the relations among nations can be friendly or hostile, friendliness is not the same as friendship, which is not a possible relationship among such entities as nations or governments. Could two nations or governments ever fall in love?

One of the moral consequences of the fact that persons have psychologies is that they have certain special needs, including the need to form certain relationships. Meeting these needs and forming these relationships are among the highest goods of human life and, for that reason, are among the central aims of morality. At least one reason why self-directed moralism is objectionable at the personal level is that it is likely to interfere with realizing some of these goals. Someone who always acted on principle, who kept spontaneous urges always under control, would find it difficult to display the natural feelings crucial for developing desirable personal relationships. Moralistic attitudes are also unnecessary to the extent that people have strong and natural psychological motivations to realize the goods that result from normal psychological and emotional development.

Governments and nations do not have these natural interests, and they do not form these natural relationships. To the extent that a nation has any interests at all, its interests are determined by and depend upon the interests of the people who are its citizens. National interests are usually ways of promoting the interests of a nation's citizens, and these involve primarily looking after themselves and their relationships with one another. A nation, then, does not have natural moral inclinations that reach beyond self-interest; and the source of the interests it does have—the interests of its citizens—is not likely to lead inevitably to an adequate concern for its responsibilities to the rest of the world, responsibilities that result from its own actions as well as those that derive from the weaker obligations to give aid.

If a nation, or a government, lacks a psychology that includes such morally relevant features as the drive toward natural relationships, it is, nevertheless, run by individuals who do have the appropriate kind of inner life. But these individuals are themselves representatives, furthering the interests that we have come to expect governments to express. A government responsive to its citizens can be expected, as a result of the pressure of the citizens' representatives, to respond to their morally justifiable claims. Outsiders, however, are poorly represented, if at all, and will not naturally see their interests protected in the policies a government sets for a nation, policies directing actions that can and probably will affect outsiders.

It is because of such facts about nations and governments that explicit and perhaps moralistic laws are needed in order to make moral values a part of a nation's aims. This may be the only way to assure that a government obeys its moral constraints. Certainly the history of our foreign policy and its effects, where moral values have not been made into enforceable goals to be promoted, tends to support this line of argument.

It is by overextending the analogy of governments with individuals that the promotion of human rights as a principal goal of a government's interaction with other governments appears excessively moralistic. If moralism is excessive, and if it interferes with our other goals as a nation, then it is wrong. But the analogy between a government and an individual human being is not complete enough to support this type of criticism. It is not reasonable to expect governments and persons to fulfill their responsibilities in the same way. A better way to extend the analogy would be to see a government as like a person, but a socially re-tarded one, who *can* do what he should, but only with effort and only in an entirely self-conscious way.

The charge of crusading moralism involves different issues, which raise questions about sovereignty and about the autonomy of individual nations and cultures to determine their own values. I shall begin responding to them by considering a case that involves only individuals.

Suppose someone has conclusive evidence that his neighbors are beating one of their children. This child is helpless, the parents show no signs of stopping the practice, and the other children—the only other members of the household— are too confused and frightened and perhaps too weak to do anything about it themselves. What is the knowledgeable neighbor's duty in such a case? It is obvious, I think that for him to do nothing would be seriously wrong. Even though it is in some sense a family matter, this goes far beyond anything that could be dismissed as strictly a domestic concern. The knowledgeable neighbor might have legitimate qualms about barging in and rescuing the child, not the least of which might be a reasonable fear for his own safety. (We might even imagine that the child's father owns the store in which this man works so that it involves a serious risk for him even to mention it directly.) Fortunately, he has another alternative open to him; he may report the matter to the local police. They are able to take care of such matters, and to protect the informer's ano-nymity. He has an obligation at least to do this. If the neighbor happened also to be paying this family's rent, or giving them the food they need, or providing them with an automobile, he might by virtue of this more involved relationship have additional obligations to exert leverage on his own to stop the brutality.[13]

How is this different from a case in which our government knows that another government is seriously violating the rights of its citizens? Child-beating is not just wrong, it is against the law; and socially sanctioned enforcement mechanisms carry out the law. These enforcement agencies do not exist on an international level, except in very weak and rudimentary forms.[14] The offend-ing father could not claim that child-beating is nobody else's business, for even if no individual neighbor has a legal duty to intervene, the police certainly do. And the nieghbor has a moral, if not a legal, duty to inform the police that they are needed. Suppose that the father said he did not see anything so bad about his actions—that he thought this was the only way to instill discipline in an unruly child—and for that reason it is wrong of other people to impose their values on him. He is in fact mistaken about child-rearing, but that is not the essential point; what he did is both wrong and against the law, and the law applies to him. The wrongness of his act does not lie in what his neighbors simply happen to believe. The social consensus which makes it wrong, and which determines the values of society, is supported by social institutions and by common belief, as well as by facts about what causes harm or suffering. If a government made a similar claim about torturing its citizens, no matter how ridiculous the claim is, there is an important difference, since there is no comparable broader society of which that government is a part.

Such differences between these cases rest on two closely related claims. The first is that some moral principles apply to all the members of a society because they are the society's values. If this claim is to be noncontroversial, then in a broader sense it must apply to only those values that it would be extremely unlikely that anyone in the society would in fact deny. They must be such that if somebody does in fact deny them, we have more reason to wonder about the person than about the value. The second claim is that these values might not apply to all nations or societies, because individual societies are not organized and determined by any broader structure as the citizens within each society are.

The larger issue involved here is that of ethical relativism, the claim that no moral values are universal because all values are culturally determined and cultures are different. To my knowledge, however, it has never been demonstrated that cultures are in fact different enough to make the logical possibility of relativism into a moral thesis with any application.[15] Regardless, the debate about moral relativism is simply not relevant here, for we could accept relativism as the correct moral theory and still rebut the charge that our foreign policy embodies crusading moralism. We need only to recognize that there are some positive duties, that somebody ought to come to the aid of the victims of oppressive governments. There is no question about evaluating types of governments and imposing the type we happen to like on other nations or cultures, not unless torturing and detaining political dissidents without trial are essential to some types of government that a culture supports.

Perhaps this is unfair to the critics of the human rights movement. After all, they are not committed to ignoring torture wherever it occurs in the world. The charge of crusading moralism does not have to rely on ethical relativism and does not have to deny that our nation has positive duties, even though some of the criticism of the legislation seems to imply these claims. The objection that the legislation is moralistic really questions whether the strong and explicit language of the laws—that one of our country's "principal goals" is to "promote increased observance" of certain values—is justifiable.

It is important to remember that the rights in question have been recognized by nearly all nations and have the status of international law. That status, however, is different from a status of domestic law in crucial respects. There is no comparable enforcement mechanism, no international police force with anywhere near the power or authority of domestic police.

The lack of a strong multilateral enforcement mechanism may not be a weakness of international law at all; there may be good reasons for not allowing such a police force to be formed. How would the scope of its authority be determined? To whom would it be accountable?

Most likely, some forms of multilateral enforcement of international law are possible and desirable, but to the extent that these are not sufficient means of enforcement the burden falls to individual governments to do what they can. Individual governments are working in a setting different from the setting of individuals within a society, and they must assume different sorts or responsibilities and duties. Because of the lack of socially sanctioned enforcement mechanisms at an international level, nations must assume the moral burden of using what leverage they can to enforce international law. Rigid provisions for action, built explicitly into a nation's laws, as in 502B, appear in this light to be reasonable ways to meet this requirement. If this means moralism in the international arena is necessary for the enforcement of international law, then there is nothing wrong with this kind of moralism.

Objections to the human rights legislation are increasing and the current laws will almost certainly be revised. My claim is that there is nothing wrong in principle with the stand the Congress has taken, and the question of the best strategy for promoting respect for human rights is an open one. There are other important considerations to keep in mind, as the critics often assert. The one I have emphasized is the legitimate goal of constraining what our government may do as it pursues the national interest.

Notes

1. Stanley Hoffman, "The Hell of Good Intentions," *Foreign Policy*, 29 (Winter 1977-78), 3.
2. *Washington Post*, February 5, 1979, p. A17.
3. 75 Dept. State Bull. 603 (1976).
4. Ibid.
5. See, for instance, Dean Acheson, "Morality, Moralism, and Diplomacy," *Yale Review* 47 (Summer 1958), 481-493.
6. Address before the B'nai B'rith Convention, September 8, 1976.
7. "Human Rights: A World Perspective," address by Patricia M. Derian before the National Association of Human Rights Workers, October 15, 1978.
8. See "But Does the Junta Really Want to Listen?" *New York Times*, January 1, 1978, sec. 1, p. 4. "But such sanctions [reductions in American

economic aid and suspension of U.S. arms sales] have now been imposed against
Chile and other authoritarian Latin nations—Uruguay, Argentina, and Brazil
[sic] —and, in the view of one diplomat, 'the United States has lost its leverage.'"

9. In all three instances, a regime we supported was overthrown, resulting
in an overall decline of U.S. influence in the country. For a detailed examination of one of these instances (Greece), see Lawrence Stern, *The Wrong Horse:
The Politics of Intervention and the Failure of American Diplomacy*, (Times
Books, 1978).

10. See J.O. Urmson, "Saints and Heroes," in *Essays in Moral Philosophy*,
ed. A.I. Melden (Seattle: University of Washington Press, 1958), pp. 198-216.

11. For an interesting version of this criticism, see Bernard Williams, "A
Critique of Utilitarianism," in Smart and Williams, *Utilitarianism: For and
Against* (Cambridge, Eng.: Cambridge University Press, 1973), esp. sections 3
and 5.

12. See, for example, Philippa Foot, "Morality as a System of Hypothetical
Imperatives," *Philosophical Review*, 81 (1972), 305-316.

13. This elaboration on the example was suggested to me by William
Wipfler.

14. Even though some human rights documents, such as those embodied
in the U.N. Charter, are binding in international law, they are difficult to enforce. Although many nations have ratified the U.N. Covenants on human
rights, only six governments have committed themselves to the U.N. complaint
procedure.

15. A logically coherent relativism is defended by Gilbert Harman, "Moral
Relativism Defended," *Philosophical Review*, 84 (1975), 3-22. To show the
difficulties of applying the theory, I would have to show that Harman's inner/
outer distinction does not cover the range of application of all moral principles,
that is, that nobody can be rational and "beyond the pale" to an extent that no
moral judgments apply.

**Part III
Principles: International Issues**

8

Domestic Jurisdiction, Intervention, and Human Rights: The International Law Perspective

Thomas Buergenthal

Introduction

Discussions of international human rights policies and practices invariably produce references to "intervention" and "domestic jurisdiction." These terms are also invoked, with predictable regularity, by governments accused of violating human rights as well as by governments unwilling to use their influence to prevent such violations.

As a matter of fact, the claim that this or that action or statement constitutes an "intervention in matters falling within our domestic jurisdiction" appears to be the most frequently relied-upon response to charges of governmental violations of human rights. It is consequently of utmost importance to examine the meaning of this international law concept and to determine what legal consequences it has for international efforts to ensure that governments respect human rights. This chapter will address these issues.

Prohibition against Intervention in the Domestic Jurisdiction of States

The prohibition against intervention in matters within the domestic jurisdiction of states is expressly recognized in all major international instruments dealing with the rights and obligations of states. The same is true of agreements establishing international organizations; its member states seek thereby to ensure that these entities are denied the authority to adopt measures or take action amounting to such intervention. Article 2(7) of the United Nations Charter is probably the best known of these provisions.[1] It reads as follows:

> Nothing contained in the present Charter shall authorize the United Nations to intervene in matters which are essentially within the domestic jurisdiction of any state or shall require the Members to submit such matters to settlement under the present Charter; but this principle shall not prejudice the application of enforcement measures under Chapter VII [of the Charter].

The Charter of the Organization of American States contains a similar, albeit a more explicit, prohibition. It declares:

> No State or group of States has the right to intervene, directly or indirectly, for any reason whatever, in the internal or external affairs of any other State. The foregoing principle prohibits not only armed force but also any other form of interference or attempted threat against the personality of the State or against its political, economic and cultural elements.[2]

The Member States of the Organization of African Unity proclaim, in like manner, their adherence to the principles of "non-interference in the internal affairs of States" and "respect for the sovereignty and territorial integrity of each State and for its inalienable right to independent existence."[3]

Some important international political instruments also give expression to the principle of nonintervention. Among the better-known recent pronouncements on this subject is the Helsinki Final Act. Its domestic jurisdiction clause[4] reads as follows:

> The participating States will refrain from any intervention, direct or indirect, individual or collective, in the internal or external affairs falling within the domestic jurisdiction of another participating State, regardless of their mutual relations.

> They will accordingly refrain from any form of armed intervention or threat of such intervention against another participating State.

> They will likewise in all circumstances refrain from any other act of military, or of political, economic or other coercion designed to subordinate to their own interest the exercise by another participating State of the rights inherent in its sovereignty and thus to secure advantage of any kind.

> Accordingly, they will, inter alia, refrain from direct or indirect assistance to terrorist activities, or to subversive or other activities directed towards the violent overthrow of the regime of another participating State.

This language of the Helsinki Final Act draws on the pronouncement on intervention found in the Declaration on Principles of International Law concerning Friendly Relations and Co-operation among States in Accordance with the Charter of the United Nations, which was adopted by the General Assembly in 1970.[5] On the subject of intervention the declaration provides, in part, as follows:

> No State or group of States has the right to intervene, directly or indirectly, for any reason whatever, in the internal or external affairs of any other State. Consequently, armed intervention and all other forms

of interference or attempted threats against the personality of the State
or against its political, economic and cultural elements, are in violation
of international law.[6]

These pronouncements on the impermissibility of intervention in the domestic jurisdiction of states by other states or by intergovernmental organizations
are, on the whole, little more than the codification of a well-established rule of
general international law. It has its source in the doctrine on sovereign equality
and independence of states, which is one of the fundamental principles of international law.[7] This principle presupposes the right of each state to exercise its
governmental functions within its territory or jurisdictional sphere in whatever
manner it sees fit, unimpeded by competing foreign governmental entities, provided only that its activities do not interfere with the rights of other states or
otherwise violate its international obligations.[8] The proviso is critical, for a
state which has assumed international obligations, either by treaty or under
general international law, with regard to a subject previously within its domestic
jurisdiction has to that extent internationalized that subject.[9] Thus, for example, the undertaking by the participating states in the Helsinki Final Act that
they "will refrain from an intervention . . . in the internal or external affairs
falling within the domestic jurisdiction of another participating State," does not
apply to those matters which these states have internationalized in treaties concluded by them.[10]

It is important to note that, in this context, the question of what constitutes
"intervention" becomes relevant only *after* one has concluded that a given subject matter falls within the domestic jurisdiction of a state.[11] That is to say, to
the extent that a matter has been internationalized, the traditional prohibition
against "intervention in the domestic jurisdiction of a state" is inapplicable.
Other prohibitions relating to the conduct of states in general remain applicable, of course. One such example is the prohibition against the threat or use
of force,[12] but it is relevant whether or not the matter in dispute is domestic
or international in character.[13]

Claims by governments that their conduct affecting human rights is a matter
solely within their domestic jurisdiction frequently suggest that, under international law, "human rights" are by their very nature domestic issues. Implicit
in this claim is the proposition that some matters are inherently domestic and
consequently not "internationalizable." This view finds no support in contemporary international law and was authoritatively rejected long ago by the
Permanent Court of International Justice. In its *Tunis and Morocco Nationality
Decress* opinion, the court declared that "the question whether a certain matter
is or is not solely within the jurisdiction of a State is an essentially relative
question; it depends upon the development of international relations."[14] The
court's analysis indicates that the phrase "the development of international
relations" has reference to the legal obligations assumed by states with regard

to a specific subject.[15] A contemporary statement of the rule, adopted by the Institute of International Law, thus quite properly declares:

> The reserved domain is the domain of State activities where the State is not bound by international law. The extent of this domain depends on international law and varies according to its development.[16]

It is clear today that under international law neither "human rights" nor any other subject matter is deemed to be inherently domestic in nature. Whether or not human rights matters fall within the domestic jurisdiction of a state depends on the extent to which international law has internationalized the subject. The prohibition against intervention in the domestic jurisdiction of a state consequently applies to efforts by one government to have another government stop human rights violations only if, as between these states, neither human rights in general nor the specific conduct is the subject of international obligations. This conclusion demonstrates the importance of ascertaining the extent to which human rights have been internationalized.

The Internationalization of Human Rights

The adoption of the United Nations Charter ushered in a process leading to the gradual internationalization of human rights. This is not to say that under international law as it existed in the pre-World War II era all human rights issues were solely matters of domestic jurisdiction.[17] Some international human rights law obviously predates the charter. Among that law are the treaties outlawing slavery and the slave trade, the conventions for the protection of certain national, religious, and linguistic minorities, as well as various humanitarian law principles applicable in time of war. A large body of international law relating to the treatment of aliens had also evolved long before the adoption of the charter. But these international obligations were either very limited in scope or concerned only certain special groups of people or countries. On the whole, however, international law, as it existed in the pre-World War II era, did not impose on states any general obligations regarding the manner in which they were to treat their own nationals.[18] Issues concerning such treatment consequently involved matters within the domestic jurisdiction of the particular state. This being the case, the prohibition against intervention applied, enabling many a government to engage in brutal violations of basic human rights without having to answer for its conduct to other governments or before intergovernmental organizations. The doctrine of humanitarian intervention, which proclaims the right of states to put an end to governmental conduct "shocking the conscience of mankind,"[19] might be regarded as an exception to this general proposition, but it never commanded the acceptance necessary to proclaim it a rule of international law.[20]

The U.N. Charter effected a significant change in the preexisting legal conceptions by requiring the member states "to pledge themselves to take joint and separate action in cooperation with the Organization" in order "to promote . . .universal respect for, and observance of, human rights and fundamental freedoms for all without distinction as to race, sex, language or religion."[21] These provisions of the charter are drafted in language that is intentionally vague. They nevertheless impose legally binding obligations on the member states.[22] To the extent that the charter creates these obligations, no U.N. member state can claim that human rights as such are a matter within its domestic jurisdiction.

But the U.N. Charter does not internationalize all violations of human rights. It is consequently necessary to determine what human rights obligations U.N. member states are deemed to have assumed under the charter. As has been noted, the charter requires the member states "to promote universal respect for, and observance of, human rights and fundamental freedoms for all without distinction as to race, sex, language or religion." Although the charter does not define "human rights and fundamental freedoms," today it is generally accepted that the rights proclaimed in the Universal Declaration of Human Rights and other major international human rights instruments supply the missing definition.[23] U.N. member states consequently have an international legal obligation "to take joint and separate action in cooperation with" the U.N. "to promote" universal respect for, and the observance of, the human rights proclaimed in these instruments. This undertaking does not require the member states to enforce each and every right listed in these instruments, if they have not also ratified them. But U.N. lawmaking practice indicates that the obligation "to promote" these rights will be deemed to be violated if a state systematically pursues governmental policies denying the enjoyment of these rights on a large scale, particularly rights that are most basic.[24] The term of art used in the U.N. refers to governmental policies evincing "a consistent pattern of gross violations of human rights."[25] This interpretation of the charter, which has evolved very gradually over the past thirty years, compels the conclusion that, as between member states, the prohibition against intervention in matters within the domestic jurisdiction of a state does not apply to governmental acts or policies involving a consistent pattern of gross violations of human rights.[26]

A valid domestic jurisdiction defense can today as a result no longer be founded on the proposition that the manner in which a state treats its own nationals is *ipso facto* a matter within its domestic jurisdiction. Moreover, such a defense must also be deemed to be inapplicable to allegations relating to individual human rights violations or cases, provided it appears that, rather than being isolated instances, they are merely symptomatic of or result from the proscribed policies. It is consequently not impermissible for Government A to file an official protest relating to the manner in which Government B treats one of B's nationals and to threaten economic sanctions lest his conditions improve, if it can be shown that the conduct complained of is characteristic of B's overall human rights policies.

In addition to the U.N. Charter, there exist numerous treaties today that establish specific human rights obligations binding on the parties thereto.[27] No governmental measure, whether general or specific, which appears to violate the rights these treaties guarantee can consequently be deemed to fall within the domestic jurisdiction of the states that have ratified these treaties. Some of these agreements, notably the Genocide Convention and the U.N. Racial Convention, have been ratified by close to 100 countries. The number of states adhering to the International Covenants on Human Rights and many other human rights instruments is not yet as large; it is increasing daily, however. Thus, although it is entirely unrealistic to believe that all or even a majority of these states live up to their obligations under these treaties, it cannot be doubted that, among themselves, these states have internationalized the vast catalog of individual and collective human rights proclaimed in these instruments. This internationalization of human rights has greatly reduced, if not made practically insignificant, the domestic jurisdiction defense that was available to states under the international law of the pre-World War II era.

Intervention

A widely accepted interpretation of the international law meaning of "intervention" is that put forth by Lauterpacht, which reads as follows:

> Intervention is a technical term of, on the whole, unequivocal connotation. It signifies dictatorial interference in the sense of action amounting to a denial of the independence of the State. It implies a peremptory demand for positive conduct or abstention—a demand which, if not complied with, involves a threat of or recourse to compulsion, though not necessarily physical compulsion, in some form.[28]

According to this view, intervention can, but need not, involve the threat or use of force. It is, however, more than mere meddling, that is, commenting on this or that policy of another government. A formal diplomatic protest, accompanied by the threat, for example, that "if your government does not remedy the situation, we shall have to suspend our economic aid," might well meet Lauterpacht's criterion of "recourse to compulsion." But the matter is not free from doubt, particularly when we are dealing with human rights. The U.N. Declaration on Friendly Relations is relevant in this regard, for example, when it declares that "no State may use or encourage the use of economic, political or any other type of measures to coerce another State in order to obtain from it the subordination of the exercise of its sovereign rights *and* to secure from it advantage of any kind" (emphasis added).[29] Whether economic coercion seeking to compel a state to change its human rights policies, for example, comes within this definition would under the declaration depend on

one's interpretation of the phrase "to secure from it advantage of any kind."
The answer might well depend upon the ideological context shaping the
relations between the governments involved.

To argue, as some have done,[30] that intervention is unlawful only if it
involves the use of force or is backed by a threat of force is untenable. The
U.N. Charter outlaws the threat or use of force by member states in their "international relations."[31] This prohibition thus governs whether or not the subject
matter of the intervention is "domestic" or "international" in character. But the
injunction against intervention in domestic affairs applies, both under general
international law and the U.N. Charter, only to matters within a state's domestic jurisdiction. It follows that acts of intervention that are impermissible when
a matter is domestic must be deemed permissible when the subject has been
internationalized. Intervention, if defined as "dictatorial interference," which
is probably the most widely held view, must therefore encompass governmental
measures that are less severe than the threat or use of force.[32]

Conclusion

In discussing the human rights implications of U.S. foreign policy, it is vital to
emphasize that the prohibition against intervention applies only to those human
rights matters that have not been "internationalized." This means that the
prohibition cannot be validly invoked by governments pursuing policies amounting to a consistent pattern of gross violations of human rights. Consequently,
as long as the U.S. government, for example, ties the pursuit of its foreign policy
objectives in the human rights field to measures designed to discourage gross
violations of human rights, it will not run afoul of the prohibition against intervention in the domestic jurisdiction of other states. This is not to suggest that
any and all measures taken by the United States in the furtherance of this
objective will therefore necessarily be lawful. The use of armed force would be
unlawful, for example, but its illegality is attributable to the fact that the United
States has assumed specific international law obligations not to use force except
in self-defense.[33] Cutting off diplomatic or military aid, for example, would not
be unlawful in this context, and neither would other economic or diplomatic
pressures designed to get states to comply with the human rights obligations
they assumed under international law.

This analysis, if it is sound, suggests that U.S. government measures, not
otherwise unlawful, designed to compel or encourage the observance of human
rights, should be related directly to efforts to enforce human rights obligations
accepted by the international community in the U.N. Charter and other international instruments. Such an approach, besides disposing of the intervention
issue, will also refute the oft-heard charges that the United States seeks to
impose *its* human rights values on the rest of the world. In the long run, the

success or failure of an effective U.S. human rights policy may well depend on the extent to which the United States succeeds in convincing the world that it is committed to promoting the human rights that embody mankind's shared aspirations rather than "American" or "Western" human rights as such, whatever they may be.

Notes

1. See, generally, Ermacora, Human Rights and Domestic Jurisdiction (Article 2, § 7, of the Charter), 124 *Recueil des Cours* 371 (1968); R. Higgins, *The Development of International Law through the Political Organs of the United Nations* 58 (1963); Preuss, Article 2, Paragraph 7 of the Charter of the United Nations and Domestic Jurisdiction, 74 *Recueil des Cours* 547 (1949).

2. OAS Charter, as amended, Art. 18. Note too that Article 19 of the OAS Charter proclaims that "no State may use or encourage the use of coercive measures of any economic or political character in order to force the sovereign will of another State and obtain from it advantages of any kind."

3. OAU Charter, Arts. III(2) and III(3).

4. Helsinki Final Act, Guiding Principle VI. The Final Act was signed on August 1, 1975. The text is reproduced in 14 *Int'l Legal Materials* 1292 (1975). For an analysis of Guiding Principle VI as it relates to human rights, see Henkin, Human Rights and "Domestic Jurisdiction," in T. Buergenthal, *Human Rights, International Law and the Helsinki Accord* 21 (1977).

5. U.N. General Assembly, Res. 2625 (XXV) of October 24, 1970, [1970] *United Nations Juridical Yearbook* 105 (1972). On the lawmaking aspects of the Declaration, see Sohn, The Shaping of International Law, 8 *Geo. J. Int'l and Comp. L.* 1 (1978).

6. Res. 2625 (XXV), [1970] *United Nations Juridical Yearbook* 105, 108 (1972).

7. I. Brownlie, *Principles of Public International Law* 284 (2d ed., 1973).

8. L. Oppenheim, *International Law,* vol. I, 286-290 (8th ed., Lauter-pacht, 1955).

9. Waldock, General Course on Public International Law, 106 *Recueil des Cours* 1, 178-179 (1962).

10. Henkin, p. 26.

11. Ermacora, p. 431; Waldock, p. 185.

12. U.N. Charter, Art. 2(4).

13. See, generally, J.N. Moore, *Law and Civil War in the Modern World* (1974); W. Schaumann, *Völkerrechtliches Gewaltsverbot und Friedenssicherung* (1971).

14. Nationality Decrees Issued in Tunis and Morocco, Advisory Opinion of 7 February 1923, Permanent Court of International Justice, Series B, No. 4, at 24.

15. See Waldock, pp. 178-179.

16. [1954] *Annuaire de l'Institut de Droit International,* vol. II, at 150.

17. See, generally, L. Sohn and T. Buergenthal, *International Protection of Human Rights* (1973), where much of the pre-World War II international law relating to human rights is reviewed and extensive bibliographies are provided on this topic.

18. Oppenheim, p. 736.

19. See generally on this subject, E. Stowell, *Intervention in International Law* 51 (1921); Sohn and Buergenthal, p. 137.

20. Brownlie, Humanitarian Intervention, in Moore, p. 217. But see Lillich, Humanitarian Intervention: A Reply to Dr. Brownlie and a Plea for Constructive Analysis, in Moore, p. 229. See also R. Lillich, *Humanitarian Intervention and the United Nations* (1973); Franck and Rodley, After Bangladesh: The Law of Humanitarian Intervention by Military Force, 67 *Am. J. Int'l L.* 275, 277-295 (1973).

21. U.N. Charter, Arts. 55 and 56.

22. Sohn, The Human Rights Law of the Charter, 16 *Texas Int'l L. J.* 129, 131 (1977); Schwelb, The International Court of Justice and the Human Rights Clauses of the Charter, 66 *Am. J. Int'l L.* 337, 346-350 (1972).

23. Sohn, pp. 132-138; T. Buergenthal and J. Torney, *International Human Rights and International Education* 45-46 (1976).

24. For a review of this practice, see Henkin, pp. 26-27; A. Verdross and B. Simma, *Universelles Völkerrecht* 599-606 (1976). See, generally, *United Nations Actions in the Field of Human Rights* (U.N. Publ. No. E.74.XIV.2, 1974).

25. See, for example, U.N. ECOSOC Res. 1503 (XLVIII) of May 27, 1970, reproduced in L. Sohn and T. Buergenthal, *Basic Documents on International Protection on Human Rights* 111 (1973).

26. Buergenthal and Torney, pp. 75-79; Henkin, p. 27.

27. The principal international and regional texts are reproduced in Sohn and Buergenthal, *Basic Documents.* For the basic U.N. instruments, see *Human Rights: A Compilation of International Instruments* (U.N. Publ. No. E.78.XIV.2, 1978).

28. H. Lauterpacht, *International Law and Human Rights* 167 (1950).

29. See note 5, above. The Helsinki Final Act uses similar, albeit somewhat more ambiguous, language. See text, p. 112.

30. See, for example, Henkin, p. 36, who appears to espouse that view.

31. U.N. Charter, Art. 2(4).

32. It may well be that part of the confusion in the literature relating to the meaning of intervention results from the fact that in international diplomatic practice this term is used in a manner which suggests a dual meaning. One usage of the term intervention appears to refer only to military intervention and acts of a similar character. The other usage of the term is always contextually

tied to the notion of "domestic jurisdiction." That usage suggests diplomatic measures rather than the threat of or resort to military force. The latter type of intervention is not unlawful, moreover, if the subject matter is not "domestic," which suggests that in this context the term is not intended to encompass the use of force. Although this is not the place to explore the dual meaning of intervention and the validity of the above assumptions, it is clear that an analysis along these lines might provide a sounder explanation of otherwise very confusing diplomatic practice than is to be found in current literature on this topic.

33. U.N. Charter, Arts. 2(4) and 51.

9 The Ethics of Intervention: Two Normative Traditions

J. Bryan Hehir

The human rights focus of President Carter's foreign policy has renewed interest in the idea of intervention among nations. The tone and orientation of the president's policy was exemplified in his speech at the United Nations in March 1977:

> All signatories of the U.N. Charter have pledged themselves to ob-
> serve and respect basic human rights. Thus, no member of the United
> Nations can claim that mistreatment of its citizens is solely its own
> business. Equally, no member can avoid its responsibilities to review
> and to speak when torture or unwarranted deprivation of freedom
> occurs in any part of the world.[1]

The clarity of this statement is intellectually and politically refreshing. The complexity of implementing it involves a host of questions, among them the relationship of intervention and human rights policy in a world still devoid of a centralized political or juridical authority. This paper examines two moments in the development of the normative doctrine on intervention. The purpose of the comparison is twofold: first, to show how different political premises led to diverse normative conclusions about intervention; second, to indicate how these traditions relate to the human rights-intervention debate. The two normative traditions will be compared in terms of (1) their idea of political community; (2) their ethic of war; and (3) their implications concerning intervention.

The Moral Tradition: The Just-War Doctrine and Intervention

The traditional normative doctrine on intervention flourished in the High Middle Ages. The political concept which sustained that tradition envisioned European society as the *Respublica Christiana*; within this Christian common-wealth the prevailing ethic of war was the just-war doctrine. These two ideas produced a normative case which made intervention a moral duty for political authorities.

The Political Concept: Respublica Christiana

The political system known as the Respublica Christiana took shape in the High Middle Ages. Its roots lay in the Carolingean period and remnants of its structure endured until the sixteenth century. The distinguishing note of the Respublica Christiana was that it was a political community and a religious entity; it was both church and state. Political loyalties were understood in terms of religious beliefs, and faith was a prerequisite for full participation and membership in the society.[2] The unity of society was confirmed and consecrated by a shared perspective of faith visibly embodied in the role the church fulfilled. Both the role of law in society and the structure of authority combined to highlight the idea of a single organic community. The source of all law was the *lex aeterna* or divine plan for history. The *lex aeterna* was grasped through the medium of natural law, whose fundamental principles and deduced premises constituted the "higher law" against which all positive law was tested. The unified legal system in turn was reflected in the structure of political authority in the Respublica.

The problem of political authority was cast in terms of spiritual and temporal power, or church and state,[3] but the unity of society was the presumption upon which all discussions of church and state were based. This presumption was reflected in the way medieval authors interchanged terms which to us convey distinct and separate realities. One commentator on the period has found that "from Carolingean times onward the words 'world,' 'empire,' 'mankind,' 'Church,' and 'Christendom' were often used as synonymous."[4]

The convergence of these themes produced an ethical mind-set of solidarity in the Respublica that described societal relations in familial terms; this in turn imposed upon the members of society a duty of responsibility for others. This philosophical bond of duty in turn was then reinforced by the Christian ethic of love,[5] and the church was the visible organizational structure through which the relations of responsibility were coordinated and exercised. The Pope as principal power in the Respublica insured solidarity by assuming the role of guardian of the rights of states, guarantor of treaties, and architect of the principles governing the laws of neutrality and the rights of neutrals.[6]

The Ethic of War: Just-War Doctrine

The executive power of the papal office included the right to use coercive measures, including the *ultima ratio*, the use of military force. When faced with the dilemma of reconciling the use of lethal force with the Gospel ethic, the preeminent theorist of Respublica doctrine, Thomas Aquinas (1224-1274), argued that force could be used to protect the unique needs of the political community, namely, security, order, and defense. The right of the state to use force is based upon the responsibility of the state for the public order of society. The content of this public responsibility has two dimensions for Aquinas. The first is the police function of maintaining order within society. The second, closely patterned on the police model but distinct from it, is the power to make war against those threatening the commonwealth from outside. The ethical argument is cast in terms of a police power model. War is not a right of the state or the sovereign to be used at will for any and all purposes; it is a specifically delineated power to be utilized in well-defined circumstances.[7] A moral consensus in the medieval system established a unified world of discourse for evaluating and justifying the use of force in the political community. Commonly recognized moral categories, authoritatively interpreted by the Pope, provided the means for designating specific forms of behavior as a threat to the community and for galvanizing other forces in the community to restrain, repel, and/or punish the culpable party. The just-war doctrine made it possible for states both to identify categories of action as substantial threats to the commonwealth and to legitimize the use of military force as a defensive or punitive measure. The final determination of which empirical situations called for the use of force was entrusted to the Pope as head of the Christian commonwealth.

Intervention in the Respublica Christiana

An exposition of the ethics of intervention based on the medieval model of Respublica Christiana can be divided into two distinct phases of development: The first phase is represented by Aquinas, the second by Francisco de Vitoria (1483-1546) and Hugo Grotius (1583-1645). The basis of the distinction between Aquinas and the later authors is the emergence of the modern state.

Aquinas on Intervention. Aquinas never explicitly evaluated intervention. In the face of this absence of explicit texts, we are forced to rely on inference.[8] Aquinas justifies the use of force as a power inherent in the state for the purpose of protecting the political community. The limits on using force are set by the boundaries of the political community in question. The key question is: How broadly does Aquinas define the political community? Is it a local unit? Does it extend to all of Christendom? Does it extend to the welfare of those beyond Christendom?

To answer this question it is necessary to take account of two distinct themes in Aquinas's political writings which are held in tension and never explicitly resolved by him. On the one hand, as Ernst Troeltsch argues, Aquinas assumed the existence of a Christian society. The medieval themes of a universal society, characterized by moral solidarity, an organic conception of the social system, and the subordination of the state to the church within the social system were integrally woven into the fabric of Aquinas's political and social doctrine. These were the themes that constituted the Respublica Christiana. The logic of these themes did move toward an interventionist position of universal scope: the bond of solidarity was the basis of the obligation, the note of universalism defined the scope of responsibility in terms of the known Christian world, and the doctrine of the just war as interpreted by the Pope specified the conditions under which the bond of solidarity became operative. The conclusion of this position was that every prince is somehow responsible for the welfare of the total Respublica as well as for his own specifically defined territory. Consequently, he may be called upon to resist aggression or unjust treatment of subjects any place in the Respublica Christiana. In these cases, intervention became a duty fulfilled in the name of the wider community.

The thrust of this dimension of Aquinas's thought, however, cannot be analyzed in isolation from another less explicit but countervailing set of ideas. This second theme indicates that Aquinas was not unaware of the political forces that were to supplant the medieval form of polity. The fragile alliance which these themes created in the mind and thought of Aquinas is described by Thomas Gilby in the following manner:

> As a theologian, St. Thomas proclaimed the unity of all men in the Church, and as a philosopher, the unity of the world under divine government; but he stood at a time when western Europe was breaking into separate nations, and as a political writer, he never refers to the universal empire desired by Dante two generations later. Instead, the political unit is the *civitas*, the *regnum* or the *provincia*, a self-governing, self-contained community, possessing the attributes of the Greek city described by Aristotle, but enlarged to territories much larger than those of Athens or Sparta.[9]

The relationship between the *regnum* and the Respublica is the critical variable in determining the substance and scope of Aquinas's conception of intervention. Because he assumed the existence of a unified Christian civilization, it seems inconceivable to think of Aquinas adopting anything resembling the later positivist doctrine of nonintervention which would isolate the *regnum* from the Respublica. On the other hand, Aquinas clearly did not identify himself with the prevailing canonist doctrine of his day which amounted to a papal monarchy, attributing to the Pope the right "to command and issue binding decrees to all nations," and to intervene extensively, using the military forces of designated Christian princes in the affairs of territories, kingdoms, and regions, even beyond the frontiers of Christendom.

Somewhere between these polar types of the positivist and canonist positions, it is legitimate to infer that Aquinas held an interventionist position, tempered and limited by his sense of the rising demands of national sovereignty. The theological and philosophical premises of the Thomistic ethic would establish, first, an obligation toward the neighbor in need which would transcend the bounds of the *regnum*, encompassing not only the Respublica, but Christians living in non-Christian lands. Secondly, Aquinas limits the scope of exercise of the obligation in his discussion of the just-war doctrine. If the justification for the use of force is the requirements of the public good, the scope of the public good is defined not in terms of the Respublica but in the more limited trilogy cited by Gilby: *regnum, civitas, provincia.*

In addition, however, Aquinas proposes a specific set of reasons to justify religious wars, which often involve a form of intervention outside the frontiers of Christendom. Aquinas would legitimate, and even command, at times, an interventionary course of action beyond the *regnum* in the service of the Respublica.

We can conclude that the elements for an interventionist position are inherent in the political ethic proposed by Aquinas. The approval of intervention in principle does not appear to be a problematical issue for him. On the other hand, Aquinas had a fundamental respect for the rights of sovereigns which logically would preclude an interventionist position as broadly drawn as Regout and Beaufort assert. What we do not find in Aquinas is how this balance between an affirmation of the substance of the right of intervention, and a limitation of its scope would work out in specific cases. The casuistry of intervention is found in two later authors, Vitoria and Grotius.

Vitoria and Grotius on Intervention. Francis de Vitoria (1483-1546) lived and wrote at a time when the political framework of Respublica Christiana, so congenial to the just-war premises, had collapsed, and the moral doctrine identified with that framework stood in need of a new defense if it was to remain viable. Vitoria, the first of the classical moralists to confront the modern doctrine of sovereignty, probed the question of intervention in a much more explicit and extensive way than Aquinas had. The reason for his interest derived first of all from the exploration of the New World by his Spanish countrymen. What right, if any, did the colonizers have to intrude into a new land and take possession of property, exercise political dominion, establish trading centers, and subordinate the native population to a status little better than slavery? How was the Christian world to evaluate this use of force?

Faced with these questions, Vitoria used the structure of the just-war teaching to articulate an ethic of intervention. He took the basic categories in terms of which just cause was defined (*defensio, punitio,* and *recuperatio*) and he extended their applicability beyond the *regnum* to a wider frame of reference.[10] Vitoria expanded the standard medieval categories of defense to include the idea of defense of innocent people wherever they are in need. Using a text from the book of Ecclesiasticus, which reads: "Gods has laid a charge on every individual concerning his neighbor," Vitoria comments, "and they are all our neighbors."[11]

In his commentary on Aquinas's concept of just cause, Vitoria cites the traditional reasons of recovering property, vindicating rights, and punishing crimes. Then he asks about the scope of these causes: is it permitted to use force to fulfill a treaty with an ally or to aid someone else who is suffering an injury? Vitoria responds affirmatively and gives two reasons for his response. The first justification for aid in these cases is that "a man's friends are in a certain sense one with himself." The second justification is drawn from the existing practice among nations: "If one should suffer injury, it would be permissible to call upon the Portuguese for aid; and therefore, it is in like manner permissible for us to aid them."[12]

Vitoria used the ethic of solidarity and the biblical theme of the needy neighbor to define community in terms of the human community, thereby universalizing the principle of solidarity. His reasoning was that the people in question are innocent people and that, by natural law, princes may and can defend the (whole) world, lest injury be inflicted upon it.[13]

In lieu of a centralized organ possessing the authority and means to act in the name of the world community, Vitoria proposes to invest each state with the authority to punish criminal action in the name of others under specified conditions. He analyzed eight cases that can be classified as legitimate interventionary action. Two cases of intervention are clearly cases of *defending innocent lives* in which force is justified: to prevent human sacrifice or cannibalism.[14] Three other cases of intervention fit both categories of *defense* and *punishment*. They include the following:

1. the right to intervene by force to prevent the harassment of missionaries preaching the Gospel;[15]
2. the right to use force to prevent the persecution of Christians by unbelievers; and
3. the right to guarantee that those seeking Christian faith are not hindered from conversion.[16]

The sixth case involves intervention where a given populace is not capable of self-government. The dangers of rationalization inherent in such a judgment made Vitoria ambivalent about extending this right to outside powers; his marginal justification of the move was based on the precept of charity, requiring us to go to the aid of those who cannot provide for themselves.[17] Finally, Vitoria seeks to preserve the right of innocent passage and free trade, even at the cost of using force to do so.[18]

Although these are very specific examples drawn from Vitoria's historical context, we can extract from them a substantive principle and a style of analysis. The principle is the extension of the right of using force beyond the instances of defense of one's own polity or vindication of its rights; Vitoria asserts this in much clearer terms than Aquinas. The method of analysis involves using the range of just-war categories to limit, qualify, and apply the substantive principle to concrete cases. This method of limitation or qualification is evident in Vitoria's discussion of the right to intervene to ensure the preaching of the Gospel and unhindered access to faith; this right is limited by the principle of proportionality and the principle of right intention in using force.

This mode of analysis, similar in style and substance to the just-war reasoning process, allowed Vitoria to formulate a doctrine of intervention based on the political premises of the Respublica Christiana, but shaped to fit the conditions of the emerging state system.

Hugo Grotius, the Dutch jurist who spent most of his adult life in exile from his native land, lived almost a century after Vitoria's death (1583-1645). Although he is regarded as the founding father of modern international law, Grotius is classified here as a representative of the medieval rather than the modern period of international ethics.[19] The reason for this choice can be understood only if we distinguish the political views of Grotius from his ethical vision.

Politically, Grotius is very much a man of the modern period of interstate relations; he was confronted with the finished product of the process that Aquinas had intuitively sensed and Vitoria had grudgingly accepted, the development of the sovereign state. Ethically, however, Grotius was more an heir of the medieval tradition than the forerunner of the modern era. He recognized that the political structure which had supported the medieval ethic was incompatible with the fully developed doctrine of sovereignty, but he sought to rescue the substance of the medieval ethic by providing it with a new foundation. His doctrine of intervention is rooted in his desire to preserve the medieval moral vision.

By the time Grotius wrote *De Jure Belli ac Pacis* (1625), the Respublica Christiana had passed into history. The international system was not an interdependent community in which states had some independent existence, it was a group of independent states in search of some minimal form of community to halt the escalating violence engulfing seventeenth-century Europe. This transformation of political life was in part the result of the demise of the church as an acknowledged center of authority in the life of states. The religious and ecclesiastical context in which the natural-law and just-war ethic had held sway had been severely eroded by the combined influences of political change (sovereignty), religious strife (the Reformation), and cultural transformation (the Renaissance).

Grotius held to the natural-law ethic as strongly as Aquinas and Vitoria, but he faced a new problem which had both epistemological and organizational dimensions. Epistemologically, the unified religious world-view which had supported the natural-law ethic had been divided, if not dissolved, by the doctrinal struggle of the Reformation. If the natural-law ethic were going to stand, it would have to stand on its own (as it claimed it could), for it could no longer rely on universally held religious beliefs for justification. Organizationally, the existence of a center of religious and political authority that served as both teacher and judge in the political community was now destroyed.

Grotius sought to save the moral and legal order from the demise of religious authority after the Reformation by creating a surrogate for the religious community, which had been the foundation of political community in the medieval period. He recognized a continuing bond of solidarity among Christians, but the source of that bond was no longer the Church. It was a legal bond, the law of nature, which created a universal legal community among men. This idea was analogous to the concept of Respublica Christiana, but the distinctive difference in Grotius is that there is no central authority to interpret or enforce the dictates of natural law. The new problem was to demonstrate the existence of a legal order among states: an order of international law. It was Grotius's attempt to grapple with this problem that earned him the title of "Father of International Law."

The fundamental purpose behind this elaborate intellectual exercise of preserving the medieval substance while accepting the modern structure of international life was to keep alive in the minds of people and the actions of states the principles of solidarity, responsibility, interdependence, and charity which Grotius believed were the enduring legacy of the Respublica Christiana. If these principles were to be preserved, the concept of intervention as a moral as well as a political reality also had to be preserved. Recognizing this fact, Grotius set forth his doctrine of the laws and limits of intervention in the international arena.

The basic principle governing intervention was, for Grotius, the right to punish wrongdoing. The extension of the right to punish into the right to intervene was made in Grotius's general discussion of punishment found in Book II of *De Jure Belli ac Pacis*:

> It is also proper to observe that kings and those who are possessed of sovereign power have a right to exact punishment not only for injuries affecting immediately themselves or their own subjects, but for gross violations of the law of nature and of nations, done to other states and subjects.[20]

As Grotius defined their role, kings, "besides the care of their own immediate states and subjects, may be regarded as protectors of the human race."[21] The *scope* of the right to intervene in the Grotian doctrine extended to every part of the human community.

Paradoxically, Grotius, the last of the medieval expositors, set forth the most fully developed articulation of the medieval model of interventionist policy, and cast it in much broader and less restrictive terms than either Aquinas or the later scholastics used.

The similarity between Grotius and Vitoria is clear. Under the rubric of the right of public authorities to punish crime, Grotius reinforced Vitoria's conclusions that the following cases were instances of justifiable intervention:

1. to prevent instances of human sacrifice or cannibalism;[22]
2. to prevent harassment of believers or missionaries preaching the Gospel;[23]
3. to guarantee the right of innocent passage, freedom of the seas and the right of free trade.[24]

Additional possible causes for intervention, affirmed by Grotius and either omitted or disapproved by Vitoria, were:

1. to suppress idolatry and/or atheism in some forms if either or both were harmful to society;[25] to suppress immoral sexual conduct;[26]
2. to punish, under specific conditions, a treaty violation or doing harm to diplomatic personages;[27]
3. to punish those trading with an enemy belligerent;[28]
4. to punish pirates.[29]

Finally, Grotius supplemented his casuistic discussion of intervention and justifiable causes of warfare with an analysis of two other themes relating to intervention: "The Causes for Undertaking War for Others";[30] and "Respecting Those Who Are Neutral in War."[31] Both of these chapters served to emphasize the close connection of the just-war doctrine and the doctrine of intervention. The reasons for undertaking war in behalf of others are given in terms of just-war *principles*: "The causes therefore which justify the principles engaged in war, will justify those also who afford assistance to others."[32] Then Grotius proceeds to use just-war *criteria* to evaluate the following questions:

1. *whom should we aid*: a state is not bound to aid or support unjust wars, even of an ally;[33]
2. *when should we aid*: a state is not bound to give aid if there is no possibility of success,[34] or if the use of force would violate the principle of proportionality.[35]

The same just-war categories are highly visible in Grotius's discussion of the doctrine of neutrality, a subject which does not appear in either Aquinas or Vitoria. From the premise that no state could be absolved of the obligation of making a moral evaluation of the justice of warfare, Grotius established two rules for guiding the conduct of a neutral nation:

1. it is not permissible to aid the party devoid of just cause, nor to obstruct the party which has a just cause;
2. in cases of doubt, neutrals ought to observe strict impartiality.[36]

In summary we can say of just-war teaching on intervention that the political premises of the medieval polity, most visibly embodied in the Respublica

Christiana of the eleventh to the thirteenth centuries, sustained the political and ethical vision of authors such as Vitoria and Grotius long after the polity had disappeared. The importance of this continuity for the doctrine of intervention resides in the fact that the political premises were the product of, and the channel for, a set of ethical values bearing upon intervention.

The Legal Tradition: International Law and Intervention

The post-Grotian tradition of international law moved decisively away from Grotius's teaching on intervention. International society was conceived as a world of sovereign states, each with the right and capability to resort to war in the diplomatic moment of truth. In this context nonintervention was affirmed as the duty of all states; the medieval normative doctrine had been reversed.

The Political Concept: State Sovereignty

The movement from the medieval commonweath to the modern state system involved the interplay of three major forces: political structures, philosophical ideas, and religious institutions. The political dimension was the appearance and consolidation of the territorial state; the philosophical dimension was the development of a theory of sovereignty; the religious dimension was the division of Christendom by the Reformation.

Ernest Barker described the period from the thirteenth to the eighteenth century in Europe as the movement from Kingdom to State.[37] The kingdoms recognized by Aquinas as distinct political entities rested securely within the Respublica. The exact relationship of the *regnum* to the Respublica was always less than clear, but the unity of the commonwealth was not seriously questioned. By the eighteenth century, when the kingdoms had become states, in fact and in law, the unity of the medieval world was eviscerated.

The key element in the transition from kingdom to state was the emergence of the doctrine of sovereignty exemplified most notably in Bodin's *Six Livres de la Republique* (1576). Bodin located supreme authority within the nation. The consequence of this view for international relations was that the sovereign state accepted no higher political authority than itself. Faced with this new factual and theoretical reality, each of the normative theorists from Grotius to Vattel sought to salvage the role of natural law in the community of nations. Pufendorf (1632-1694) substituted the state for the role of moral authority previously played by the Church, while Wolff (1679-1754) left the formulation of positive law to scholars, since no universally accepted authority any longer existed.[38] In a broadly drawn critique, Leo Gross evaluates the normative consequences of the transition from the Respublica to the Westphalia system (1648) in the following manner:

> Instead of heralding the era of a genuine international community of nations subordinated to the law of nations, it led to the era of the absolutist states, jealous of their territorial sovereignty to a point where the idea of an international community became an almost empty phrase and where international law came to depend upon the will of states more concerned with the preservation and expansion of their power than with the establishment of a rule of law.[39]

Each of the sovereign states possessed the attributes of independence, equality, and the right of self-preservation which formed the basis of the principle of nonintervention. The third attribute, declaring each state free to preserve its independence and sovereignty in ways it saw fit, provided the foundation of the new ethic of war: *competence de guerre.*

The Ethic of War: Competence de Guerre
and the Norm of Nonintervention

The shift in normative doctrine from *bellum justum* to *bellum legale* was effected by the authors whom James T. Johnson calls the "secularizers" of just-war doctrine, principally Pufendorf, Wolff, and Vattel.[40] In Aquinas the use of force is a police action which only those with proper authority can initiate in the name of the political community and in response to an act which is both objectively wrong and subjectively culpable. Vattel's conception departed completely from this penal model. The right to make war belonged to each sovereign ruler, who could resort to force whenever he judged it to be in the interest of his state. This is the substance of *competence de guerre*, which Johnson defines as the right and authority of each sovereign to decide when just cause for war existed.[41] By the eighteenth century war was a policy measure and an act of self-help, not an instrument of vindictive justice.

The changing conception of war and politics is reflected in normative writings after Grotius. Lacking both a sense of international community and a substantive ethic of force, the post-Grotian authors shaped an ethic of intervention which was the antithesis of the traditional view. For Pufendorf, the only justification for intervention was an act of self-help to enforce a state's own rights. Both Pufendorf and Wolff rejected any intervention based on a penal model of community enforcement as an unwarranted intrusion on the equality and liberty of each state. In the name of protecting the independence and liberty of states, the post-Grotian lawyers affirmed a norm of nonintervention.

Nonintervention as the Norm

Emmirich Vattel (1714-1767) and the positivist school inherited and used the doctrines of state sovereignty and *competence de guerre* in their normative evaluations of intervention. Vattell established the framework regarding sovereignty, war, and intervention from which the later positivist position developed.

For Vattel the law of nations was simply the natural law applied to the life of states. The law of nations is in turn divided into the necessary and the positive law. The positive law applies the necessary law to the mutual relations of states: it differs from the necessary law in the kind of obligation it imposes and the content of its commands. As Vattel defines the necessary law of nations it seems to correspond in binding power and content to the full scope of natural law. The gap between the necessary and the positive law of nations is the concession Vattel makes to the independence of states. The weight that he gives to the liberty of nations requires that the necessary law be diluted to accommodate state behavior.[42] Rather than the Respublica conception of international community within which members have a place and a degree of freedom shaped by responsibilities toward others in the society, Vattel's conception assumes a situation of independent states whose responsibilities toward each other and relationships with each other are principally determined by the standard of preserving the maximum amount of liberty for each. In rejecting Christian Wolff's hypothetical construct of a *civitas maxima,* Vattel contrasted the nature of domestic and international life.

> It is true that men, seeing that the laws of Nature were not being voluntarily observed, have had recourse to political association as the one remedy against the degeneracy of the majority, as the one means of protecting the good and restraining the wicked; and the natural law itself approves of such a course. But it is clear that there is by no means the same necessity for a civil society among Nations as among individuals.[43]

For Vattel, liberty was the concept which joined the idea of state sovereignty and the duty of nonintervention. To be sovereign is to be independent; since states equally possess this right of independence, the norm of nonintervention must govern their relationships so that each may enjoy liberty and preserve sovereignty.

Vattel's evaluation of intervention involved two steps: affirming a rule of nonintervention, then specifying two exceptions to the rule. Following Grotius and Vitoria, he asserts that a state could use force for the three traditional reasons of defense, punishment, and the redress of grievances. Vattel proceeds immediately, however, to exclude intervention from the three legitimating reasons for using force:

It clearly follows from the liberty and independence of Nations that each has the right to govern itself as it thinks proper, and that no one of them has the least right to interfere in the government of another. Of all the rights possessed by a Nation that of sovereignty is doubtless the most important, and the one which others should most carefully respect if they are desirous not to give cause for offense.[44]

Some consequences of this nonintervention principle include: no state has the right or the responsibility to judge or seek to change the internal administration of another sovereign ruler;[45] ". . .no one may interfere, against a Nation's will, in its religious affairs without violating its rights and doing it an injury;"[46] and, finally, intervention could not be justified by the restriction or harassment of missionary activity.

In summary, Vitoria and Grotius defended both secular and religious reasons for intervention. Vattel rejected in principle both sets of reasons as infringements on the liberty of the sovereign state. The authors who stood in the Christendom tradition would probably have adapted as their commentary on Vattel's work the observation of Albert de Lapradelle: "His work, permeated with the spirit of liberty, is not sufficiently imbued with the spirit of solidarity."[47]

Yet, even as Vattel laid the basic principles for the doctrine of nonintervention which prevailed in the next two centuries of international law, he acknowledged two exceptions to the principle. The exceptions illustrate how Vattel stands as a bridge between the natural-law tradition and the positivist school of international law. In one exception he reflected, almost in spite of the rest of his writing, a dependence on Grotius. The justifying cause in this instance was intervention on behalf of cities rebelling against tyrannical rule. Vattel makes clear that this is an exceptional case: the injustice on behalf of the sovereign must be an "insupportable tyranny"; the citizens themselves must revolt and request or accept outside aid; and Vattel adds the final caution that "this principle should not be made use of so as to authorize criminal designs against the peace of Nations."[48]

The second exception to the nonintervention principle acknowledged by Vattel was intervention to preserve the balance of power. In recognizing this exception Vattel was building upon Westphalia, which established the basis of the balance of power system, and he was anticipating the writings of the positivists who adapted the principle of nonintervention to succeeding forms of the balance of power system.

Nonintervention seemed to belong to the balance of power system.[49] Yet, even the positivists did not hold to an absolute rule of nonintervention. In the view of T.E. Lawrence, author of a standard text of international law in the positivist period, an absolute adherence to nonintervention is unworkable in a community of states. Intervention should be used sparingly, but it needs to be used effectively at times.[50] The determination of when intervention should and could justifiably be used in a legal sense engaged all the major authors of the period. The structure of their normative response was patterned on Vattel's approach, but they significantly expanded the number of exceptions to the nonintervention principle. The principal categories of exceptions were: humanitarian intervention; counterintervention or intervention to preserve the balance of power; intervention to enforce treaty rights; and intervention in the name of self-preservation.[51]

Entering the twentieth century, the rule of nonintervention was in possession; it was part of a whole systemic perspective on international affairs. World War I called that perspective into question and inaugurated a series of proposals and programs, from the League of Nations through the United Nations, designed to shape a different conception of sovereignty, the use of force, and the meaning of international community. The premises upon which the principle of nonintervention had rested were called into question. The principle today remains part of the contemporary international order, but it has been placed in a new context.

Two Traditions: The Implications for Foreign Policy and Human Rights

The prevailing normative doctrine on intervention is not identical to either of the positions we have examined here. The doctrine in possession today is the evaluation of intervention in the United Nations Charter. If one examines the charter on the three categories used in this chapter, however, it is clear that it draws selectively from the two traditions we have examined.

The charter's premise on sovereignty and force sets it off from the presumptions of unrestricted independence and *competence de guerre* which characterized the positivist doctrine. At the same time, the U.N. system is qualitatively less integrated and less restrictive of members' sovereign rights than the medieval normative doctrine. The limits on sovereignty in the charter are significantly more restrictive than Vattel or the positivists would allow, but substantially less constraining than the Respublica of Aquinas or the *Societas humana* of Grotius.[52] The restrictions on recourse to force in the charter contradict *competence de guerre*, but the model of collective use of force is much less ambitious than the penal model of Aquinas or Grotius.[53]

The ethic of intervention manifests the same reflection of the two traditions. It is set by two controlling texts, Article 2(7) and the declaration of nonintervention contained in the General Assembly Resolution 2125 (24 October 1970), which join the principle of nonintervention to other principles in the U.N. system. The two principles are directed toward two distinct sets of relationships within the international system. Article 2(7) controls the relationship of the U.N. as an organization toward its member states through the concept of domestic jurisdiction. The article reads:

Nothing contained in the present Charter shall authorize the United
Nations to intervene in matters which are essentially within the domestic jurisdiction of any state or shall require the Members to submit
such matters to settlement under the present Charter; but this principle
shall not prejudice the application of enforcement measures under
Chapter VII.[54]

In American political parlance this would be defined as a "states rights"
article; the presumption of political authority rests with the sovereign state's
right to control its affairs; the burden of proof in this article rests with the
U.N. to show cause for intervention.

It is possible to find in the U.N. Charter other reflections of the mix of the
medieval and modern ethics. The medieval system, universalist in principle and
procedure, accorded the presumption of law to the central authority; in the
medieval relationship of *regnum* and Respublica, it was the *regnum* which was
subordinate; the charter reverses this dynamic. At the same time the charter
does place the domestic jurisdiction principle within a setting of law, responsibility, and obligation which the nineteenth-century understanding of sovereignty
would not acknowledge.

The "states rights" premise of the charter is tested most severely in the U.N.
system by the case of human rights. The charter and the Universal Declaration
of Human Rights are universalistic in intent, declaring each person to be the
subject of a spectrum of rights which states are then bound in principle to
respect. This assertion of the human rights of individuals in a document designed
for the international community penetrates the traditional shell of state sovereignty and reflects the Grotian conception that the *societas humana* is first a
community of persons, then a society of states.

The potentially radical nature of this conception of rights and law is tempered, however, regarding enforcement of rights. The enforcement issue brings
human rights claims up against the domestic jurisdiction claims of states. The
compromise, as Vincent has observed, is that for any measures beyond moral
persuasion, the principle of domestic jurisdiction holds, unless it can be
demonstrated that the denial of human rights constitutes a threat to peace and
calls for enforcement procedures under chapter VII of the charter.[55]

This nuanced relationship between the themes of human rights and intervention in the charter severely restricts the capability of the U.N. itself to protect and defend the principles on human rights espoused by its member states.
In this situation the burden of activity falls in large measure on what the states
themselves are prepared to do in their separate foreign policy measures.

The human rights debate exposes contending conceptions of foreign policy.
The school of classical diplomacy, whether reflected in the actions of statesmen
or the analysis of scholars, has always found the human rights issue a problematical issue for foreign policy. The premises of the classical view accord closely
with normative primacy of the state, the unique role of force, and the governing
norm of nonintervention.

Although there have always been normative objections raised against this conception of policy, the striking fact today is that even policy analysts now question its adequacy. In a world marked by increased transnational activity and transnational problems, the role of the state and use of force are placed in a different context. The debate between the "classicists and modernists" (as Stanley Hoffman describes them) is now quite extensive.[56]

In his U.N. speech the president sided with the modernists in his emphasis on transnational responsibility for states. Such an affirmation neither decides the debate nor solves the problem of policy implementation. The state is still unique in world politics; force still functions as an effective instrument in some cases; transnational links are still fragile. But even to espouse the idea of transnational responsibility in a normative way brings back some of the premises of the older tradition about international community, force and justice, and solidarity among states and people. The guiding norm is still nonintervention, and there are empirical and ethical reasons to espouse this in a world of states. But the pressure on the principle will grow and the resource of the two normative traditions will be needed to determine in principle and practice how foreign policy should be conducted to keep the peace among states while still preserving the rights of people.

Notes

1. President Carter, Speech at the United Nations; *New York Times* (18 March 1977), p. A-10.

2. For an exposition of the premises and philosophical position which sustained the Respublica cf. A-H Chroust, "The Corporate Idea and the Body Politic in the Middle Ages," *Review of Politics*, 9 (1947) 423-452; M. Wilks, *The Problem of Sovereignty in the Late Middle Ages* (Cambridge: University Press, 1963); G. Ladner, "Aspects of Medieval Thought on Church and State," *Review of Politics*, 9 (1947) 403-420.

3. For an analysis of the church-state issue as it was perceived in the Middle Ages cf. Y. Congar, *Catholicisme, Hier, Aujourd'hui, Demain*, vol. III, s.v. Eglise et Etat, pp. 1430-1441 (1952); J.C. Murray, *We Hold These Truths: Catholic Reflections on the American Proposition* (New York: Sheed and Ward, 1960), pp. 197-211.

4. G. Tellenbach, *Church, State, Society at the Time of the Investiture Controversy* (New York: Harper and Row, 1959), p. 63.

5. For a discussion of how philosophical and theological themes were woven in a theory of society based upon a patriarchal model of the family, cf. E. Troeltsch, *The Social Teaching of the Christian Churches*, 2 vols. (New York: Harper Torchbooks, 1960) I, pp. 284ff.

6. The political and juridical role of the papacy in the medieval system is

extensively explored in M. Zimmerman, "La Crise de l'Organization Internationale a La Fin du Moyen Age," Academie de Droit International, *Recueil des Cours,* 44 (1933), 319-434; cf. also Wilks, cited.

7. The just-war theory appears in Aquinas in a sparsely delineated form. For a detailed treatment of his theory cf. L.B. Walters, Jr., *Five Classic Just-War Theories: A Study in the Thought of Thomas Aquinas, Vitoria, Suarez, Gentili and Grotius.* Unpublished Ph.D. Dissertation, Yale University, 1971. The analysis of Aquinas, Vitoria, and Grotius in this chapter draws extensively from Walters's superbly constructed work.

8. R. Regout, *La Doctrine de la Guerre Juste de Saint Augustin a Nos Jours d'Apres les Theologiens et les Canonistes Catholiques* (Paris: A. Pedone, 1934); D. Beaufort, *La Guerre Comme Instrument de Secours ou de Punition* (The Hague: Martinus Nijhoff, 1933). While both authors assert that Aquinas would hold for the right of a state to intervene anywhere on behalf of those in need, neither indicates how, on the basis of texts from Aquinas, to justify intervention not carried out to defend or vindicate the state executing the intervention.

9. T. Gilby, *Between Community and Society* (London: Longmans, Green & Co., 1953) p. 58.

10. The pertinent texts are the following: F. de Vitoria, "De Potestate Civili," 13, in J.B. Scott, *The Spanish Origin of International Law: Francisco de Vitoria and His Law of Nations* (Washington, D.C.: Carnegie Institute, 1917), p. lxxxii, Appendix C; "De Jure Belli," 33, in E. Nys, ed., and J.B. Pate, trans., *Francisci de Vitoria, De Indis et De Jure Belli Relectiones* (Washington, D.C.: Carnegie Institute, 1917), p. 178. Future references to *De Jure Belli* will be cited DJB, with the paragraph number and the page number from the Nys edition; future references to *De Indis* will be cited DI, with the section, paragraph, and page numbers from the Nys edition.

11. Vitoria established the rationale for intervention in his commentary, "On St. Thomas Aquinas, Summa Theologiae Question 40: On War," in J.B. Scott, cited. (Future references to this work will be cited *On War,* with the article, paragraph number, and page number from the Scott edition.) In *De Indis,* Vitoria evaluated specific cases of intervention. This quotation is taken from DI, III, 15, p. 159.

12. *On War,* I, 5, p. cxvii.

13. *On War,* I, 6, p. cxviii.

14. DI, III, 15, p. 159.

15. DI, III, 9, 12; pp. 156, 157, 158.

16. DI, III, 12, 13; pp. 157, 158.

17. DI, III, 18; pp. 160-161.

18. DI, III, 2, 3, 10; pp. 151, 152, 153.

19. Grotius's two major works were *De Jure Praedae Commentarius,* trans. G.L. Williams and W.H. Zeydel, Classics of International Law, 2 vols. (Oxford: Clarendon Press, 1950); *De Jure Belli ac Pacis,* trans. A.C. Campbell (Washington,

D.C.: M.W. Dunne, 1901). Future references to this work will be cited JBP, with book number, paragraph number, and page number from the Campbell edition.

20. JBP, II, 20, p. 247.

21. JBP, II, 20, p. 249.

22. JBP, II, 20, p. 253; JBP, II, 20, p. 247.

23. JBP, II, 20, p. 254.

24. JBP, II, 2, pp. 95-96; II, 2, pp. 89-90; II, 3, p. 104; *De Jure Praedae*, XII.

25. JBP, II, 20, pp. 252-253.

26. JBP, II, 20, p. 247; p. 249.

27. JBP, III, 20, pp. 393-400; II, 18, pp. 202, 212.

28. JBP, III, 1, pp. 293-294.

29. JBP, II, 20, p. 247.

30. JBP, II, 25, pp. 285-289.

31. JBP, III, 17, pp. 377-378.

32. JBP, II, 25, p. 285. Having established the obligation to aid others in need, Grotius articulates a hierarchy of people who have a claim on a state; the list runs from subjects of the state, to allies, friends, and finally, those whose claim is "the common tie of our nature, which alone is sufficient to oblige men to assist each other." JBP, II, 25, pp. 285-288.

33. JBP, II, 25, p. 287.

34. Ibid.

35. JBP, II, 25, p. 285.

36. JBP, III, 17, p. 49.

37. E. Barker, *Church, State, and Study: Essays* (London: Methuen & Co., Ltd., 1930) p. 67.

38. For a discussion of Pufendorf and Wolff, cf. W. Schiffer, *The Legal Community of Mankind: A Critical Analysis of the Modern Concept of World Organization* (New York: Columbia University Press, 1954), chapter 3.

39. L. Gross, "The Peace of Westphalia, 1648-1948," in R. Falk and W. Hanrieder, eds., *International Law and Organization: An Introductory Reader* (Philadelphia: J.P. Lippincott Company, 1968) p. 64.

40. J.T. Johnson, *Idealogy, Reason and the Limitation of War* (Princeton: Princeton University Press, 1975), p. 16. Cf. also J. Kunz, "Bellum Justum and Bellum Legale," *American Journal of International Law*, 45 (1951), 528-534.

41. Johnson, cited, p. 16.

42. It must happen, then, on many occasions that nations put up with certain things although in themselves unjust and worthy of condemnation, because they cannot oppose them by force without transgressing the liberty of individual nations and thus destroying the foundations of their natural society. *The Law of Nations or the Principles of Natural Law* (1758). Edited and translated by C.G. Fenwick (Washington, D.C.: Carnegie Institute, 1916) 21, p. 8. Hereafter cited as LN, with section, paragraph, and page numbers.

43. LN, preface, p. 92.

44. LN, II, 54, p. 131.

45. LN, II, 55, p. 131.

46. LN, II, 59, p. 133.

47. The introduction to *The Law of Nations* in the Carnegie edition is by A. de Lapradelle, p. liv.

48. LN, II, 56, p. 131; cf. also LN, III, 296, p. 340.

49. The preeminent author in the positivist tradition of international law described the relationship in the following manner: "Thus the natural antagonism between the most powerful states seems to guarantee the observance of the principle of nonintervention." Lassa Oppenheim, quoted in Schiffer, cited, p. 93.

50. T.E. Lawrence, *The Principles of International Law* (Boston: D.C. Heath & Co., 1911) p. 135.

51. For classifications of the exceptions cf. Ellery C. Stowell, *Intervention in International Law* (Washington, D.C.: Byrne, 1921); H.G. Hodges, *The Doctrine of Intervention* (Princeton: The Banner Press, 1915); W.E. Lingelback, "The Doctrine and Practices of Intervention in Europe," *Annals, American Academy of Political Science*, 16 (1900), 1-32.

52. R.J. Vincent surveys the contemporary legal literature and concludes that the prevailing view of the sovereignty today is that of "relative sovereignty." Within this perspective of the political order, the principle of nonintervention fulfills a dual role: "It expresses the idea that states are to be immune from interference by other states and it stands at the frontier between international law and domestic law—where international law respects sovereignty, but conceives it as 'that competence which remains to states after due account is taken of their obligation under international law.' " *Nonintervention and International Order* (Princeton: Princeton University Press, 1974) p. 297.

53. The controlling texts in the Charter governing the use of force are Article 2(4) and Article 51. Article 2(4) prohibits the use or threat of force against the territorial integrity or political independence of any state. The countervailing text, Article 51, reserves to states the right of individual or collective defense. Both of these provisions are then complemented by Chapter VII of the Charter, which provides for the authorization of collective defense through a competent organ of the United Nations.

54. Charter of the United Nations, Article 2(7), *Charter of the United Nations and Statute of the International Court of Justice* (New York: U.N. Office of Public Information, n.d.), p. 4. In relations among states the declaration of nonintervention is absolutist in tone and content; it provides for no exceptions to the nonintervention principle, yet the practice of states manifests varied interpretations of the principle.

55. Vincent, cited, p. 309.

56. Hoffman, "Choices," *Foreign Policy*, 12 (1973), 6-12.

10 Human Rights and Intervention

Mark R. Wicclair

It is fairly common to believe that it is morally wrong for nations to intervene in the affairs of other nations. This belief has played an important role in the current debate about whether the promotion of human rights should be a fundamental goal of U.S. foreign policy.[1] There are those who object to giving U.S. foreign policy a human rights orientation on the grounds that this would be "interventionistic." Ernest Lefever, for example, has argued:

> Making human rights the chief, or even major, foreign policy determinant carries dangers. . . . International law forbids any state from interfering in the internal political, judicial and economic affairs of another. Fundamentally, the quality of life in a political community should be determined by its own people. . . .[2]

As Lefever rightly indicates, international law prohibits certain forms of interventionary activity. And those who argue that the promotion of human rights should not be a basic aim of U.S. foreign policy sometimes claim that such a policy would commit the United States to a violation of principles of international law. But for the purposes of this discussion, I will not consider what international law has to say on the subject of intervention.[3] Instead my concern is with the claim that, *independent of what international law proscribes or prescribes,* intervention on behalf of human rights is *morally impermissible.*

Those who have argued against the legitimacy of intervention have rarely, if ever, argued for an absolute prohibition against interventionary activity. Two types of qualifications have generally been acknowledged. On the one hand, there are what might be termed *general* exceptions to a comprehensive nonintervention rule, whereby specified types of interventionary activity are thought to be excluded from the rule. On the other hand, there are what might be termed *special* exceptions, whereby it is conceded that extraordinary circumstances can override a presumption against interventionary activity of a specified type. Among the standard general exceptions which have been recognized at one time or another are the following: intervention for the purpose of (legitimate) self-defense; intervention to protect citizens of one state

The author would like to thank Peter Brown and Douglas MacLean for their many helpful comments and criticisms.

when they are within the territory of another state; intervention in the interests of the balance of power; and intervention in response to illegitimate intervention (intervention to enforce nonintervention).[4] Defenders of a general rule of nonintervention normally have not recognized intervention on behalf of human rights, a subclass of what is commonly referred to in the literature as "humanitarian intervention," as a general exception to the rule of nonintervention. However, even though they do not recognize intervention on behalf of human rights as a general exception, defenders of a comprehensive nonintervention rule commonly allow that certain cases involve such flagrant abuses of human rights (for example, the treatment of Jews in Nazi Germany) that the presumption against humanitarian intervention is overridden. Nevertheless, it is not uncommon for such a statement to be followed by the reminder that these cases are indeed "extraordinary."

In this paper I shall argue that the case for a moral presumption against intervention on behalf of human rights is unconvincing. I will examine what I take to be the major standard moral arguments against intervention;[5] and I will claim that whatever their merits with respect to other types of interventionary activity, none of these arguments provides a conclusive basis for a presumption against intervention on behalf of human rights.

However, before proceeding, a few preliminary remarks about the notion of intervention are in order. The literature on the subject of intervention includes a wide range of definitions of the term. Sometimes intervention is interpreted narrowly to mean "coercive interference" involving "the use or threat of force,"[6] and the target of interventionary activity has been identified as "the structure of political authority in the target society."[7] An even narrower interpretation of intervention would restrict it to the use or threat of *military* force. On the other hand, intervention is sometimes construed broadly to include almost any instance of interference by one state in the affairs of another.[8] A somewhat narrower definition restricts intervention to attempts by the government of one state to compel the behavior of the government of another state.[9] The fact that such diverse definitions of the term have been offered has prompted one writer to observe: "Notwithstanding the voluminous literature on intervention, there appears to be no agreement whatsoever on the phenomena designated by the term."[10]

Clearly, if a nonintervention rule is to function as a moral constraint upon the formulation and execution of foreign policy and as a serviceable principle for assessing the behavior of states toward one another, some criterion for determining instances of intervention must be fixed. As a first step toward formulating an interpretation of intervention for the purposes of this discussion, I will proposed the following condition: To say that the behavior of a state S_1 toward another state S_2 is "interventionary," implies that S_1 undertakes some action[11] for the purpose of either (1) producing a change in S_2, or in the behavior of S_2, or (2) preventing a change in S_2, or in the behavior of S_2.[12]

However, if no further condition were added, the claim that efforts to promote human rights in other countries are generally illegitimate because they are "interventionary" could be dismissed out of hand, for international relations involve continual efforts by states to influence other states, and certain efforts to influence (for examples, through negotiation or "quiet diplomacy") are commonly accepted as legitimate. One possibility at this point is to add the condition that an act is interventionary only if force is used or threatened. But the following considerations suggest that this condition is unsuitable for the purpose of this discussion. First, it can be argued that there are strong independent reasons for prohibiting the use or threat of outright force as an instrument of foreign policy. Thus, it is important to consider whether there are substantial moral reasons for supporting a qualified presumption against attempts by one state to produce or prevent changes in another state, even if no use or threat of force is involved. Second, it seems to me that those who object to giving U.S. foreign policy a strong human rights orientation on the grounds that it would commit the United States to an "interventionistic" foreign policy are not merely invoking the specter of marines or clandestine agents landing or operating on foreign soil. Rather, their objection seems to be of a more general nature, namely, that it is illegitimate for the United States, or any country, to "meddle" in the affairs of another nation.[13] Third, the public debate over whether the United States should seek to promote human rights in foreign countries has not been occasioned by proposals by policymakers to send military units to, or to finance clandestine operations in, foreign countries. Rather, it has focused primarily upon measures such as imposing conditions on bilateral military and economic assistance to, and imposing economic and other sanctions on, governments which have poor human rights records.[14] That is, by and large the controversy has concentrated on the legitimacy of efforts by the United States to compel foreign governments to improve their human rights records.[15]

This suggests the following as the additional condition for which we have been looking: the behavior of S_1 toward S_2 is interventionary only if S_1 attempts to *compel* the government of S_2 to act in a manner desired by S_1. Compulsion, it is important to recognize, need not involve force or the threat of force. Rather, it occurs whenever an attempt to modify behavior contrary to an agent's wishes is carried out by the production of, or a threat to produce, undesirable states of affairs in the event of noncompliance. Thus, for example, S_1 attempts to compel the government of S_2 if it seeks to get the latter to act contrary to its wishes by terminating or threatening to terminate part or all of S_1's military or economic assistance to S_2. Accordingly, intervention can now be defined in the following manner:

The behavior of S_1 toward S_2 is interventionary if and only if: (1) S_1 undertakes some action for the purpose of either (a) producing a change in S_2, or in the behavior of S_2; or (b) preventing a change in S_2, or in the behavior of S_2; and (2) in order to achieve this end, S_1 either compels or attempts to compel the government of S_2 to act in an appropriate manner.

It might be objected, however, that this definition of intervention is too narrow. For it fails to include those cases in which a state attempts *directly* to produce or prevent changes in another state, or in the behavior of that state, by, say, financing opposition candidates, disseminating hostile propaganda, or supporting insurgency movements. Since such attempts directly to produce or prevent changes do not involve efforts to compel or coerce (current) governments to modify their behavior, they could not be termed instances of intervention according to the above definition. But this seems both arbitrary and counter-intuitive.

This objection can be met by construing conditions (1) and (2) above as sufficient, not necessary and sufficient, conditions of intervention. To do so will suffice for the purposes of this discussion. For, as my earlier comments suggest, the issue of intervention has entered into the public debate about whether the United States should seek to promote human rights abroad primarily in the context of questioning the legitimacy of efforts by the United States to *compel* foreign governments to improve their human rights records. Since such efforts have been opposed on the grounds that they are "interventionistic," I think that it is important to consider whether convincing arguments can be provided for a moral presumption against attempts to compel foreign governments to improve their human rights records; and this is what I propose to do in the remainder of this chapter by examining various arguments against intervention.

Arguments against intervention can be divided into two broad categories, consequentialist and nonconsequentialist arguments. Consequentialist arguments claim that intervention, or certain types of interventionary activity, should be prohibited because of the undesirable consequences which flow from intervention. Insofar as they rest upon a claim that intervention, or specified types of interventionary activity (normally) produce certain types of effects, consequentialist arguments are empirical in nature. Nonconsequentialist arguments, on the other hand, claim that, independent of the effects produced by interventionary activity, there are conclusive reasons for recognizing a nonintervention rule. Arguments of this type, then, do not rely upon empirical claims concerning the likely effects of intervention. Moreover, whereas consequentialist arguments cite certain undesirable effects as reasons for prohibiting intervention, nonconsequentialist arguments attempt to establish that interventionary activity is intrinsically wrong. In this section I will examine nonconsequentialist arguments against intervention, and in the following section consequentialist arguments will be discussed.

The first nonconsequentialist argument which I shall consider is an argument against intervention in general. It invokes an analogy between individuals and a principle which is commonly referred to as the "harm principle," on the one hand, and nations and a general rule of nonintervention on the other hand. To begin with the case of individuals, the argument runs as follows. Each person is entitled to respect from all other persons as a free (autonomous) and equal moral agent. This principle, the principle of respect for persons, is a basic moral principle. Now the harm principle is a rule which expresses the appropriate respect to which each person is entitled. According to the harm principle, except for the purposes of self-defense or to prevent harm to others, it is illegitimate for one person x to interfere with the conduct of any other person y. In particular, x's belief that y is acting, or is about to act, in a way which is detrimental to y's mental and/or physical well-being or to y's happiness, does not justify x's interfering with y's conduct. To compel y to act in a way contrary to y's will in such cases would involve a failure on the part of x to recognize y's freedom to select his or her own values and to acknowledge y's capacity to choose for himself or herself. In short, if x were to interfere in such cases, x would fail to respect y as a free and equal moral agent. Thus, the argument concludes, the harm principle should be recognized as a basic norm of interpersonal relations.

To turn now to the case of states, an argument for a nonintervention rule based upon a purported analogy with individuals and the harm principle can be formulated as follows. States are personlike entities in that states can be said to have goals and ends and to act. To be sure, it is individuals who determine what become the goals or ends of a particular state at any given time; and it is individuals acting in certain capacities or roles who act for the state. But it is still proper to say that the state as a whole has or pursues certain goals or ends (for example, in its domestic or foreign policy). And insofar as it is correct to say in particular instances that specified individuals are acting as representatives or agents of some state or other, it can be said that their actions (for example, signing a treaty or issuing a declaration of war) comprise actions of the state they represent. Now since they are personlike entities, states, like individuals, are entitled to respect as free and equal moral agents. This means that each state is entitled to have its autonomy or sovereignty and moral equality recognized by all other states. And, the argument concludes, the fact that a general rule of nonintervention is a suitable analog to the harm principle recommends it as a basic norm of interstate relations.[16]

This argument is open to a number of objections, but I will restrict my remarks to the following two points. First, there is a significant disanalogy between the harm principle and a rule prohibiting intervention among states. The harm principle prohibits interference to prevent individuals from acting in ways which others believe to be detrimental to the agent himself or herself. But it does not prohibit interference to prevent harm to individuals by others (third parties). In cases where human rights violations occur as a result of governmental policies, for example, it would be false to say that a person (the state) is harming itself. Rather, in those cases, individuals (citizens) suffer harm as the result of the actions or omissions of other individuals (government officials and their agents and supporters), and the harm principle would not proscribe interference in such cases. Hence, it is misleading to invoke an analogy with the harm principle to support a general rule of nonintervention which includes a presumption against intervention on behalf of human rights.

Second, the foregoing argument fails to make a conclusive case for *any* nonintervention rule. Even if it were conceded that states are personlike entities in the respects claimed, it would not follow that states and persons have similar moral rights and duties. Whereas it might be plausible to claim that the principle of respect for persons is a basic moral principle, it is not plausible to assert that a principle which expresses respect for the autonomy or sovereignty and moral equality of nation-states is a basic moral principle. In any event, an argument is needed to show why collectivities like nation-states should be recognized as objects of respect and subjects of rights on an analog with persons.

Alternatively, one might try to derive a general nonintervention rule directly from the principle of respect for persons, that is, without invoking a claimed analogy between individuals and states. One such argument proceeds as follows. States are associations of individuals, and the particular cultural traditions and institutional arrangements of a state reflect the unique historical circumstances of that country and the values of its citizens. Now if the government of a state S_2 were to compel the government of S_1 to alter the institutional arrangements of S_1, this would be tantamount to interfering with the autonomy of the citizens of S_1 and their ability to shape the destiny of their nation in accordance with their own values. But this is clearly illegitimate, for it violates the principle of respect for persons, a basic moral principle. Consequently, the argument concludes, there is good reason for recognizing a principle of state autonomy or sovereignty, and a general rule of nonintervention.[17]

Leaving aside a consideration of its merits with respect to other types of intervention, this argument fails in the case of intervention on behalf of human rights. The primary reason for this is a failure to distinguish between just and unjust institutional arrangements. This point can be illustrated with the aid of the following example. Suppose that the traditions and institutions of a particular state have supported the unjust treatment of a racial minority for several decades. Further, let us suppose that this unjust treatment consists in part in gross and systematic human rights violations. In this case it cannot plausibly be claimed that the cultural traditions and institutions of that state reflect the values of the racial minority; nor can it plausibly be claimed that those institutions respect their autonomy. Hence, they might welcome foreign intervention to help them shape the destiny of their nation. Further, the majority cannot legitimately invoke the principle of respect for persons to protect their cultural traditions and the institutions they value from external intervention. For by hypothesis the majority has consistently failed to respect the freedom and moral equality of minority group members, and it would be nothing less than a cruel irony to invoke the principle of respect for persons to justify perpetuating violations of that very same principle. Thus, the principle of respect for persons does not afford the majority a right to perpetuate unjust institutional arrangements; nor does it afford them a right to be free from external intervention to alter those arrangements. Consequently, the foregoing argument cannot be used to support a moral presumption against intervention to compel foreign governments to change unjust institutional arrangements which support human rights violations.

The social contract or consent account of the legitimacy of government interference with individual liberty might be used to generate another nonconsequentialist argument for a general nonintervention rule.[18] However, since it is implausible to claim that citizens give or have given their expressed or tacit consent to violations of their rights or that they would never consent to interference by foreign governments, this argument need not be considered here. Instead I will discuss an argument in which the notion of actual (explicit or tacit) consent is replaced by the notion of *hypothetical* consent. This will be the final nonconsequentialist argument which I shall consider.

Since John Rawls is the leading contemporary spokesman for social contract theory, my discussion will focus upon his formulation of the contract strategy.[19] Rawls employs the device of a hypothetical social contract to derive and justify principles of social justice. These are principles which assign basic rights, liberties, and duties and which specify entitlements and conditions of access to wealth, occupations, and so on. By his account, to ask whether the political and economic institutions of a particular society are just is not to ask whether the members of that society have given their explicit or tacit consent to those institutional arrangements. Rather, it is to ask whether those institutions are compatible with principles which they *would* acknowledge if they were to adopt the perspective of a *hypothetical* situation which Rawls terms the "original position."

What must we do in order to adopt the perspective of persons in the original position? Among other things, it would be necessary for us to don what Rawls refers to as "the veil of ignorance." In so doing, we would develop a fairly severe case of temporary amnesia. For as a result of the veil of ignorance, we would no longer know elementary facts of the following sort: the particular characteristics of our own society; our position in society (for example, our class, status, occupation, and income); our particular interests and preferences; our physical characteristics, personality traits, intelligence, and capacities

Now despite the fact that Rawls employs the device of a hypothetical contract, he asserts that the outcome of this thought experiment is not devoid of moral significance. For largely as a result of the veil of ignorance, when assuming the perspective of the original position, individuals relate to one another as free and equal moral persons, and any agreements reached by them

will be fair. As Rawls puts it, when actual social arrangements satisfy principles
which would be selected from the perspective of the original position, the members of that society "can say to one another that they are cooperating on terms
to which they would agree if they were free and equal persons whose relations
with respect to one another were fair."[20] This, then, is the basis of the claim
that by adopting the perspective of persons in the hypothetical original position,
we can address fundamental ethical questions.

Rawls's primary concern is with principles of justice which apply to the
basic political, economic, and social arrangements of nation-states, not to relations
among those states. Accordingly, the question Rawls asks is: Which principles
would be selected by the parties to a hypothetical domestic social contract?[21]
But the question of particular interest to us is this: Would the parties to a
hypothetical *international* social contract agree to a nonintervention rule which
includes a presumption against intervention on behalf of human rights? The
claim that they would constitutes another argument for a general nonintervention rule.

Like the other nonconsequentialist arguments we have considered so far,
this argument also fails. For suppose it is assumed that: (1) the parties to the
contract agree that the world should be divided into separate and politically
independent nation-states, and they have already selected principles of justice
which apply to the basic institutional arrangements of particular states;[22] (2) the
principles of justice which have been selected recognize certain fundamental
rights, that is, "human rights"; and (3) the contractees assume that citizens
of actual states are sometimes subject to serious human rights violations and
that in some cases citizens are unable to bring about a timely end to those rights
violations without external assistance from foreign nations.[23] Then the parties
to the international social contract would recognize that if they selected a nonintervention rule which included a presumption against intervention on behalf
of human rights, citizens of nation-states would run the risk of being indefinite-
ly subject to serious human rights violations. On the other hand, they would
recognize that this risk could be avoided by selecting a limited intervention rule
which permitted intervention on behalf of human rights. Thus, if they were to
consider none of the possible side-effects of permitting nation-states to intervene
in the affairs of other nation states on behalf of human rights, the parties to the
contract would select that limited intervention rule.[24] Thus, from a contractarian
perspective, the case against intervention on behalf of human rights requires consequentialist considerations.

Consequentialist arguments will be examined in the next section. In this
section I have analyzed a number of nonconsequentialist arguments for a nonintervention rule. To be sure, I cannot claim to have examined every conceivable nonconsequentialist argument. For there are an indefinite number of
such arguments. Still, my selection of the arguments I discussed was not
arbitrary, for an effort was made to reconstruct the standard arguments in the

literature. Thus I think it is warranted to conclude that none of the commonly advanced nonconsequentialist arguments for nonintervention establishes a presumption against intervention on behalf of human rights.

To turn now to consequentialist arguments, the standard argument of this type for a general nonintervention rule involves the claim that intervention threatens world peace and stability. According to this argument, recognition of a general rule of nonintervention in a world of politically independent nation-states is a condition of peace and stability among those states. Leaving aside a consideration of the merits of this argument as it applies to other types of interventionary activity, can an argument of this nature be used to defend a presumption against intervention on behalf of human rights?

To begin with, it should be noted that an argument from world peace and stability in the case of intervention on behalf of human rights can cut both ways. Hersch Lauterpacht, for example, argues that "ultimately, peace is more endangered by tyrannical contempt for human rights than by attempts to assert, through intervention, the sanctity of human personality."[25] A more important point is this. It must be recalled that the term "intervention" includes a wide range of measures, from military force to economic sanctions. It might well be plausible to claim that *military* intervention generally threatens world peace and stability. Thus, for example, considerations of world peace and stability might rule out sending marines into the Soviet Union to help evacuate Jews who wish to emigrate to Israel. But it is less plausible to claim that there is a serious threat to world peace and stability whenever economic sanctions are employed. To be sure, world peace and stability might be threatened if economic sanctions are applied in order to promote the domestic interests of one state at the expense of another. But it remains to be shown that there is a similar danger whenever economic sanctions are imposed on behalf of human rights. This is not to deny that considerations of world peace and stability should enter into a state's decision on how to act in particular cases. But to admit that such prudential considerations can *sometimes* weigh against intervention clearly does not commit one to the acceptance of a general presumption against all forms of intervention on behalf of human rights. To claim that world peace and stability require a presumption against all forms of intervention on behalf of human rights, is comparable to treating international society like an extremely fragile house of cards which would come crashing down as a result of anything from a sneeze to being hit by a baseball bat.

At this point it might be claimed that although it is possible in principle to distinguish between prudent and imprudent or permissible and impermissible instances of intervention and to formulate appropriate rules, states generally cannot be trusted to make distinctions or to observe rules. And a claim of this sort might then be used to support a *general* rule of nonintervention. But this line of reasoning would prove too much, for the unqualified skepticism which underlies an argument of this sort would support the two following broad propositions: (1) states *generally* cannot be counted upon to distinguish between prudent and imprudent courses of action in matters related to world peace and stability; and (2) states cannot be trusted to observe *any* rules. The first proposition suggests that the continued existence of a world society divided into sovereign states whose relations are governed by a general nonintervention rule is itself a threat to world peace and stability. And the second proposition implies that it would not matter what sort of rule concerning intervention, whether it be a general nonintervention rule or a limited intervention rule, were acknowledged in theory.

In addition, it is important to recognize that even in the unlikely event that it could be shown that a presumption against intervention on behalf of human rights is necessary for world peace and stability, the case for nonintervention would still be inconclusive. For the absence of interstate conflict and international instability insures neither that international arrangements, nor that political and economic arrangements in particular states, are *just*. It cannot be denied that world peace and stability are desirable ends. But from a moral perspective, considerations of justice must be taken into account as well. Thus, depending upon the extent to which injustice prevails in the world, it is conceivable that a period of conflict and instability would be justified, all things considered.

The three remaining consequentialist arguments which I shall consider directly address the case of humanitarian intervention. Each of these arguments attempts to show that intervention is generally not in the best interests of its would-be benefactors. The first of these arguments is that of John Stuart Mill. In a short essay entitled "A Few Words on Non-Intervention,"[26] Mill offers a consequentialist argument against intervention to "aid the people of another [country] in a struggle against their government for free institutions"[27] which might be used to support a presumption against intervention on behalf of human rights. Mill distinguishes between two types of cases: (1) those cases in which an oppressive regime would not be able to remain in power without receiving external assistance from one or more foreign countries; and (2) those cases in which such assistance is neither required nor received. In the former instance, according to Mill, intervention by some third party or parties is already taking place. Further intervention in such cases is justifiable, not on behalf of the victims, however, but in order to enforce the norm of nonintervention. As Mill says, "Intervention to enforce non-intervention is always rightful, always moral, if not always prudent."[28] However, in the latter instance, Mill claims that intervention is, as a general rule, illegitimate. Mill offers the following justification for this claim:

> The reason is, that there can seldom be any thing approaching to assurance, that intervention, even if successful, would be for the good of the people themselves. The only test possessing any real value, of a people's

having become fit for popular institutions, is, that they, or a sufficient
portion of them to prevail in the contest, are willing to brave labor and
danger for their liberation.[29]

According to Mill, it is in the (successful) struggle for liberty against their oppressors that individuals are most likely to develop a "spirit of liberty" or "the
virtues of freemen," that is, dispositions essential to maintaining institutions
which secure the basic political rights and liberties of citizens. Since "it is
during an arduous struggle to become free by their own efforts" that these
dispositions "have the best chances of springing up," "the liberty which is
bestowed on them by other hands than their own [that is, with the aid of
foreign intervention] will have nothing real, nothing permanent."[30]

Now one might object to the fact that Mill stresses individual dispositions
over all other factors (for example, level of economic development, distribution
of wealth, class structure) which determine the practical feasibility of particular
political arrangements in a given society. However, for the sake of argument, let
us grant that certain dispositions are essential for maintaining institutions which
secure the basic political rights and liberties of citizens. Still, Mill fails to make
a plausible case for the claim that the ability to topple a repressive regime is
generally correlated with the possession of those dispositions. Suppose a
repressive regime commands a large, well-financed, well-trained, and highly
efficient security apparatus which is equipped with sophisticated weapons and
communications technology. Then its ability to put down insurgency movements
without the aid of foreign assistance does not necessarily indicate that the
insurgents lack organization, self-discipline, or any of the other dispositions
which one might claim are essential for maintaining institutions which secure
basic political rights and liberties. Conversely, if a regime's forces are ill-
equipped, undisciplined, and poorly organized, a victory on the part of insurgents
can hardly be said to demonstrate that they possess "the virtues of freemen."
In addition, Mill fails to show that the experience of fighting an oppressive
regime (with or without foreign assistance) will foster dispositions of "freemen."
What is the connection, say, between the abilities, training, and experiences
of revolutionaries, guerrillas, or urban terrorists and such dispositions?

Moreover, suppose it is conceded *arguendo* that if the victims of human
rights violations on the part of oppressive regimes are incapable of putting an
end to those violations without foreign intervention, then an extended period
of foreign assistance and supervision will be required to minimize the prospects
of a recurrence of oppressive practices. Still, given the seriousness of human
rights violations, even an extended period of foreign supervision might well be
preferable to allowing human rights violations to continue unabated.

A second consequentialist argument against intervention on behalf of
human rights on the grounds that it is not in the best interests of the victims
of rights violations can be formulated as follows. Nations are neither altruistic

nor impartial. That is, in formulating and executing foreign policy, domestic interests, that is, the interests of individuals and groups at home, are decisive, and the interests of foreign nationals are of relatively minor significance. Consequently, when "one state meddles in another's affairs, the nationals of the victim are rarely considered on the same footing as those of the interfering state. The latter treats them rather as means for its own ends."[31] As a result, when a nation intervenes in the affairs of another nation for the stated purpose of aiding the victims of human rights violations, its interventionary activity will favor the interests of individuals and groups in the intervening state, rather than the interests of the victims of human rights violations. Hence, the argument concludes, it is in the interest of the victims of human rights violations to recognize a presumption against intervention.

Now one might object to the rather cynical picture of international affairs which underlies this argument. But for the sake of this analysis, I will not dispute it. Still, the argument is not valid. Suppose it is generally the case that when states intervene in the affairs of nations for the stated purpose of aiding the victims of human rights violations, the decision to intervene is shaped primarily by domestic interests.[32] Nevertheless, it does not follow that intervention does not generally (also) benefit the victims of human rights violations. Indeed, domestic interests (for example, an interest in promoting stability to protect foreign investments, a concern for a state's "image" in the world, or domestic political considerations) might only be served if the rights situation of persons in the target state is actually improved. Thus, advocates of a moral presumption against intervention on behalf of human rights cannot rest their case upon the mere claim that states are neither altruistic nor impartial. Rather, they must demonstrate further that the victims of human rights violations generally fail to benefit from, or are generally made worse off by, intervention. Given the seriousness of what is at stake in the case of human rights violations, in the absence of conclusive empirical evidence to this effect, it is irresponsible to advocate a presumption against intervention on behalf of human rights.

The last of the consequentialist arguments which I shall examine is an argument from lack of sufficient knowledge, and it can be formulated as follows. "Outsiders," that is, the citizens and governments of foreign states, lack the information, insight, and understanding which are required to know what is best for the citizens of other states. Hence, "the claims of a state's members will generally be better served if they are left to work out their own salvation."[33] Consequently, the argument concludes, even if persons in one state sincerely believe that persons in another state are suffering from human rights violations, it is generally in the best interests of the latter for the former to refrain from intervening.

Two logically distinct claims account for the apparent plausibility of this argument. One, a form of moral relativism, is a claim to the effect that the values shared by the members of one state are often significantly different from and as valid as the shared values of persons in other states. And the second is a claim to the effect that persons in one state generally lack sufficient knowledge of the particular circumstances in other states to allow them to determine how to succeed in actually improving conditions in those states.

To begin with the first of the two claims, I certainly do not wish to deny that outsiders who claimed to be bringing the "fruits of civilization" to various "backward" regions of the globe during the colonial era, or even in the recent past, were at worst attempting to mask their true interests, and at best grossly insensitive to cultures, traditions, and institutions significantly different from their own. In this respect, I think the foregoing argument might well serve as a helpful caution against what might be termed "cultural imperialism." However, if it is to be used to argue against intervention in cases of purported *human rights violations,* advocates of that argument would have to deny that there are *any* transcultural (universal) moral rights, that is, human rights. This in turn would imply that intervention could *never* be justified by citing claimed human rights violations which it is avowedly designed to eliminate. But those who argue against "humanitarian intervention" rarely, if ever, take such an absolutist position. Insofar as exceptions to the rule are allowed (for example, in the case of the treatment of Jews in Nazi Germany), there is a tacit admission that there are certain fundamental transcultural moral rights, the violation of which justifies intervention. But if it is conceded that there are *some* human rights, then an argument from moral relativism cannot be used to defend a presumption against intervention on behalf of those rights.[34]

Finally, let us consider the claim that persons in one state generally lack sufficient knowledge of the particular circumstances in other countries to allow them to determine how to succeed in actually improving conditions in those countries. I do not wish to deny that there are real problems in determining what means, if any, will bring about a significant improvement in the situation of victims of human rights violations. But I think that it is at least arguable that "outsiders" are no less equipped to make such determinations than "inside" ruling elites who have shown a persistent disregard of the rights and legitimate claims of large segments of the population. Surely, it is implausible to claim, say, that the U.S. government should generally take at face value claims put forth by repressive regimes that in view of the particular circumstances in their countries, no significant improvements in human rights are feasible in the foreseeable future; or that they are doing everything practically feasible to improve conditions. This is not to say that such claims are never warranted by the facts. Rather, I only want to suggest that it is unwarranted to maintain that nations like the United States do not have the capacity, and therefore should not even attempt, to determine independently whether such claims have merit.

I have argued that none of the consequentialist and nonconsequentialist arguments which I have considered establishes a convincing case for a general moral presumption against intervention on behalf of human rights. This discussion suggests that it is irresponsible to dismiss in advance efforts to compel foreign governments to improve their human rights records on the grounds that such efforts are "interventionistic." If intervention on behalf of human rights is morally wrong, then it is wrong because it would not serve to promote justice, all things considered, in particular cases. This suggests that it is morally unobjectionable to include among the goals of U.S. foreign policy the promotion of human rights, and that what is urgently needed is a careful study of the feasibility of achieving this goal in particular cases.

Notes

1. The International Security Assistance and Arms Export Control Act of 1976 specifies in part that "a principal goal of the foreign policy of the United States is to promote the increased observance of internationally recognized human rights by all countries" (P.L. 94-329, 90 STAT. 748).

2. The Rights Standard," *New York Times*, January 24, 1977, "Op-Ed" page.

3. The status of human rights violations in international law has been the subject of considerable controversy. For a discussion of the legal status of intervention, see the essay by Thomas Buergenthal in this volume.

4. See R.J. Vincent, *Nonintervention and International Order* (Princeton: Princeton University Press, 1974), pp. 283-293.

5. I will not consider arguments which attempt to show that it is in the interest of particular states to adopt a policy of nonintervention.

6. Vincent, p. 8. This definition derives from Oppenheim. See L. Oppenheim, *International Law*, 8th ed., ed. by H. Lauterpacht (London: Longmans, 1955), vol. I, *Peace*, p. 305. Winfield states that intervention "occurs where one state interferes by force or threat of force in the affairs of another state." Percy H. Winfield, "Intervention," *Encyclopedia of the Social Sciences*, Vol. 8 (New York: Macmillan, 1932), p. 236. See also J.L. Brierly, *The Law of Nations*, 4th ed. (Oxford: Clarendon Press, 1949), p. 284.

7. James N. Rosenau, "Intervention as a Scientific Concept," *Journal of Conflict Resolution*, XIII: 2 (June 1969), 161.

8. Thomas and Thomas observe that "some authorities would include in their definition of intervention almost any act of interference by one state in the affairs of another. For example, it has been said that mere official correspondence carried on by one state with another concerning some action of the other amounts to intervention, while conversely it has also been intimated that a failure of a state to concern itself with the affairs of another might amount to negative intervention." Ann Van Wynen and A.J. Thomas, *Non-Intervention: The Law and Its Import in the Americas* (Dallas: Southern Methodist University Press, 1956), p. 67.

9. According to Thomas and Thomas, intervention involves "actions taken by one state to impose its will upon another against the latter's wishes. . . . The essence of intervention is the attempt to compel" Thomas and Thomas, pp. 68-69, 72.

10. Rosenau, p. 152.

11. Insofar as intentionally refraining from acting in order to achieve a specified end is construable as "action," this condition does not preclude counting a state's failure to act in certain contexts as an instance of intervention.

12. This condition is suggested by Rosenau. See Rosenau, p. 159.

13. John Vorster, the then Prime Minister of South Africa, apparently thought that he would win the sympathy of some Americans when he made the following statement in the course of an interview: "It is fast reaching the stage where we feel that the United States wants to prescribe to us how we should run our country internally and that is of course unacceptable to us. It is a fool who doesn't listen to advice but nobody can allow outsiders, however well-intentioned, whatever their motives, to meddle in their internal affairs." *New York Times*, September 17, 1977. It goes without saying that Vorster's remarks were directed against economic and other sanctions short of outright force.

14. The International Security Assistance and Arms Export Control Act of 1976 referred to in note 1 above contains the following additional provision: "It is further the policy of the United States that, except under circumstances specified in this section, no security assistance may be provided to any country the government of which engages in a consistent pattern of gross violations of internationally recognized human rights."

15. It is sometimes assumed that military and economic assistance programs give the United States considerable leverage over foreign governments. Accordingly one of the aims of withholding or threatening to withhold assistance to governments with poor human rights records is to compel those governments to change their policies. This construal of the purpose of imposing conditions on aid appears to assume that the United States shares no responsibility for human rights violations. Those who believe that the United States has directly or indirectly contributed to rights violations might advocate imposing restrictions on aid to end U.S. complicity. It would be disingenuous to charge those who take this position with advocating "interventionary" policies. For a discussion of U.S. involvement in the cases of Iran and the Philippines, see the contributions of Richard Cottam and Richard Claude to this volume. Still another aim of terminating aid, or severing all relations with governments with poor human rights records, may be to disassociate the United States from those governments. On this view, the termination of assistance is not necessarily associated with the expectation that it will improve the rights situation of foreign nationals.

16. Christian Wolff, a natural law theorist who is regarded as among the first to have written a treatise on international law which explicitly recognized a general rule of nonintervention, at one point asserts that "nations are regarded as individual free persons living in a state of Nature. . . . Therefore . . . nations

also must be regarded in relation to each other as individual free persons living
in a state of nature." Christian Wolff, *Jus Gentium Methodo Scientifica Per-
tractatum*, 1764, trans. by Joseph H. Drake (Oxford: At The Clarendon Press,
1934), Prolegomena, section 2. In a later passage, Wolff draws the following
analogy: "[J]ust as by force of natural liberty it must be allowed to every man
that he abide by his own judgment in acting, consequently also in the exercise
of his right, as long as he does nothing which is contrary to your right, so likewise by force of the natural liberty of nations it must be allowed to any one of
them to abide by its own judgment in the exercise of sovereignty" (chapter II,
section 255).

Vincent, citing Benn and Peters, also draws an analogy between individuals
and states. See Vincent, pp. 344-345, and S.I. Benn and R.S. Peters, *Social
Principles and the Democratic State* (London: George Allen & Unwin, 1959),
p. 361.

17. An argument along these lines is suggested by Benn and Peters, p. 361.

18. According to Wolff, "since civil sovereignty arises from the stipulation
by which men have united into a state and by force of which individuals have
bound themselves to the whole, because they desire to promote the common
good; the obligation of individuals has regard only to the whole; and the right of
the whole over individuals, which is sovereignty, belongs only to the whole, who
have contracted one with the other: consequently there is absolutely no natural
reason why a certain nation should share any of this right with another nation"
(Wolff, chapter II, section 255).

Vattel, a follower of Wolff, states that "liberty and independence belong to
man by his very nature, and . . . they cannot be taken from him without his
consent. Citizens of a state, having yielded them in part to the sovereign, do not
enjoy them to their full and absolute extent. But the whole body of the Nation,
the State, so long as it has not voluntarily submitted to other Nations, remains
absolutely free and independent." Emer de Vattel, *The Law of Nations or the
Principles of Natural Law*, 1758, trans. by Charles G. Fenwick (Washington:
The Carnegie Institution of Washington, 1916), Book I, Introduction, section 4.

19. Rawls's contractarian theory is systematically developed in *A Theory of
Justice* (Cambridge, Mass.: Harvard University Press, 1971).

20. Rawls, p. 13.

21. In the course of a discussion of conscientious refusal in time of war,
Rawls asserts that it should be possible "to relate the just political principles
regulating the conduct of states to the contract doctrine and to explain the
moral basis of the law of nations from this point of view" (p. 377). However,
Rawls does not attempt systematically to carry out this project in *A Theory
of Justice*. For some insightful suggestions along these lines, see Charles R.
Beitz, "Justice and International Relations," *Philosophy & Public Affairs*, No. 4
(Summer 1975), 360-389.

22. One might suggest another alternative: The parties to the hypothetical

contract are to be thought of as individuals who do not assume that the world is or should be divided up into independent nation-states. As Barry observes, this would leave open the question whether nation-states should be "the units within which 'principles of justice' operate. . . ." Brian Barry, *The Liberal Theory of Justice* (Oxford: Clarendon Press, 1973), p. 129. I think that this is an important point, but I cannot pursue it further here.

23. The veil of ignorance does not exclude what Rawls refers to as "general facts." The parties to the contract "understand political affairs and the principles of economic theory; they know the basis of social organization and the laws of human psychology. . . . There are no limitations on general information, that is, on general laws and theories. . ." (pp. 137-138). It seems plausible to claim that both of the propositions mentioned in (3) could be inferred from the sorts of "general laws and theories" which pass through the veil of ignorance.

24. It might be argued that the parties would recognize a rule which imposes an *obligation* on foreign governments, or on an international organization, to intervene in certain specific circumstances.

25. Hersch Lauterpacht, *International Law and Human Rights* (New York: Frederick A. Praeger, Inc., 1950), p. 32.

26. J.S. Mill, *Dissertations and Discussions: Political, Philosophical, and Historical* (London, 1875), Vol. III, pp. 153-178.

27. Ibid., p. 258.

28. Ibid., p. 261.

29. Ibid., p. 258.

30. Ibid., p. 258-260.

31. Benn and Peters, p. 361.

32. One might claim that the prospects of "impartiality" would be significantly enhanced by entrusting decisions to intervene to an international organization like the United Nations. But, given the realities of international politics, this remains doubtful. Moreover, the prospects that intervention on behalf of human rights would *ever* be approved might then be seriously reduced.

33. Benn and Peters, pp. 362-363.

34. It is beyond the scope of this discussion to formulate a list of "human rights," or to determine *which* rights U.S. foreign policy should promote. Other essays in this volume address these important issues.

Part IV
Applications: Information and Interpretation

11   ". . .in the National Interest"

Peter G. Brown

Introduction

My overall purpose in this chapter is to examine critically the concept of the "national interest" as a source for the moral authority of the foreign policies of the United States and other governments. In particular, I want to show that the concept (1) is too inclusive in ways that can mask important—even crucial—differences which should matter from a moral point of view; and (2) when used in an unqualified way as a source of moral authority to override human rights concerns does violence to the idea of human rights.

In the course of developing the two arguments anticipated above I will show why certain language contained in Section 502B of the Foreign Assistance Act of 1961 as amended provides inadequate guidance to policy and why certain portions of that act reverse the proper order between considerations of national interest and concerns for human rights. The act states that

> the United States shall, in accordance with its international obligations
> as set forth in the Charter of the United Nations and in keeping with
> the constitutional heritage and traditions of the United States, promote
> and encourage increased respect for human rights and fundamental
> freedoms throughout the world without distinction as to race, sex,
> language, or religion. Accordingly, a principal goal of the foreign
> policy of the United States shall be to promote the increased obser-
> vance of internationally recognized human rights by all countries.

And 502B (c)(1)(C)(ii) invites the secretary of state to determine whether, notwithstanding human rights violations that would otherwise justify the denial of such assistance, "on all the facts it is in the national interest of the United States to provide such assistance."

I will summarize my objections to some assumptions embodied in portions of that act at the conclusion of this paper.

In the setting of policy and in common usage "the national interest" refers to the physical security of the United States, its economic well-being, and the

---

I am indebted to Peter French, Robert Kudrle, Henry Shue, and Mark Wicclair for useful criticisms of earlier drafts of this paper. Douglas MacLean was untiring in helping me focus the final argument. Defects are, of course, my own.

preservation of its institutions and values. In the passage quoted above it serves as a moral excuse from obligations imposed by the rest of the act.

I should make clear at the outset that I do not assume that the national interest of the United States and human rights of the citizens of other nations must always conflict. Such conflicts may indeed be the exception rather than the rule. The discussion that follows is directed to the question of what to do when there is such a conflict.

The Concept of the "National Interest"

In this section I will show that the concept of "national interest" is too inclusive. Because this term serves as a justification for policies this overinclusiveness can lead to serious imbalances and lack of discrimination in the conception and execution of our foreign policies.

At bottom the problem is that the word interest seems so broad as to include any (rational) desire. It fails to be adequately specific about what is at stake. In *Shattered Peace: The Origins of the Cold War and the National Security State,* Daniel Yergin notes the lack of discrimination in the related concept of "national security":

> We must remember that "national security" is not a given, not a fact, but a perception, a state of mind.
>
> And what characterizes the concept of national security? It postulates the interrelatedness of so many different political, economic and military factors that developments halfway around the globe are seen to have automatic and direct impact on America's core interests. Virtually every development in the world is perceived to be potentially crucial. An adverse turn of events anywhere endangers the United States. Problems in foreign relations are viewed as urgent and immediate threats. Thus, desirable foreign policy goals are translated into issues of national survival, and the range of threats becomes limitless. The doctrine is characterized by expansiveness, a tendency to push the subjective boundaries of security outward to more and more areas, to encompass more and more geography and more and more problems. It demands that the country assume a posture of military preparedness; the nation must be on permanent alert.[1]

At first glance "national security" appears to refer to only a portion of the universe designated by the "national interest." A nation is secure when it can repel or deter actual or potential adversaries and sufficiently protect raw material sources and markets to prevent catastrophic economic collapse. What Yergin points to is the way the boundaries of this conception tend to expand so that potentially adverse consequences of nearly any sort are perceived as threats to *security.*

"National interest" has all the problems of "national security," but it has
them in spades. By referring to any sort of well-being of the citizens of a nation,
"national interest" can serve to sound the alarm for the slightest actual or
potential incursion on present or prospective privilege.

There are two related problems with relying on "national interest" as
a source of justification for our policies: (1) the concept "national interest"
is homogeneous and limitless; and (2) when used in regard to a nation with far-
flung military and economic interests it justifies a great diversity of actions and
reactions all over the globe—actions and reactions that might appear in a different light if even elementary moral distinctions were taken into account.

Let me develop these two points in turn. At the conceptual level the fundamental problem is that the concept of "national interest" lumps together under
one word matters of very different moral standing as if, in all relevant ways, they
are homogeneous. We may speak of the interest the nation has in securing
reliable access to certain raw materials abroad, for example, leather or liquid
natural gas.[2] Such a policy may be in the interests of individual citizens, since
it may make for more reliable and/or less expensive products, and so on. However, we may also refer to preventing a Soviet first strike at our defense installations and population centers as being in the national interest. Yet, the two are
obviously issues of entirely different orders, though both may truly be described
as being in the national interest.

In what morally relevant ways are they different? Is it just that one
outcome—nuclear war—is dramatically more unpleasant than the other—absence
of inexpensive goods? I think the difference clearly goes beyond this in the
following way: assuming the United States is not involved in, or about to undertake, unwarranted belligerence against other nations, the difference consists
precisely in the difference between satisfying something that is an interest only,
and protecting something that is a right as well as an interest. The difference I
am emphasizing is the difference between promoting the national interest by
guaranteeing that inexpensive durable materials and suitable energy sources are
available, and promoting the national interest by protecting the rights to security
of the nation's citizens. The former promotes a national good by satisfying
widely held preferences; the latter promotes a national good by guaranteeing
that citizens can in fact enjoy their rights. Both types of goods are in the
national interest but they do not stand on the same moral foundations. On
whatever account of human rights one accepts, some of which are depicted in
other chapters of this volume,[3] it is a violation of those rights to launch an unprovoked attack on civilian population centers.

I do not intend to imply, of course, that protection from unprovoked attacks is the only right that Americans enjoy. The list of genuine rights is surely
broader. I need not designate the scope of this list to make the point that the
concept of the national interest as currently used includes in one bundle at
least two very different kinds of things: (1) matters that are in the national

interest because they pertain to the satisfactions of citizens but do not involve the protection or promotion of their rights; and (2) matters that are in the national interest because they affect in significant ways the rights of American citizens.

At the policy level the treacherous breadth and homogeneity of the concept of the national interest serve as the intellectual rationale for widespread overt and covert policies designed to protect and promote that interest. It is difficult to overestimate the damage to ourselves and others that has been wrought in the name of the national interest. From Watergate to Chile to Vietnam and in countless other areas, the "national interest" has been invoked to justify policies and individual acts that would not have appeared justified if it had been explicitly recognized that we have been eroding or eliminating the rights of our own citizens or those of the citizens of other nations in the pursuit of policies that even on the most charitable interpretation were undertaken in the pursuit of mere interests. These abuses spring, at least in part, from the inherent lack of discrimination in the concept. As long as the national interest can be advanced by the satisfaction of preferences that are not also rights, it can be thought to justify nearly any policy which might enhance the well-being of Americans.

In the next section I wish to show why the widely held belief that human rights regarding policies should be constrained by the national interest reverses the proper relation by which the one concept should serve as the basis for constraints on the other.

The National Interest over Human Rights?

I will argue in this section that one nation should not simultaneously and consistently take as a goal of its policies protecting and/or enhancing the human rights of the citizens of other nations and allow considerations of national interest that are not also rights to override actions otherwise conducive to the protection and promotion of human rights.

At least two occasions where rights regarding objectives can conflict with the national interest are: (1) when the United States is supplying—and it is in our interest so to supply—some technology or techniques which are directly or indirectly being used to subvert human rights (for example, electronic devices being used in torture); and (2) when the United States, by withholding (or threatening to withhold) something deemed desirable by another country, could be influential in improving the behavior of the government of that country as that behavior bears on human rights, but withholding the things in question would be detrimental to the national interest of the United States. An example of this could be withholding helicopters desired by a regime when the sales could have positive effects on U.S. balance of payments and employment.

As the chapters in the preceding section of this volume make clear, there is considerable debate over the criteria to be employed in deciding what should be regarded as a human right. Further, as the chapters by Bedau, Beitz, and Shue amply illustrate, answering the question of which rights satisfy those criteria requires a complex set of arguments and judgments. In what follows I assume that there are at least some human rights—I need not decide which they are; and that standards can be specified for setting aside the spurious rights claims from the genuine rights claims.

I will assume that it is an uncontroversial feature of a right (whatever the most defensible list of rights turns out to be) that a right, to use Ronald Dworkin's phrase, can serve as a veto over an interest.[4] That is, a right cannot be set aside for the purpose of satisfying or advancing something which is an interest only, or for reasons of promoting overall social utility.

An example will illustrate how rights serve as a veto over interests. Take two individuals; one person is blind and the other person has perfect vision in both eyes. It is very much in the interest of the blind person to have a donation of a healthy eye from the person who is not blind, and his interest in receiving the eye which would then restore sight to him far outweighs the loss to the person who would be giving up the one eye. While the latter's vision would be impaired, he is not rendered blind or anything close to it. But one could not reasonably argue that the overall increase in welfare outweighs the right of the sighted individual who can see to keep both of his eyes. For we believe that a person has a right to bodily integrity that outweighs the overall increase in welfare that might result from a more efficient distribution of bodily parts.

Dworkin states this point in a general form:

It follows from the definition of a right that it cannot be outweighed by all social goals. We might, for simplicity, stipulate not to call any political aim a right unless it has a certain threshold weight against collective goals in general; unless, for example, it cannot be defeated by appeal to any of the ordinary routine goals of political administration, but only by a goal of special urgency.[5]

As the blind/sighted analogy suggests, Dworkin's definition is correct to indicate that it is part of what we mean by a right that it cannot be overridden by an interest that does not enjoy some kind of special urgency. The nature of rights themselves serves as a constraint on the pursuit of interests. We can state this principle as follows: In every case of conflict between the promotion of an interest to which no one has a right and the promotion of a right, the right takes priority over the mere interest. I will call this the rights over interests principle.

What is it about human rights that gives them this special status? It is that they are human rights: to disregard them is to treat the rights-holder not as a person but as a thing. It is no accident that traditional rights theorists take liberty to be a central right because liberty in the sense of being able to set and pursue goals for oneself is a defining feature of what we mean by human personhood. Rights thus serve to designate the boundaries of being a person, boundaries which serve as a shield.

What then can override a right? The question makes sense, of course, only to those who do not believe that rights are also absolute, for if they were absolute nothing could override them.

"Special urgency" (to use Dworkin's phrase), I should like to argue, refers to circumstances like war or the clear and present danger thereof, actual or highly likely widespread civil disorder, dire threats to essential natural systems such as the water supply, and so on. What these circumstances have in common is that they involve setting aside some rights, for instance freedom of movement or of the press, in order to secure other rights placed for one reason or another in a position of priority. If the relation between rights and interests is properly characterized by Dworkin, and if what justifies setting aside some rights is appeals to others, then only rights may override rights. I will call this the rights over rights principle.

When we can promote the human rights of the citizens of other nations we cannot fail to use the effective means at our disposal because they conflict with elements of our national interest to which we have no right. This is by no means the same as saying that we should put the rights of the citizens of other nations ahead of, or even necessarily on an equal footing with, some rights of American citizens. It is to say that we cannot pass up opportunities to promote effectively human rights abroad merely by showing that it is in the national interest to do so. In applying the rights over interests principle to foreign policy the qualification "consistent pattern of gross violations" should be added to avoid imposing the obligations of monitoring every form of human intercourse—which is practically impossible—and responding to single transgressions against rights—which would render foreign policy chaotic.

A critic might concede that the rights over interest principle does imply that the rights of the citizens of other nations should serve a *constraint* on pursuing the national interest. That is, we should not pursue our national interest in ways that impair the rights of the citizens of other nations. However, he might argue that it is a very modest claim: it is quite a different thing to assert that, when our duty to *promote* rights conflicts with our national interest, promoting rights should take precedence.[6] This criticism depends on the distinction between causing harm and failing to prevent it. It is taken to be morally different to cause harm than to fail to prevent it effectively when the means to prevent it are at one's disposal.

I do not need to deny the general importance of this distinction to show why it does not undercut the rights over interest principle. Why is this so? For the purpose of argument suppose that there are positive rights of some sort, rights that entitle one to receive something—for example, income. If there are any such rights there is no distinction between respecting a right and promoting it when a person is lacking it. What would it mean to respect someone's right to income unless we tried to provide it or insure that he or she had the means to attain it? In the case of positive rights the way to respect them is to promote them.

In the case of forbearance rights the distinction between causing and failing to prevent harm may appear to be more applicable. It may appear that we can respect a right without promoting it simply by leaving the rights-holder alone. But as Henry Shue[7] has pointed out, respecting at least some forbearance rights may be indistinguishable from promoting them. In the case of having a right to free speech, for instance, respecting that right will involve establishing institutions with the legal authority and power to prevent one person from under-cutting the right of some other person to exercise that right. In a word, respecting the right involves promoting it.

It follows from this that we may not justifiably pass up opportunities to protect and promote the rights of the citizens of other nations simply because it is in the national interest to do so.

In what follows I will consider two objections. First, that the principle cannot be applied in practice; and second, that it is too strong.

Can the Principle Be Applied?

However, a serious complication arises in the application of this principle. Some nations that are human rights violators have shown a resistance to being deterred from their practices by threats that U.S. assistance will be withheld because of knowledge that the assistance can be obtained elsewhere. What if a decision on the part of the United States to refuse to sell helicopters to Argentina be-cause of its human rights record simply induced that nation to turn to a French manufacturer to purchase similar equipment? Under these circumstances the threat has no effect, and it is likely to be detrimental to U.S. interests such as maintaining a favorable balance of payments, and high levels of employment in the aircraft and related industires. Does my argument oblige us to undertake such pointless sacrifices? (I do not rule out that we might want to make such sacrifices simply to avoid complicity.)

I think not. In the first place the conclusion only requires that we must not waive *effective* opportunities to promote human rights simply because it is in the national interest to do so. But here it might appear that the exceptions will swallow the rule. That is, it could be argued, at least in regard to security assistance, that the rights over interests principle will find few if any applications because of the multiplicity of suppliers of arms. (Similar arguments could be made in regard to economic assistance if nations could easily secure such assis-tance from numerous sources.)

But this view overemphasizes the exception to the principle. Acting in accordance with the principle in regard to such claims would require shifting the burden of proof to those who would stress the ineffectiveness of U.S. threats of terminated or reduced assistance to demonstrate that options are open to other nations such that U.S. leverage is undercut. Moreover, the principle requires that we cannot fail to pressure third parties who engage in arms exports to exert their leverage in reducing human rights abuses simply because it is not in the U.S. national interest to exert such leverage unilaterally. A justifying excuse could be advanced along these lines only by showing that exerting such pressure will be ineffective or is likely to undermine the rights of Americans.

These complications do suggest that the United States may properly fail to protect and promote human rights in the name of the national interest only when there is clear evidence that attempts to influence alternative suppliers would endanger the rights of Americans and not their interests only. Truly ineffective sacrifice is not required by the rights over interests principle, but difficult obligations are imposed in insuring that bilateral and multilateral attempts to secure leverage have been exhausted.

Is the Principle too Strong?

Another objection to the principle, which points in a different direction, might well stress that the principle commits us to too much. A critic might ask: Doesn't the principle impose an obligation to intervene in a large number of nations worldwide? Wasn't the idea of the United States as the world's policeman adequately discredited by the Vietnam War?

I do not believe the principle is overreaching in this manner for four reasons. First, a large number of the world's nations are not significant human rights violators and hence no action is required in regard to them. Second, and more importantly, the principle as I have stated it does not require that we sacrifice the rights of Americans to secure the rights of the citizens of other nations. It is much weaker than this, requiring only that we not fail to promote rights when there is a conflict between promoting rights and something to which we have an interest only. For instance, conscripted foreign wars are not required to promote the rights of the citizens of other nations because of the effects of such wars on the rights of those who unwillingly serve in them.

Of course, tracing all the implications of the rights over interests principle for foreign policy would require specifying a list of genuine human rights, and describing the order and the nature of the relation between them when the rights themselves come into conflict with each other.

Third, we should not lose sight of the fact that the principle is a rights-regarding principle. It does not commit us to foreign policies such as the Vietnam War which may violate more rights of more individuals than they protect.

Exactly where interests only leave off and rights begin will obviously involve some difficult line-drawing problems and will depend upon exactly what list of rights one accepts. I only wish to show in what follows that—and this is my fourth point—the rights over interests principle does not impose an endless list of obligations. There is a symmetry in respect to obligations and excuses: the broader the list of rights of others one accepts the wider is the list of rights of one's own citizens that can figure in justifiable excuses for not discharging those obligations. For instance, if citizens of other nations have economic rights then *comparable* economic rights of Americans need not be sacrificed to protect or promote those rights.

There is, however, a difficult related problem as to whether citizens have *special* rights in respect to their government which can override the *human* rights of others. It might be claimed, for instance, that, insofar as governmental legitimacy is based on tacit consent, certain promises are implied between the governed and governing. These promises might take the form, for instance, of promises to advance the interests of the citizens. The U.S. government might be thought to have the duty to promote the interests of Americans in a stable supply of petroleum over the human rights of Iranians.

I am not prepared to say that special rights (for example, those that exist between family members) can never override human rights. However, I do believe that two responses are possible. First, while I would accept that some promises do create rights in the person to whom the promise is made I would point out that persons and governments are not necessarily justified in making all the promises they do make either explicitly or tacitly. Certain promises are unjustified because they conflict with other values which enjoy some greater moral authority. Thus even if there are such promises between governments and citizens their existence alone would not be sufficient to show that these promise-generated obligations are stronger than those to promote or enhance human rights.

I am not prepared to say where the boundary on legitimate promises between the government and its citizens ought to be. To do so would require an account of how intranational obligations are weighted when they conflict with international obligations. To my knowledge the theoretical work which would be required to justify criteria for such decisions has not been done.

However, I think we can state where the burden of proof ought to be. We can presume that one cannot justifiably promise to disregard the human rights of another person unless one's promise is to protect one's own human rights or those of another. For instance, one could justifiably promise to serve in a war against an aggressor which would violate some rights of some persons. But one cannot justifiably promise to disregard the human rights of another person unless another human right is at stake because that is precisely to deny the humanity of that person whose rights are disregarded.

In light of this last objection the rights over interests principle can be slightly modified to state: It may be presumed that in every case of conflict between the promotion of an interest to which no one has a right and the promotion of a right, the right takes priority over the mere interest. A government can justifiably disregard this presumption only in the unlikely event that it could be shown that explicit or tacit promises between a government and its people could appropriately disregard the rights of other individuals in the name of mere interests of its citizens. Of course, it should be remembered that on the basis of what I have argued we are *not* obliged to sacrifice the rights of American citizens to protect the rights of the citizens of other nations.

Conclusion

The language of Section 502B states that effective opportunities for improving the human rights record in other countries can be ignored if it is in the national interest to do so. There are two problems with this point of view. First, it invokes an amorphous concept which, as I have argued, conceals important moral differences. Second, if interests cannot be traded off against rights, this is a mistaken way of expressing what is in part a legitimate concern.

The United States has an interest in a number of things, including access to reliable raw material markets at low prices, strategic stability, ready access to consumers in other nations, and so on. While by all accounts we have a right to national security, few would argue that we have a *right* to coffee at $2.00 a pound, or to dump wheat abroad without regard to its effect on domestic markets in other nations—though pursuing such objectives or engaging in such actions may be in the national interest.

We can avoid the ambiguities involved in the concept of national interest, and appropriately express our true regard for human rights by requiring in legislation or in subsequent policy that the opportunity to improve the human rights situation in other nations can be set aside only when such policies would adversely affect the rights of Americans.[8] This, of course, leaves open the task of setting out criteria for distinguishing spurious human rights claims from the genuine, as well as specifying the priorities among rights. Such work, especially in the area of international relations, is a formidable endeavor. If this paper has been successful in undercutting the careless use of the concept of the national interest in these circumstances, it has accomplished enough for now.

Notes

1. Daniel Yergin, *Shattered Peace: The Origins of the Cold War and the National Security State* (Boston: Houghton Mifflin Co., 1977), p. 196.
2. How, in ambiguous situations, do we determine what is in the national

interest? One view, and the one to which I want to take exception, is that we can count on the political process to bring to the attention of elected officials how various groups would like foreign policy to enhance or protect their interests. I call this view "interest group decision-making," for it implies that we can maximize the collective interest by insuring that the political process is responsive to various groups that come forward in behalf of their own interest. On this view, one does not need any systematic understanding of what the public interest is, but can trust to hitting on this interest by letting the political process run its course.

A problem with this point of view can be illustrated with an example. It is strongly in the interest of the steel industry to see to protective tariffs to curtail the importation of lower priced foreign steel into the United States. Instituting these tariffs simply means higher profits. Consequently, they will engage in well-organized and probably expensive attempts to convince Congress and executive agencies of the need for tariffs. If they are successful, the price of steel will be higher than it otherwise would have been, and consumers will pay a slightly higher price for products containing steel. Yet the disadvantage of the tariffs to any given consumer will be slight compared to the enormous advantage to the industry of having the tariffs. As a consequence it is not in the interests of consumers to undergo time and money costs associated with opposing—or seeking the repeal of—the tariff. However, it could easily be the case that lower prices for steel could contribute to the overall well-being of the citizens.

We can generalize from this example to support the following position: highly organized special interest groups can take advantage of the high cost of forming a coalition to oppose them to press successfully for policies which will deviate substantially from the national interest. It follows from this that insofar as we rely on interest group decision-making we can count on an oversupply of policies that are not in the national interest.

3. See Bedau, Beitz, and Shue especially.

4. Ronald Dworkin, *Taking Rights Seriously* (Cambridge, Mass.: Harvard University Press, 1977)

5. Ibid., p. 92.

6. See Douglas MacLean's chapter in this volume.

7. Henry Shue, *Basic Rights: A Philosophical Perspective on Some Foreign Policy Choices* (forthcoming), chapter 2.

8. Introducing such language in legislation might make coalition formation difficult or impossible.

12 Monitoring Human Rights Violations: How Good is the Information?

John Salzberg

In this chapter I will describe and evaluate the sources of information available to the Congress in the field of human rights and explore whether there might be additional sources of information for Congress to utilize. I will begin by focusing on the information utilized by the Subcommittee on International Organizations of the House Committee on Foreign Affairs. This subcommittee, which was chaired by Congressman Donald M. Fraser from 1971 to 1978 and for which I served as a staff consultant, is the only committee of the Congress which has held extensive hearings in the human rights field. It is fair to assert, therefore, that it is the only congressional committee which has systematically acquired information on the status of human rights in particular countries. Later in the chapter I will discuss the information provided to Congress by the Department of State. It consists of annual reports that the department has been required, since 1976, to present to Congress on the human rights conditions in each country that receives security assistance from the United States.

The Fraser Subcommittee began its heavy emphasis on human rights in August 1973. A first series of hearings, from August to December 1973, consisted of fifteen hearings and approximately forty-five witnesses. The subcommittee focused both on general problems in the international protection of human rights and measures to improve the effectiveness of international organizations in this field, as well as the situations in a number of particular countries. Following these hearings, a report with recommendations was adopted by the subcommittee.

Since those initial hearings, the subcommittee has continued to look into individual country situations. Since 1973 the subcommittee has held over 150 hearings.

In addition to receiving testimony from the Department of State and other government witnesses, the subcommittee has received testimony from a variety of public witnesses. Public witnesses have included representatives of non-governmental organizations (many of whom had recently undertaken a field investigation of the situation in the particular country under study), exiles from the country (many of whom had been deported because of their active defense of human rights), U.S. missionaries abroad who were closely identified with and knowledgeable of the human rights movement in particular countries, professors with special knowledge of the country concerned, former U.S.

government officials, and members of Congress who may have visited the
country concerned.

Public Witnesses

I will discuss briefly each of these categories of public witnesses. Each kind
of witness has its own virtues as well as its own difficulties.

1. Nongovernmental Organizations. The nongovernmental organization representatives may be roughly divided into two subcategories. First, there are those
witnesses representing international human rights organizations. The subcommittee has received testimony from three such organizations: Amnesty International, the International Commission of Jurists, and the International League
for Human Rights.

The subcommittee has received testimony from Amnesty International
concerning Chile, South Korea, Uruguay, Paraguay, and the Philippines. In all
of these cases, Amnesty International had sent a mission to the country and the
witness was a member of that mission. The witness reported to the subcommittee the findings of the mission. Obviously, in that situation, the subcommittee usually agreed to receive testimony from Amnesty International prior
to the mission's departure for the country in question. In one instance, the
publication of the mission's report was timed to coincide with the testimony,
thus increasing the press attention to the mission's report.

The International Commission of Jurists has testified before the subcommittee on the situations in Chile, Iran, and South Africa. With respect to Chile
and Iran, the testimony was based on a recent field mission to those countries.

The International League for Human Rights testified before the subcom-
mittee on Paraguay. (Former Deputy Assistant Secretary of State for Inter-
American Affairs Ben Stephansky and Professor Robert Alexander of Rutgers
University conducted the field mission.)

The relationship between the subcommittee and the international nongovernmental organizations has been one of mutual benefit. The subcommittee
obviously benefits by having firsthand accounts of the human rights situations
presented by organizations with a well-respected international reputation. At
the same time, testifying before the Congress has helped the organizations get
their viewpoint across not only to the Congress, but through the Congress to the
Department of State. Through testifying before Congress, it is likely that the
organizations' views are given more credibility and importance by the Department of State.

The second subcategory of nongovernmental witnesses are the churches,
particularly the Catholic and Protestant denominations. The subcommittee
has received testimony from the U.S. Catholic Conference, the National Council

of Churches, as well as individual Protestant denominations. Testimony from the U.S. Catholic Conference has focused particularly on Latin America, where the Church is frequently in the forefront of the human rights movement. The National Council of Churches testified on the South Korean situation, where the Protestant church is under government attack. B'nai B'rith of the Anti-Defamation League spoke on anti-Semitism in Argentina.

2. U.S. Missionaries. U.S. missionaries who have lived for extended periods of time in the country under study have also testified before the Fraser Subcommittee. Frequently these missionaries have been closely supportive of dissident factions in the country and hence are intimately aware of the repressive nature of the regime. Compared with the persons whose firsthand knowledge is based on a short-term field visit, missionaries are obviously in a position to speak with greater knowledge about the situation. A number of witnesses were themselves the victims of oppression. Revered Philip Devlin and Reverend Daniel Panchot were both detained in Chile, Reverend Francisco Gilchrest was detained in Paraguay, and Father James Weeks was detained in Argentina. Although none of these persons were tortured, some were mistreated and witnessed the torture of others. Fred Morris, a former Methodist missionary, who at the time of his arrest was a free-lance journalist and businessman, was tortured in Brazil. Father James Sinnott and Reverend George Ogle were two missionaries in South Korea who were expelled from that country for their identification with the human rights movement. Because their own lives have been affected by government oppression, these witnesses provide human interest in the situation. Their testimony frequently attracts interest by the press.

3. Exiled Nationals. The subcommittee has received testimony from at least fifteen persons exiled from the country concerning which they are invited to testify. These persons testified on the following countries: Chile, Indonesia, Soviet Union, Iran, El Salvador, India, Uruguay, and Argentina. Some were political prisoners in their country; others served as defense lawyers for political dissidents; others were opposition political party leaders. All were steadfastly in opposition to their government, but most could be vigorously defended as being credible in their criticism of their government. Their intimate knowledge of the human rights situation in their own country, as well as the dramatic upheaval in their own lives as a result of their defense of human rights, make their testimony particularly convincing and moving.

Obviously, the subcommittee needs to be especially careful to check the testimony from exiles for accuracy and for impartiality. Given their personal involvement and the unhappy circumstances which caused them to leave their country of origin, some of these witnesses may be prone to exaggerate in criticizing their country's government. However, their testimony can be counterchecked for accuracy through questions by the chairman or other members of the subcommittee, through comparison with testimony of other public witnesses, and through balancing their testimony with countertestimony from other witnesses who are known to be favorably inclined toward the government concerned.

4. Progovernment Nationals.   The witnesses in each of the categories already discussed almost invariably have been critical of the governments concerning which they are testifying. If the subcommittee received testimony from only these witnesses, it might be said to be willing to hear only the negative perspective on the country in question. Therefore, the subcommittee has frequently received testimony from witnesses who either argue that human rights are not being seriously violated or that the violations are a necessary evil, due to extenuating circumstances. The views of these witnesses often coincide with the positions taken by the government in explaining its human rights performance. The only drawback in this practice is that many of the progovernment witnesses are so uncritical of their government that they have little credibility. Often these witnesses are selected upon recommendation of the government's embassy in Washington, and are nationals of the country. These witnesses are also planning to return to their country, and because of the nature of many of the governments studied by the subcommittee, this fact would, in itself, dissuade most persons from criticizing their government, even if they so desired.

It is worth noting that among non-U.S. nationals only a very few critics of their governments have testified and returned to their country. Father Fernando Cardinal of Nicaragua was one such witness. As a result of his testimony, he was highly criticized by progovernment forces in his country and threatened with dismissal from his university teaching position. Fortunately, this was not carried out. Other persons, who were *not* returning to their countries, were nevertheless the victims of other actions: Shrikumar Poddar, an Indian national residing in the United States, had his passport lifted; Gustavo Roca, an Argentine national, was charged in absentia with violating a law which prohibits persons from advocating sanctions against Argentina; Mr. Wilson Ferreira-Aldunate, of Uruguay, was faced with a court suit to confiscate his property.

5. Nonnationals.   The subcommittee has also received testimony from persons who are neither nationals of the United States nor of the country concerning which they are testifying. We had James Dunn of Australia talk about East Timor—a territory acquired by Indonesia through force.

The subcommittee has also relied upon persons from the universities, and others with professional competence relating to the subject under consideration for testimony. Lawyers and political scientists have been most frequently relied upon, as well as anthropologists and area specialists.

6. Former State Department Officials.   A final category of public witness has been the former State Department official. Testimony has been taken, for instance, from the former director of the Office for Korean Affairs, and the legal advisor and the ambassador to El Salvador. Their testimony has provided valuable insight not only into the human rights situation of the country in question, but also into the workings of the Department of State in human rights.

Evaluating the Testimony of Public Witnesses

One of the questions which must be addressed by the subcommittee is how to evaluate the authenticity of the information provided by the nongovernmental organizations and other public witnesses. Probably the most credible sources are the nongovernmental organizations, who are apolitical, who are themselves competent to evaluate human rights, and who have a reputation for being critical of governments of all political persuasions—countries of both the political left and the right. The individuals they select to take part in field missions are persons of reputation and experience and are not partisan in their political affiliations. Generally, their assertions are based on evidence obtained during the course of field missions or from sources of information within the country concerned who are considered to be reliable. Nevertheless, there is no sure litmus test for validating the accuracy or completeness from any public witness. For this reason, the subcommittee usually calls upon several witnesses to testify on the subject. To the extent that their testimony corroborates one another's assertions, this lends validity to the information which they provide.

Moreover, in order to test the accuracy of this information, the subcommittee frequently invites witnesses who are known to take opposite positions. Consequently, we invite persons who will assert that violations in human rights do not exist in a particular country, or do not exist on the same scale as is alleged by other persons or organizations. The accuracy and completeness of this kind of testimony must be given the same scrutiny. Judgment as to which testimony is providing a more accurate description of the human rights situation in a country is determined by comparing the credibility of the various testimonies. Thus, an evaluation of the quality of the information is determined through an advocacy situation, with competing sources of information vying for acceptance.

Whether the testimony by the public witnesses represents isolated occurrences of human rights violations, or whether it suggest a consistent pattern of gross violations of human rights is one of the difficult questions the subcommittee must determine. It is only when the latter conditions are met that a country becomes ineligible for military aid and possibly development aid. Most of the testimony before the Fraser Subcommittee concerns patterns of violations, and not isolated incidents. The non-governmental organizations generally present a wide range of information and incidents. Moreover, they provide documentation which suggests that the violations of human rights are a consequence of governmental indifference or governmental complicity in the practices being reported.

U.S. Department of State Testimony

In most instances, testimony from public witnesses precedes testimony from the Department of State. This practice enables the subcommittee to have the benefit of outside sources of information, as well as opinions concerning U.S. policy, prior to reviewing testimony from the department. In requesting testimony from the department, the subcommittee will often send a list of written questions for written response by the department prior to the hearing. The responses are either contained in a separate document or appear in the opening statement delivered by the department witness at the hearing. Questions usually concern such matters as the status of human rights in the country concerned, including the incidence of torture, arbitrary detention, violations of due process, freedom of the press, and so on. The subcommittee also frequently asks about the nature of U.S. assistance programs and how the status of human rights affects our relations with the government in question. The questions serve to direct and focus the subcommittee's attention and to indicate to the department its particular concerns. Receiving the department's answers to these questions prior to the hearing enables the subcommittee to obtain some knowledge of the department's positions prior to the hearing, and can help to sharpen the questions addressed at the hearing.

During the Nixon and Ford administrations, the subcommittee on International Organizations was frequently frustrated in its efforts to obtain frank and complete testimony from the department on human rights violations in particular countries. The department has two competing objectives: to provide an honest and open account to the Congress on the status of human rights, while maintaining friendly relations with the country concerned. The latter objective often outweighs the priority of giving Congress complete information.[1] Referring particularly to the department under Secretary Henry Kissinger, Mr. Patrick Breslin of the Carnegie Endowment reported: "State [Department] frequently sought to keep Congress in the dark about human rights violations by regimes receiving U.S. aid . . . . State often appeared before Congress as an apologist for the abuses of dictators . . . . State seemed generally more defensive about a nation's human rights record the more the United States was associated with its regime." He noted that the State Department was forceful and its criticism of such regimes as Cuba and North Korea but defensive and evasive with respect to U.S. aligned countries such as Iran, Nicaragua, Paraguay, and Uruguay. He did acknowledge that occasionally the department would come out with a more critical statement of an aligned country, such as testimony on South Korea in 1974, but these appear to be the exceptions.

Although it is true that the Carter administration has been more explicit and frank about human rights violations in many countries, its record is not even. In 1977 the subcommittee received testimony from the department on the situations in El Salvador, Cambodia, Indonesia (East Timor), and Thailand. The department gave quite a candid account about El Salvador, departing from past practice of the Inter-American Bureau, which had been particularly protective of its client states. Deputy Secretary Charles Bray referred, *inter alia,* to the occurrence of abritrary arrests and detentions, the forced exile of opposition party candidates, and the department's "disquiet" at the suspension of certain rights following the elections in that country. As would be expected, given our absence of diplomatic relations with Cambodia, testimony by the department was particularly frank and specific. Normally the department is very reluctant to estimate the number of deaths or incidents of torture in another country; however, in this case, the department stated that deaths had been in the tens of thousands, if not hundreds of thousands. In an unprecedented move, the department permitted testimony by a junior officer from our embassy in Bangkok who is watching events in Cambodia. He detailed the information he obtained from interviewing thousands of Cambodian refugees.

A negative impression of the department's frankness on human rights testimony may be gained by reading its testimony on East Timor, a province Indonesia acquired by force. Whereas, with respect to Cambodia, the department felt competent to estimate the number of deaths since the Communists took control, it was considerably more reserved with respect to the East Timor conflict. Initially the department estimate was "a few thousand," then it was revised to "under 10,000." Despite its assertion that it had little information to make an estimate, it remained convinced that estimates of deaths at more than 10,000 were "greatly exaggerated." More significantly, the department has chosen to accept Indonesia's acquisition of East Timor by force, and the denial of the Timorese people's right of self-determination. U.S. interests in maintaining friendly relations with Indonesia have been the explanation for ignoring this situation.

Testimony on Thailand sought to put the best possible light on the military takeover and the severe restrictions on human rights. An effort was made to disassociate the military takeover from the violence governmental and quasi-governmental forces had inflicted upon the demonstrators at Thammasat University. Rather than acknowledging a political prisoner population, the department asserted that most persons arrested since the coup have been "petty criminals."

State Department Reports

Largely in response to congressional pressure for better information on the status of human rights in particular countries, the department began in 1974 to require from the embassies of all aid-recipient countries a report on the status of human rights. These reports were classified and hence were not of much value to congressional committees. In 1976 the Congress attached a formal reporting requirement to the human rights and security assistance provision of the Foreign Assistance Act. As part of the congressional presentation of materials for the security assistance requests, the department was required to prepare a report on the status of human rights in each security assistance-recipient country. The first reports were issued early in 1977.

As in the hearings, the reports tended to shy away from reaching conclusions concerning the severity of human rights violations in particular countries. Emphasis was placed on recounting the allegations of international human rights organizations—such as Amnesty International, the International Commission of Jurists, and Freedom House—without the department's reaching its own conclusions.

Also, the Congress has unfortunately not taken the opportunity to review and criticize the accuracy of the reports. The only explanation that can be provided for this omission is the pressing nature of other demands upon the time of the committees. The Subcommittee on International Organizations did ask the Congressional Research Service of the Library of Congress to prepare human rights reports on fifteen countries. Many of these countries are security assistance recipients; others were leftist, totalitarian countries such as North Korea and the Soviet Union. These reports provide a brief review of political events in the country and a description of the status of human rights, including such questions as torture, prolonged detention, and due process. The information is based to a considerable extent on the congressional hearings, but also on nongovernmental reports and press accounts. The CRS reports are library research pieces and did not involve sending a staff to the countries to obtain firsthand information. The reports also review U.S. government response to the human rights situation.

The CRS reports were, unfortunately, issued several months after the State Department issued its reports. The subcommittee has issued a new request to the CRS to prepare reports on a selected number of countries, approximately fifteen, which are to be issued at the same time the department issues its new reports. Under the recent legislation adopted by the Congress, the department reports now include both security assistance-recipient countries as well as development assistance-recipient countries. The first such reports, which were also the first administration reports prepared wholly by the Carter administration, were issued in January 1978. Although showing some improvement, these State Department reports have also been criticized for having the same shortcomings as previous reports. They are biased in favor of assistance-recipient countries, and they are incomplete both in the rights they discuss and in their unwillingness to draw conclusions. Clearly the department needs to reach its own conclusions on the state of human rights in aid-recipient countries. It is not adequate simply to cite the conclusions of nongovernmental organizations and other sources.

David Weissbrodt, in an article entitled "Human Rights Legislation and U.S. Foreign Policy,"[2] makes a number of criticisms of the State Department reports, including the department's uncritical reliance on information provided by the aid-recipient governments. He also points out that the primary emphasis in these reports is placed on the integrity of the person rights, notwithstanding the fact that the amendment asks them to report their information concerning human rights and fundamental freedoms in general. These are fair and reasonable criticisms of the State Department reports.

Moreover, it would be useful for the Congress to engage in a more critical review of the department reports, since this is probably the best remedy for discouraging incomplete or inaccurate reporting. There is no question that the reporting requirement is generally not enthusiastically received by the department. Very likely, the reports would not be issued at all unless they were required by Congress. On the other hand, the reporting requirement does give the department an opportunity to speak frankly about human rights practices in particular countries, which it might not do except if it were required. There may very well be incidents where the department would like to speak publicly on the human rights conditions in a specific country but is reluctant to do it voluntarily. The reporting requirement thus provides the opportunity for public and critical comments. The aid-recipient government also, of course, may undertake some positive measures to improve its human rights practices if it knows that a forthcoming report is going to be issued by the department on the human rights situation in its country.

International Organizations

Congress has made relatively little use of reports by international organizations on human rights conditions. An exception would be Chile, which has been the subject of special reports by the OAS as well as various U.N. agencies, including the Commission on Human Rights. Part of the reason for this is the fact that the United Nations fails to review, in most instances, serious violations of human rights in particular countries. The OAS Inter-American Commission on Human Rights has been better in this regard. One limitation which might be borne in mind is that, because of the separateness of international organizations from individual governments, it would be difficult to have those organizations formally testify before a committee of Congress. It might be possible to have persons who serve on these commissions testify, provided they testified in their personal capacity.

Prospects for Obtaining New Sources of Information

In summary, the Congress has both increased the utilization of already existing sources of information and has sought to add new sources. Obviously, prior to the congressional and executive branch interest in human rights the nongovernmental organizations, exiles, American missionaries, and other sources of information were in existence. The congressional interest has increased the public attention and the importance placed upon these sources, both by the Department of State as well as by the governments involved, which are both criticized as well as praised in these reports. It may very well be that because of the congressional as well as executive branch interest in the findings of these organizations, they are now obtaining greater financial resources to undertaken their work. The Ford Foundation's recent funding in this area is a case in point.

In 1978 Congressmen Fraser and Dante B. Fascell introduced a bill[3] to establish an Institute for Human Rights and Freedom. This institute would administer a modest amount of public funds to support nongovernmental organizations and individuals working in the human rights field. The Committee on Foreign Affairs adopted legislation to establish the Institute. Unfortunately, it was defeated on the floor of the House. The Senate Committee on Foreign Relations held a hearing on the question of establishing such an institute but did not take legislative action. Given the meager resources of most nongovernmental organizations, such an institute could be very helpful, provided political considerations could be divorced from the commission's operations. A suggestion has also been made that such an institute itself could prepare reports on individual country situations, just as the Commission on Civil Rights prepares reports on the status of civil rights in this country. Given the hesitancy of the Department of State to issue frank reports, because of the political effects such reports would inevitably have on our foreign relations, an institute with a quasi-autonomous nature might be able to speak with more frankness.

Notes

1. The Carnegie Endowment for International Peace did an extensive study of Departmental testimony on human rights and reached similar conclusions. (See "Human Rights: Rhetoric or Action?" by Patrick Breslin, *Washington Post,* February 27, 1977, p. C1.

2. *Georgia Journal of International and Comparative Law,* 7 (1977), 263-274.

3. H.R. 11326, introduced March 7, 1978. See Congressman Fraser's discussion of this institute in "Freedom and Foreign Policy," *Foreign Policy,* No. 26 (1977), 155ff.

13 Human Rights Violations and U.S. Foreign Assistance: The Latin American Connection

William L. Wipfler

One major unscientific obstacle confronts any study that establishes the conclusion that the United States consciously or unconsciously, contributes to the violation of human rights elsewhere. It is the myth of the inherent goodness and ultimate triumph of American moral values, which continues to be generally accepted in spite of the barrage of revelations that document questionable involvements in destabilizations and coups, in drug experiments and assassination attempts, in the organized violation of the rights of U.S. citizens through unwarranted surveillance and other invasions of privacy, and in even more violent acts against those who protested the war in Vietnam or demanded their civil rights. The myth portrays the United States as an exception in the midst of a violent and immoral world, generally motivated by good intentions, and only occasionally guilty of an error in judgment. Objective data that demonstrate the participation of the United States or its representatives in deplorable undertakings are frequently rejected, filed away, or hidden under the veil of national security because they represent an assault on the myth.

It is the purpose of this study to demonstrate that in at least one important area of the world the myth is unfounded, that in fact U.S. foreign assistance tends to support human rights violators. I will show why an honest assessment of the intentions and goals of U.S. assistance programs will show why any credible and effective linkage of foreign assistance to human rights conditions will require many profound changes in the objectives and the conduct of U.S. foreign policy. Such conclusions are not apparent from the data alone, which are in any case difficult to interpret. Even where they demonstrate strong trends in U.S. support of gross violators of human rights, thus suggesting a marked U.S. preference for granting aid to repressive regimes, the data often fail to account for the factors that motivate the decisions to provide such assistance. Such data likewise fail to indicate whether certain elements in the relationship between the United States and aid recipients exacerbate the human rights problems in those countries. My aim is to make explicit some of these factors in order to show how promoting human rights turns out to be inconsistent with some other U.S. foreign policy goals.

Specific situations in certain countries are discussed elsewhere in this volume. I shall discuss a general trend that is evidenced in a geographic region: Latin America. That broad a perspective is necessary in order to reveal broad and general tendencies that sustain the conclusion that the United States tends to support human rights violators. Further, I shall discuss other evidence that demonstrates that this tendency is consistent with the intentions of U.S. policy-makers, rather than existing in spite of those intentions.

It is common knowledge that U.S. aid to Latin America has flowed heavily to some of the worst violators of human rights. Our unabashed support of the military junta in Chile was, in fact, the single most important case for focusing public attention on the problem of U.S. complicity with governments that were grossly violating human rights. In other countries, too, such as Brazil, Argentina, and Guatemala, where reports on human rights conditions have been most depressing, it turns out that U.S. relations with the governments of these countries have been very friendly, and they are at the top of the lists of recip-ients of our bilateral economic and military assistance in Latin America.[1]

Once we confront the facts that show U.S. foreign assistance flowing to some of the Latin American governments which engage in gross violations of internationally recognized human rights as defined by aid legislation, the more difficult questions of causation arise. Is the selection of repressive governments purposeful? What benefits accrue to the United States by this selection? Does U.S. foreign aid stimulate the violation of human rights? Is foreign assistance a reward to a repressive government for providing some advantage to the U.S. national interest as perceived by the policymakers? How significant is foreign assistance in the complex multilevel relationships between the United States and other nations?

What is necessary to answer these questions is a perspective that considers particular situations as they relate both to regional and global interests of the United States and to the historical situation in Latin America. We must examine the comments and ideas of major actors rather than just "official" policy.

What emerges clearly from such an investigation is that the principal pur-pose of U.S. aid to Latin America has been the creation and maintenance of stable governments in that region. Although the justification for this effort usually refers to both "security" and "development," we shall attempt to keep two questions before us: Whose security? Whose development? These ques-tions are critical and can assist us in discovering what the real motives were in promoting the types of stable governments that have come into being in Latin America. Furthermore, they can help us assess the costs of such a policy inso-far as human rights are concerned.

The early 1960s are a crucial period in the history of U.S.–Latin American relations and of particular importance in the development of the U.S. foreign assistance program to that region. January 1, 1959, marked the victory of the revolutionary forces in Cuba, and a great deal of subsequent U.S. activity was clearly in reaction to that situation. In 1961, President John F. Kennedy an-nounced his Alliance for Progress, a special and highly extolled effort in coopera-tion for the development of Latin America, which ostensibly aimed at social and political reform. At the same time a conscious decision was made to strengthen the police and military of the region. This was clearly in response to the Cuban revolution, but was made at a time when the spirit and trend in Latin America was toward greater democratic change. The then *New York Times* correspondent, Tad Szulc, referred to it as the "twilight of the tyrants." As the Alliance was proposed, elected administrations with at least an expressed desire for social reform governed in Argentina, Bolivia, Brazil, Chile, Colombia, Costa Rica, Honduras, Mexico, Peru, Uruguay, and Venezuela, and the Dominican Republic would join them the following year. A number of them were experienced in democracy, but several were fragile experiments having recently emerged from harsh personalistic or military dictatorships and faced with difficult economic problems. The original thrust of the Alliance for Progress appeared to be designed to respond to the economic concern while reinforcing the democratic trends and the desire for social reform.

In spite of this, the anticommunist paranoia and fear of "another Cuba" were so prevalent at the time that the military of Latin America was identified as the power to back. A U.S. Senate study mission that toured Latin America in late 1961 advised the administration to

> take a more favorable attitude toward the military groups in Latin
> American countries. . . . We are convinced that the military are not
> only the sole forces of stabilization, but they also promote democratic
> institutions and progressive changes of a socio-political nature.[2]

By 1964, with the spate of military coups that would eventually engulf most of Latin America now well underway, President Johnson's Assistant Secretary of State for Latin American Affairs, Thomas Mann, announced a "realistic" U.S. policy that would support any regime compatible with U.S. economic and security interests and opposed to communism. Democratic development, while a necessary element of the rhetoric justifying the continued granting of foreign assistance, was subordinated to the goal of stability.

In view of this and the fact, which is discussed below, that the U.S. business sector was successful in recapturing the economic assistance program as an instrument to facilitate and often subsidize increased private investment, aid to the police and military of Latin American countries takes on more significance. It is apparent that the growing volume of private investment carried with it the concomitant risk of larger losses in the event of radical political change and, therefore, required greater guarantees of protection. Two major elements for meeting this need have been the U.S. Security Assistance Program, which provided grants and credits for military training, arms, and other equipment, and the AID Office of Public Safety, which provided equipment and training to police and internal security forces. The latter program was terminated by the Congress in 1973.

The Office of Public Safety was funded by AID under the general heading of "development assistance." It provided training within the host country for police personnel, special courses of instruction for senior officers at the International Police Academy in Washington, D.C., and made available weapons and specialized equipment for riot control, counterinsurgency, and sophisticated communications. During the decade of the Alliance it expended $50.2 million in Latin America.[3] In his presentation to the Senate Committee on Appropriations in 1965, AID Administrator David Bell described the rationale of OPS. He said:

> Maintenance of law and order, including internal security, is one of the fundamental responsibilities of government. . . .
>
> Successful discharge of this responsibility is imperative if a nation is to establish and maintain the environment of stability and security so essential to economic, social and political progress. . . .
>
> Plainly, the U.S. has very great interests in the creation and maintenance of an atmosphere of law and order . . . When there is need, technical assistance to the police of developing nations to meet their responsibilities promotes and protects these U.S. interests. . . .
>
> In order to deal with the dynamics of internal security situations, the public safety program has developed and utilized methods to deliver to threatened countries, in a matter of days, urgently needed assistance including equipment, training, and technical advice.[4]

By 1970 the OPS program was becoming an embarrassment for the Congress because of the voluminous documentation it was receiving that denounced the gross violation of human rights being perpetrated by the police in a majority of the Latin American countries that were beneficiaries of the OPS. Brazil had been the major recipient of OPS largesse. By the end of FY '70 it had received $7.5 million, 523 officers had received training in the United States, and 100,000 federal and state police had been locally trained by resident public safety advisors in Brazil.[5] In the same year, it became the object of international outrage. Cases of torture, disappearances, and assassinations were documented by the score. Amnesty International, the International Commission of Jurists, and other human rights organizations and major religious bodies in the United States and Europe published reports on the deteriorating situation in Brazil, indicating the responsibility of the police and military. In spite of this, AID presented an OPS request for Brazil for 1971 that was the largest in the proposed budget.[6]

Similar denunciations were made regarding the public safety programs in Guatemala and the Dominican Republic, also among the principal grantees. Increased police repression and brutality, the use of torture, and the appearance of right-wing paramilitary groups known to be composed of off-duty police and military hunted down and carried out "justice" on alleged subversives and opponents of the regimes. Like the "Death Squad" of Brazil, the "White Hand" of Guatemala and "The Band" of the Dominican Republic were increasingly familiar names to those who followed events in those countries. In 1971 the senior staff member of the Subcommittee on Western Hemisphere Affairs of the Senate Foreign Relations Committee, Mr. Pat Holt, visited the Dominican Republic and Guatemala to examine the impact and results of the OPS and military assistance programs. In his report, which was a harsh and devastating criticism, he wrote of Guatemala:

> The argument in favor of the public safety program in Guatemala is that if we don't teach the cops to be good, who will? The argument against is that after fourteen years, on all evidence, the teaching hasn't been absorbed. Furthermore, the U.S. is politically identified with police terrorism. Related to all this is the fact that the Guatemalan police operate without any effective political or judicial restraints, and how they use the equipment and techniques which are given them through the public safety program is quite beyond U.S. control. . . . On balance, it seems that AID public safety has cost the United States more in political terms than it has gained in improved Guatemalan police efficiency.[7]

Mr. Holt's estimate of the program's effects in the Dominican Republic was equally negative.

In spite of AID and State Department arguments a majority of the Congress was soon convinced that the OPS could not be continued. It was obvious that programs designed to increase the effectiveness of security forces in countries where there was "governmental violence" and where human rights and due process were consistently ignored were no longer tenable. When the testimony of former U.S. AID and Army officials linked similar examples of torture and assassination in Vietnam to police training there, the pressure was too great. Congress halted all overseas programs in December 1973, and a year later terminated OPS and closed the International Police Academy in Washington.

The much larger factor in the U.S. effort to promote stable governments in Latin America has been provided through U.S. Military Assistance and related programs. The Department of Defense, with congressional approval, has been a very generous benefactor to the military establishments of those countries, providing more than $2.56 billion through 1975.[8] Until the time of the Cuban revolution the emphasis of military assistance under the Mutual Security Act of 1951 was hemispheric defense. After 1960, however, counterinsurgency became the focus. Robert S. McNamara, the secretary of defense, stated at the 1967 congressional hearings on the Foreign Assistance Act that

> the primary objective [of the Military Assistance Program] in Latin America is to aid, where necessary, in the continued development of

indigenous military and paramilitary forces capable of providing, in conjunction with police and other security forces, the needed domestic security.[9]

Although the dollar amounts expended for arms and equipment through the various military assistance transactions (grants, transfers, credits, sales, and so on) far exceed the amounts spent for training Latin American military personnel, the latter is the single most important element in the aid budget. In his presentation of the military assistance budget in 1962, Defense Secretary McNamara emphasized the importance of this program in the following statement:

> Probably the greatest return on our military assistance investment comes from the training of selected officers and key specialists at our military schools and training centers in the United States and overseas. These students are handpicked by their countries to become instructors when they return here. They are the coming leaders, the men who will have the knowhow and impart it to their forces. I need not dwell upon the value of having in positions of leadership men who have first-hand knowledge of how Americans do things and how they think. It is beyond price to make friends of such men.[10]

According to the Department of Defense, between 1950 and 1976 more than 77,000 Latin American military personnel had been trained in the Panama Canal Zone, the United States, or elsewhere under this program.[11] In 1973, that department still presented MAP training as the best "dollar for dollar" investment the United States could use for influencing Latin American armed forces.[12]

In view of the fact that military men who had been trained in the program had overthrown democratically elected governments and were leading increasingly repressive regimes, one might well ask, "Influence for what?" Clearly, the influence that was desired was not merely the ability to nurture a pro-democratic and anticommunist attitude in the Latin American military. Rather the goal of influence was the imposition of a U.S.—defined model of economic development that required the creation of a stable climate favorable to private investment, that is, capitalism. The "stable climate" had to be not only noncommunistic but totally unsympathetic to any Marxist influence.

One needs only to review the statistics contained in the annual presentations for Foreign Assistance Appropriations made to the Congress by the administration to affirm this appraisal. In case after case U.S. economic and military assistance has risen dramatically after a military coup or assumption of power by a military-backed civilian (for example, Brazil in 1964, Dominican Republic in 1966, Guatemala in 1954 and 1970, Uruguay in 1971). The clearest example is that of Chile, a heavily documented illustration of the political purposes of the foreign assistance program, where the manipulation of security assistance was a major factor leading to the 1973 military coup.

It is a matter of record that when Salvador Allende's Marxist government was elected in September 1970 the United States engaged in numerous covert actions to prevent him from taking office, including a CIA-directed attempt at a military coup d'etat. In October the CIA station chief in Santiago was advised by cable, "Military solution is objective," a message that initiated energetic attempts by the CIA to persuade the military to move against Allende. When the coup failed to occur the Nixon administration manifested its displeasure by cutting back on security assistance in order to remind the Chilean military of its dependence on the U.S. for spare parts for weapons, training opportunities, and sophisticated armaments. After the first eight months of the Allende administration the United States ended its chastisement of the military and demonstrated through the restoration of military assistance that it would back the Chilean armed forces *against* the Marxist government. As the U.S. drastically reduced economic assistance from the 1970 level of $80.3 million to $10.1 million by 1973, in the same period security assistance rose from $3.3 million to $23.8 million.[13] The military coup that overthrew Allende in September 1973 was the culmination of a U.S. -nurtured destabilization. "Since 1974, Chile's military junta has received more than $686 million in all forms of direct American assistance, including generous debt reschedulings,"[14] a substantial reward for responding appropriately to U.S. "influence."

What are the benefits that accrue to the United States through the establishment and support of stable, noncommunist, non-Marxist, and nondemocratic regimes in Latin America? To put it simply, Latin American countries have enormous economic potential, and it has been the belief of U.S. policymakers that they could best be developed through private investment. The stability and security that were sought were felt to be necessary to attract foreign investors and assure protection for their investments. It is not surprising, therefore, that stable governments favored by the United States to receive the bulk of economic and military assistance are often military dictatorships, governments that have suspended the constitutional guarantees of their countries and now rule under some form of martial law. Although these are the regimes that are the most flagrant violators of human rights, they can also be counted on to maintain law and order while private enterprise taps new resources and creates new markets. It is within this context that the U.S. foreign assistance program must be viewed and understood.

The decision to create a foreign assistance program was not a magnanimous decision unrelated to the desire and necessity of U.S. economic sectors to invest overseas. Further private investment with government backing was to be the primary instrument for holding back the "Communist threat."

It is understandable why the U.S. business community was deeply disturbed when the original design of the Alliance for Progress was announced in 1961. Emphasizing social and political reform, it relied heavily on government planning for development rather than private investment. The business sector was alarmed. Their congressional allies enacted legislation that tied aid eligibility to restrictive investment guarantees and provided for harsh, punitive measures against countries that nationalized U.S. property. Lobbying was frenetic and, after less than two years of experimentation with the original emphasis of the Alliance, private investment was restored as the major channel for assisting development. Private capital was invested overseas at a faster rate than ever.

Evaluating this response, Chase Manhattan's David Rockefeller, a recognized spokesman for U.S. business interests in Latin America, wrote:

> In my view, a primary reason for this relatively good performance [increased investment] is a change in the policy which prevailed in the early years of the Alliance, placing too much emphasis on strictly government-to-government assistance. This approach, while it took account of the fact that there is a genuine and urgent need to do away with social inequities, did not encourage the conditions which are essential to stimulating private investment and economic growth. Revolutionary change which shakes the confidence in the fair treatment of private property is incompatible with rapid economic expansion. Now that the vital role of private enterprise is being recognized in a number of Latin American nations, we see the development of a more favorable business climate.[15]

Mr. Rockefeller does not enumerate those factors that are beneficial to such a "favorable business climate," but it is apparent that they are not congenial to change that would alleviate social inequities.

It was clear that the Alliance for Progress was unable to fulfill any of the goals in the original proposal in spite of the tremendous expenditure of aid funds. This was a cause of serious concern for its supporters, and several evaluations were undertaken in 1970 and 1971. One result was that the 1972 Foreign Assistance Bill was initially rejected, with its major critics pointing to the confusion of public funds and private investment as its key weakness. In opposing the bill, Senator Frank Church stated:

> I could understand—though perhaps not condone—a foreign aid program that is essentially self-serving. We live, after all, in a selfish world. But the present program is designed primarily to serve private business interests at the expense of the American people. In far too many countries, as in the case of Brazil, we poured in our aid money for one overriding purpose: to furnish American capital with a "favorable climate for investment." . . .Moreover, the risk of loss due to political instability, riot, revolution or expropriation has been largely shifted from the investor to the U.S. Government . . . [and] the American taxpayer. Our foreign aid program has become a spreading money

tree under which the biggest American businesses find shelter when
they invest abroad.[16]

The bill was approved after the addition of modifications that permitted recipient nations greater flexibility in the utilization of appropriations. By 1972,
however, the bulk of foreign assistance was habitually granted to the most
repressive regimes in Latin America.

U.S. foreign economic assistance was clearly limited in its potential for
assuring a "favorable business climate." The stabilization of Latin American
governments amenable to U.S. investment through the strengthening of their
security forces has been a major purpose of the Military Assistance Program
and related elements of military aid. The arguments that are presented to the
Congress during the hearings prior to the approval of the annual Foreign Assistance Bill do not generally emphasize this fact. Professionalization of the
armed forces, the modernization of their equipment, increased democratization,
influence, and numerous other justifications are offered. Nevertheless, in 1968,
General Robert Proter, the commander of the U.S. Southern Command with
responsibility for virtually all aspects of U.S. -Latin America military cooperation, made explicit reference to the political purposes of military assistance
as well as support for Latin American police. Addressing the Pan American
Association, he said:

> Many of you gentlemen are leaders and policymakers in the businesses
> and industries that account for the huge American private investment
> in Latin America. . . . Some misguided personalities and groups in our
> own country and abroad call you capitalists who seek profit. Of course
> you do. . . . You can help produce a climate conducive to more in-
> vestment and more progressive American involvement in the hemi-
> sphere. . . .
>
> As a final thought, consider the small amount of U.S. public funds that
> have gone for military assistance and for AID public safety projects as
> a very modest insurance policy protecting our vast private investment
> in an area of tremendous trade and strategic value to our country.[17]

By 1973 that insurance policy covered a direct investment with a book value of
$14.8 billion and markets that received $9.3 billion of exports from the United
States.[18]

It is this situation that has led a number of analysts to suggest that the
nature of the training received through the military assistance program has not
only contributed to the rash of military coups but also to the repressive nature
of the resulting regimes. Dr. Miles Wolpin, in a major study on the affects of
military aid on the Third World, concludes that in addition to military objectives
the purposes of training are to:

(1) develop a propensity to solicit and/or acquiesce in American policy suggestions; (2) structure a definition of national interest that precludes nonalignment; and (3) inculcate an ideology of development which stresses subsidies and hospitality to transnational corporations.[19]

They provide an answer to the earlier question, "Influence for what?" And they are clearly goals that would be applauded by Mr. Rockefeller as being harmonious with his view on private investment as an instrument for the "development of Latin America. The ideological indoctrination that permeates all of the training was summed up in a statement made by Wolpin at a congressional hearing:

> Military aid is not limited to the provision of equipment and technical instruction in its use. The third dimension of MAP is ideological indoctrination. Although the process is multi-faceted, of particular importance is a portrayal of communism as a diabolical edification with a consequential imputation of supernatural potency. Given the careerism, anti-intellectualism and social conservatism that usually characterize officer corps, there is a good basis for ready assimilation of such frightening stereotypes. Since potentially effective reform coalitions generally utilize egalitarian slogans and just as often incorporate at least some radical elements, one can predict that they will catalyze the fears of many politically oriented officers.

> The forementioned antipathies are reinforced by other aspects of MAP indoctrination which inculcate distrust for public enterprise, stress the alleged role of the military rather than civilians in "nation building," omit almost all reference to civilian supremacy, categorically reject nationalism as an economically rational option for underdeveloped countries, and purport to distinguish between a "loyal" and an allegedly "disloyal" opposition.[20]

General William Westmoreland illustrates the use of a number of these same ideological issues in a rather remarkable speech he delivered to the Eighth Conference of the American Armies in Rio de Janiero, September 25, 1968:

> I feel that the prospects of repeated "Viet Nams" around the world present a very real danger to the security of every freedom loving people. For this reason I believe that the techniques of insurgent warfare are high on the list of threats which each of us must consider. . . . We must not expect to find the patterns identical or the techniques always similar. . . . Two things, however, are likely to remain the same: the propaganda describing each insurgency will picture what they term as "oppressed" people rising to overthrow the alleged oppressor. The objective—a Communist dictatorship—will persist. . . . The world has many dissatisfied people whom the Communists can exploit in their quest for destruction of free society. This poses a threat that will be present for a long time. . . .

Although nation building sounds like a function of civil agencies, it has been our experience that military forces—our own and those of the nation we are seeking to help—must often play a role and make use of the special equipment and capabilities to help the people help themselves.[21]

It is apparent that within such a narrow ideological framework there is no room for opposition and barely space for criticism. Military messianism, which has characterized the attitude of the Latin American coup-makers, is a crusading spirit that seeks converts, not critics. When their own mission is supported by the most powerful nation in the world, they know they are right. When U.S. foreign assistance to a nation is dramatically increased immediately after the military takes power, or if military aid is boosted or even held steady when a country has been denounced throughout the world for the gross violation of human rights, it cannot be understood by the regime as anything but a stamp of approval of its actions. And in that case, those who decide to grant such aid ultimately share in the responsibility for the violations that take place.

These are depressing conclusions, especially for those who thought—and perhaps intended—that U.S. government funds that started flowing to Latin America in the early 1960s, under the banner of the Alliance for Progress, might succeed in improving the lives of some of the millions of needy people there, instead of giving to them trained and professional rulers who have little regard for their welfare or respect for their rights. In April of 1970, Senator Edward Kennedy expressed his own disappointment when he delivered the annual Mansfield Lecture at the University of Montana. The burden of his speech was an evaluation of the alliance which had been initiated by his brother nine years earlier. His remarks were a litany of defeats in every aspect of the program. He stated:

And so today it is a personal tragedy that I can repeat nearly the same somber facts about Latin America that President Kennedy cited in 1960 and that Robert Kennedy cited in 1966. The Alliance for Progress has been a human failure. More than 30 percent of the population still die before their fortieth birthday.

The Alliance has been an economic facilure. Even our hopes for economic development are far from realization. The rate of economic growth per capita has averaged 1.8 percent for the decade, lower than it was in Latin American in the years when there was no Alliance. . . .

The Alliance has been a social failure. Land remains in the hands of a minute percentage of the population. In some countries less than 10 percent of the people own 90 percent of land. . . .

The Alliance has been a political failure. It was intended to write a new page of political history in Latin America, to end the depressing chapter of family dictatorships and military coups. Instead, thirteen constitutional governments have been overthrown in nine years. . . .

And the spirit of the Alliance has failed here at home. Despite our strong traditions of democracy, the United States continues to support regimes in Latin America that deny basic human rights. . . .

For decades, the Pentagon, the State Department and our intelligence agencies have urged the United States to intervene on the side of stability in Latin America out of fear that an end to the hegemony of the oligarchs would throw open the door to communist revolution. . . .[22]

From this perspective, it is no accident or mere coincidence that U.S. assistance to Latin American countries flows most freely and abundantly to the most repressive regimes. It is, rather, the expected result of the policy's design. There is a Latin American connection between human rights violations and U.S. foreign assistance.

Notes

1. Reports on the human rights conditions in these countries can be found in: *Amnesty International's Reports* for 1975-76 and for 1977 (Amnesty International Publications); U.S. Department of State, *Country Reports on Human Rights Practices* (Washington, D.C., Feb. 3, 1978); and in the report of the Center for International Policy, *Human Rights and the U.S. Foreign Assistance Program: Fiscal Year 1978*, Part I—Latin America (Washington, D.C., 1978). This last study also includes U.S. Foreign Assistance data for those countries. Complete data on Foreign Assistance is contained in: U.S. Agency for International Development, *U.S. Overseas Loans and Grants and Assistance from International Organizations*, 1975, 1976 (Washington, D.C.: USAID, 1977) and Department of Defense Security Assistance Agency, *Foreign Military Sales and Military Assistance Facts* (Washington, D.C., December 1976).

2. U.S. Congress, Senate, "Study Mission to South America (November-December 1961)," 87th Congress, 2nd Session, Document 91 (Washington, D.C., U.S. Government Printing Office, 1962), n.p.; cited by John Saxe-Fernandez, "The Central American Defense Council and Pax Americana" (paper read at the Spring Colloquium on Latin America, Brandeis University, May 12, 1967, Waltham, Mass.), pp. 8-9.

3. U.S. Agency for International Development, Statistics and Reports Division, *Operations Report*, data as of June 30, 1969; U.S. Agency for International Development, *Program and Project Data Presentations for Fiscal Year 1971* (Washington, D.C., U.S. Government Printing Office, 1970).

4. U.S. Congress, Senate, *Foreign Assistance Appropriations, FY 1965* Hearings before the Committee on Appropriations, pp. 72, 75.

5. U.S. Agency for International Development, Statistics and Reports Division, *Operations Report*, data as of June 30, 1971 (Washington, D.C.: USAID, 1971).

6. U.S. Agency for International Development, *Program and Project Data Presentations to the Congress For Fiscal Year 1971* (Washington, D.C.: USAID, 1970).

7. Pat Holt, *Staff Memorandum on Guatemala and the Dominican Republic*, Staff Report for Senate Foreign Relations Committee, Subcommittee on Western Hemisphere Affairs (Washington, D.C.: Government Printing Office, December 30, 1971), pp. 6-7.

8. U.S. Agency for International Development, *U.S. Overseas Loans and Grants*, July 1, 1945-June 30, 1974 (Washington, D.C., 1975); 1975 data only: U.S. Congress, Senate, Committee on Appropriation, *Foreign Assistance Appropriations for Fiscal Year 1976*, Hearings, 94th Congress, 1st. Session, 1975 (Washington, D.C.: U.S. Printing Office, 1975), pp. 1448-1518.

9. U.S. Congress, House of Representatives, *Foreign Assistance Act of 1967*, Hearings, Committee on Foreign Affairs, 90th Congress, 1st Session (Washington, D.C.: U.S. Printing Office, 1967), p. 17.

10. U.S. Congress, House of Representatives, *Foreign Operations Appropriations for 1963*, Hearings before the Committee on Appropriations, 87th Congress, 2nd Session (Washington, D.C.: U.S. Printing Office, 1963), p. 359.

11. U.S. Defense Security Assistance Agency, *Foreign Military Sales and Military Assistance Facts* (Washington, D.C.: 1977), pp. 30-31.

12. U.S. Department of Defense, *Military Assistance and Foreign Military Sales Facts:* 1973, p. 2, cited by Don L. Etchison, *The United States and Militarism in Central America* (New York: Praeger, 1975), p. 110.

13. Center for International Policy, *Human Rights and the U.S. Foreign Assistance Program: Fiscal Year 1978*, Part 1, Latin America (Washington, D.C., 1978), pp. 44-48.

14. Ibid., p. 45.

15. David Rockefeller, "What Private Enterprise Means in Latin America," *Foreign Affairs*, April 1966 (reprint).

16. Frank Church, "Farewell to Foreign Aid: A Liberal Takes His Leave," *Congressional Record*, October 29, 1971 S17179-S-17186 (reprint), p. 9.

17. General Robert Porter, "Address to the Pan American Society," New York, March 26, 1968; reprinted in U.S. Congress, House of Representatives, *Foreign Assistance Act of 1968*, Hearing before the Committee on Foreign Affairs, 90th Congress, 2nd Session (Washington, D.C.: U.S. Government Printing Office), pp. 1204-1205.

18. U.S. Congress, Senate, *U.S. Relations with Latin America*, Hearings before the Subcommittee on Western Hemisphere Affairs of the Committee on

Foreign Relations, 94th Congress, 2nd Session, February 21, 1975 (Washington, D.C.: U.S. Government Printing Office, 1975), p. 103.

19. Miles D. Wolpin, *Military Aid and Counter-revolution in the Third World* (Lexington, Mass.: D.C. Heath, 1972), p. 11.

20. U.S. Congress, House of Representatives, *Human Rights in Nicaragua, Guatemala, and El Salvador: Implications for U.S. Policy*, Hearings before the Subcommittee on International Organizations of the Committee on International Relations, 94th Congress, Second Session, June 8 and 9, 1976 (Washington, D.C.: U.S. Government Printing Office, 1976), p. 95.

21. Cited in Gary MacEoin, *Revolution Next Door* (New York: Holt, Rinehart and Winston, 1971), p. 138.

22. Edward Kennedy, "Beginning Anew in Latin America," *Saturday Review*, October 17, 1960, p. 18ff.

**Part V
Applications: Problems of
Implementing a Human Rights Policy**

14

Can a Human Rights Policy Be Consistent?

Abraham M. Sirkin

The Carter administration's human rights policy has been greeted, both at home and abroad, with a mixture of praise, criticism, and skepticism.

The praise has come for real accomplishments. The policy has raised consciousness in regard to persistent inhumanities that the world was beginning to accept as normal. Prisoners in several countries have been released and some governments have improved their behavior. In many important quarters, the former reputation of the United States as a supporter of freedom is being restored, replacing its more recent image as a patron of tyranny.

The policy has been attacked abroad for its "interference" in the domestic affairs of sovereign states, accused at home of causing injury to other U.S. vital interests, and criticized generally for its apparent inconsistencies. It has been condemned simultaneously for pressing too heavily on our right-wing "friends" and for serving primarily as a cold-war ploy against Communist nations. An inconsistency has been seen also in the alleged tendency of the administration to "pick on" small, powerless nations and to be more cautious in its human rights strictures against larger countries in which the United States has significant interests.

The potential dangers of the human rights policy and the ostensible inconsistencies in its application have contributed to skepticism about its durability. Whether or not the current human rights effort will survive the Carter presidency will depend largely on the perception by the American people, the U.S. Congress, and subsequent administrations of the results of this administration's experiment. It may depend also on their understanding of what an effective U.S. government policy on human rights must entail and on the impediments that exist to its consistent application.

The purpose of this essay is to analyze what a realistic human rights policy must reckon with in terms of objectives, means, decision factors, limits, and risks and to relate these factors to the recurring question of consistency.

A Variety of Objectives

At first blush, one might think that the goal of "improving observance of human rights" is a simple and clear objective. As one enthusiastic young foreign service officer put it in the early days of the Carter administration, "All that needs to be done is to cable U.S. Embassies around the world: 'The U.S.

Government now stands for human rights. Now go ahead and do it.'" Unfortunately few things in life are that simple, least of all the planning and execution of a human rights policy. The complexity begins right at the start, in determining the more specific objectives of such a policy.

Is the main purpose of the policy to save or help individual victims of oppression? Is it to raise the standards of human rights observance generally by repressive regimes? Is it to push vigorously for the introduction of democracy and its attendant freedoms in all countries? Is it to dissociate the United States publicly from oppressive governments in order to enhance the U.S. posture internationally on human rights issues? Should the United States be pressing governments to honor the social and economic rights of their people as well as their civil and political rights?

It would be pleasant and tidy if actions taken to serve any one of these objectives would invariably serve the others as well, but this is not always the case. To take one example, the U.S. government may meet resistance in interceding with a repressive regime to protect individual victims if American officials are at the same time busy publicly excoriating that regime in order to dissociate from it. Each objective may be a proper and reasonable component of a human rights policy but a decision has to be made as to which of them is more important to pursue at a particular time.

The maximum human rights agenda—the democratization of all the nations of the world and the fulfillment of the basic needs of their people—is clearly unattainable in the short term. It is therefore essential to set priorities among the rights to be protected and to be established as primary objectives. The United Nations and the U.S. Congress have come to the sensible conclusion that certain violations of human rights—summary executions, torture, prolonged imprisonment without fair trial, massive officially sponsored racial discrimination—are more egregious than other forms of repression and therefore need to be attended to, in most cases, with a greater sense of urgency. Nevertheless, situations do occur where it will be highly desirable for the U.S. government to nudge a regime, for example, toward free elections. Thus, the priorities are not universally applicable and therefore not consistent.

The objective of "dissociating" from repressive regimes that the United States has tended to support is specifically mentioned in the legislation requiring reductions in aid to such government. Dissociating has several potential benefits: the regime involved may be induced thereby to change its way; the regime's opponents, who may some day come to power, have a good indication that the United States no longer "supports" their oppressors; the United States reduces its own complicity in the regime's repressions; and the United States strengthens its posture in the East-West ideological contest and improves its image among present, and especially future, leadership elements in other countries.

Dissociating, however, can bring problems as well as benefits. It can be applied only to "friendly" nations to which the United States has provided arms or economic assistance or both. It therefore contributes to the charge of inconsistency. The chances are that, because of various decision factors noted below, the U.S. government will find itself dissociating from some human rights violators and not from others equally culpable, even among the "friendly" nations.

The objective of supporting social, economic, and cultural rights as well as civil and political rights raises a different set of issues and obstacles to consistency. The American people have long accepted their obligation toward fulfillment of these rights by providing billions of dollars in aid to developing countries since World War II, although, in the past decade, regrettably, the volume of U.S. foreign aid has been in decline.

The practical distinction between civil-political rights and social-economic rights has to be kept in mind, however. In most cases governments have it within their power to stop killing and torturing their own people and denying them their civil and political rights. Outside pressure may induce such governments to behave more decently. Most governments in developing countries, however, do not have it in their power to feed, clothe, house, heal, and educate their people properly even if they wanted to do so. If the physical resources, economic infrastructure, and managerial skills are missing, outside pressure can accomplish little. Yet there are two things a foreign government can do to enable developing nations to meet the basic needs of their people. One is to provide them more economic aid, either directly or through such international financial institutions as the World Bank. The other is to see that the aid is managed so as to improve the conditions of poor people in the developing world and to contribute to the economic growth needed to reduce poverty in future generations.

There is no warrant either in logic or in fact to the claims of dictatorships of both Right and Left that social and economic rights need to be fulfilled before civil and political rights can be granted and protected and that political repression is an essential precondition to economic development. Nevertheless, for its human rights policy to be credible in much of the developing world, the U.S. government needs to demonstrate its practical concern for the basic economic needs of people. It has to honor the objectives related to their economic rights as it presses their governments to stop violating their civil rights.

In determining the appropriate human rights objectives that the U.S. government should pursue in a particular country, judgment needs to be exercised on a case-by-case basis. The specific goals for U.S. policy are likely to differ, therefore, from one country to another. As a consequence, the groundwork is laid for an apparently "inconsistent" human rights policy from the very start—in the setting of different goals for different countries.

Available Means

The types of positive or negative actions the U.S. government can take to influence the internal behavior of another government include: quiet diplomacy, public statements, manipulation of economic and military assistance, increase or decrease of diplomatic and other relations, and actions in international forums.

Within each of these categories the intensity of the action taken can range from the very mild to the very sharp. This makes possible many adjustments in the means employed to meet the requirements of particular circumstances.

Quiet diplomacy is now held in disrepute by some human rights supporters because the term has been used in recent years to cover situations in which nothing at all was being done on behalf of human rights. The fact remains, however, that discreet diplomatic approaches by various foreign governments and by various U.S. administrations, including the several most recent ones, have helped to free, or ease the condition of, prisoners in a number of countries and to enable thousands of individuals to emigrate from lands governed by oppressive regimes. Many times, of course, quiet approaches do not work and the option of going public has to be considered.

Public statements and symbolic acts may be potent weapons. They *may* induce a regime to improve its behavior, and they serve the purpose of "dissociation." But they are double-edged instruments. They may cause authoritarian regimes to persist in their harassment in order to demonstrate, to their own people and to the world, their sovereignty and their independence. This can be as true of proud world powers, such as the USSR, as of "macho" juntas in small Latin American "republics." If overused, public criticism may lose its impact, especially if the public chiding rarely leads to stronger action or to improved behavior. Official public statements on human rights violations in foreign countries can be extremely effective in certain situations, but they need to be handled with circumspection.

The means most favored by the U.S. Congress to affect the human rights situation abroad is the manipulation of foreign aid. This is natural since Congress appropriates the money for military and economic assistance and is able to attach to its appropriations whatever strings it desires.

Military assistance is a highly visible form of association. If the only objective is to dissociate from a government receiving U.S. arms, withholding the arms would be a simple answer. Moreover, repressive regimes often have no compunction about taking the U.S. military supplies intended for defense against foreign aggression and using them to crush domestic dissent. This tends to make the United States a partner in the regime's repressive behavior and to insure the bitter enmity of the opposition elements, who may one day come to power. But other considerations do intrude. One is national security, either our own or that of the recipient country, or both. The very term, of course, is now suspect. It has been used in recent years to cover the invasion of the rights of our own citizens as well as the delivery, at least up to 1974, of police equipment to the internal security forces of dictators. The fact is, however, that some nations under authoritarian regimes whom we supply with arms— South Korea, for example—are confronted at their borders by powerful, expansionist states whose governments are even more repressive. We need to be circumspect about the nature and volume of arms we supply, but denying arms altogether to such endangered nations would serve neither our own security interests nor human rights objectives.

Most of the repressive regimes to which we provide weapons and other security assistance are not so directly challenged. But even in these cases it would be prudent, before deciding to withhold arms, to estimate the impact of such an action on the various elements in the receiving nation's power structure, both within the armed forces and in the country generally. The arms denial card needs to be played shrewdly by knowledgeable American officials who have the insight to decide whether, when, and how to use the threat of an arms cutoff to achieve a desired objective.

The manipulation of economic aid in behalf of human rights gives rise to a different set of considerations. The United States provides economic aid to foreign nations, among other more self-serving reasons, in order to help the receiving nations meet the basic human needs of their citizens, to speed economic development that will benefit future generations, or to do both. Since this aid is generally channeled through governments, it enhances their power and prestige. If these governments are authoritarian, as many of them are, the aid, though intended to help entire nations, can be viewed as "supporting" repressive regimes.

The dilemma this poses cannot be solved by any generalized, simplistic formulas. It is unreasonable to insist that economic aid must be provided under all circumstances, regardless of how much it may contribute to the strengthening of a repressive regime and the continued gross violation of rights. It is equally unreasonable to decree that aid should be cut off to repressive governments regardless of the impact of this action on the present and future economic and social conditions of their people.

The Congress recognized this dilemma in stating that aid should not be eliminated if it "directly benefits . . . needy people," but that hardly solves the problem. There is no sure way to determine which type of aid does, and which does not, directly help needy people. Does construction of a road network that enables poor farmers to get their produce to good markets qualify? Suppose the same road accommodates tanks and limousines? Should that kill it? Does construction of a dam to provide irrigation to grow more food directly aid needy people? How about construction of a factory that gives jobs to needy unemployed? In order to comply with the letter as well as the spirit of the law, a U.S. government interagency committee has been struggling with the problem and has had to make rather arbitrary decisions.

There is, however, a deeper problem. One of the important moral and political tasks in the world today is to reduce the gap between the rich countries and the poor countries and to shrink the percentage of the world's population that lives below the poverty line. The Third World is pressing for a New International Economic Order, which involves, among other things, a substantial transfer of resources from the industrialized countries to the developing nations.

Over the past decade, economists, bankers, diplomats, and politicians have been engaged in a worldwide debate over the most efficient and equitable way to achieve this end. Should the model of development emphasize rapid industrialization as represented by the modern economic history of Western Europe, the United States, Japan, and the USSR? Or should this model be ignored, and replaced by a model that aims at meeting "basic human needs" and that emphasizes agricultural and rural development, "appropriate technology," and labor intensive small industry?

The argument for moving in this "new direction" is that industrialization in some countries, at least in the short run, has led to greater prosperity for the wealthy and middle classes but has done little to improve the living conditions of the mass of the people. The U.S. Congress some years ago decided that all bilateral U.S. economic aid should head in the "new directions." President McNamara of the World Bank has also been urging more attention to the alleviation of poverty as a major development goal. Leaders of several developing countries have opted for agricultural priorities and a basic-needs strategy for economic growth and development, but the support for this approach in the Third World is far from unanimous.

Critics of this approach come from the right and left. Conservative economists fear that concentration of resources on improving the conditions of the poor now will delay the building of the infrastructure needed to reduce the numbers of the poor in future generations. This criticism is echoed by government leaders of many Third World countries and intellectuals of the left who see in the "basic human needs" strategy a revival of Western imperialism. The colonial powers were once accused of exploiting the raw materials of their colonies, of unduly emphasizing the primacy of their agriculture and of deliberately preventing them from industrializing. The "basic human needs" approach, say these Third World critics, is stifling their modernization and development just as surely as did the old imperialism. The picture is further complicated by the question of the extent to which the governing elites of most developing countries can be persuaded to include the goal of income redistribution as one of the objectives of their development strategy.

While the theoretical debate continues, what the world seems to be moving toward in practice is a mix of development strategies and projects that is directed at both greater current equity and future growth, at what the Congress would call "direct" benefits to the needy of this generation combined with the investment required to reduce the poverty of future generations. Exempting aid for the currently needy from mandated sanctions on economic assistance does not therefore meet the whole issue.

Another factor has to be kept in mind in considering sanctions on economic aid in behalf of human rights. Most economic assistance programs, apart from food shipments, take several years of continuity and build-up to achieve their developmental, or even their current welfare, goals. A stop-and-go economic aid policy can destroy its effectiveness. Thus a decision to interrupt the flow of aid in the name of one set of human rights objectives may well become a serious obstacle to meeting another set of rights objectives.

Despite all these complexities, the question of stopping economic aid to repressive regimes is viewed by some observers as a cut-and-dried matter. Their reasoning is neat and simple: If American aid to a country is substantial enough for the repressive regime to feel "dependent" on it and thus provides the American government with "leverage," the aid should be cut to activate the "levers." On the other hand, if a regime does not feel that it "needs" the aid, and thus does not offer the donor any leverage, the aid should be stopped in order to avoid U.S. complicity in the regime's violations.

The trouble with this simplistic approach, designed apparently to achieve a mechanical consistency, is that it ignores all the complex factors that should go into a decision to reduce or eliminate economic assistance. Ironically it would give the repressive regime itself the primary power of decision as to whether it "needs" the aid. One can be sure its "needs" will be calculated, not on its oppressed people's requirements for current well-being and future economic improvement, but on its own imperatives for survival in power.

Decisions on terminating economic aid because of human rights violations ought to do justice to the various moral, economic, and political factors involved. To make such careful judgments, decision-makers need wide knowledge of actual conditions, a broad commitment to human rights objectives, a long-range perspective, and considerable flexibility in implementation.

Sanctions on international trade and investment would clearly have a stronger impact on repressive regimes than would cutoffs of economic aid. But they would also have a stronger impact on the populations of the countries governed by the gross violators, on the sanctioning country itself, and on the world economic scene generally. Such action has been seriously considered so far only in a few cases—for example, in regard to the massive and brutal racial discrimination in South Africa and the butcheries in Uganda.

Economic sanctions are a reasonable means to employ to achieve human rights objectives. They are likely to be effective, however, and avoid serious counterproductive results only if they are wielded with skill, circumspection, and full awareness of their far-ranging implications.

Stepping up or reducing educational, cultural, and scientific exchanges can have symbolic value, as can increasing or decreasing diplomatic contacts or representation. However, the cost-benefit ratios in operating these levers on behalf of human rights will differ greatly from one case to another.

American efforts to bring pressure on gross violators need not be confined to bilateral measures. A strong case can be made for working patiently at building the international machinery that may some day call the worst violators to account. The opportunities to do this now are limited. At the United Nations the deck has been stacked against consideration of any human rights cases other than the three favorite targets—South Africa, Chile, and Israel—of the current U.N. majority, although there are intimations that a somewhat broader view may be developing in U.N. forums. In the Inter-American Human Rights Commission, nations presently under authoritarian management constitute a majority and hesitate to create precedents which might someday be used against themselves, though the record of the commission for courageous and forthright reporting is gradually improving. The development and strengthening of effective international institutions committed to protection of human rights ultimately may turn out to be the surest way to achieve lasting results in the struggle to expand the area of freedom and to meet basic human needs.

In implementing U.S. human rights policies generally, the variety of means employed to suit varying circumstances of individual countries inevitably results in an inconsistent pattern of treatment of human rights violations. This is particularly true when public statements are made or public actions are taken in some situations and quiet diplomacy is exercised in other cases of apparently equal gravity. To appreciate the need for this differentiated treatment, it is useful to examine some of the factors that have to go into human rights policy decisions.

Complex Decision Factors

Every decision on the American reaction to a serious human rights situation inevitably requires answers to two questions: Does the particular situation warrant the attention of the U.S. government? If so, what should the U.S. government do about it?

To answer the first question the factors to be considered are these: the seriousness of the violations; the degree to which the situation is improving or worsening; the authenticity of an external or internal threat to the society justifying *some* restrictions on liberty (torture and summary executions never being justified); the willingness of a government to admit outside inquiry; and the stage of a nation's political and cultural development. This latter point remains highly controversial in theory. In practice, however, reality does and will prevail. For example, one might reasonably look for free elections in Uruguay, Chile, and the Philippines, whose people have had the voting habit, before expecting them in Saudi Arabia, where the ballot box is virtually unknown. History and common sense compel a double standard.

After the decision is reached that a government's human rights behavior requires the attention of the U.S. government, the next question is: What should be done about it? The answer demands consideration of the following factors:

1. The Likely Consequences.   In deciding how to respond to serious human rights violations, responsible officials do not have the option of simply adhering to one particular "principle" without regard to the consequences. They have to ask: What will be the likely impact of the means selected on the human rights situation itself? Will it help or hurt the victims? Will it succeed in influencing a regime to improve its behavior or will it trigger a backlash? Will the contemplated action strengthen or weaken potential liberalizers within a regime? Will it achieve the aim of dissociating the United States from the repression? Where the consequences of diplomatic moves are not predictable, risks have to be calculated and sometimes may have to be taken. But American human rights advocates would have little cause for moral satisfaction if the actions they advocated were invariably adopted and resulted in augmenting the volume of repression in the world, even if the United States then washed its hands of the results.

2. The Degree of U.S. Influence or Leverage.   Some governments are unlikely to be swayed by anything the U.S. government does. A certain few governments are heavily dependent on U.S. aid or arms or moral support. All the others range along a continuum between these two poles. In this increasingly interdependent world, the United States has to rely on a number of foreign nations for its own national needs—energy, for example, or raw materials or air bases. The presumed U.S. leverage in some cases comes down to the calculation of who needs whom more. Our policy makers may have been too ready in the past to decide that we needed particular dictators more than they needed us.

3. The U.S. Relationship to the Regime.   Some of the noisiest debates on human rights policy revolve about this factor. Groups with a leftist orientation want all the emphasis placed on the crimes of the rightist dictatorships. Conservative groups want to use human rights policy to belabor Marxist regimes. Myopic as these two positions are, each has a partial point.

On the one hand, the United States does have a special need, as congressional legislation insists, to dissociate itself from the practices of authoritarian regimes it has supported, generally as a real or presumed bulwark against communism, and for whose actions it is therefore to some degree responsible. The goal of dissociating is not relevant in respect to U.S. relations with most Communist regimes. Far from supporting them, the United States spends billions to defend itself against them and continues to make them the targets of its international diplomacy and broadcasting efforts. American concern over the spread of communism, in fact, is another reason for dissociating from right-wing dictatorships.

Repressive regimes of the right almost invariably succeed in radicalizing and polarizing their people, especially their youth, so that when they are toppled it is the extreme left opposition that has the best chance of benefiting. Dissociating the United States from such regimes in good time may help to slow down or even to halt this radicalization process, by encouraging power-sharing and giving heart to moderate elements.

On the other hand, in the long run, it is the totalitarian regimes of the left that pose the more dangerous threat to human rights around the world. Once a Communist government fastens itself on a nation, it is extremely difficult to break its iron grip, as distinct from the rightist dictatorships, most of which tend to be looser and more prone to collapse. With due attention to other important U.S. interests, U.S. public or quiet pressure on Communist regimes over their human rights practices needs to be carefully modulated but rarely, if ever, completely relaxed.

A balanced human rights policy has to deal with the dangers from both directions and to employ the means most appropriate to the different political relationships between the United States and the various types of repressive regimes.

4. Special Regional Conditions. In dealing with human rights situations in at least two regions of the world, U.S. policymakers have to keep in mind the particular historical and psychological contexts in which its actions on behalf of human rights may be viewed. Because of the long history of U.S. "interventions" in Latin America, many governments and peoples in that region are sensitive to U.S. pressures on individual governments to conform to American wishes, although some opposition elements will welcome intervention on *their* side for a change. In Africa, any American initiative to obtain international cooperation to focus on outrages in any black African state will find little support among East, West, and Central African nations as long as the intense and odious patterns of racial discrimination persist in the Southern African states. The choice of means to respond to serious human rights conditions in these two continents must take these sensitivities into account.

5. Other U.S. Interests. This is by far the most difficult element to deal with in the set of decision factors. The Carter administration is accused by some of wrongly subordinating other important national interests to moralistic posturings on human rights. Advocates of a strong human rights policy argue, on the contrary, that the administration rhetoric is inadequately reflected in its actions and that other interests, of a crasser nature than human rights, are in fact repeatedly found to be overriding in official responses to violations.

It may be instructive to identify these other interests and to divide them candidly and realistically into two groups, one characterized primarily by national or sectional self-interest and the other affected as well with high moral international purpose.

In the first group one could place: the promotion of U.S. exports, including arms sales, to provide profits for some, jobs for others, and an improved balance of payments for the nation as a whole; a substantial volume of profitable U.S. investment overseas; the oil imports needed for U.S. factories, farms, homes, and cars; and the continued use of overseas bases regarded as essential for the defense of the United States. Whatever one may think of such considerations, the likely cost to some or all Americans of a particular move in behalf of human rights abroad is a factor no administration in our democracy can afford to ignore.

The second group of U.S. interests, which go well beyond selfish U.S. concerns, would include: reduction of the danger of nuclear war; control of the proliferation of nuclear arms; preservation of peace in areas of potential conflict around the world; protection of independent nations against foreign aggression; meeting basic human needs of the world's poor; abating the growth of the world's population; and promotion of economic and social progress of developing nations. If protection of human rights is an ethical good, so is each of these objectives. In fact, those having to do with the peace of the world may have an even stronger claim to ethical virtue.

The unfortunate fact is that certain of the means employed to advance the ethical good of human rights observance may well prove to be a stumbling block to the achievement of one or another of the goals on this list of high moral purposes. For example, if stopping arms aid to a repressive regime will predictably induce it to go nuclear, which aim should be controlling? As is to be expected in a period of one-issue politics, some human rights purists refuse to recognize the existence of such conflicts. Policymakers, however, have no choice but to examine the available trade-offs and to determine which of the competing interests is most compelling at a particular moment.

It is the need to consider the objectives, means, and decision factors appropriate to each human rights situation that makes a case-by-case approach imperative. Since each case differs, in some respects at least, from every other, an intelligent human rights policy, sensitive to the different combination of factors in each situation, requires a deliberate "inconsistency" in its application. The criticism of the Carter administration for inconsistencies in the execution of its human rights policy thus misses the mark. In many instances the critics are less interested in consistency per se than in using the argument to press the government either to punish their favorite target countries or to ease up on their special friends.

Limits and Risks

As should be evident by now, a positive human rights policy can be neither open-ended nor cost-free. Certain considerations involving the limits and risks of a human rights policy generally have to be kept in mind by policymakers deciding on possible actions in individual cases.

The potential risks of an activist program could come from overzealousness, impatience, or inflexibility on the part of the congressional legislators or the executive formulators and implementers of human rights policy. Some of the risks are these:

1. If the United States should find itself in open confrontation with a large number of countries at one time over their human rights violations, the result could be a concerted international backlash. A wholesale approach could stiffen the determination of the world's numerous dictatorships to resist jointly what they continue to regard as foreign interference in their internal affairs. Moreover, such a reaction might spur a coordinated move by authoritarian regimes to emasculate the U.N. Declaration and the U.N. Covenants that provide the diplomatic and legal underpinnings for international action on behalf of human rights. Constituting a majority of the world's governments, the authoritarians of right and left could combine to adopt declarations reemphasizing the primacy of national sovereignty, downgrading civil and political rights and setting the international human rights movement back by decades. Some recent moves at the United Nations are already pointing in that direction.

2. Most developing countries are currently under authoritarian rule; a substantial number might qualify as gross violators. A vigorous U.S. human rights policy that takes too many of them to task over their domestic practices could cut across American efforts to improve the North-South dialogue. Better communication and cooperation between the industrialized nations and the poorer countries of the world have become increasingly important aims of American foreign policy in recent years. As a result, the number of developing countries selected as targets for public U.S. criticism or action over human rights offenses in any one period may have to be limited.

3. Congressional mandates in the human rights field can make it difficult if not impossible for executive policymakers to decide how to deal effectively with each serious human rights situation in ways most appropriate to the individual case. When the motive for such legislation was to prod an administration that had little interest in human rights, it was understandable. To continue pressing for legislation that denies essential flexibility to an administration committed to a positive human rights policy risks forcing the U.S. government into action that could harm various other national interests and could backfire on the human rights enterprise itself. The apparent purpose of such legislation is to institutionalize an activist human rights policy. There would seem to be no virtue, however, in institutionalizing a simplistic and counterproductive rigidity that prevents policymakers from coping intelligently with the complex issues involved.

4. The efforts of elements in the Congress to manipulate the operations of the World Bank, the regional development banks, and the International Monetary Fund (IMF) on behalf of human rights can result in serious injury to these institutions and to the purposes of development and world financial stability that they serve. Some human rights supporters in the Congress have sought to withhold U.S. funds from going through the international development banks to nations run by repressive regimes. Approval of such a move would subvert the multilateral character of the banks, violate the bank charters that we helped to frame, and cripple these major channels for the transfer of resources from the rich to the poor nations.

Moves of this type are supported in the Congress by a bizarre coalition of single-minded human rights enthusiasts and hard-core isolationists. The latter are delighted at any opportunity to slash foreign aid and to wipe out the U.S. contributions to the multilateral agencies. In this odd coupling, the right-wing opponents of foreign aid would seem to be the more clear-eyed about their objectives and about the most effective legislative means to achieve them.

This is not to say that the impact of the activities of the development banks and the IMF on human rights is always beneficial. Problems may exist with the level and handling of development loans to some of the more repressive regimes and with the austerity programs having an impact on human rights that some countries have to institute if they want to be bailed out of their financial difficulties by the IMF. The danger is that the mandatory legislative remedies being proposed to cure these ills, if adopted, would result in harming the patient. The state of civil and economic rights in the world will not be bettered if the development banks and the IMF are undermined.

5. A vigorous human rights policy requires, and has received, broad popular support. A domestic backlash could develop, however, if the program is perceived as jeopardizing other vital U.S. interests, such as SALT negotiations, control of proliferation of nuclear arms, national security arrangements, or international trade. A good part of the public, for a time, at least, could turn against the policy if economic sanctions were repeatedly used and resulted in lost orders for U.S. products and consequently in lost jobs for American workers. This may put a ceiling on the extent to which economic sanctions can be used as a human rights "lever." These are the realities of political life which policymakers cannot brush aside.

6. The most serious risk in an activist human rights program is the possibility that it may be blamed for some appalling disaster for U.S. foreign policy. The event most likely to attract such blame would be the collapse of a conservative, undemocratic regime in some country and its replacement by more repressive rulers, perhaps of a Marxist bent. The fiasco would be worse if it followed public U.S. government pressure on the crumbling regime to relax its internal controls. The likelihood is, however, that the human rights policy would be blamed even if such pressure had never been applied. If the collapsing government were one that the United States had strongly supported as a supposed bastion against communism, the culpability for the debacle should attach to previous U.S. policies and to the U.S. diplomatic, military, and security elements that carried it out in mindless, short-sighted ways. In several countries, U.S. officials have nurtured and encouraged right-wing authoritarian leaders, who for purposes of their own aggrandizement and survival in power proceeded unchecked to suppress all moderate opposition, and thus to radicalize their own people and prepare the ground for an ultimate takeover by well-organized extremist or totalitarian elements. The Carter administration has had to deal cautiously with the gross violations of regimes headed by leaders regarded by previous U.S. administrations as "indispensable" for stability and therefore untouchable but whose ground has begun to shake beneath them. It is caught in a vise created by the mistakes of previous policy and the failure to dissociate in good time. The administration, consequently, has had to be careful about taking any action that might be interpreted as pulling the rug from under foundering dictators where there is danger that the alternative regimes might be more repressive and ultimately, perhaps, come under Soviet control.

All the risks that may be faced as a result of doing the wrong things or doing too much all at once argue for certain limits on human rights initiatives. These limits in turn make for further inevitable inconsistencies in the execution of the policy.

The one way to achieve some measure of consistency is to do nothing at all about human rights. This, however, is not a viable option either. It has proven in the recent past to have its own serious costs and risks, which would again come into play, if the policy reverted to its former inactive state. For example:

1. The foreign policy of the U.S. government would lose domestic public support in the long run if it did not properly reflect the values of the American people. Respect for human rights is deeply ingrained in the American psyche.

2. The United States would alienate many people around the world, especially idealistic young people, by its revived image as the patron and supporter of repression. It would consequently be at a disadvantage in the ideological competition for the minds of future leaders in many countries.

3. In individual nations, continued U.S. official support of authoritarian leaders would turn even moderate opposition elements into enemies of the United States. Whenever such opposition groups come to power, U.S. interests may well suffer.

4. Failure of the U.S. government to use its prestige and influence to hold the line against the spread of authoritarianism in the world could facilitate the advent of an international political climate that would be adverse to U.S. interests and to the survival of freedom on the entire planet.

Obviously the task of planning and carrying out an effective human rights policy is no simple matter. Those entrusted with this task have to endure both the barbs of the cynics tied to a short-sighted, ultimately self-defeating "realpolitik" and the indignant protests of the idealists still wedded to the twin illusions of American omnipotence and instant societal perfectibility. The maneuvering space between the Scylla of overdoing and the Charybdis of underdoing is narrow indeed. In the face of all the complexities, difficulties, dangers, and limits, can the positive human rights policy initiated by the Carter administration survive?

The answer is yes. It can survive if it is realistic, carefully planned, skillfully executed, sensitive to the domestic and international contexts in which it must function, and, above all, lucky.

Its survival may depend on what happens in critical situations abroad well beyond its control. Its chances of enduring will be determined also by the extent to which it is characterized by realizable objectives, a sense of priorities, a restrained rhetoric that does not arouse exaggerated expectations, a long-range view, and a cooperative approach that shares with other freedom-loving nations the common task of enlarging the area of liberty, justice, and economic equity in the world.

The public support needed for the survival of a vigorous human rights policy would be strengthened if the complexities and inconsistencies inherent in its execution were more widely understood and accepted. With this improved understanding, the overall balance, integrity, and coherence of the policy—and of its implementation—might be better judged and appreciated.

15 Security Assistance in Perspective

Howard M. Fish

Security assistance has been a tool of U.S. national policy for over three decades. It is neither a policy goal, nor an end in itself. It serves only as a means for furthering U.S. interests. Its fundamental purpose is aptly defined by the following excerpt from the Foreign Assistance Act of 1961.

> In enacting this legislation, it is therefore the intention of the Congress to promote the peace of the world and the foreign policy, security, and general welfare of the United States by fostering an improved climate of political independence and individual liberty, improving the ability of friendly countries and international organizations to deter, or, if necessary, defeat Communist or Communist supported aggression, facilitating arrangements for individual and collective security, assisting friendly countries to maintain internal security, and creating an environment of security and stability in the developing countries essential to their more rapid, social, economic and political progress. . . .[1]

In sum, in providing defense articles and services to others, security assistance has been central to the fundamental concept of collective security which has been, and remains, the keystone of U.S. national security policy.

Security assistance has not only helped develop the defensive strength of our allies and friends, it has served other U.S. security interests as well. It has helped facilitate the cooperation of other countries in permitting the United States to use facilities to support U.S. forces abroad and it has helped maintain regional balances where important U.S. interests could be threatened by hostilities.

The continuing importance of security assistance was reflected in President Carter's policy statement on arms transfers in May 1977. While pressing for restraint in the world's arms trade and making clear that arms sales would be used only as "an exceptional foreign policy implement," the president made equally clear that U.S. arms would continue to be available to strengthen the security of our allies and friends and, through them, our own security.

As an integral part of his policy, the president stressed that

> in formulating security assistance programs. . . , we will continue our efforts to promote and advance respect for human rights in recipient countries.[2]

Ideally, U.S. security interests and U.S. human rights objectives would be equally well served by security assistance. But there are times when measures to promote human rights by refusing security assistance would run counter to other U.S. interests.

It is not the purpose of this paper to try to weigh the relative merits of human rights and other U.S. policy objectives. U.S. interests and objectives will have differing weights in various parts of the world. Each case must be considered on its own merits. Instead, this paper is intended to put security assistance into perspective—to give some dimension to its nature and scope, as a measure of its usefulness as a policy tool.

"Security Assistance" is not a precise term. It can generally be described, however, as having six components. Four are administered by the Defense Department.

One comprises grants of combat equipment and other material, most commonly known as MAP; it made up the bulk of the Security Assistance Program for many years.

The second component is the International Military Education and Training Program—a self-explanatory term—known by the acronym IMET. This program provides training for foreign students, mainly in U.S. military schools and facilities alongside U.S. personnel. They receive the same training and are measured against the same standards of academic excellence established for U.S. military personnel.

The third component of security assistance is credit financing provided by the U.S. government—in the form of either direct loans or guarantees to lending institutions—to assist in financing the purchase of U.S. defense equipment and services; the purchase can be made directly from U.S. contractors or through U.S. government channels.

Sales through government channels, known as Foreign Military Sales or FMS, are the fourth element of security assistance. They permit the purchasing government to use the procurement services of the Defense Department. The purchasing governments pay any direct costs that may be associated with a particular purchase, plus a general administrative surcharge to meet U.S. costs of operating the EMS system.

There are two other components of security assistance that are not administered by the Defense Department. One is Security Supporting Assistance, a form of economic assistance primarily for certain countries in the Middle East, administered by the Agency for International Development. The other is the direct commercial export of items controlled by the State Department Office of Munitions Control through the International Traffic in Arms Regulations.

Only three of the six forms of security assistance are any burden to the taxpayer. Sales through government channels and direct exports controlled by the State Department are normally for cash. Those that are financed with credit are reimbursed in full, with interest calculated at the cost of money to the U.S. government (plus a small administrative charge). There has been only one default in the entire twenty-two-year history of the credit program. Certain credits extended to Israel, however, have been "forgiven" by the Congress.

All six forms of security assistance share one common feature: they are all under the policy control and direction of the Secretary of State. It is he who has the statutory responsibility for determining whether there will be a grant program for any country and the level of that program. He also is responsible for approving or denying all proposed sales, whether through FMS channels or directly by U.S. contractors. Similarly, he has the responsibility for initially setting the levels of credit and security-supporting assistance earmarked for individual countries.

The Defense Department is necessarily involved in program decisions that it must implement and which affect U.S. defense programs and resources. The Department of Defense therefore plays an active role in providing advice to the State Department on matters that are peculiarly within its competence. It provides advice, for example, on the impact that a proposed program or sale may have on regional military balances, on the ability of another country to use and maintain the equipment in question, and on the effect, if any, on military capabilities and readiness of our own forces. But the primary role of the Defense Department is that of the program manager, carrying out a multiplicity of administrative tasks—including procurement training, accounting, and reporting—once a program or sale has been approved by the State Department.

There have been some major changes in security assistance since its inception. Its purposes have remained fairly constant, but there have been marked changes in the relative components of the program and among its recipients.

Some twenty-five years ago, when the cold war was at its height, the United States embarked on a massive program of rearming its allies, mainly in NATO Europe. The Congress appropriated today's equivalent of more than $13 billion annually in the early 1950s for grants of military assistance. As our European allies were rearmed and their economies strengthened, the focus of grant assistance shifted to other allies, primarily in East Asia and the Middle East. As MAP recipients in these areas grew militarily and economically stronger, levels of grant assistance declined—Indochina aside—but, over the years, approximately seventy countries received some measure of grant material assistance.

Today, the grant materiel program is only a shadow of its earlier years. In FY '78, $170 million was allocated to programs for seven countries. (A $48 million program also was authorized for Turkey but embargoed by the Congress.) In five of the eight countries—Greece, Turkey, Spain, Portugal, and the Philippines—U.S. forces enjoy the use of military facilities and operating rights. In addition to the country programs, the Congress approved $55.6 million to cover the costs of administering the program in FY '78, including the delivery of items funded in earlier years.

The grant training program—IMET—also has been reduced, though not to the same degree. In recent years, the Congress reduced the administration's requests for funds by almost 25 percent. The impact of those reductions has been magnified by the greatly increased costs of the training program stemming from inflation and new pricing criteria set by legislation. Over the years, the United States has trained approximately 492,000 students under the program; in FY '78 it trained 4,542.

In the latter part of the 1960s, the levels of credit financing rose as a means of helping other countries shift from grant assistance. It has remained essentially at the same level in recent years. For FY '78, the Congress approved about $2.1 billion of credit financing for twenty-eight countries.[3] Israel received $1 billion out of this total, of which one-half will be "forgiven." Jordan and three base-rights countries—Spain, Greece, and Turkey—received credits of about $510 million and Korea, no longer a grant recipient, received $275 million. That left $316 million in credit financing for twenty-two other countries, including Indonesia, Thailand, Kenya, Morocco, and the Philippines. Figure 15-1 shows the levels of credit financing authorized or extended during FY 1950-1977 in constant FY '77 dollars.

Sales were practically nil twenty-five years ago when the grant program was at its height. In FY '64, sales exceeded grants for the first time. They rose most markedly in the mid-1970s—reaching a peak in FY '75 when sales orders in FMS channels reached over $12 billion and exports through commercial channels directly by U.S. contractors totaled about $547 million. Sales declined in the following two years, though commercial exports increased to over $1 billion.

The upswing in sales is attributable to several factors. First, former major grant recipients, such as Taiwan and Korea, have shifted from grants to sales. Second, the United States has engaged in a multi-year effort to refurbish Israeli forces in the aftermath of the October 1973 Arab-Israeli War. Third, several of the major oil producing states, particularly Iran and Saudi Arabia, undertook extensive programs to modernize and enlarge their defensive forces. Aside from programs with certain of our NATO allies, such as the F-16 cooperative effort, sales elsewhere throughout the world have risen modestly and, in some cases, have declined.

Figure 15-2 shows the levels of foreign military sales agreements from FY 1950-1977, in constant FY 1976 dollars, compared with grant military assistance programs during the same period.

Program levels are somewhat misleading. They probably suggest to some that deliveries were made during the years in which the programs are reported. In fact, deliveries normally span a number of years. About $39 billion of foreign military sales orders placed through FY '77 remained undelivered at the end of FY '77. In other words, there was a backlog of about $39 billion—including $7 billion in construction for Saudi Arabia—with projected deliveries not to be fully completed until the mid-1980s. Figure 15-3 shows deliveries

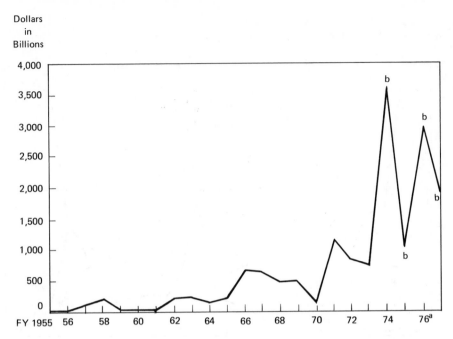

Dollars
in
Billions

^aIncludes transitional quarter (FY 1971).

^bIncludes amounts "forgiven" Israel of $1.5 billion in FY 1974; $100 Million in FY 1975; $850 million in FY 1976; and $500 million in FY 1977.

Figure 15-1. Foreign Military Sales Financing Program, FY 1955-FY 1977
(Constant $—FY 1977)

under grant and FMS programs during the period FY 1950-1977, in constant FY '76 dollars.

Program levels are also misleading in another way. Gross figures give no inkling of what type of equipment or services are involved. They are usually interpreted in terms of tanks, fighter aircraft, and other combat equipment. As a practical matter, normally only about 40 percent of the grant and FMS material programs comprise weapons, ammunition, and munitions. The remaining 60 percent includes a broad range of goods and services, a number of which serve a dual purpose in meeting civilian as well as military needs. Table 15-1 shows a percentile breakout of FMS orders of articles and services, by region, worldwide, during FY 1950-1977.

While gross figures have limited utility we can gain a better appreciation or

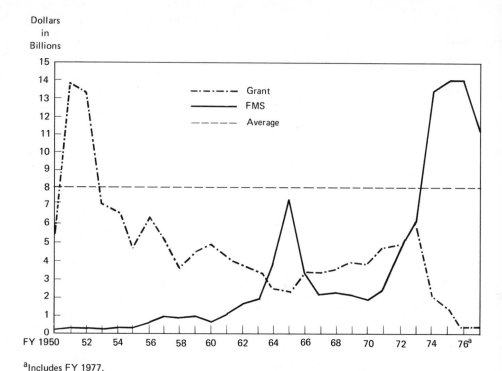

Figure 15-2. Grant/FMS Programs, FY 1950-FY 1977 (Constant $–FY 1977)

perspective of security assistance by breaking down those figures on a region-by-region and program basis.

In Latin America, security assistance has been modest indeed. Grant materiel programs for Argentina, Brazil, Chile, Columbia, and Peru ceased in the late 1960s. The small grant materiel programs maintained in recent years in nine countries, which totaled in the aggregate around $4 million per year, were discontinued in FY '77. Credit financing in Latin America has ranged from $39 million to $158 million during FY 1973-1977, with total sales (cash and credit) vacillating between $82.2 million and $214.9 million during that period. This is in sharp contrast with the extensive Latin American purchases from Western Europe and, in the case of Peru and Cuba, from the USSR.

In Africa south of the Sahara, U.S. security assistance also has been quite modest. Grant assistance focused primarily on Ethiopia and now has been discontinued given the current state of relations with Ethiopia. There have been

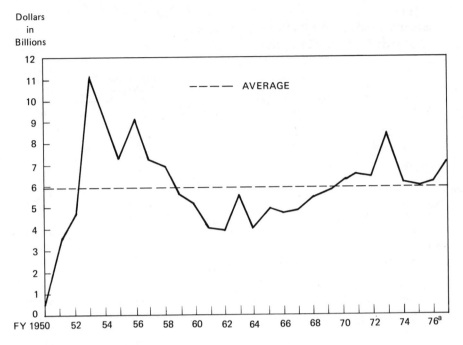

Dollars
in
Billions

Figure 15-3. Grant/FMS Deliveries, FY 1950–FY 1977 (Constant $–FY 1977)

Source: 68-77, *1977 Facts Book.*
[a]Includes FY 1977.

credit-financed programs for Gabon, Kenya, Liberia, Zaire, and, most recently, Cameroon. In FY '78, these countries were extended $40 million in credit financing, with sales agreements totaling $35 million. In addition, in FY '78, there were cash sales of $187 million to Sudan.

In East Asia, grant materiel assistance has been reduced substantially. For FY '78, the Congress approved $41.1 million for the Philippines, Thailand, and Indonesia, with the expectation that only the Philippines would be programmed for grant materiel assistance in FY '79. Cash and credit financed sales have risen—primarily as Taiwan and Korea have shifted away from grant assistance. Credit assistance for Korea will probably continue at substantial levels—about $275 million— as Korea continues its forced modernization, to cope with advances in North Korea's armaments.

In South Asia, the U.S. has had no grant materiel program since FY '67. No credit financing has been extended to South Asia since the India-Pakistan

Table 15-1
Percentile Breakout of FMS Orders of Articles
and Services Worldwide by Region

Worldwide Total	Weapons and Ammunition[a]	Spare Parts	Supporting Equipment[b]	Supporting Services[c]
FY 1950-1977	40	20	10	30
FY 1977	39	21	5	35
Regional Totals				
East Asia				
FY 1950-1977	41	33	14	12
FY 1977	47	33	9	11
Nesa				
FY 1950-1977	38	15	7	40
FY 1977	39	18	3	40
Europe				
FY 1950-1977	49	24	12	15
FY 1977	41	26	9	24
Africa				
FY 1950-1977	33	22	24	21
FY 1977	2	27	53	18
American Republics				
FY 1950-1977	34	24	25	17
FY 1977	34	23	18	24
Canada				
FY 1950-1977	22	40	24	14
FY 1977	13	43	11	33

[a]Weapons and Ammunition—fighter aircraft, bombers, destroyers, submarines, tanks, artillery, machine guns, rifles, all ammunition and missiles.

[b]Supporting Equipment—training and cargo aircraft, tankers, tugs, barges, trucks, trailers, radar, communications equipment and other equipment and supplies.

[c]Supporting Services—construction, supply operations, training, technical and administrative services.

conflict in FY '71, and only since February 1974 has the U.S. resumed selected sales to either country. North Africa and the Middle East, including the Persian Gulf, have accounted for the bulk of the security assistance programs over the past four to five years. As mentioned earlier, this was due for the most part to the need to refurbish Israeli forces after the October 1973 war, and to the programs that Iran and Saudi Arabia had undertaken to modernize their forces. Jordan is the only country for which grants of materiel continue. Israel normally receives $1 billion in credit, with one-half "forgiven"—in effect, grant aid. (By FY '78, about $3.45 billion in credit had been forgiven Israel since the October 1973 war.

Tables 15-2 and 15-3 show the levels of grant assistance and total FMS sales for the period FY 1973-1977 on a regional basis and the component breakdown of sales to countries with sales totaling $50 million or more during FY '77.

An overall perception of U.S. security assistance would benefit by a comparison of U.S. programs—particularly to the developing countries of the world—with those of the Soviets and other suppliers in Western Europe. We can make such a comparison most effectively by looking at deliveries of major items of

Table 15-2
Worldwide Foreign Military Sales and Grant Aid[a]
(dollars in millions)

	FY 1973	*FY 1974*	*FY 1975*	*FY 1976[b]*	*FY 1977*
Total FMS	$4,477	$10,545	$12,306	$13,168	$11,190
Total Grant Aid	4,250	1,577	1,095	299	280
East Asia and Pacific					
FMS	308	322	667	1,742	1,276
Grant aid	4,085	1,397	942	129	56
Near East and South Asia					
FMS	3,076	8,738	6,114	9,615	8,526
Grant aid	40	44	74	58	58
Europe					
FMS	800	1,138	5,176	1,341	1,051
Grant aid	80	81	17	38	84
Canada					
FMS	90	105	97	57	74
Africa					
FMS	3	14	27	231	114
Grant aid	10	12	13	8	6
Latin American Republics					
FMS	110	215	190	89	83
Grant aid	13	15	15	16	10
International Organizations					
FMS	90	15	34	92	67

Note: Totals may not add due to rounding.

[a]Includes MAP, MASF, and IMET.

[b]Includes transitional quarter (FY1976).

[c]Includes North African countries: Egypt, Libya, Morocco, and Tunisia as displayed in the Congressional Presentation Document (CPD).

Table 15-3
Countries with Foreign Military Sales Totaling
$50 Million or More in FY 1977[a]
(dollars in millions)

Area	Total Sales Agreements	Weapons and Ammunition	Supporting Equipment	Spare Parts	Supporting Services
Near East and South Asia	8,055.1	3,295.0	264.4	1,563.1	2,932.6
Iran	5,803.1	2,069.4	178.1	1,380.9	2,174.7
Israel	552.0	443.5	19.0	50.1	39.4
Jordan	117.0	13.9	6.7	14.2	82.2
Pakistan	137.9	70.7	13.9	30.3	23.0
Saudi Arabia	1,804.7	634.1	43.0	74.0	1,052.7
East Asia	1,094.2	545.8	94.3	343.2	110.9
China (Taiwan)	153.0	42.0	9.2	81.2	20.6
Korea	654.0	336.2	52.9	202.6	62.3
Philippines	58.0	31.0	12.2	9.7	5.1
Singapore	113.7	75.8	1.4	29.2	7.3
Thailand	103.8	61.2	18.4	13.6	10.6
Europe	221.2	138.2	7.7	57.3	18.0
Spain	95.0	27.4	4.1	55.2	8.3
Switzerland	88.6	79.8	1.4	.2	7.2
Africa	113.6	2.2	60.5	30.4	20.5
Sudan	91.9	–	53.4	27.8	10.7

[a]Excluding NATO, Japan, Australia, and New Zealand.

equipment, such as combat aircraft, tanks, artillery, and combat vessels. This is an area where we have concrete information, which permits a more realistic method of comparison than trying to assess relative dollar values.

Again, if viewed regionally, we find that:

In Africa South of the Sahara, the Soviet Union has been the dominant supplier over the past five years in almost all categories.

The USSR also had a commanding lead in deliveries to North Africa, with extensive programs in Algeria and Libya.

Similarly, the USSR had a commanding lead in deliveries to the confrontation states in the Middle East and to South Asia.

The U.S. leads in deliveries only to the Persian Gulf and to East Asia (in the latter case, mostly Korea, Taiwan, and the Philippines).

It is Western Europe and Canada (and the USSR in the case of Peru) that lead in deliveries to Latin America.

On a worldwide basis, the Soviet Union is the leading supplier of tanks and self-propelled guns, artillery, guided missile patrol boats, supersonic combat aircraft, and surface-to-air missiles. France has sold a significant quantity of armored personnel carriers and armored cars, guided missile patrol boats, supersonic combat aircraft, and helicopters. The United Kingdom has been a significant supplier of tanks and self-propelled guns, major and minor naval surface combatants, subsonic combat aircraft, and other aircraft. The United States has been the predominant supplier only of major naval vessels—almost all used, rather than newly constructed vessels provided by other suppliers—subsonic combat aircraft, and antiaircraft missiles.[4]

Soviet arms are substantially lower in price—often discounted—than comparable Western equipment, with the list price apparently based primarily on what the Soviets estimate the market will bear. Credit is extended on favorable terms. Payments usually have been over eight to ten years, after a grace period of one to three years, with interest at 2 to 2.5 percent. Moreover, the USSR has been willing to accept payment in commodities or local currency, and has frequently reduced or postponed payments when the recipient was unable to meet them.

In contrast, except for the Israeli program, U.S. sales are either for cash or with credit financing with interest rates, as pointed out earlier, equal to the cost of money to the U.S. government. U.S. legislation requires payment in advance or on delivery for sales and the payment of interest on net arrearages on sums due. The law also requires that the United States add a surcharge to sales, to assure that the United States recoups the cost of administering the overall sales program.

Western European suppliers sell either for cash or on credit terms. They do not normally discount prices, but Western European governments will extend credit on generous terms if needed to conclude an arms sale that they consider important. Several Western European countries, notably France and the United Kingdom, are committed to indigenous arms industries. But their own forces are too small to support those industries and arms exports are important to their survival. Western European suppliers produce a full range of equipment for land, sea, and air forces. While their equipment is not as technologically advanced in some cases as U.S. equipment, the lesser developed countries can find in Europe a wide selection of equipment for modern conventional forces. In sum, since the early 1950s and 1960s we have seen a lessened dependence by others on U.S. arms and equipment. Western Europe provides much of the equipment needed by Western European forces; it also provides an alternate source of arms to others. The Soviets, too, offer an alternate source.

Despite certain changes over the years, security assistance continues to be an important national security policy tool. There have been shifts in the focus and nature of that assistance, but its fundamental purpose remains the same: to help assure the security of this country through developing the defensive strengths of its allies and friends. It also remains a useful tool in maintaining regional balances where U.S. interests are threatened, such as the Middle East, and it is an important factor in our relations with several key countries, including those that provide facilities for use by U.S. forces.

The question now is how security assistance relates to human rights. Secretary of State Vance made clear in an address at the University of Georgia that the advancement of human rights is a central part of our foreign policy.[5] President Carter's statement on arms policy made equally clear that, in formulating our security assistance programs, we will continue our efforts to promote and advance respect for human rights in recipient countries.[6] To the extent that there are favorable developments on human rights in a given country, the United States can be forthcoming in security assistance. Conversely, where there are unfavorable developments, there will be constraints on what we will do.

It is firm policy that the United States will not provide equipment or training, either through MAP or FMS, to carry out civilian law-enforcement functions. For example, there is a complete bar against training in any phase of civilian law enforcement, either on an individual or unit basis. In fact, we do not provide training of any kind to any individual unless satisfied that the individual will not be then assigned to a unit with civilian law-enforcement functions.

Further, there is a complete bar against providing defense articles, defense services, or training of any kind to units that are not a part of a nation's defense forces under the direction and control of the Ministry of Defense. For units under the Ministry of Defense, there is a general bar against the provision of defense articles, defense services, or training to any unit that has ongoing civilian policy functions.

Finally, there is a general rule or ban against the provision, to any units, of riot control agents, given their possible use to quell civilian disturbances. In short, U.S. policies are intended to insure that security assistance is not used as a means of violating or repressing human rights.[7]

These policy guidelines are designed for universal application. They can be applied in a simple and straightforward manner in all cases. It becomes more difficult, however, to set universal or general guidelines about when or how security assistance should be suspended in any given case where a violation of human rights has occurred. In his recent address at the University of Georgia on human rights policy,[8] Secretary of State Vance identified three broad areas that should be weighed when determining whether and how to act.

"First," he said, "we will ask ourselves, what is the nature of the case that confronts us?" What are the kinds and the extent of the violations? Are there given patterns or trends in support, or in deprivation, of human rights? What is the degree of control and responsibility of the government concerned? In short, how serious is the situation?

The second set of questions that he identified concerns the prospects for effective action. In his words, "Will our action be useful in promoting the overall cause of human rights?" Put in terms of security assistance, would an embargo—or threat of embargo—provide effective leverage in the case at hand?

The third set of questions is designed, as Secretary Vance put it, "to maintain a sense of perspective." In his words, "Have we been sensitive to genuine security interests, realizing that outbreak of arms conflict or terrorism could in itself pose a serious threat to human rights? Have we considered all the rights at stake? If, for instance, we reduce aid to a government which violates the political rights of its citizens, do we not risk penalizing the hungry and poor who bear no responsibility for the abuses of their government?" Again, in terms of security assistance, this means we must examine carefully whether an embargo—or threat of an embargo—would change the military balance in a sensitive area to the extent that it might heighten the danger of conflict, or whether there would be a real risk that other countries in the area might perceive a diminished U.S. commitment to peace and security in that area.

There are no pat or simple answers to these questions. Each case must be examined on its own merits and in its own context. They serve, however, to highlight the need to marshall all of the resources available to us—including the support of other governments and international organizations—if we are to be successful in persuading others to improve their human rights records.

Notes

1. The Foreign Assistance Act of 1961, as amended, Sec. 501, PL 87-195, approved on September 4, 1961, 75 Stat. 424.

2. The text of President Carter's statement on Conventional Arms Transfer Policy, issued on May 19, 1977, is contained in a "Report to Congress on Arms Transfer Policy Pursuant to Sections 202(b) and 218 of the International Security Assistance and Arms Export Control Act of 1976." The report was submitted by the Secretary of State to the Congress on June 30, 1977. The Senate Committee on Foreign Relations issued the report in a Committee Print, *Arms Transfer Policy,* dated July 1977.

3. The Foreign Assistance and Related Programs Appropriations Act, 1978, PL 95-148, approved on October 31, 1977.

4. These conclusions are based on data contained in *World Military Expenditures and Arms Transfers 1966-75,* published by the U.S. Arms Control and Disarmament Agency.

5. Speech by Secretary of State Cyrus R. Vance on Law Day before the University of Georgia's Law School, April 30, 1977, at Athens, Georgia.

6. See note 2 above.

7. *Department of Defense Military Assistance and Sales Manual.* Part II, Chapter C, 4.f., and Part III, Chapter B, 3.a. (23).

8. See note 5 above.

16 Human Rights in the Philippines and U.S. Responsibility

Richard P. Claude

Introduction

In the field of foreign policy, the American is often beset by difficulties because, on the one hand, he is apt to believe in the independence of nations and, on the other hand, he would like to see the extension internationally of freedom and democracy. But emphasis on noninterference with others, results in tolerating oppression, while pressing freedom and human rights on others leads to international tensions. Whether this is a real or only apparent dilemma is a topic of current debate in the United States and elsewhere, and its outcome is by no means clear.

Debate over the role of foreign policy in the promotion of human rights focuses more on means that upon ends. Optimists are divided by a line separating those who call for activism and those who call for restraint, not between those who support human rights and those who do not.

Former Secretary of State Henry A. Kissinger, who dominated foreign policy for nearly a decade, regularly argued against linking human rights questions to foreign policy decisions. He said that he was for human rights, but that American commitments abroad had to be based not primarily upon moral considerations, but on national security judgments.[1] Those calling for restraint in promoting human rights internationally have argued that, given worldwide cultural and legal diversities, the criteria for judgment are not yet established whereby one country can confidently condemn another on human rights grounds. These pessimists say that neither public threats nor condemnation by one country of another are appropriate, given the evidence that all countries are, to some degree, human rights violators, and judgments of degree in such matters are difficult to make in any but the most obvious cases of large-scale gross violations. They insist that going so far as to cut off foreign aid in the name of human rights is counterproductive, involves questionable leverage, and results not in human rights gains, but in fruitless confrontation.

Case Study Approach. A debate which largely focuses on problems of selecting effective means ordered to agreed-upon goals is best advanced by "getting down

The author wishes to acknowledge indebtedness to his undergraduate research assistant, Mr. Jonathan David, for his uncommonly effective aid as fact-gatherer, analyst, sounding board, and sleuthhound.

229

to cases." In this essay, the example of relations between the United States and the Republic of the Philippines will be examined.

U.S.-Philippine relations supply an apt case study because, as I shall attempt to demonstrate, in this instance, the pessimist's cautions carry minimum weight. First, the view that the diversity of cultures, legal systems, and values makes it impossible to discern criteria for judgment in the field of human rights does not apply by virtue of historical circumstances. Until recently, the Philippine constitution was based upon that of the United States; for five decades Philippine children were taught standards of justice in terms of the United States Bill of Rights. Second, as indicated by published reports of the International Commission of Jurists and by Amnesty International, the recent human rights record in the Philippines is not one involving marginal, borderline, and therefore tenuous judgment.[2] It is a country where a consistent pattern of gross violations of internationally recognized human rights is patently evident and substantially documented. Third, the matter of whether American military assistance generates an available sanction with high or low leverage capability is barely open to doubt, in view of the continuous record of American security assistance, and the notorious history of public safety projects.

Systematic Debasement of Human Rights in the Philippines

After twenty-six years of free and independent political life, martial law was declared on September 22, 1972. From that time to the present, the Philippines has had no free press, no free election for representatives, no union organizing, and a galloping inflation rate of over 50 percent. Virtually all political opponents of President/Premier Ferdinand Marcos have been jailed at one time or another. Offering legal assistance to political detainees is highly risky.[3] A state of widespread fear prevails which chills expression as well as creativity (the Philippines' only nuclear physicist is imprisoned at Bicutan Rehabilitation Center).[4] International organizations estimate that over 53,000 people have been arrested or detained since 1972 for political reasons, and torture is a standard procedure. Civil and political rights in the Philippines have disintegrated.

In a nationwide radio-television address on December 11, 1974, President Marcos stated emphatically: "No one, but no one has been tortured. . . . None has reason to complain that his dignity has been violated, or that his convenience has not been looked after."[5]

Soon after the president's speech, some twenty-one young men and women were subjected to torture in military camps and "safehouses."[6] The details of the torture of many Camp Olivas detainees were exposed by Father Edicio de la Torre, a Catholic priest, whose Christmas 1974 hunger strike received international publicity. Subsequently, Sister Lourdes Palma, a medical doctor, was able to examine twenty-one torture victims, and their cases are presented in the report of the Association of Major Religious Superiors. Of the twenty-one documented cases, one will be reviewed here in detail for illustrative purposes. The case is from the personal testimony of Armando Enriquez Teng, twenty-five, a former student of the University of the Philippines.[7]

The Case of Armando Enriquez Teng. Armando was arrested together with his wife, Leonarda, at about 3:00 P.M. on 13 December 1974 at No. 710 Granate Street, Quiapo, Manila. They were entering Teng's brother's house at 3:00 P.M. when they noticed that a stranger was standing at the door. Teng was about to ask the man where his brother was, when suddenly several plain-clothesmen with drawn .45 caliber pistols entered.

Without explanation, one of them, Eddie Abolos, hammered Teng's hands with his gun and told him and his wife to keep quiet or else they would be shot. The Tengs assumed the intruders were burglars. Suddenly, Abolos directed Teng to stand up, stuffed a sheet of paper into his mouth, and ordered him to swallow it. Teng testified, "he asked many questions which I could not understand. All the while he kept hitting me." Leonarda Teng begged the armed men to stop the senseless violence and "free us because our one-and-a-half-year-old baby was waiting at home." They answered negatively and took the Tengs for interrogation to the Military Intelligence Unit of the Philippine Constabulary at Camp Crame.

They reached Crame at about 7:00 P.M. and were brought into an air-conditioned office. There they were questioned about alleged subversive activities in which they were said to be accomplices. Teng explained: "I had no knowledge about what they were talking." After a companion of Abalos struck Armando Teng, he lost consciousness. When he awakened, he faced Clifford Noveras, who had an army crank-operated field telephone. The wires leading from the power unit were cut, exposing two electrodes, through which power was transmitted when the crank was turned. According to Teng:

> Clifford Noveras forced me to sit at one corner of the office and connected a live telephone wire to my thumb and penis. He turned the telephone crank-shaft until more than 110 volts of electric current flowed up and down my whole body. He did this several times and again I lost consciousness. . . . Then they brought me to Brigadier General Tomas Diaz's house in front of Luna Hospital, Quezon City. General Diaz asked me if I was a certain Nick or Pepe. I answered "no." Then I was brought to the garden of the house by a certain Art Gonzales. He aimed his gun at me and said, *"Umamin ka no!* [Admit it]." When I said, *"Wala akong alam diyan sa sinasabi ninyo"* [I do not know what you are talking about]," he boxed me in the solar plexus several times until I fell to the ground breathless and moaning in pain. Gonzales picked up a big marble stone and hit my shoulder

twenty to twenty-five times. . . . Then a certain Alejandro Flores told
me that he would rape my wife, Leonarda, if I did not confess. Then
Espino dragged me back into the car.

Armando Teng's wife subsequently disappeared. At 1:00 A.M., on December 14, he was taken to Camp Olivas where he was deposited for incarceration in
a state of shock.

Teng's case, along with others, became publicly known through church
groups. In a letter to Major General Fidel Ramos, the Archbishop of Manila,
Jaime Cardinal Sin, requested that an impartial team including representatives
named by him formally investigate twenty-one reported torture cases, including
the case of the Tengs. The petition was denied, and the military announced that
they would undertake their own investigation. No report has been published.
At the time when Amnesty International was scheduled to visit the Philippines
(late November 1975), a hearing was hastily organized at Camp Olivas, during
which some detainees were asked to recount their torture experience and were
cross-examined by the military panel. Thereafter, Defense Secretary Juan Ponce
Enrile said that those responsible for any maltreatment would be disciplined. In
fact, Second Lieutenants Espino and Noveras were thereafter promoted to the
rank of first lieutenant. Major Patalinghug, who offered well-paying jobs and
release to tortured detainees if they would cooperate as state witnesses against
Father de la Torre, was promoted to the rank of lieutenant colonel.[8]

According to the report of the Association of the Major Religious Superiors
in the Philippines, nearly 6,000 persons were in jail in 1976 without benefit of
habeas corpus. The report, entitled *Political Detainees in the Philippines*, acknowledges that data are "next to impossible" to secure on the number of
detainees. Nevertheless, the association's newsletter and unpublished newsletters of various rehabilitation center detainees estimate that over 50,000 persons
have been detained at one time or another over the years of martial law. There
are no reliable and comprehensive data on the number of those tortured, though
one of the functions of these "underground" newsletters is to circulate the
names of detainees and those who have been tortured, and such names total
over 400 since 1970. The Association of Religious Superiors avers: "There is
an undetermined number of safehouses where detainees are brought for 'tac-
tical interrogation,' and some are not heard from again."[9] Over 90 percent of
those taken to "safehouses" and detention centers in the Greater Manila Area
have undergone torture. The following methods of torture are reported to be
used with regularity: application of lighted cigarettes to various parts of the
body including the ears and genital areas; electric shocks on different parts of
the body, including the genital areas; stripping and sexual abuse (and sometimes
rape) of female detainees; beating with fists, gun buts, and rubber hoses; pressing a hot iron against the sole of the foot; holding the victim's head under water
until he or she loses consciousness; smashing the fingers with bullets inserted
between them.

In 1977, the International Commission of Jurists published a report entitled *The Decline of Democracy in the Philippines*. Among its many damning conclusions was the judgment that the Marcos regime "has not yet taken effective steps to prevent the use of torture by security units of the Philippine military establishment when interrogating suspects."[10] Moreover, according to the ICJ Report, the Philippine government, using military authority, has otherwise denied to the Philippine people their basic rights under the constitutions of 1935 and 1973.

Analysis of American Responsibility

The deplorable state of human rights in the Philippines raises the question of relations with other nations and what posture others should assume in response to the debasement of internationally recognized standards. Do others bear some responsibility to show disapproval or to seek to remedy wrongs?[11]

In individual relations as in international relations, freedom is conditioned upon the range of available choice, and responsibility is conditioned by past, present, and future commitments.

On any given human rights situation abroad, the United States has the option of doing and saying nothing, of quietly and privately seeking redress of violations, of publicly speaking out on violations, of severing economic, military, and political ties, and of seeking international action of some kind, or any combination of these. Those who would advocate a strong, active American concern with human rights (congressional Democrats such as Donald Fraser of Minnesota,[12] Robert Drinan of Massachusetts, and so on) are willing to use the leverage of withholding American foreign assistance as a sanction against human rights violators. They point to Article 1, Section 3 of the United Nations Charter, a binding treaty, which commits member nations "to promote and encourage respect for human rights and for fundamental freedoms." They also argue that the weight of responsibility is greater for a country such as the United States—deeply involved in international programs of foreign assistance. Such aid, they say, should be tied to worthwhile goals such as the promotion of human rights, because to do otherwise would show blindness to the consequences of the ways in which American money is spent abroad.

If the weight of American responsibility toward the Philippines is calibrated by the concededly loose obligations of international law and the vague goal of tying aid programs to characteristically American values, then rather little should be expected. As Under-Secretary of State for Economic Affairs Richard Cooper said on September 11, 1977, to an Asian development conference (ASEAN), "Human rights are not the 'be all and the end all' of [American] government objectives."[13] The burden of responsibility, so lightly freighted, may be sufficiently carried by resort to "quiet diplomacy," support for international human rights fact-finding processes, and applying appropriate sanctions where convenient. But this states the case too weakly by linking lightweight response-options to minimal responsibility.

Rather than passing neutral judgment over Philippine human rights viola-tions, the United States—perhaps unwittingly—has stood at the supply end of a flow of repressive technology. At least in part because of Ferdinand Marcos's cunning, the United States continues under President Carter to support the mailed fist of authoritarian abuse in the Philippines. U.S. responsibility trans-cends the bonds of international law and the unilateral freedom of donor in relation to the client. More should be expected because we are linked to Philippine human rights abuses by a web of past, present, and future ties which place our weight behind the debasement of rights and liberties. The link be-tween American policy and Philippine repression has important elements of causality which bring to mind the proposition of the philosopher Gabriel de Tardé: "The problem of responsibility is connected with the philosophical search for causes and is but an application of the latter, but a very arduous one, to the study of the facts relative to man living in society."[14] Let us examine this causal web of past, present, and future American commitments which in some Filipino eyes generates responsibility out of culpability at most or con-tributory negligence at least.

The Past: Law Enforcement American Style. The history of Philippine-Ameri-can relations involves a uniquely close colonial link. That link, according to Philippine Supreme Court Justice Enrique Fernando, was reinforced at the core by "traditional civil liberties which in our country date back juridically speaking from the inception of the American tutelage on April 11, 1899."[15] In the postcolonial period, a relationship of continuing tutelage can be seen in the development of legal formalities. For example, the 1973 Revised Constitution accords a guarantee against self-incrimination which reads: "No person shall be compelled to be a witness against himself. Any person under investigation for the commission of an offense shall have the right to remain silent and to counsel, and to be informed of such right. No force, violence, threat, intimida-tion, or any other means which vitiates the free will shall be used against him. Any confession obtained in violation of this section shall be inadmissible in evidence" (Article 6, Section 20). With enthusiasm, Justice Fernando com-ments: "The epochal American Supreme Court decision in *Miranda* v. *Arizona*, the opinion being rendered by Chief Justice Warren, is thus now a part of our fundamental law."[16]

The Philippine equivalent of *Miranda* v. *Arizona* involves an intriguing example of legal transplantation, but its significance for the protection of citi-zens against police abuse is academic so long as martial law prevails. Under these circumstances, the most substantial contribution which can be said to have been made by the United States to the Philippine criminal justice system was made by the Public Safety Program. In 1962, President Kennedy established the

Office of Public Safety (OPS) in the Agency for International Development (AID).[17] Its purpose was to supply arms and training to selected foreign police forces, on the theory that the police were the first line of defense against subversion in troubled Third World countries. The OPS established the International Police Academy (IPA) in Washington, D.C., and sent "Public Safety Advisors"—former U.S. military men and police officers—to about forty developing countries.[18] A total of 8,855 foreign policemen received training at the Washington IPA and various police schools throughout the United States.[19] The academy began training foreign police officers in 1963 and continued until 1974. During its final years, there were allegations that the academy encouraged the use of brutality, taught the use of torture methods, and promoted the creation of police states.[20] U.S. officials persistently denied these allegations, and an independent review by the General Accounting Office found no supporting evidence other than the showing of the film *Battle of Algiers* that dealt with inhumane methods of interrogation.[21] Between 1969 and 1974, when the IPA was discontinued, 284 Filipino police officials were trained in Washington, D.C. The largest single group, thirty-five during 1973, was graduated at the end of the first year of Philippine martial law. Public Safety allocations for the Philippines amounted to $12.3 million by the time the program was phased out in 1974.[22]

Under the chairmanship of Juan Ponce Enrile, the National Police Commission was set up before the martial law period under the joint sponsorship of the Office of the President of the Philippines and the AID Office of Public Safety.[23] Its task was to improve the organization, administration, and operation of local police agencies by exerting greater centalized control. American Public Safety assistance supporting the effort to integrate police activities fell into four major categories: training, communications, police improvement, and records. The post-martial law impact of these American investments in public order are difficult to assess. Nevertheless, a clear view on this matter is given by the American-based group the Friends of the Filipino People. In their publication of 1976 entitled *The Logistics of Repression* they conclude that the Philippine Public Safety project sponsored by the United States

> can most probably take credit for helping to institutionalize the most advanced techniques of information and confession-extraction from political suspects, like the common use of electric shock, subtle psychological torture, and selective beating—methods remarkably similar to those employed in Brazil, Korea, Vitenam, Iran and Uruguay, all of which have received significant amounts of OPS assistance and training.[24]

The hand-held electric transceivers used in the Teng case detailed earlier were of the same sort as those supplied by U.S. AID assistance. With regard to these devices of horror, the 1974 Public Safety Project Report on the

Philippines says antiseptically, "No maintenance problems are anticipated since each city has technicians trained on this equipment and sufficient spare parts are on hand."[25] The bizarre theory of the United States supplying the training, the funding, the equipment, indeed the spare parts, for instruments of torture is widely believed in the Philippines, especially among human rights groups interviewed by the author. Such ironies were perceived in the United States as well. As early as 1971, a staff report of the United States Senate Committee on Foreign Relations concluded that in Guatemala and the Dominican Republic the OPS program had no result more obvious than identification of the United States with political violence and governmental repression.[26] Human rights groups and anti-Vietnam War protestors combined to bring pressure upon Congress, which voted in 1973 to ban the use of foreign aid funds for police training abroad.[27] On the basis of additional revelations—including allegations that OPS helped to forge the police apparatus with which President Marcos destroyed civil liberties in the Philippines—Congress voted to abolish all Public Safety Programs, including training in the United States.[28] As a result of these provisions of the Foreign Assistance Act of 1974, the International Police Academy was closed on March 1, 1975.

The Present: More of the Same. The Foreign Assistance Act of 1974, which abolished the International Police Academy, also contained a "sense of Congress" motion, Section 502, calling for the termination or reduction of military aid to any government which "engages in a consistent pattern of gross violations of internationally recognized human rights."[29] Undoubtedly, this expression of sentiment by Congress constituted an innovative forward step in congressional policymaking. Nevertheless, two important notes of realism should be sounded to avoid excessive expectations and romanticism about the law. First, insomuch as Section 502B was enacted in substantial part to right the past wrongs of the OPS and IPA, the emphasis in the statute on human rights defined in terms of freedom from torture and inhumane treatment is understandable.[30] The relative insensitivity of the statute to other social and economic rights spelled out in the U.N. Declaration of Human Rights is not to be explained as mere oversight. Second, it should be noted that the law did not end all forms of police aid to many countries, including the Philippines.

Between 1972 and 1976, U.S. narcotics control aid to the Philippines totaled $1.28 million.[31] This aid continues police assistance under the International Narcotics Control Program run jointly by AID and the Drug Enforcement Agency (DEA).[32] The human rights challenge in this area for the United States involves monitoring and control over training equipment, and technical support. Skills, material, and money acquired in narcotics control can easily be diverted for surveillance and the apprehension of political dissenters. To administer AID support, the Philippine Constabulary Anti-Narcotics Unit was established in 1972 as a special section of the Philippines Constabulary.[33] The latter is the principal enforcement arm of the martial law regime. In 1976, a *Report* to Congress by the General Accounting Office stated ominously that aid earmarked for narcotics control can too easily be shared with nonnarcotic foreign police elements.[34] The Friends of the Filipino People concluded their report of 1977 with the view that, because of the narcotics program, "sophisticated police communications equipment, vehicles, and light weaponry have been channelled to such bodies as the Philippine Constabulary and the military-dominated National Police Commission."[35]

Another problem that continues to bedevil American foreign policy is military aid. The question of security assistance policy related to human rights is complex where the Republic of the Philippines is concerned. The special difficulties associated with analyzing Section 502B considerations were succinctly identified by Robert B. Oakley, Deputy Assistant Secretary of State for East Asian and Pacific Affairs. In his appearance before the Subcommittee on Foreign Operations of the House Appropriations Committee, he said on April 5, 1977:

> We have major military bases in the Philippines, the maintenance of which is important both for the defense of the Philippines from external attack and for the broader security interests of the United States Government. U.S. security assistance has long been viewed by the Philippine Government as an implicit *quid pro quo* for our use of these facilities.[36]

This *quid pro quo* relationship makes it clear that U.S. reliance upon some twenty American military installations, including Clark Air Field and Subic Naval Base, has given the Philippine government considerable leverage over the United States to influence the flow of American security assistance. An irony associated with this situation is that Section 502B was designed to give leverage to the United States over the human rights record of recipient countries. In the politics of bilateral relations, it is not unusual to find leverage available to both parties over the other. The question for political analysis then becomes, which party uses its leverage with skill and success. That the Philippines have attempted to use the leverage of U.S. bases to increase security assistance is the unspoken assumption of the statement of Lester L. Wolff, Chairman of the Subcommittee on Asian and Pacific Affairs, made on March 10, 1977:

> I spoke to General Romulo when I was out in the Philippines last, and I said that I did not think that the American people would stand idly by if there was an attempt to blackmail us—and I used that word—for continuation of the bases in the Philippines.[37]

Months earlier, Foreign Secretary Carlos Romulo, chief negotiator for the Marcos government, had tentatively accepted an offer by Secretary of State

Kissinger of $1 billion over five years as rental payment for continued use of American bases in the Philippines. Half of that amount was to take the form of military aid and half, economic aid. President Marcos, however, overruled his subordinate to turn down the offer, claiming the billion dollars was inadequate and stating furthermore that he would consider accepting $1 billion in military aid alone, with the amount of economic aid to be negotiated above and beyond that.[38] Negotiations on the terms for maintaining U.S. bases in the Philippines have foundered on many points of difference. Among other things, President Marcos, sensitive to U.S. leverage through aid, has demanded that Americans surrender their leverage; that is, he has insisted that any security and development package be considered "rent" for bases in the Philippines. Not falling in the category of "aid," it would thereby not be subject to cuts by Congress.[39]

Turning to the United States, we may ask, how has it used its available leverage to achieve its stated goals? The Philippine Republic has been a recipient of U.S. military aid since 1947. However, since the imposition of martial law by President Ferdinand Marcos, U.S. military aid has escalated from $80.0 million in the four-year period preceding martial law (fiscal years 1969-72) to $166.4 million in the four-year period succeeding martial law (fiscal years 1973-76).[40] This represents an increase of 106 percent. The Carter administration has expressed support for the phaseout of the Military Assistance Program (MAP), but President Carter asked for a $2.6 million increase for the Philippines for fiscal 1978.[41] The Republic of the Philippines is the only country in the world, including many military allies with more nearly exemplary human rights records, where Military Assistance Program requests have increased. In an October 1977 effort spearheaded by Congresswoman Yvonne Burke to reduce Philippine military aid in the spirit of 502B, the Carter administration expressed opposition. According to the Executive Branch Position Paper on HR7797, cuts in military aid to the Philippines "would have a serious impact upon important programs with a treaty ally which allows us the use of valuable military facilities."[42] Thus no effort was made by President Carter to exert leverage upon human rights by way of arms aid; at the same time, President Marcos's reliance upon military bases as leverage to increase security assistance prevailed in the White House, as suggested by the quotation above.

Lack of administration leadership in tying together human rights and military aid was met by successful opposition in the United States House of Representatives. Congressman Long of Maryland, for example, argued that the Carter administration justification for increased aid "is, supposedly, demonstration of continued U.S. support in defense of the Philippines. But even the Pentagon admits that the Philippines is not subject to any viable external threat. It seems that the defense envisioned is, rather, the defense of the Marcos regime."[43] In fact, the "Philippine Amendment," which Representatives Long and Burke supported, was passed in the House by roll-call vote on October 18, 1977.[44] With modifications agreed upon by the Senate, the Appropriations Bill was signed into law by President Carter with a total military appropriation for 1978 in the Philippines of $26.9 million, instead of the $41.4 million which the administration requested.[45]

In the first year of his administration, President Jimmy Carter and Secretary of State Vance projected a new and heightened human rights profile in American foreign policy, and they indicated that arms transfer policies would be significantly affected thereby in the future. However, the enactment in 1977 of the "Philippine Amendment" over presidential objections raised serious questions about such policy. During the president's first month in office, arms transfer restrictions for Argentina, Ethiopia, and Uruguay were proposed (although Uruguay had already been excluded under the 1976 Foreign Assistance Appropriations Act) on human rights grounds.[46] On March 11, Brazil angrily denounced the U.S. accusations of Brazilian violations of human rights, and terminated U.S. military aid, while other Latin American countries followed suit.[47] By contrast, Secretary of State Vance announced in 1977 that "whatever the human rights violations" in the Philippines, aid would not be cut off because of "overriding security considerations."[48]

The Future: Pipelines, Backlogs, and Coproduction. In the first four years after Philippine martial law commenced (1973-1976), all categories of U.S. security aid remained high or have been substantially increased. This is shown in table 16-1. The "business as usual" profile, where regimentation permeates civic life, may not be disturbing in the short term. However, as the *Report to the Congress* by the Comptroller General (GAO) stated in 1976, where martial law has been imposed for an extended period of time a closer look is appropriate.[49] Relying upon the table, a comparison of pre-martial law help with post-martial law aid certainly opens the United States to criticism for pursuing a policy of rewarding repression.

The effectiveness of American human rights policy where military aid is concerned is further called into question if one contemplates an admittedly speculative question. What would happen if arms agreements and appropriations were cut off to a recipient country such as the Philippines? If that were to happen, the flow of arms would nevertheless continue into the future. How long into the future is suggested by the right hand column in the table identified as Backlog Carry Forward. This indicator shows the length of time that the average martial law period demand per annum would continue to be met by "orders in the pipeline" or precommitted credit. Thus, lag time is a critical aspect of arms transfer policy, because it means that an aid cut off may take years to execute. In the case of Chile, for example, there were $100 million in the military assistance "pipeline" when restrictions on arms transfers began in 1974. Were it not for specific congressional intervention, it would be after 1979 when this pipeline would finally go dry.[50]

Table 16-1

Pre-Martial Law (1955-1971) and Post-Martial Law (1972-1976) U.S.-Philippine Foreign Military Sales and Military Assistance
(*in thousands of dollars*)

	1970	1971	1972	1973	1974	1975	1976	1972 and 1976	1955 and 1976	Post-Martial Law as of 1955-76	Backlog Carry Foward[a]
1. Foreign Military Sales											
Credit (direct)					8,600			8,600	8,600	100%	
Foreign Military Sales Credit (guarantee)						14,000		14,000	31,400	44.6%	
2. Foreign Military Sales											
Agreement	843	1,107	468	1,159	4,896	13,809	30,157	68,489	79,401	86.3%	
Foreign Military Sales Deliveries	841	1,309	728	84	1,680	5,412	10,387	18,291	31,985	57.2%	
FMS backlog	+2	−202	−206	+1,075	+3,216	+26,397	+19,970	+50,198	+47,416		4.6 Yrs.
3. Military Assistance Prog.											
(not training)	15,614	14,517	13,152	16,457	14,784	18,975	18,700	82,068	511,165	16.1%	
MAP deliveries	15,867	12,051	15,936	14,816	14,820	12,529	13,506	71,607	474,417	15.1%	
MAP backlog	−253	+2,466	−2,784	+1,641	−36	+6,446	+5,194	+10,461	+36,948		2.7 Yrs.
4. Excess Defense Articles											
Program	3,699	2,333	2,688	15,671	2,470	1,340	4,649	26,818	98,125	27.3%	
EDA deliveries	639	5,233	1,432	4,318	15,014	1,139	5,533	27,436	97,228	28.2%	
EDA backlog	+3,060	−2,900	+1,256	+11,353	−12,544	+201	−884	−618	+897		.6 Yr.
5. International Military Education and Training Program	795	825	989	813	544	473	736	3,555	32,538	10.9%	
IMET deliveries	816	684	978	739	584	597	742	3,740	32,504	10.1%	
IMET backlog	−21	−141	−11	+74	−60	−124	−6	−185	+34		.22 Yr.

Source: Defense Security Assistance Agency, *Foreign Military Sales and Military Assistance Facts, 1976*, (Washington, D.C.: Department of Defense, 1976).

[a] Average martial law period demand per annum (deliveries and expenditures) divided into the total 1955-1976 backlog.

How is the future of 502B leverage over human rights affected in terms of the five components of security assistance as identified in the table?[51]

1. FMS Credit. Military hardware, services, and training bought from the United States may be purchased on credit, classified as either "direct" or "guaranty."[52] Direct credits come from the Department of Defense and finance the entire cost of a purchase. Guaranty credits are used to back loans worth ten times the amount of appropriated funds. Thus $8.6 million direct credit to the Philippines will buy $8.6 million worth of equipment, service, and training. But $14 million guaranteed credit will buy $140 million (nearly half of the 1976 Philippine Gross National Product). Although the Philippines cannot possibly use all available FMS credit in any one year, these credits are transferable and may be called upon years after they were initially appropriated. The future is thus assured despite possible action by congressional "meddlers."

2. FMS Agreements. Like FMS credit, sales agreements also use the Department of Defense procurement system, but sales are for cash. There is no legal limit to the amount purchaseable by the buyer in any one year, and classified or government-manufactured equipment is available only through this Pentagon source. FMS Agreements for 1977 for the Philippines are $71 million.[53] The difference between agreements (contracts) and deliveries is referred to in the table as the "FMS Backlog." It acts like mortgage insurance in the sense that if the United States were to refuse to enter into agreements as of 1976, the Philippines would still have sufficient backlog to meet average demand for the next 4.6 years. This figure gives substance to the cynical observation made by Philippine opposition leaders that "Marcos plans to outlast the four-year term of any American president."

3. MAP Equipment. The United States retains title to all Military Assistance Program equipment. MAP is scheduled to end in 1980 on the congressional view that foreign governments should bear the cost of their own defense. A presumption is raised that the intent of 502B is violated where the Philippines is concerned by virtue of its being the only country to enjoy projected increases in this category. While MAP equipment is not supposed to go to the constabulary units which enforce martial law, the 1976 GAO *Report* found that the constabulary use of MAP equipment was uncontrollably in violation of the Foreign Assistance Act of 1973 which forbids mixing police with military functions.[54]

4. EDA Grants. The grant program for Excess Defense Articles is the Pentagon's "bargain basement" aid in the form of grants at reduced rates of military equipment. Annual appropriations from Congress are not required, but there

is a $100 million annual ceiling.[55] EDA grants to the Philippines in the first
four years of martial law were three times larger than in the preceding four
years.

5. IMET Program. This involves instruction of foreign military officers by
officers or employees of the United States. The instruction takes place in the
United States and overseas. IMET funds are appropriated annually by Congress.
Before 1976, the International Military Education and Training Program was
a part of MAP. But when Congress voted to phase out MAP, it decided to perpetuate the training program as one which could be continued separately. Half
of the torturers identified by the 1976 Amnesty International Report were
IMET graduates.[56]

The weaponry and training provided under these programs are intended to
help the Philippines defend itself against external attack. But studies conducted
by the GAO, the Friends of the Filipino People, and the Center for International
Policy in Washington, D.C., have all found that arms-export policy simply helps
perpetuate Philippine martial law and the Marcos regime. These groups detail
examples whereby American security aid is diverted for internal use to combat
rebellious minorities or to crush dissident movements.[57]

Even if efforts were made to pull back where aid is concerned, one American contribution that remains to be identified has passed the point of no return.
Increasingly U.S. industries are exporting their technical expertise by way of
"coproduction" projects with arms producers. Such joint production efforts
involve both American and foreign producers. According to the Stockholm
International Peace Research Institute, U.S. coproduction in the Philippines
involving the manufacture of 150,000 Colt M-16 rifles is now under way.[58] The
problem with this kind of enterprise lies in the fact that the transfer of technology is irrevocable, it increases the number of arms suppliers a belligerent can
turn to in wartime, and it generates new demands which are beyond the control
of the technological donor. Thus coproduction, which in the Philippines is
fostered for the purpose of "making the Philippines self-reliant" in small arms
production, may in some regards be more dangerous than direct arms transfers.[59]
By building local arms industries in such countries as the Philippines, coproduction has the effect for the foreseeable future of reducing any potential leverage
that arms aid might have in the promotion of human rights.

Four Views from Manila Bay

Complex interrelationships between the Republic of the Philippines and the
United States have been reviewed above with an effort to present an ample
range of factual detail. However, to paraphrase Justice Holmes, the facts do
not speak for themselves. They must be interpreted.

In a summer 1977 lecture tour in East Asia, I encountered many interpretations of U.S.-Philippine relations. But I think that four views of these matters which merit summary stand out clearly, each putting the "facts" in a different light. The four perceptual patterns set out below are hardly consistent, one with another. They are arrayed, at the one extreme, from views based on assumptions about the need for abrupt if revolutionary change, to views on the other side, which reflect preferences for incremental if traditional modes of societal change. The attitudes reported below reflect the disparate opinions of forty well-educated, urban Filipinos—technocrats, lawyers, church people, academics, and members of professional and political elites. My interviews and meetings in the Philippines were extensive and involved a broad spectrum of government as well as opposition leaders. Because of possible political recriminations, however, I shall eschew standard scholarly annotation practice and refrain from identifying by name the sources of many opinions summarized.

The four views of human rights which I encountered may be labeled: (1) The "Figleaf" Theory (which sees the Philippine experience as a process of arms race victimization masked by diverting rhetoric); (2) The "Bread and Freedom" Theory (which sees U.S.-Philippine relations in terms of a tragedy of modern liberalism stemming from ignorance over the conditions requisite to promote economic development); (3) "The Children of Light and the Children of Darkness" Theory (which sees Carter-Marcos rivalry in politico-moral terms); and (4) the "It's Working" Theory (which takes satisfaction in finding progress toward the "normalization" promised by President Marcos, explained at least in part by effective U.S. diplomatic action "behind the scenes.")

The "Figleaf" Theory of Human Rights. The volume of arms trade with Third World countries has grown consistently in the 1970s. Far from being a carefully controlled instrument of foreign policy in the service of human rights, the international market for arms has grown wildly in recent years. To stave off recession and to recover capital flowing from the United States to oil-producing countries, U.S. arms sales have burgeoned. In just three years, 1973-1975, the United States secured firm orders for military equipment and services valued at $13.7 billion from OPEC countries (Organization of Oil Producing Countries).[60] The patina of human rights activism which covers this activity with legitimacy diverts attention from two considerations which are politically sensitive in the United States: first, the role of U.S. responsibility for building repressive regimes through the reckless Public Safety Program of the late 1960s; second, the enormity of arms sales to Arab (OPEC) countries which is inconsistent with U.S. avowals of support for Israel. The question of whether arms-transfer policy is in service of human rights or whether the reverse is the case can be analyzed in terms of the figure below. If we are interested in human rights violators over whom the United States has high policy leverage through security assistance, then we shall be concerned with those recipient countries which fall in matrix cell A (see figure 16-1). Iran and the Philippines would be examples. In fact, not one arms recipient falling into matrix cell A has been the object of serious arms cuts. Each has been exempted on the excuse of overriding American national interest considerations. Indeed, in the cases of Iran and the Philippines, both have enjoyed ever-increasing assistance in most categories of arms aid said to be under the influence of human rights considerations. In the words of one Philippines intellectual, "All of this human rights hypocrisy is simply a cover for unpopular military policy and massive transactions in arms hardware. First, there was Admiral Dewey, then General MacArthur. We don't need to be saved by American military force a third time."

The "Bread and Freedom" Theory. In the *Termination Phase-Out Study* of the Public Safety Program in the Philippines, the Evaluation Team noted that the build-up of a centralized and coordinated law enforcement capability was an appropriate corollary to guiding development theory relied upon by the American Agency for International Development in the 1960s. The *Report* specified the corollary in these terms: "As the economy continues to expand, prices of basic commodities rise, and wage scales remain static, crimes against property can be expected to escalate accordingly."[61] Philippine technocrats have followed President Marcos in accepting the assumption that economic development is a deeply destablizing force in society and political and social dislocation must accordingly be anticipated by vigorous and, if necessary, coercive control.

In this connection, the Development Academy of the Philippines—"President Marcos's think-tank"—has many scholars who take seriously the writings of Samuel P. Huntington of Harvard. They interpret his *Political Order in Changing Societies* (1968) to amount to a Third World prescription applicable to the Philippines, namely: establish a strong central authority before worrying

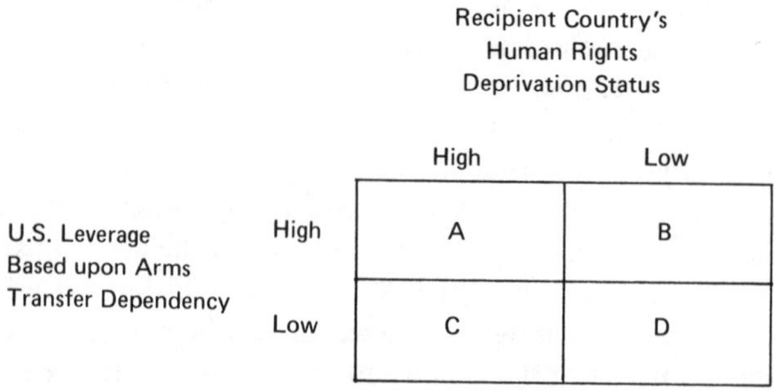

Recipient Country's
Human Rights
Deprivation Status

		High	Low
U.S. Leverage Based upon Arms Transfer Dependency	High	A	B
	Low	C	D

Figure 16-1. U.S. Assistance and Human Rights Deprivation

about representation and the Western luxury of civil liberties.[62] This view is presented with skill by O.D. Corpus, President of the University of the Philippines. His essay "Liberty and Government in the New Society" is required reading for Philippine technocrats.[63] Arguing that "the human societies for which Locke and Jefferson were the eloquent intellectual architects exist no more," Corpus concludes his intellectual manifesto in terms designed to cut ideological links to the United States. "That tradition of liberty and freedom in which we all have been schooled," he wrote, "is inadequate for the development of humanity and civil life under modern conditions." The essay seeks to justify as "historical necessity" the Marcos regime in terms of its building popular support. This it has done through the development of effective economic and social programs instead of through a preoccupation with a "licentious press" and the "corruption" of political party machinations. A variation on the Corpus thesis that human rights must be secondary to economic development is the criticism that Americans do not understand human rights development even in their own country. "Don't tell us about your version of human rights," said a relative of President Marcos in a private interview. She continued:

> We are already patterning ourselves upon the United States, except, we are at the stage of development which you reached in the late nineteenth century. We need a few Rockefellers, Carnegies, and Hills to speed things up. After they have done their job, we will bring them under control through tax policy and then worry about freedom of the press. That's the American version of human rights which we understand.

American contributions to Philippines economic development, tied as they are to an authoritarian ideology, have a counterproductive effect, according to some dissident Philippine critics. Continued aid helps to consolidate the Marcos dictatorship in three ways, they say. First, its massive volume serves to signal American approval of the regime. Second, it allows the government of the Philippines to divert resources otherwise earmarked for economic ends to military purposes. Third, a significant portion of it, for example, in the narcotics control program, is used for internal security ends. The fact that the impact of American policy in these three facets is known and not acted upon in the United States shows, according to Philippine critics, that Americans have not thought through their own human rights policy. Human rights must be promoted as part of a strategy to achieve economic development. "If you Americans can't do that," according to one, a mid-level government employee, "then you should stop all this talk of human rights, as if you had something important to say."

"The Children of Light and the Children of Darkness" Theory. At a breakfast meeting with the pastor of one of Manila's largest Protestant churces, the observation was made that President Carter had styled himself an intellectual follower

of Reinhold Niebuhr, the theologian. The pastor raised the question of whether it seemed likely that Jimmy Carter had gotten the point of Niebuhr's celebrated book *The Children of Light and the Children of Darkness* (1944).[64] The title is taken from St. Luke's observation (chapter 16, verse 8) that "the children of this world are in their generation wiser than the children of light." This meant, said the pastor, that the pursuit of morally worthy goals must not founder on naiveté. The righteous must cultivate cunning as effective as that of their opponents, but their actions must also show sincerity of purpose.

An editorial by Teodoro Valencia in the *Philippines Daily Express* (February 17, 1977) carried the theme of Carter's disingenuousness. The author wrote in the state-controlled newspaper:

> Filipinos, including some Church leaders, had hoped to use U.S. President Carter's announced abhorrence of violators of civil rights and human rights to needle President Marcos. Even the latest pastoral letter carried rings of warning that the President of the USA may look with disfavor on some of the practices of martial law. But these colonial-minded Filipinos must have suffered a shock when President Carter called down the U.S. State Department for denouncing Russia's imprisonment of writer Andrei Sakharov. . . . Obviously, America is to have a double standard, one for big guys like Russia and China and another for small ones like the Philippines, Indonesia and Singapore.[65]

An opposition senator who had been involved in the Plaza Miranda affair expressed deep disappointment over the absence of American "follow-through" in advancing human rights. He said:

> While America is our best friend, you cannot string us along with moral promises and then expect equanimity when you fail us. Indeed, the level of cynicism over U.S. human rights posturing is so deep that if I were running for office today, I could only get elected from my constituency by adopting an anti-American position.

Many Philippine observers with whom I spoke were fearful that American policymakers would be "outfoxed" by Marcos's efforts to coopt the human rights theme—his human rights address soon after the election of President Carter, his announcement of the lifting of travel bans on Filipino citizens and the cynical substitution of a $100 airport tax on travelers, his sponsorship of the "World Peace through Law Conference" in Manila in August 1977. According to a young Manila attorney, "It was in a spirit of abject bluff that Marcos told the Board of Governors of the Asian Development Bank in April 1977 that he could not be faulted in his view that human rights and economic development go hand in hand." President Marcos's comment had been: "There can be no trade-off of human rights with economic development."[66]

The Theory That "It's Working." President Carter has suggested that a foreign policy, to be durable, must reflect the values of its constituent people. The United States as a moral force in the world must not be reluctant to be forthright in promoting human rights, whatever the short-run consequences, and despite occasional embarrassments. "Endurance in pursuit of a high goal, not a scoreboard count of wins and losses, will make the difference in the long run." This is the attitude which I met among American embassy personnel at the post in Manila. They thought that President Marcos had already relented somewhat on human rights standards: new disciplinary actions brought against alleged torturers, willingness of the Marcos government to admit visitors to rehabilitation centers, and announcements after August 1977 that President Marcos would make new efforts toward "normalization."[67] "Of course, we are using assorted diplomatic measures in support of human rights," I was told.

One of those who have welcomed President Carter's heightened profile of human rights is Dr. Salvador P. Lopez. He participated in the formulation of the United Nations Declaration of Human Rights in 1947. For that reason, and also because he has remained a fearless spokesman during the period of martial law, he is affectionately known by students at the University of the Philippines and by many others in the Philippines as "Mr. Human Rights." In a February 1977 comment on "United States Foreign Policy and Human Rights," he stated sagely: "In the end, the Filipino people must accept the self-evident truth that their own salvation as a free people, the future of freedom and democracy in the Philippines, cannot be left to the intentions of an outside power, however well-meaning and generous. It lies solely in their own hands."[68]

Among Filipinos with whom I spoke, the observation was unexpectedly but widely made that "Carter's talk of human rights has made talk of human rights here legitimate." The point of subtle analysis underlying this view is that verbal behavior in politics does bring about marginal changes which can be important. Before Carter, public discussion of human rights was politically suspect, as was all political talk in public. The effect of subversion charges applied to anti-Marcos gatherings, as well as detention without charges for political disputation, had the inevitable "chilling effect" of discouraging the most innocent political exchange. "But now," according to a young sociologist, "human rights groups are springing up all over." An attorney made a similar observation: "Since so much can now be done in the name of 'human rights' which previously was forbidden, it is not surprising that there is much curiosity about these human rights." U.S. influence on human rights remains potentially strong in such Asian countries as the Philippines and South Korea. But despite their military ties to the United States, both allies have demonstrated the limits of such pressure. Whether changes in verbal behavior on the part of grass-roots Filipinos who are now eager and animated in their newly open ventilation of human rights issues signify the dawn of changing public policy remains to be seen. There are those who say of American human rights policy that, through the interest it has heightened, if not through the exercises of political, economic, or military leverage, "it's working." Of course, when their voices are heard in a free Philippine press, in open and independent courts, in classrooms marked by academic freedom, and in chambers of elected legislative representatives, then we shall know that "it's working."

Conclusion

American human rights initiatives are not likely to be effective unless they are coupled with a rational arms transfer policy. When arms transfers are said to be a tool of foreign policy, as in the United States, then the instrument chosen must be suited to the goal and used consistently. Although the refusal to sell arms to a nation on account of human rights violations will not, by itself, ensure the redress of human rights grievances, it may prove effective in conjunction with the application of other policy instruments. But an impediment stands in the way of this strategy. That impediment is that the United States does not have an arms transfer policy. A vacuum remains evident in place of clear-cut common standards for review of the proposed recipient's stance. The executive branch is better equipped to develop such criteria in combination with international human rights policy than is the legislative branch. But a case-by-case approach, without consistently weighted policy criteria, has been predominant under both Republican and Democratic administrations. When a decision is made without reference to a generally shared and clearly stated policy, then flexibility is gained, but at potentially great cost. The prospect for friction between Congress and the executive is increased, and serious expectations abroad regarding the promotion of human rights are disappointed.

On the whole, the United States is likely to be accepted by Third World countries, such as the Philippines, as a partner in the development of human rights. But in such a partnership they should be able to expect that the United States will be on tap, not on top, and they should be able to expect from the United States clear policy and consistent action.

Notes

1. "U.S. Blocks Rights Data on Nations Getting Arms Aid," *New York Times*, November 19, 1975, pp. 1, 14.

2. William T. Butler, John P. Humphrey, G.E. Bisson, *The Decline of Democracy in the Philippines* (Geneva: International Commission of Jurists, 1977); Amnesty International, "Report of the Mission to the Republic of the Philippines, 22 November-5 December 1975" (London: Amnesty International,

1976). See also the Committee on International Relations, Hearings before the Subcommittee on International Organizations, "Human Rights in the Philippines: Report by Amnesty International," Testimony by Thomas C. Jones, member, Amnesty International Mission to the Philippines; 94th Cong., 2d Sess., Sept. 15, 1976, p. 11. And see Richard P. Claude, "The Decline of Human Rights in the Republic of the Philippines," *New York Law School Law Review* 24 (1978), 201-223.

3. Interview by the author with President Marcelo B. Fernan of the Integrated Bar Association, Manila, July 26, 1977.

4. Association of Major Religious Superiors in the Philippines, *Political Detainees in the Philippines*, Book 2 (mimeo) 31 March 1977, Appendix 1, p. xiii. "Torture during arrest is still being reported. E.g., Roger Posadas,–only doctor of nuclear physics in the Philippines, arrested Jan. 6, 1976. Kept 70 days in 'safehouse' where he was subjected to beatings with fists and .45 caliber pistol."

5. *Manila Bulletin Today*, 12 December 1974, p. 1.

6. Major Religious Superiors, *Political Detainees*, "Torture, Deaths and Disappearances," pp. 22-47.

7. Ibid., pp. 24-26.

8. Ibid., p. 27. The vast majority of those imprisoned and tortured under martial law have been Catholics. Jovito R. Salonga, a Protestant spokesman and one-time opposition senator, has commented upon this and related ironies. In 1977, he said, "The Muslim rebels, who have inflicted serious losses on the Armed Forces, are not being arrested or prosecuted today for rebellion, subversion, or illegal possession of firearms. In fact, the government continues to negotiate with them and has agreed to grant amnesty to and release all Muslim political prisoners. Why should Christian, non-Muslim prisoners, most of whom have not even taken up arms, be treated differently?" "For a More Credible Human Rights Posture," Speech delivered before the Makati Rotary Club, June 28, 1977, p. 7.

9. Major Religious Superiors, pp. 7-8, 28. For related analysis, see Richard P. Claude, "Reliable Information: The Threshold Problem for Human Rights Research," *Human Rights* (Journal of the American Bar Association), 6 (1977), 169-177.

10. International Commission of Jurists, *Decline of Democracy*, p. 47.

11. See the analysis of "contributory responsibility" by Joel Feinberg in *Doing and Deserving, Essays in the Theory of Responsibility* (Princeton: Princeton University Press, 1970), p. 222, in chapter 9, "Collective Responsibility."

12. Donald M. Fraser and John P. Salzberg, "Foreign Policy and Effective Strategies for Human Rights," in *Universal Human Rights*, 1 (Jan.-Feb. 1979), 32-40.

13. Lewis M. Simons, "U.S. to Skirt Rights Issue Aid to Friends," *Washington Post* A 23, col. 6 (Sunday, September 11, 1977).

14. Gabriel de Tardé, "Theory of Responsibility," in Herbert Morris, ed., *Freedom and Responsibility* (Stanford: Stanford University Press, 1961), p. 47.

15. Justice Enrique Fernando, "The Revised Constitution as Fundamental Law," in Mendoza, *Perspectives*, p. 106.

16. Ibid., p. 118. *Miranda* v. *Arizona*, 384 U.S. 436 (1966).

17. U.S. Department of State, Agency for International Development, *AID General Notice*, November 30, 1962.

18. Comptroller General of the United States, *Report to the Congress* "Stopping U.S. Assistance to Foreign Police and Prisons" (Washington, D.C.: General Accounting Office, 1976), p. 1.

19. Ibid., p. 15.

20. Ibid., p. 16. See especially Thomas Lobe, "Adventures in Social Control in the Third World," *United States National Security Policy and Aid to the Thailand Police* (Denver: University of Denver Graduate School of International Studies, *Monograph Series in World Affairs*, vol. 14, book 2, 1977), pp. 3-11.

21. Ibid., p. 16. The underlying Kennedy administration "Counter-Insurgency Theory" is difficult to fault as to the original intention, which was to minimize coercion. The police, using less powerful weapons and more peaceful methods than the armed forces, were thought less likely to alienate the civilian populations of developing countries. With proper use of police, a government could apply the lowest level of violence necessary to suppress disorder. In practice, however, the theoretical distinction broke down. On the one hand, the Pentagon had more funds and personnel than the Office of Public Safety. On the other hand, many Third World governments were controlled by the military, or soon came to be, and the police were then used in ways to blur the distinction.

22. Jeter Williamson and Paul Katz, Evaluation Team, *Termination Phase-Out Study*, Public Safety Project, Philippines, (Washington, D.C.: Office of Public Safety, 1974), pp. 52-55.

23. Ibid., p. 12. The predisposition of Filipino law enforcement personnel to an autocratic attitude in police decision-making is reported by the Civil Service Commission, *Special Annual Report on Local Police Personnel Management*, 1965 (Manila: Civil Service Commission, 1966), pp. 78-79. On Asian police attitudes and human rights, see David H. Bayley, *Forces of Order* (Berkeley: University of California Press, 1976).

24. Walden Bello and Saverina Rivera, eds. *Logistics of Repression* (Washington, D.C.: Friends of the Filipino People, 1977) p. 30.

25. Williamson and Katz, *Termination Study*, p. 34. Equipment description is found in AID Project 492-11-710-231, "Internal Security, U.S./Philippines, 1970-1973."

26. Senate Committee on Foreign Relations, Staff Memorandum, *Guatemala and the Dominican Republic*, 92d Cong., 1st Sess., 1971.

27. 22 USC. 2420, Sec. 660 (Sec. 30(a) of the Foreign Assistance Act of 1974).

28. Benedict Kerkvliet, "Statement for the Friends of the Filipino People," House Committee on Foreign Affairs, *Fiscal 1975 Foreign Assistance Request* (Washington, D.C.: Government Printing Office, 1974), p. 775.

29. 22 USC. 2304, Sec. 502B. Reflecting the link between arms aid gone awry and used for internal repression and human rights emphasizing personal liberty, the law formerly read:

Sec. 502B, Human Rights—It is the sense of Congress that, except in extraordinary circumstances, the President shall substantially reduce or terminate security assistance to any government which engages in a consistent pattern of gross violations of internationally recognized human rights, including torture or cruel, inhuman or degrading treatment or punishment; prolonged detention without charges; or other flagrant denials of the right to life, liberty, and the security of the person.

But in 1976 it was broadened to read:

Sec. 502B. Human Rights—(a)(1) It is the policy of the United States, in accordance with its international obligations as set forth in the Charter of the United Nations and in keeping with the constitutional heritage and traditions of the United States, to promote and encourage increased respect for human rights and fundamental freedoms for all without distinction as to race, sex, language, or religion. To this end, a principal goal of the foreign policy of the United States is to promote the increased observance of internationally recognized human rights by all countries.

(2) It is further the policy of the United States that, except under circumstances specified in this section, no security assistance may be provided to any country the government of which engages in a consistent pattern of gross violations of internationally recognized human rights.

30. "Our most concentrated attention over the years and recently has been involved with the violations of integrity of the person—officially sanctioned murders, tortures, and detentions without trial." Statement of Warren M. Christopher, Deputy Secretary of State, Senate Committee on Foreign Selections, Hearings of the Subcommittee on Foreign Assistance, "Human Rights," 95th Cong., 1st Sess., March 7, 1977, p. 63.

31. Senate Foreign Relations Committee, Subcommittee on Foreign Assistance, "Foreign Assistance Authorization: Arms Sales Issues," 94th Cong., 2d Sess., 1976, p. 39.

32. Friends of Filipino People, *Logistics*, pp. 30-32.

33. Williamson and Katz, *Termination Study*, pp. 51-55.

34. Comptroller General, *Report to Congress*, pp. 25-27.

35. Trials, *Logistics*, p. 31.

36. Statement by Robert B. Oakley, Deputy Assistant Secretary of State for East Asian and Pacific Affairs, House Subcommittee on Appropriations "Foreign Assistance and Related Agencies Appropriations for 1978," 95th Cong., 1st Sess., 1977, p. 612.

37. Committee on International Relations, Hearings in Subcommittee on Asian and Pacific Affairs, "Foreign Assistance Legislation for 1978," Comment by Chairman Lester L. Wolff, 95th Cong., 1st Sess., 1977, p. 24.

38. Senate Committee on Foreign Relations, Staff Report "U.S.-Philippine Base Negotiations" (Washington, D.C.: Government Printing Office, 1977), p. 3.

39. Center for International Policy, *Human Rights and the U.S. Assistance Program, Fiscal 1978, Part 2–East Asia* (Washington, D.C.: Center for International Policy 1977), p. 34. "Marcos Said End of Martial Law Will Depend on Carter's Policies, Especially on Pact on Philippine Bases," *New York Times*, Feb. 13, 1977, p. 11, col. 1, See, also, "Accord Reached on 2 U.S. Bases," *Washington Post*, January 1, 1979, p. 1, col. 4.

40. Data Management Division, *Foreign Military Sales and Military Assistance Facts* (Washington, D.C.: Department of Defense, Security Assistance Agency, 1976).

41. Committee on International Relations, Report of a Special Study Mission to Asia, April 8-21, 1977, "Security Assistance to Asia for Fiscal 1978," 95th Cong., 1st Sess., June 19, 1977, p. 1.

42. Executive Branch Position Paper on HR-7797 (Senate Amendment 74), October 18, 1977.

43. *Congressional Record* (daily) United States House of Representatives, 95th Cong., 1st Sess., October 18, 1977, p. H11211. "U.S. Study Questions Pacific Bases' Value," *New York Times*, April 10, 1977, p. 7, col. 1.

44. Ibid., p. H11212.

45. "6.8 Billion Foreign Aid," *Washington Post*, October 19, 1977, p. A-18, col. 3.

46. "Brazil Cancels Treaty," *New York Times*, March 12, 1977, p. 1, col. 1.

47. "U.S. Says Six Nations Curb Human Rights," *New York Times*, January 2, 1977, p. 1, col. 1. The sequence of developments can be conveniently reviewed by reliance upon the *Congressional Quarterly* (Weekly edition, vol. 35, 1977), No. 2, p. 79 (January 8); No. 10, p. 406 (March 5); No. 19, p. 886 (April 7); No. 25, p. 1205 (June 18); No. 26, p. 1283 (June 25).

48. House Appropriations Committee, Subcommittee on Foreign Operations, "Foreign Assistance," 95th Cong., 1st Sess., March 2, 1977, p. 48.

49. Comptroller, *Report*, pp. 34-35.

50. 22 U.S.C. 2370, Foreign Assistance Act of 1974, Sec. 25, as amended, International Security Assistance and Arms Export Control Act of 1976, June 30, 1976.

51. Each is explained in Data Management, *Military Sales*, p. 1. See also "Security Assistance to Asia for 1978," pp. 21-27.

52. Center for International Policy, *Human Rights*, p. 6.

53. Ibid., p. 32; see also *Statistical Abstract of the U.S. 1976* (Washington, D.C.: U.S. Department of Commerce, 1976), pp. 836-838.

54. Comptroller General, *Report*, pp. 28-36.

55. Center for International Policy, *Human Rights*, pp. 6, 32.

56. Friends of Filipino People, *Logistics*, p. 30.

57. Comptroller, *Report*, pp. 22-23, 32-34; Friends, *Logistics*, pp. 23-28, 54-58, 76-77; Center, *Human Rights*, pp. 31-36.

58. Stockholm International Peace Research Institute, *World Armaments and Disarmament, SIPRI Yearbook, 1976* (Cambridge: M.I.T. Press, 1976) p. 36. Since 1974, the Department of Defense, with Colt Industries of Connecticut, has been coproducing M-16 rifles in the Philippines, with the aid of FMS credits totaling $21.8 million. The Philippines purchased 10,000 and assembled 140,000 rifles, plus spare parts over the period 1975-1979.

59. Interview by Jonathan David with Kenneth Bleakley, Political-Military Advisor, Philippine Desk, Department of State, November 10, 1977. On the penetration of the Philippines and other Third World countries by multinational firms, see Robert B. Stauffer, *Nation-Building in a Global Economy* (Beverly Hills: Sage Professional Paper, 01-039, 1973).

60. SIPRI *Yearbook*, pp. 136-137.

61. Williamson and Katz, *Termination*, p. 3.

62. Samuel Huntington, *Political Order in Changing Societies* (New Haven: Yale University Press, 1968).

63. O.D. Corpus, "Liberty and Government in the New Society" (Quezon City: University of the Philippines, 1975). A mélange of more recent uncensored views may be found in the very interesting symposium volume *Human Rights in the Philippines*, edited by Purification Valera-Quisumbing and Armando F. Bonifacio (Quezon City: University of the Philippines Law Center, 1977).

64. Reinhold Niebuhr, *The Children of Light and the Children of Darkness* (New York: Scribner Brothers, 1944).

65. Teodoro F. Valencia, "We Stand to Gain," *Philippine Daily Express*, February 17, 1977, p. 4, col. 1.

66. Ferdinand E. Marcos, "Human Rights and Economic Development," address at the Annual Meeting of the Board of Governors of the Asian Development Bank, Philippine International Conference Center, April 1977.

67. "President Ferdinand Marcos Relaxes Martial Law," *Washington Post*, A13, col. 2, August 22, 1977. "Promises, Promises in Manila," *New York Times*, August 25, 1977, p. 18, col. 1. "Marcos Establishes New Party," *New York Times*, February 2, 1978, p. 10, col. 4.

68. Salvador P. Lopez, "U.S. Foreign Policy and Human Rights" (unpublished mimeo, February 25, 1977).

17 Arms Sales and Human Rights: The Case of South Korea

Jerome Alan Cohen

Like the Shah's Iran, the Republic of Korea too must be a special case for Americans. True, General Park Chung-Hee's overthrow of Korea's shortlived democratic government in 1961 cannot be attributed to American intervention. Indeed, had the legitimately elected President Yun Po-Sun asked his American ally to suppress the usurpers, the United States would probably have done so. Yet, once the new leaders seized power, the American attitude toward them gradually changed from suspicion and hostility to unenthusiastic acquiescence to strong support, despite their increasingly repressive rule. And in South Korea American support has been indispensable to the survival of any government and of the Republic itself.

Of course, the special responsibility of the United States for basic freedoms and other fundamental human rights in South Korea long antedated the advent of the Park regime. Americans not only played the key role in liberating Korea from Japanese colonial oppression at the end of World War II but also agreed to the Soviet occupation of the northern part of the peninsula while U.S. forces occupied the southern part. As the USSR and its Korean sympathizers converted the North into a totalitarian Communist system, the American occupiers taught people in the South as much about authoritarian practices as about democratic principles in the process of bringing order out of chaos and creating a government that would be responsive to both American interests and ideology. When postwar attempts to establish a unified government for the entire peninsula failed, it was the United States that took the initiative in establishing the Republic of Korea under U.N. auspices in the South while the Communists established the Democratic People's Republic of Korea (DPRK) in the North, thus perpetuating the novel and tragic division of the Korean people. When, following the 1948 withdrawal of U.S. forces from the ROK, its Communist rival sought to unify the peninsula by force in 1950, the United States led the foreign coalition that under the U.N. banner went to the defense of the ROK. At the end of that bloody stalemate, the United States concluded the Mutual Security Treaty of 1954 with the ROK, obligating the United States to come to the defense of South Korea "in accordance with its constitutional processes." Washington thereafter continued to provide military and economic aid to the ROK that at last report totaled over $13 billion, in addition to stationing forces

The author is grateful to Professor Gregory Henderson for valuable comments on the manuscript.

at a cost that has now reached well over \$12 billion.[1] Moreover, because South Korea was alienated from all its neighbors—the Communist regimes that controlled China, the Soviet Union and North Korea and the detested Japanese colonialists—and largely isolated from the rest of the world, the overall American impact upon the ROK was immense. Americans not only became the defenders of South Koreans but, in trade, investment, politics, cultural life, and education, also became their mentors and big brothers. American contacts with South Korea are far more intimate than those with Iran, and U.S. influence over its people and their values is correspondingly greater.

From 1948 to 1965 the United States did not hesitate to use its enormous influence over the ROK for many purposes. Although the American occupation had offered only a flawed and ambiguous model of democratic rule, after the ROK was established, Washington, under both Democratic and Republican administrations, intervened on a number of occasions to press the autocratic Syngman Rhee to curb some of the worst excesses of his often arbitrary presidency. Some of these American interventions took the form of public scoldings. In March 1950, for example, Secretary of State Dean G. Acheson sharply reminded the Rhee regime "that U.S. aid, both military and economic, to the Republic of Korea has been predicated upon the existence and growth of democratic institutions within the Republic."[2] Such ad hoc admonitions and behind-the-scenes pressures could not alter the nature of Rhee's government—that was left to the students of Korea, who in the spring of 1960, after rigged national elections and subsequent cover-up, went into the streets and rocked Rhee from office. But the spasmodic American pressures, and Rhee's awareness that greater abuses might elicit even sterner reactions, did place limits upon his arbitrariness. Furthermore, they at least made clear to the Korean people that the United States did not endorse his authoritarianism. The U.S. position was surely not an irrelevant factor in the calculations of those who overthrew Rhee and gave Koreans the only year of unrestricted political freedom they have ever known.

During the first few years after Park's military coup aborted the experiment with democracy, the United States exercised its leverage over the ROK's new authoritarian rulers as it had over Rhee. Thus a combination of American and domestic pressures forced Park to don more legitimate civilian clothes in 1963 by holding a national election which he won by only the barest plurality despite his control of the government. Even after that election Park remained very unsure of the American support that was essential to his continuing in office. Nothing in his education and service in the Japanese military and his postwar Korean military experience had equipped him to deal with American politicians and diplomats. Yet in the circumstances in which he found himself the challenge of coping with them was especially great.

Not only was Washington maintaining a policy of equidistance between the new rulers and the then still active opposition forces, who were bolstered by renewed antigovernment demonstrations by the students, but Park also had to

be concerned about potential rivals within the ruling elite itself. Park sorely
needed the U.S. seal of approval to consolidate his power. If he was to prove a
more effective vote-getter at the next election, he would have to demonstrate
to his colleagues and to the people generally that he was an effective aid-getter.
In view of the pervasiveness of the felt "threat from the North," military aid was
especially crucial. If Park couldn't get it, the ROK would need someone who
could.

Moreover, given South Korea's extreme dependence on the United States
and the insecurity of the Park regime, all participants in Seoul politics were extremely sensitive to signs, cues, utterances, and gestures from American sources.
Delphic diplomatic announcements and plastic smiles and smirks of even lowly
embassy officials—not to mention explicit public criticism—made Korean hearts
palpitate violently. In South Vietnam President Diem had just been eliminated
by rivals within the elite, with what degree of American assistance Park could
not be certain.

Thus, as late as 1965, American leverage over the ROK seemed very great,
and it was coupled with the continuing will to use it, if only on occasion, to
moderate some of the regime's worst abuses against human rights and efforts to
suppress pluralistic elements in society. Of course, the United States also used
its leverage for other purposes, pressing Seoul, for example, to restore diplomatic
relations with Japan in 1965, an action that improved Park's bargaining position
in Washington.

Then came the massive American involvement in Vietnam, which markedly
changed Korean-American relations. In order to sustain that tragic adventure,
the United States badly needed Korean combat forces in Vietnam beginning in
late 1965. To be sure, troops from the ROK, a client-state and nonmember of
either the U.N. or SEATO, whose armed forces are under the command of an
American general even on Korean soil, could hardly have been expected to give
a great boost to the Johnson administration's attempt to transform the war into
an international crusade against communism. Nevertheless, the addition of the
Korean flag was useful for propaganda purposes. More important, of course, was
the actual fighting role of the fierce Korean contingents, whose presence made
the number of U.S. casualities lower than they otherwise would have been at a
time when the American public was becoming increasingly hostile to the war.

The Vietnam War would have been helpful to the Park regime even if the
United States had not needed ROK combat forces. The war proved a major
stimulus to South Korea's developing economy, generating surpluses that could
be used both to assure further prosperity and to consolidate Park's political
base. Vietnam also vividly reminded opposition parties, students, and Koreans
generally that too much internal disunity could risk defeat by their Communist
kinsmen to the north.

Yet the American request for ROK combat forces made the war a veritable
heaven-sent opportunity for Park. In view of the enormity and pervasiveness

of American influence in Korea, the total dependence of the ROK armed forces
on U.S. weapons, logistics, training, organization, and operations, and Park's
need for Washington's approval of his still shaky rule, it was probably an offer
that he could not have refused. Nevertheless, he seized this opportunity, as well
as American insistence upon Seoul's normalization of relations with Tokyo, to
wring out of the United States everything that he could have hoped for as support. Lyndon Johnson's gratitude was Texas-sized. Washington totally em-
braced Park.

Through a series of policies and public and private utterances and gestures
the United States made clear to Koreans and the world that its earlier doubts
about Park had dissipated and that American ties with the ROK were closer than
ever. Vice President Hubert Humphrey visited Seoul in February 1966 and
sought to overcome the uncertainty inherent in the U.S. treaty commitment to
come to the defense of the ROK "in accordance with its constitutional processes."[3]

President Johnson visited Seoul in November of the same year and "reaffirmed the readiness and determination of the United States to render prompt
and effective assistance to defeat an armed attack against the Republic of
Korea,"[4] a new rhetorical flourish that Koreans hopefully depicted as a significant step toward a stronger American tie. And as early as July 1965 the U.S.
commander in Korea and Ambassador Winthrop Brown had jointly pledged that
there would be no reduction in U.S. force levels on the peninsula.[5]

Spurred by the need to convince the American people that all would
eventually go well in Vietnam if only patience and fortitude were demonstrated,
Washington adopted a more upbeat evaluation of the situation in Korea in order
to show that a seemingly endless anticommunist crusade could indeed have a
happy ending. South Korea came to be glorified as a beacon of the Free World,
a shining model that Vietnam and other developing states might emulate. And
President Park, who had almost been executed for his role in a procommunist
upheaval in 1948,[6] gained acclaim as a sage of anticommunism and a strategist
of counterinsurgency, lecturing his Southeast Asian counterparts on how to
avoid appeasement and summoning the foreign ministers of the "Asian Pacific
countries" to Seoul in an effort to cajole them into a holy alliance. A common
utterance of American diplomats in Seoul in those halcyon days of Korean-
American relations was: "No man is indispensable, *but*. . . ."

The new and unabashed American support for the regime and for Park as
an individual broke many a political heart and put an end to the U.S. policy of
maintaining equidistance between the party in power and its opposition. This
crucial shift in the balance of political forces in Seoul was facilitated by the fact
that the opposition parties and intellectuals of democratic persuasion, who had
never given up the illusion that the American liberal establishment was at least
secretly with them, found themselves in the unenviable position of opposing

the single most important U.S. policy of the day regarding Korea—the dispatch of Korean troops to Vietnam. This made the regime even more indispensable to the United States.

Washington's belated enthusiasm for Park was manifested in the language best understood by South Koreans anxious about their security—military aid. It rose dramatically from the all-time low of $124 million in 1964 to a whopping $480 million in 1969 and $556 million in 1971.[7] Whatever may have been the functional utility of such lavish spending by the United States, its symbolic significance was enormous. Park was a president who could really deliver—or, rather, acquire—the goods and safeguard Korean security! Those massive military inputs further bolstered the Korean military elite whom the United States had created in 1945 and subsequently nurtured, a group that tends to view opponents of its policies as subversive elements to be disposed of by any means, without regard to legal niceties.

This sudden change in U.S.-ROK relations elicited a reaction from North Korea that further strengthened Park's hand. The influx of American military aid, the intensified U.S. defense commitment, and the increasing prosperity of the South combined with the benefits accruing from the ROK's normalization of relations with Japan to shatter DPRK dictator Kim Il-Sung's dream of "liberating" the South and unifying the country. Moreover, Park's dispatch of troops to Vietnam caused the leader of the North to suffer the ignominy of watching his countrymen resist a fraternal Communist power's effort to win a holy war of national liberation. The response of the North was to heighten the already tense situation on the Korean peninsula through a host of incidents that culminated in the doomed commando attack upon Blue House (Park's White House) and the *Pueblo* and EC-121 affairs. These actions reinforced the image shared by South Koreans and Americans of a bloodthirsty North Korea that was bent upon aggression, and this in turn facilitated Park's program for imposing unity upon the unruly, aspiring democrats in the South.

The advent of the Nixon-Kissinger-Ford administration only exacerbated the situation. When, beginning in the mid-1960s, Washington ceased exercising the leverage over Seoul that it formerly employed to curb the worst abuses of ROK authoritarianism, it did so on pragmatic grounds. The new Republican administration, however, transformed this recent practice into a matter of high principle, cynically invoking the shibboleth of "nonintervention in the internal affairs of another state" against Americans who urged their government to return to its earlier practice of applying various pressures to stimulate South Korea's rulers to grant their people certain minimal political and civil rights. This gave Park the clearest signal that he could move ahead in the early 1970s with measures far more repressive than those that he adopted during the first decade of his rule.

Thus two of the less well known casualties of the Vietnam War were democracy and human rights in Korea. The American obsession to have Korean troops in Vietnam swept away the earlier U.S. concern for the development of a relatively open society and pluralistic politics in Korea.

The Fate of Human Rights in the ROK

"Human rights practices in Korea have been carefully considered in formulating this proposed security assistance program."[8] So reads the U.S. Defense Department's "Congressional Presentation" for the fiscal year 1978 security assistance program, which attempts to justify the appropriation of $280,400,000 for military aid to the ROK.

What does this delphic statement mean? What weight should the United States attach to human rights considerations while seeking to maintain the peace and security of East Asia? What "human rights" should we be concerned with? To what extent are they being observed? What policies can we suggest to promote the observance of human rights in Korea?

President Park Chung Hee declared martial law and dissolved the National Assembly in October 1972, as the first formal steps toward ending the then existing constitutional system and substituting in its place the so-called "Yushin Constitution." Since then, Park's "revitalizing reforms" have narrowed, but not eliminated, the differences between the totalitarian North and the supposedly "free" South in their respect for human rights.

This summary of post-1972 developments will focus on political and civil rights rather than economic and social rights, for it is the former that have created the major controversy inside and outside Korea. Observers plainly differ over the costs and benefits of the ROK's developmental strategy that makes the country increasingly dependent upon foreign capital and resources, and they debate such matters as whether the ROK has done enough to raise minimum wages and to reduce income differentials among various strata of its population or to improve the status of women. Yet it seems clear that in many respects the ROK has continued to make very impressive, if uneven, economic and social progress. We would not be concerned with South Korea in this volume had the Park regime made commensurate progress in fostering political and civil rigths. Instead, what we have witnessed since 1972 is tragic retrogression, repression so thorough and comprehensive that it has created profound doubts in the United States about the long-run viability of our country's support for the Park regime and even perhaps for the ROK itself.

I will discuss three aspects: (1) state officials' arbitrary violation of the integrity of the person outside the judicial system; (2) arbitrary manipulation of the judicial system for purposes of political repression; and (3) restraints upon freedoms of expression.

Arbitrary Violations of the Person

As to the first, political murder has not become a staple of life in the South as it
has at various times in certain Communist countries and as it is today in Uganda,
to cite only the leading non-Communist example. Nevertheless, there have been
cases of "mysterious" deaths. For example, on October 16, 1973, Professor
Tsche Chong-Kil, who spent the years 1970-72 at Harvard Law School on a
prestigious Harvard-Yenching Fellowship, was picked up by the Korean Central
Intelligence Agency shortly after having lamented, in a supposedly secret faculty
meeting, police brutality against some of his colleagues and students at Seoul
National University's Law Faculty. He was never seen alive again. Four days
later the government announced that Tsche had been arrested on charges of
spying for North Korea and that after making a full confession he had committed suicide by jumping out the window of an interrogation center. Yet the
occupant of a neighboring cell, later released, claimed that he heard screams
from Tsche's cell followed by silence and the rapid summoning of medical
help; the accusation of spying was never substantiated; Tsche's supposed confession was never published; and the report of his "suicide" has been treated
with the utmost skepticism. The fact that his widow, a medical doctor, was
denied permission to examine the corpse hardly inspired confidence in what
appears to have been a hastily contrived story.[9]

Even more mysterious was the subsequent death of the ardent patriot and
intellectual leader Chang Chun-Ha. Chang, a Magsaysay Award Winner and
former National Assemblyman and publisher, had initiated a "one million
citizens' petition for a democratic amendment of the Yushin Constitution" in
late 1973. When the movement began to snowball, gathering roughly 500,000
signatures, the Park regime put an end to it in early 1974 by invoking newly
promulgated "emergency decrees."[10] They authorized up to fifteen years in
prison for any person who "asserted, introduced, proposed or petitioned for
revision or repeal" of the Yushin Constitution.[11] Chang was arrested with
his colleagues, was "hanged upside down and simultaneously . . . burned with a
flame on several parts of his body," and then sentenced to the maximum term
by a court-martial rather than regular court.[12] Domestic and foreign pressures
later forced the regime to release Chang and hundreds of intellectuals, students,
and religious and literary figures condemned by the military tribunals. Shortly
afterward, however, Chang, an experienced mountain climber who had once
conquered the formidable mountains of Western China to join the Chinese and
Korean forces resisting Japanese imperialism, was reported to have fallen to
his death from a cliff while climbing a hill near Seoul. The prosecutor's office
accepted the story of a man who had been alone with Chang just before he fell
and who claimed that death must have resulted from a hiking accident. After a
newspaper editor reported a variety of suspicious circumstances shedding doubt
on this claim, the editor was arrested. Many others were puzzled about the

death of "perhaps the only man who could have revived an effective opposition
to President Park Chung-Hee's Government,"[13] but no one could afford to be
too curious.

Kim Dae-Jung, the charismatic democrat who made such an impressive
showing against Park in the 1971 presidential election that Park put an end to
such elections, was undoubtedly targeted for a similar fate. After kidnapping
Kim from a Tokyo hotel room and spiriting him out of Japan by ship in August
1973, the KCIA was on the verge of dumping him overboard, bound, gagged, and
weighted, when a nationwide outcry in Japan and vigorous behind-the-scenes
diplomacy by the United States saved Kim's life.[14] Kidnapping itself, of course,
is one of the most flagrant violations of the person short of murder.

Obviously, mysterious deaths and kidnapping have a profoundly chilling
effect upon those who might wish to speak out against the policies of the Park
regime as Tsche, Chang, and Kim did, each in his own way. Yet far more in-
timidating has been the widespread use of torture following arbitrary arrest.
This is why Korea's only living ex-president, Yun Po-Sun, has characterized
the Park regime as "government by torture," for at least during the early and
mid-1970s it was highly dependent upon pervasive and systematic violations of
human bodies and minds to maintain its control. The "Genghis Khan cooking"
to which Chang Chun-Ha was subjected when the KCIA ran a flame over his
body is only one of many exquisite and esoteric techniques that Park's minions
have devised. The reports of Amnesty International and other organizations that
have investigated KCIA torture have documented how cold water is forced up
the nostrils through a tube, how electric shocks are applied to the genitals, toes,
and other sensitive parts, and how people are hung from the ceiling and spun
around, beaten and kicked mercilessly, stripped naked in subzero weather and
doused in water, made to stand or sit without sleep for days on end, and subjected to various forms of psychological intimidation.[15]

Most of those tortured are unkown to the press and the outside world.
Those whose detention tends to attract publicity are often better treated.
Nevertheless, even well-known persons suffer physical abuse if their behavior
is considered sufficiently provocative as occurred in the cases of Tsche, Chang,
and Kim. In 1975, after students recently paroled from jail spoke out against
the tortures they had suffered, thirteen former opposition National Assemblymen revealed that they too had been tortured shortly after President Park
seized emergency powers in the autumn of 1972. One of them, Ch'oe Hyong-U,
son of one of South Korea's most noted politicians, was paralyzed at least temporarily from the waist down as a result of this mistreatment. In his statement to the
National Assembly he noted that several cattle dealers had recently been arrested
for forcing their animals to drink a large amount of water to increase their weight
just before they were sold for slaughter. Ch'oe asked: "Why haven't the KCIA
and other agents who used water torture on national assemblymen been arrested?
Are the assemblymen less important than the cattle?"[16]

In these circumstances is it any wonder that the Park regime has gone to great lengths to hinder congressmen like Donald Fraser and agencies like Amnesty International from interviewing victims of Park's terror?[17] Of course, after they are released from interrogation centers and torture chambers, most victims are extremely reluctant to talk about their experiences, out of fear that government agents might make good their threats to retaliate against those who break their silence. In some cases shame is also a factor. For example, in his speech to the National Assembly, Ch'oe Hyong-U declined to reveal details of his wife's torture on the ground that human decency prevented him from describing it. A number of women students who protested against Park's repression have been arrested by the KCIA, tortured, and repeatedly raped, as in the case of several Ewha University students in late 1973.[18] Understandably, most of these rape victims have kept silent about their ordeal.

In many cases people have been tortured not so much to elicit information and evidence from them as to intimidate them. Large numbers of persons have been detained, interrogated, tortured, and then released after a few days, with no thought apparently given to bringing any legal proceeding against them. Like the even more widespread overt surveillance of people's homes, their activities, and their mail, this type of official action is designed to frighten Koreans into conformity.

In other cases torture has been applied for the specific purpose of obtaining evidence to be used in criminal prosecutions. One of the most grisly instances of this involved Soh Sung, a handsome Korean resident of Japan who had gone to South Korea to study at Seoul National University and who was prosecuted for espionage. By the time he appeared in court after interrogation by the KCIA, his body and face were horribly burned. His eyelids and ears had disappeared, his fingers had adhered together, and his eyeglasses had to be bound to his head. His conditon presented a certain challenge to interrogators who operated under bureaucratic requirements that the accused authenticate his confession by placing his fingerprints upon it. Since Soh had no fingers left, his captors proved as imaginative as they were punctilious by having him authenticate his confession with a toe-print.[19] The fact that the Yushin Constitution maintains the previous constitution's prohibition of torture did not lead the court to exclude the confession from evidence, for the new constitution pointedly fails to retain its predecessor's ban on the admission of coerced confessions.[20]

One could detail other gruesome cases,[21] but the point is clear—if actual deaths at the hand of torturers have been relatively few, their savageries have turned hundreds of articulate and conscientious Koreans who have been involved in the democratic movement into the living dead. They suffer from both physical damage and psychological trauma. As Koreans say, their sickness has gotten to the marrow of their bones. Although resort to torture appears to have diminished since 1976, the fear lingers on.

Arbitrary Manipulation of the Judicial Process

If such drastic methods have to be used to obtain evidence for formal legal proceedings, the pressure becomes enormous to distort those proceedings in order to prevent revelation of the methods of extracting the evidence as well as the dubious nature of the evidence itself. Thus the judicial process has inevitably become corrupted in various ways despite the continuing claim of regime spokesmen that the independence of the judiciary is guaranteed by the constitution, and is not subject to interference by anyone.[22] The classic case was the 1974 conviction of twenty-two members of the so-called "People's Revolutionary Party" for allegedly having organized to overthrow the government and replace it with a regime sympathetic to North Korea. By universal—not merely Western—standards of fairness, the judicial process by which those defendants were tried can only be termed a farce.

The trial was held not before a regular court but before a military tribunal established by the 1974 emergency decrees. Hearings were closed, with only one member of each defendant's family allowed to attend. The "confessions" were admitted into evidence, even though they were extracted under hideous forms of torture. Moreover, forty-two prosecution witnesses testified in the absence of defense lawyers, who were apparently under house arrest at the time. In any event the defense was not permitted to question prosecution witnesses and statements. No defense witnesses were allowed. Government-controlled media proclaimed the guilt of the accused before judgment was rendered. No foreign journalists were permitted at the trial because, according to the prime minister, "[t]here was too great a risk they might misunderstand and misrepresent what happened in court."[23] In April 1975, after the Supreme Court upheld the eight death sentences and all but two of the prison sentences meted out—but before the accused could exercise their rights to petition the Supreme Court for retrial and petition the president for mercy—the eight condemned to death were unlawfully hanged, despite assurances from the Public Prosecutor's Department that no executions would take place until the accused had an opportunity to exhaust their rights. The government cremated the bodies of a number of those executed, thereby preventing any examination for signs of physical torture. After a careful investigation that pieced together a coherent account of this case, Amnesty International concluded that the charges against the so-called PRP has been fabricated just as a 1964 prosecution of the same group had been.[24]

Because of the outcry at home and abroad against these judicial murders— even the normally timid U.S. Department of State protested—and because resort to courts-martial for punishing civilians is generally unattractive, military tribunals no longer enforce Park's continuing rule by emergency decree. Yet the regular courts that have had to deal with subsequent political prosecutions have behaved in a most irregular fashion. This was demonstrated by the trial of

Kim Dae-Jung and the seventeen other prestigious leaders who on March 1, 1976, issued a declaration of national conscience calling upon President Park to resign and restore democratic government. The March 1 group was immediately prosecuted for violating Emergency Decree No. 9, a Draconian catch-all that prohibits "disseminating falsehood," opposing the new constitution that guarantees Park's one-man rule, and "publicly defaming" the emergency decree itself.[25] The three levels of judicial proceedings that resulted in long prison sentences for the principal "offenders," and even longer deprivations of political and civil rights for virtually all, mocked minimal standards of fairness.

Although the accused and their families demanded an open and free trial, the admission of friends and relatives was restricted to limited numbers of ticket-holders, and the trial was conducted in what the *Washington Post* reporter on the scene called "an atmosphere of intimidation and hostility."[26] Since the defendants were charged with disseminating groundless rumors and misrepresenting facts, they sought to call a variety of witnesses to demonstrate the truth of what they had stated, but the court permitted merely three. The only defense witness allowed to testify in support of their statements on the economy was taken to the KCIA office prior to his court appearance, so that, by the time he testified, he had become a prosecution witness; this economist who had often criticized the regime's reliance upon foreign lenders and investors dropped his head and kept silent when questioned by the defense. Frustrated by the court's refusal to allow the testimony and documentary evidence they sought to introduce, defense attorneys walked out in protest. They were also outraged by the regime's refusal to allow them freely to confer with the defendants who were in detention.

The bizarre nature of the trial is best illustrated by the fact that the accused were not permitted to challenge the validity of the decree they were charged with violating because by its terms it had prohibited judicial scrutiny. Moreover, despite the fact that the prosecutors were permitted to quote passages from the March 1 declaration to support their case, the defendants were precluded from showing why those statements were accurate. Nevertheless, in the hope of giving the appearance of a fair trial, the defendants were allowed to deliver long orations, often including opinions that would bring arrest outside the courtroom, since the court was confident that the heavily censored news media would give the public no hint of the views expressed. "These aren't legal proceedings," one diplomat declared. "They remind you of showcase trials in Communist countries."[27]

There was never any danger that the defendants' arguments might persuade the court. Not only were the judges precluded by law from considering challenges to the emergency decree itself, but Park's "revitalizing reforms" have also subjected the judiciary to a "reappointment" process that has screened out the less cooperative elements. Scores of judges have been purged, including nine of the ten Supreme Court judges who constituted the majority vote in a landmark decision that aroused Park's ire just before "revitalization." Thus one can well understand why the March 1 group called for the creation of a judiciary that is truly independent of the political authorities and capable of protecting the people against tyranny.[29]

Denial of Freedoms of Expression

The March 1 group also called, among other things, for rescission of the repressive "emergency decrees" without which Park apparently believes he can no longer rule; release of political prisoners; renewal of freedom of speech, press, and assembly; restoration of the legislative system that was abolished in 1972 in favor of Park's present parliamentary charade; and enjoyment by industrial and agricultural workers of a right to organize and strike. This implicitly suggested the lack of basic freedoms of expression in the ROK. It also served as the foundation of the government prosecution of the group for violating Presidential Emergency Decree No. 9. Promulgated on May 13, 1975, that decree prohibits "fabricating or disseminating false rumors or misrepresenting facts" and "denying, opposing, misrepresenting or defaming the constitution; or asserting, petitioning, instigating or propagandizing revision or repeal of the constitution by means of assembly, demonstration or through public media such as newspapers, broadcasts or press services; or by other such means of expression such as writings, books or recordings."[30] Also prohibited is any act openly defaming the emergency decree itself. Alleged violators are subject to arrest, detention, confiscation, and search without a judicially approved warrant. Those convicted are to receive not less than one year in prison, and no maximum sentence is specified. They are also subject to suspension of civil rights, including the rights to run for office and to vote, for up to ten years.

Emergency Decree No. 9 is the capstone of an effort to suppress all dissenting views. It was surely not required in order to prohibit Communist or other revolutionary activity, for such acts had long been banned by formally enacted legislation that is itself of an all-encompassing, catch-all type. The National Security Law, enacted shortly after Park's 1961 coup, mandates harsh felony punishments for "[a] ny person who has organized an association or group for the purpose of...disturbing the State" or who has prepared or conspired to do so.[31] Such "anti-State organizations," if they "operate along the lines of the communists," are further dealt with in the companion Anti-Communist Law. That legislation provides up to seven years at hard labor for "[a] ny person who has praised, encouraged or sided with anti-State organizations or members thereof on foreign communist lines or benefited the same in any way through other means."[32]

The only requirement for conviction under the Anti-Communist Law is that the conduct in question be deemed to have benefited an anti-State

organization. No subjective intention on the part of the actor to aid such an
organization need be proved. In these circumstances, as the Amnesty report
points out, "any dissent is capable of being characterized as a benefit to an anti-
State organization. That this is no mere academic theorizing is made clear by
the government's conviction under this law of the courageous lawyer Han
Seung-Hon for publishing an essay that opposes the death penalty as morally
indefensible and of Kim Chi-Ha, the poet laureate of the democratic resistance,
for stating that the government neglects the rights of the poor and underprivi-
leged and that the KCIA uses torture to extract false confessions.

The Kim Chi-Ha case is a good example of how, under the Anti-Communist
Law, criticism of violence is regarded as more subversive than advocacy of violence. Because so much of the regime's power rests upon the apparatus of
violence—the KCIA, the Army Counterintelligence Corps, the police, and the
Capital Guard Division—to criticize violence is to challenge the existence of the
regime. Thus, as Kim Chi-Ha discovered, one can talk about torture only on
pain of himself suffering further torture and punishment. Kim, whose death
sentence was commuted to life imprisonment thanks to outraged public opinion
at home and abroad, was subsequently released. But, when he exposed the torture inflicted upon the defendants in the "People's Revolutionary Party" case,
his life sentence was revived, and he was sentenced to an additional seven years
in prison, where he today remains in complete isolation, unable to have even
toilet paper because he once used this substance to record a statement which was
then smuggled out and published. By revealing the torture of the alleged PRP
members, he was found to have benefited a supposedly "anti-State organization." Moreover, anyone who has "praised, encouraged, or sided with" Kim
Chi-Ha runs the risk of a similar conviction.

Another example of resort to the Anti-Communist Law to suppress expression is the 1978 conviction of purged university professors Paik Nak-Chung and
Lee Yong-Hui for having published a translation of a volume of academic essays
on China by respected Western scholars including Harvard professors John K.
Galbraith and Ross Terrill. The defendants were sentenced to terms of hard
labor for "inciting" sympathy for Peking and "praising" the Chinese Communist
revolution, but it seemed clear that the real reason for their conviction was that
they had both consistently published criticisms that offended the government.[34]

Emergency Decree No. 9 goes one step further than the Anti-Communist Law.
It eliminates even the objective requirement of proving that the conduct in question benefited an anti-State organization. If any person simply speaks out against
Park's "revitalizing reforms," advocates revision of the Yushin Constitution, or
criticizes the emergency decree, he or she can be convicted and sentenced to long
deprivation of freedom and loss of political and civil rights,[35] as were Kim Dae Jung
and other democratic leaders for precisely such statements. Emergency Decree
No. 9 is thus designed to freeze the political status quo of Park's unfettered rule.

Having "legally" suppressed all forms of expression at home in an effort to

prevent domestically inspired political change, the regime also has sought to
suppress Koreans' expression abroad in order to deny foreigners access to unfavorable facts and opinions concerning the regime and thereby reduce external
pressures for change. In March 1975 Park rammed a new law through his cap-
tive National Assembly, creating the crime of "slander against the state." Article
104, Section 2, of the Criminal Code now provides:

> All Koreans who commit the following crimes outside of the country
> will be liable to sentences of up to seven years of imprisonment:
> slandering any national body which has been established by the con-
> stitution or spreading rumors or distorting facts about any such body;
> also all other activities which may harm the welfare and interest of or
> defame the Republic of Korea.[36]

The new law also prohibits Koreans from committing such acts inside their
country in association with foreigners or foreign organizations and provides up
to ten years' suspension of civil rights for any violator. It is remarkable that a
regime that so often claims that it seeks to inform foreign audiences about
Korea, that it wishes foreign news agencies to report more accurately, and that
it welcomes visitors who seek the truth should go so far to frustrate attainment
of those goals. I know that I am not the only observer to note that, since
enactment of this law, a great many, though not all, Koreans have ceased engaging foreigners in frank discussions about their country, whether at home or
abroad. Indiscretion can mean seven years in prison. Moreover, in late 1977
Park's National Assembly adopted a law authorizing confiscation of the property
of those "anti-State" Koreans who "slander" the government while overseas.
Foreigners who maintain that few South Koreans complain about their plight
ought to come to grips with these facts of Korean life as well as others. As a
Korean journalist told a visiting American who asked whether he had any
message for the people of the United States: "Just say that by law, now, we are
not allowed to discuss our country with foreigners. That should tell them
enough."[37]

The effective suppression of dissent, of course, is far more than a matter of
criminal legislation and prosecution, or even of resort to occasional mysterious
deaths and widespread detention and torture. By a comprehensive program of
administrative measures—some authorized by legislation, others covert—the
regime has imposed increasingly severe restraints upon such pluralistic elements
as the highly centralized society possesses.

Just as in Communist countries, the South Korean government has curbed
the independence of the legal profession as well as that of the courts.[38] Journalists have been equally unsuccessful in resisting suppression.[39] Because no
autonomous institutions can be allowed to exist to challenge the authorities, the
regime has increasingly tightened its grip upon the universities, while groping to
develop a new Yushin ideology of "Korean-style democracy" to replace the

democratic ideals upon which the ROK was founded. Park has used both the carrot and the stick in an effort to achieve conformity among faculty and students.[40] The government has also had to devote extraordinary attention to muzzling Protestant and Catholic religious leaders, many of whom have been among the most unyielding critics of repression.[41] Although defenders of Park's repression often seek to give the impression that the only people affected by denials of human rights are politicians, intellectuals, journalists, judges, lawyers, and Christians—a bourgeois elite that is unrepresentative of the silent majority—this is refuted by the regime's obstruction of efforts by factory employees to organize unions, bargain collectively and resort to strikes in the hope of improving minimal wages and working conditions in an economy that relies on cheap labor to lure foreign investments and boost exports.[42]

Appraisal

The Yushin Constitution did not retain previous constitutional guarantees such as the requirements that coerced confessions be excluded from evidence and that detained persons be allowed judicial scrutiny of the validity of their detention—habeas corpus.[43] Yet a superficial reading of that document suggests continuing support for many basic human rights. The chapter on the rights and duties of citizens opens with a ringing declaration that "[a]ll citizens shall be assured dignity and value of human beings, and it shall be the duty of the State to guarantee such fundamental rights of the people to the utmost."[44] And there are reassuringly unqualified provisions that "[a]ll citizens shall enjoy personal liberty,"[45] and that "[n]o citizen shall be tortured nor compelled to testify against himself in criminal cases."[46] Nevertheless, a number of specific guarantees are qualified on their face. Freedoms of speech, press, assembly, and association are promised "except as provided by law," and "[t]he right to association, collective bargaining and collective action of workers shall be guaranteed within the scope defined by law."[47] Laws restricting all freedoms and rights may be enacted "when necessary for the maintenance of national security, order or public welfare."[48] Moreover, whenever the president merely anticipates a threat to the national security or public safety and order, the new constitution authorizes him to take emergency measures such as those he has promulgated that "temporarily suspend the freedom and rights of the people prescribed in this Constitution" and that prevent any judicial review of presidential actions.[49] And in similar circumstances the new constitution also authorizes the president to declare martial law and take special measures suspending basic rights.[50]

Thus the apparent constitutional protections keep the promise to the ear but break it to the hope. Indeed, even the usually resourceful and versatile Korean constitutional law scholars have confessed that the new governmental form eludes definition. One calls it "Leadership Presidency";[51] another, "Presidential Absolutism," a kind of "republican monarchy" that "has boldly put an end to the past oscillation between the classical presidential and parliamentary systems."[52] Professor Han Tae-Yon, who is known to be the legal draftsman of the Yushin spirit, is surprisingly straightforward in his treatment of "the nature of the governmental form" under the new constitution: it remains a presidential form of government, "albeit in an adulterated form. . . ; the concentration of power in the presidency inevitably entails the personalization of political power."[53]

Even more disturbing, of course, is the fact that the Park regime has systematically acted in violation of those constitutional norms that on paper it claims to respect. Finally, the new constitutional system not only frustrates any legitimate challenge to Park's monopoly of political and lawmaking powers, but also condemns as illegal and unconstitutional any attempt peacefully to alter the system. In these circumstances comparison with the theory and practice of constitutionalism in the Communist world is inevitable.

Those who defend Park's tragic record on human rights during the past five years chant a constant litany—the militant "threat from the North" requires the enforcement of strict social discipline and political unity. That is supposed to be the all-purpose, universal excuse to absolve the government of the most horrendous abuses. Mysterious deaths, unspeakable tortures, increasingly totalitarian conformity—all are justified by invoking the "threat from the North." That threat exists, to be sure, and must be taken seriously. Yet it existed long before Yushin, usually more acutely, and at times when the ROK found itself in weaker condition, absolutely and relative to the DPRK, than during the 1970s. It is difficult to escape the conclusion that the "threat from the North" has been a convenient pretext for Park's shutting down the electoral system and stifling the dissent this inevitably created. After amending the previous constitution to allow himself to run for a third term in office, Park promised the people of Korea in the 1971 election that he would not seek a further term. His opponent Kim Dae-Jung, warned that, if reelected, Park would put an end to elections and perpetuate his rule by dictatorial means. This, of course, is precisely what happened, and, to add insult to injury, Park had Kim sentenced to a year in prison for making this brash prediction and committing other supposed violations of the electoral system Park had just abolished. For former General Park the costs and uncertainties of political democracy had proved intolerable (despite the many millions of dollars in supposed political contributions gouged from the Gulf Oil Corporation and other foreign and domestic businesses).

Yet for the Korean people the costs and uncertainties of the system Park has now foisted upon them are very great. To justify his actions the president and his defenders seek to give the impression that Koreans are not yet capable of freely governing themselves and enjoying democratic rights. They emphasize the authoritarian and collectivist elements of Korea's tradition and ignore

traditional concern for justice, morality, and human dignity. They also ignore
the past century of struggle—and progress—by the increasingly educated Korean
people toward achieving some form of open society. After visiting the United
States in 1883, Yu Kil-Chun, one of Korea's early modernizers, introduced his
awakening nation to the idea that freedom means freedom of the person, of
property, and of press and assembly.[54] That idea proved very attractive to
Koreans, and during their bitter experience under Japanese colonialism and their
subsequent efforts to develop an independent nation it came to be widely
shared. Yushin has dealt a devastating blow to their hope of translating that
idea into practice.

Is this blow a coup de grace? Or are there prospects for reversing the adverse trend? The release in the summer of 1977 of two small batches of political
prisoners—but only on condition that they "repent" their alleged misdeeds—
caused certain hopes to be raised that President Carter's expressed concern for
human rights in Korea and elsewhere might be exercising some influence in
Seoul.[55] Even more suggestive was the National Assembly's mid-1977 recommendation to the president that he not only recognize a "productive and active
role" for the assembly but also extend "generous hands even to violators of the
Emergency Measures" and promote harmonious collaboration among the
assembly, the administration, and all walks of life "so as to enable the Emergency Measures to be lifted."[56] Nevertheless, although the constitution provides
that "the President shall comply with [such a] recommendation unless there
are any special circumstances and reasons,"[57] as of April 1979 Park had failed
to do so. Moreover, the poet Kim Chi-Ha and several hundred other political
offenders remain confined in difficult conditions.

The regime naturally has been trying to sit out the storm stirred up by
its policies and has taken cosmetic actions to conceal the more sophisticated
methods of repression that it has been developing. We may indeed see another phase of relaxation within the fateful downward spiral of the dignity
of man in Korea. The regime, desperate to improve whatever is left of its
"image," has been threatening, cajoling, and even begging the political prisoners
and prisoners of conscience to recant, repent their "sins," and pledge not to become "recidivists" in signed statements prepared by the government in return
for "suspension of the execution of their sentences" or presidential pardon. It
has been trying to exploit the suffering of the prisoners' families, telling them
that it is the recalcitrance and stupidity of their detained husbands, sons, and
daughters that keep the families apart. This, needless to say, amounts to forcing
the dissidents to cease being who they are and to give up what they have so
arduously lived for.

New chapters of this tragedy recur periodically. Fierce protests against the
"revitalizing reforms" that usually involve thousands of students swell the ranks
of political prisoners and temporarily close leading universities. Such events are
rarely reported in the South Korean press.

Everyone knows the root cause of the problem: the regime's monopolization of political power and truth. As long as the condition persists, the cause of human rights in Korea is hopeless.

In the meantime, in the United States, from late 1976 the preoccupation with Koreagate scandal and the Carter Administration's plan to withdraw American ground forces from South Korea obscured concern for the human rights situation in the ROK. Even more importantly, Americans became puzzled by the relation of human rights to Washington's security policy in Korea. Many recognize what democratic leaders in Seoul have long emphasized—that U.S. actions that eventuate in a North Korean takeover of the South would surely constitute no victory for human rights. Yet it is undoubtedly true, as Jimmy Carter stated during the 1976 presidential election campaign[58] and as Secretary of State Cyrus Vance pointed out in late 1977,[59] that Park regime's repugnant repression has weakened the American people's support for our Korean security commitment. Indeed, as American officials concede in private while denying it in public, Park's suppression of human rights is one of the factors that underlies our government's desire to adjust the location of U.S. ground forces in order to avoid their automatic involvement in any conflict on the peninsula. For the American people the specter of another war on the Asian mainland in support of an authoritarian dictatorship is enough to overshadow the important differences between the situations in Vietnam and Korea. As Vietnam demonstrated, in the long run the United States will not sustain costly military involvement unless its young people who are called upon to sacrifice their lives find appropriate ideological justification. Although Koreans appreciate the human rights distinctions that still exist between North and South, those distinctions are not likely to be perceived by Americans as sufficiently great to justify the supreme sacrifice. Nor is the link between the ROK's security and that of Japan likely to be regarded as sufficiently vital to warrant the expenditure of U.S. ground forces.

In the absence of the kind of ideological bond that reinforces other American ties to the West European democracies, Japan and Israel, the U.S. security commitment to the ROK can be expected to erode further. This is why, on recent visits to South Korea, I frankly told anyone who was allowed to listen that Park's human rights policy should be called the "threat from the South." It is gradually separating Koreans from their only real security and promises to add to the tragedy of a long-suffering people.

Prospects

Is there anything that can be done to improve the depressing picture? As many critics of U.S. policy toward Korea during the past decade have argued, the reduction of American military aid to the ROK would send a strong signal of official disapproval of Park's abuses. Yet early in 1977 Secretary Vance announced that the new administration would not take such action, despite its "great concern about the human rights situation in that country."[60] Because of the security situation in Korea, he said, the ROK would be exempted from the newly unveiled policy of cutting U.S. aid to governments that suppress human rights. In the current delicate circumstances of the Korean-American relationship, it was apparently feared that even a symbolic cut might signal more than intended, confirming increased American indifference to South Korea's security. After all, the projected withdrawal of U.S. ground forces was based on the assumption that, in addition to the vast sums that the United States has already expended for the modernization of the ROK military, special substantial "compensation" would have to be contributed by Washington to enable South Korea to shoulder the burden of its own ground defense without diminishing its security. If, even before Washington and Seoul had agreed upon the amount of this extraordinary "compensation," the United States began reducing already anticipated military aid, this could raise grave doubts about either ROK security or the planned force withdrawals. Thus, until the Tongsun Park affair came to a boil in the fall of 1977, the option of cutting military aid for the ROK seemed out of the question.

The pressure that the United States mobilized against the Park regime in this affair was massive, making it very clear that, even though the ROK had no legal obligation to extradite Tongsun Park, if it failed to send him back to the United States, the Congress and the executive branch would join in cutting Seoul's aid.[61] What the Tongsun Park affair demonstrated was that: (1) despite its concern for Korean security, the United States is willing to threaten withholding of military aid to Seoul if it deems the interest to be promoted thereby important enough; (2) the United States regards protection of the integrity of its legislative process as sufficiently important to warrant resort to such a threat; (3) the threat to deny military aid can be an effective lever in stimulating the ROK government to take certain desired actions; and (4) at least when confined to a period of limited duration, this sanction need not adversely affect South Korean or American security.

Now that the dust has settled from the Tongsun Park affair and its sequel— the effort to obtain the testimony of former Korean Ambassador Kim Dong-Jo— it appears that the United States is not prepared to do for human rights in the ROK what it did to protect the integrity of its own legislative process. Despite the fact that Secretary Vance warned Seoul that its repression, as well as its refusal to cooperate in the Koreagate investigation, is eroding American support, the Carter Administration seems likely to maintain the position it adopted at the outset—that security considerations preclude it from recommending the reduction of military aid as a sanction against the Park regime's repression. Of course, if the Park regime enters an even more repressive stage, that position could change. But administration refusal to follow through with its military aid would endanger implementation of its desired withdrawal of ground forces, which is still desired even though subject to reconsideration because of new concern over North Korean strength. It might be better for the human rights of the South Korean people if the United States were to retain its ground forces in the ROK and revert to the pre-1965 U.S. policy of using its leverage to moderate some of the regime's excesses. But this would put the interests of the South Korean people ahead of those of the American people, who are unlikely to be willing to fight another ground war in Asia in defense of the type of government the ROK will continue to have under Park whether or not the United States reverts to its pre-1965 policy. To choose the third option—to cut military aid while proceeding with the withdrawal—would not only court the danger of a North Korean attack but would also risk propelling the South to destabilize the entire area by developing nuclear weapons in a desperate effort to assure its defense.

To be sure, even without regard to questions of human rights, there will be every reason for Congress carefully to scrutinize whatever bargain the administration strikes with Seoul over "compensation" arrangements. Indications from Seoul suggest that the ROK may ask the United States to approve as much as $5 billion in military sales and assistance over the next five years, while Washington seems to contemplate, at least at the start of the negotiations, a total of $2.2 billion.[62] Congress will want to verify the need for whatever sum is ultimately requested, the impact that such a large new input can be expected to have on the already dangerous arms race on the Korean peninsula, and the implications for South Korean society of this further militarization. Thus, for a variety of reasons, military aid to Korea will remain a controversial question, even though revised estimates of North Korean strength in early 1979 led the debate to subside temporarily.

Of course, the military aid sanction is only one of the instruments for expressing the principles of an administration sincerely determined to promote observance of human rights abroad. Despite President Park's thorough censorship, we should not underestimate the impact upon South Korea of considered statements of policy, not mere passing remarks, by our highest leaders. If President Carter spells out our concern about human rights in Korea, the message will soon reach the people as well as their rulers. Furthermore, symbolic acts by the president are as potent in Seoul as in Moscow. A sympathetic letter from Carter to the ROK's foremost democratic politician, Kim Dae-Jung, or to its best-known poet, Kim Chi-Ha, who are both in prison, would enormously encourage democratic-minded Koreans without jeopardizing the security of anyone except President Park. And surely Carter should not visit Seoul or welcome Park to Washington in the absence of improved conditions; in November 1978 Carter reportedly informed Park that he "hoped" a meeting would take place in mid-1979 but that in the interim he expected Seoul to develop a better human rights record.[63] In an obvious response, the ROK at year's end released Kim Dae-Jung and roughly 100 other political prisoners.

Much more creative use can be made of our ambassador in Seoul. Recall of our ambassador would have been one appropriate response to Park's first steps to dismantle the political process in 1971, and we could have further shown our disapproval of the "revitalizing reforms" by maintaining only a chargé d'affaires at our embassy. When in June of 1977 Ambassador Richard Sneider invited former President Yun Po-Sun and several other distinguished members of the convicted March 1 group to a reception in honor of Under Secretary of State Philip Habib, President Park and his colleagues were reportedly furious,[64] but the message was not lost upon them or upon Seoul's underground political grapevine. A consistent pattern of similar signals by our envoys would make that message more credible. Future ambassadors should be able to communicate to the Korean people, in their language, American interest in supporting their desire for a more humane and open society.

Other pressures may also have an effect. For example, the State Department could designate South Korea as one of the countries that has consistently violated human rights and is therefore ineligible for Public Law 480 "Food for Peace" benefits unless it signs a agreement that the aid received will be allocated to the needy. Such an agreement would be tantamount to an embarrassing public admission that South Korea had indeed violated human rights.[65]

The administration should also permit private and official American contacts with North Korea, which shows signs of wanting to emerge from its dangerous isolation. Such contacts would be intrinsically important in seeking to diminish the political tension that endangers Northeast Asia and the world and that gives Park the rationale for his repression. They would also stimulate the Park regime to strive to recognize those shared values that provide the only sure guaranty of its link to the U.S.

An imaginative, resourceful administration can pursue a range of other measures never previously attempted in an effort to prod its Korean ally back onto the road toward a more humane and open society. It should recognize, of course, that, if successful, its efforts may lead to a chain of events that terminates the so-called "revitalizing reforms" and introduces a more democratic but necessarily turbulent era. Yet, at least as long as the United States maintains a credible commitment to the ROK's security and strong support for the new democratic experiment, the strains inherent in the transition from dictatorship to some form of more open society should be well within limits that the political system can tolerate. Moreover, on balance, the international environment is today less threatening to the ROK and more favorable to its political liberalization than during the brief democratic interlude of 1960-61, when the Sino-Soviet split was barely discernible, when the idea of a Chinese rapprochement with the United States and Japan seemed visionary, and when the North Korean leadership confronted fewer problems. Given the South Koreans' dynamism, impressive educational attainments, postliberation democratic values, economic and social progress, increasing entanglement with the industrialized democracies, and distaste for Park's repression, we should be confident that, even though a threat from the North persists, their next experiment with freedom will have a better chance of survival than the previous one did. Koreans have benefited from Japan's postwar experience in economic development. They might also study Japan's political system as well as those of India, Greece, Spain, Portugal, and other countries that are making the transition from authoritarianism to democracy.

Legitimation of political power in modern South Korea has been solely predicated upon pluralistic competition and protection of basic human rights. The destruction of this constitutional system has resulted in a crisis of political authority. Because persuasiveness has proved inadequate to sustain the regime, it has had to resort to terror, and this has inevitably undermined the bond of shared ideals and values between Korea and the United States that transcends any momentary coincidence of national interests. We will have learned nothing from recent experience if we fail to see this sobering causal chain. Thus, in the long run the inconvenience of short-run instability will produce a healthier and more stable society, one that enjoys not only national self-respect but also the respect of the truly free world. Such a course would offer South Korea its only sure guaranty of continuing American support and genuine security.

Notes

1. See Carter for International Policy, *Human Rights and the U.S. Foreign Assistance Program, Fiscal Year 1978, Part 2–East Asia* (Washington, D.C.), p. 46.

2. "Secretary Acheson's Aide-Memoire to the Korean Ambassador," April 7, 1950, in Donald G. Tewksbury, ed., *Source Materials on Korean Politics and Ideologies* (Institute of Pacific Relations, New York), p. 145.

3. United States Senate, "United States Security Agreements Abroad," *Hearings before the Committee on Foreign Relations*, 91st. Cong., 1971, p. 1725.

4. *Dept. of State Bull.*, Nov. 21, 1966, p. 1198.

5. S.R. Larsen and J.L. Collins, Jr., *Allied Participation in Vietnam* (Dept. of Army, 1975), p. 125.

6. See Elizabeth Pond, "South Korea's New Trouble," *Christian Science Monitor,* May 22, 1974, p. F8; Letter, "Professor Gregory Henderson to *Christian Science Monitor,*" *Christian Science Monitor,* June 20, 1974, p. F8.

7. See U.S. Agency for International Development, *Overseas Loans and Grants and Assistance from International Organizations* (Washington, D.C., 1960) p. 71; ibid. (1974) p. 73.

8. *Congressional Presentation for the Security Assistance Program*, FY 1978, Vol. I, p. 59.

9. See Jerome Alan Cohen, "A Grim Anniversary in South Korea," *Washington Post*, Oct. 9, 1974, p. A18.

10. See Robert Campbell, "Everything's Illegal," *Far Eastern Economic Review*, Jan. 21, 1974, pp. 19-20.

11. See Articles 2 and 5 of "Emergency Measure No. 1," promulgated January 8, 1974; translated in William J. Butler, *Report of Commission to South Korea for Amnesty International* (no date), p. 20 (hereafter "Butler, *Report*").

12. Butler, *Report*, note 11 *above*, at p. 26.

13. Roy Whang, "An opposition leader's mysterious death," *Far Eastern Economic Review*, Sept. 12, 1975, p. 18.

14. Jerome Alan Cohen, "Huh? What? Who, Me? Free Kim Dae Jung," *Los Angeles Times* August 8, 1978, Part II, p. 5.

15. See, for example, "Report of an Amnesty International Mission to the Republic of Korea" (hereafter cited as "Amnesty International Report") in "Human Rights in South Korea and the Philippines: Implications for U.S. Policy," *Hearings before the Subcommittee on International Organizations of the Committee on International Relations*, House of Representatives, 94th Cong., 1st sess., May 20-June 24, 1975, pp. 55-56 (hereafter cited as "1975 Hearings").

16. "Truth About the Politics of Torture," *Dong-A-Ilbo* (East Asian Daily), Feb. 28, 1975 (in Korean).

17. See, for example, Father James Sinnott, "Congressman Fraser Visits Political Prisoners in South Korea," April 6, 1975, printed in *Hearings*, 1975, p. 357.

18. There is a discreet and guarded Korean-language account of the widely known Ewha incident by the then Dean An In-Hee of the College of Education, Ewha Women's University, in *Yosong Dong-A* (Women's East Asian Monthly), Feb. 1974, pp. 110-115.

19. See Butler, *Report*, note 11, p. 27.

20. See the statement of Professor Gregory Henderson, "Human Rights in South Korea: Implications for U.S. Policy," *Hearings before the Subcommittee on Asian and Pacific Affairs and on International Organizations and Movements*, Committee on Foreign Affairs, House of Representatives, 93rd Cong., 2nd sess., July 30, Aug. 5, Dec. 20, 1974, p. 86 (hereafter "1974 Hearings"). For an English translation of the pre-1972 Constitution, see *Laws of the Republic of Korea* (Korean Legal Center, Seoul, 1969), pp. 1-30.

21. See John Saar, "Confession in Seoul: A Tale of Terror," *International Herald Tribune*, July 7, 1977, p. 4.

22. See, for example, John Saar, "Abusing the Law in Korea," *Washington Post*, Aug. 1, 1976, p. C5.

23. The statement was made by Prime Minister Kim Jong-Pil in the National Assembly in October 1974. He also explained that the secrecy of the trial was due to lack of court space. *1975 Hearings*, p. 64.

24. "Statement of Brian Wrobel, Amnesty International, London," *1975 Hearings*, pp. 72-73.

25. Article 1 of the Emergency Decree. An English translation of the entire decree may be found in *1975 Hearings*, pp. 6-7.

26. John Saar, "S. Korean Trial: Christians Put Park Dictatorship in Dock," *Washington Post*, Aug. 9, 1976, p. A8.

27. Ibid.

28. In the landmark decision, the Korean Supreme Court held unconstitutional a new statute restricting judicial review of legislation. The new statute had required that in order to decide upon constitutionality a quorum of two-thirds of the entire court had to hear the case and that two-thirds of the judges present had to concur. The Supreme Court Plenary Collegiate Session, Decision of June 22, 1971. The revamping of the judiciary was carried out during 1972 as part of the Yushin "revitalizing reforms."

29. For a brief account of the March 1 Declaration and its consequences, see Jerome Alan Cohen, ". . . and a letter from Carter to Kim," *Christian Science Monitor*, March 1, 1977, p. 27.

30. Article 1(B), note 24, above.

31. Article 1. For an English translation of the National Security Law, see *Laws of the Republic of Korea* (3rd ed., Korean Legal Center, Seoul, 1975), pp. 772-775.

32. Article 4 (1). For an English translation of the Anti-Communist Law, see *Laws of the Republic of Korea*, note 31, above, pp. 776-780.

33. See Amnesty International Report, *1975 Hearings*, p. 51.

34. See "South Korea: Bad Reviews," *Newsweek*, July 31, 1978, p. 34.

35. See p. 51, note 25, above.

36. For a discussion of this provision, see *1975 Hearings*, pp. 51-52. In order to adopt the bill containing this provision, the majority of the National Assembly's Committee on the Judiciary and Legislation met secretly to consider the bill in the Library of the Assembly while the opposition committee members were kept locked in the committee room. The plenary session that considered the bill was held in the cloakroom while opposition members were kept locked in the main Assembly chamber (p. 52).

37. "Statement of the Reverend James P. Sinnott," *1975 Hearings*, p. 46.

38. For an account of the bar associations' efforts to protest, written before they succumbed to the regime's pressures, see Jerome Alan Cohen, "Lawyers, Politics and Despotism in Korea," *American Bar Association Journal*, June 1975, p. 730.

39. For an observer's account of the vain struggle of Korea's leading newspaper, see Sinnott, note 37, above, pp. 45-47.

40. See Andrew H. Malcolm, "400 Professors Ousted in Korea," *N.Y. Times*, March 14, 1976, p. 1.

41. Amnesty International Report, *1975 Hearings*, p. 57.

42. Testimony of Rev. George E. Ogle, *1974 Hearings*, p. 145.

43. Article 10 (5) of the pre-1972 Constitution, repealed by the new

Constitution, had contained the guarantee of habeas corpus, and Article 10 (6) had prohibited reliance on coerced confessions.

44. Article 8.

45. Article 10 (1).

46. Article 10 (2).

47. Article 8 and Article 29.

48. Article 32 (2). Obviously this provision is designed to expand the constitutionally permissible limits of restricting basic rights through "laws." The term "laws" herein denotes statutes passed by the legislature and meeting the requirements of generality and specificity. It is noteworthy that the 1972 Constitution does not retain its predecessor's provision that even a law restricting liberties and rights in the public interest cannot be constitutionally valid if it infringes "the essential substances of liberties and rights." Article 32 (2) of the pre-1972 Constitution.

49. Article 53 (2) and (4).

50. Article 54 (1) and (3).

51. Park Il-Kyong, *The Yushin Constitution* (Seoul, 1973; in Korean), pp. 1, 297.

52. Mun Hong-Ju, *The Korean Constitution* (Seoul, 1973; in Korean), p. 332.

53. Han Tae-Yun, *A Study of the Constitution* (Seoul, 1973; in Korean), p. 390.

54. Yu Kil-Chun, *A Travelogue of the West* (Seoul, 1976; in Korean), pp. 116-118.

55. See, for example, "South Korea Frees 14 Foes of Regime," *New York Times*, July 25, 1977, p. 1.

56. For an official English translation of the National Assembly's Recommendations, see "Recommendations, Resolutions," *Korea Herald,* July 5, 1977, p. 4.

57. Article 53 (6).

58. See "Excerpts from Carter's Speech and His Replies," *New York Times* June 24, 1976, p. 22.

59. See Richard Halloran, "Grand Jury on Korea Hands up Sealed Report as Term Expires," *New York Times*, Dec. 7, 1977, p. A16.

60. See Jerome Alan Cohen, "Putting the Heat on Seoul," *New York Times*, March 2, 1977, p. 21.

61. See, for example, "Bell Plans New Plea for Korean's Return," *New York Times*, Sept. 15, 1977, p. 1; Richard Halloran, "House Panel Urges Seoul to Aid in Bribery Inquiry," *New York Times*, Oct. 28, 1977, p. A12; "Carter Says Seoul Impedes U.S. Justice over Tongsun Park," *New York Times*, November 6, 1977, p. 1; and "Park Probe Cooperation or Aid Cuts, O'Neill Says," *Japan Times*, Dec. 13, 1977, p. 1.

62. See note 1, above.

63. William Chapman, "Carter Plans to Meet Head of South Korea," *Washington Post*, Nov. 8, 1978, p. A2.

64. A Correspondent, "Habib's Cocktail Mix Upsets Park's Men," *Far Eastern Economic Review*, June 10, 1977, pp. 10-11.

65. See Seth A. King, "Link to Food-Aid Program Helping Carter's Human-Rights Campaign," *New York Times*, Dec. 18, 1977, p. 3.

18 Arms Sales and Human Rights: The Case of Iran

Richard W. Cottam

Should American foreign policy seriously address the goal of encouraging the support of human rights in every part of the globe? Anyone seeking to think through this question should consider carefully the case of Iran. In any ranking of states in 1977 according to the degree of freedom of expression granted its citizenry, Iran would fall into one of the least free categories.[1] Dissenters within such nonfree states as South Korea, the Philippines, and the Soviet Union in 1977 were able to attract a great deal of attention, albeit at great personal risk. But their counterparts in North Korea, Cuba, the PRC, Uganda, Cambodia, and Iran lacked even that degree of freedom. The Iranian regime shared its low ranking with many other regimes. But Iran nevertheless must be a special case for Americans. The regime that denied the Iranian people freedom of expression came into power as a direct result of American intervention. Indeed, a useful exercise for the student of human rights would be a comparison of the Iranian press of early 1953, before the August 19 coup, and the Iranian press of early 1977. Of course, it cannot be asserted that, had there been no American-supported coup, there would have been freedom of expression in Iran. But there is at least the possibility that Iran might have remained free. In any case, the denial of human rights in Iran was to some degree a direct American responsibility. Did we, then, have a special obligation to encourage the restoration of human freedom to the Iranian people?

There is much irony in this dilemma. For most Americans, even including the best informed, consciousness of Iran evolved slowly during the Cold War and only achieved depth in the period of the energy crisis. Pre-World War II Iran was for those few Americans with any consciousness of it, the successor to that grim, Oriental despotism, the Persian Empire, which, we were told by our teachers, almost snuffed out Western civilization in the fifth century B.C. when it attempted to conquer Athens. It is a little difficult, therefore, to think of Iran as a focus of a struggle over human rights. But the facts are that Iran has had three periods in this century in which there was genuine freedom of expression. In each case the period came to an end with an episode that involved foreign intervention. Both Americans and the British were involved in all three cases, but only in the last case, the coup of August 19, 1953, were the Americans and the British on the same side. In 1912 and 1921 the United States appeared to Iranians to be the advocates of freedom for Iran. That image of the United States was of such strength that it endured even after the overt American intervention in 1953. So strong was the image of an America supportive of

freedom in Iran that Iranians could believe a picture in which well-meaning but
innocent Americans were duped by their clever and deceitful British cousins.
Consequently, possibly nowhere else in the nonfree world was the Carter administration's human rights position taken more seriously than in Iran.

Yet the image was never really deserved. In 1906 an alliance of Iranian
merchants, liberal religious leaders, and intellectuals were able to extract from
a weak, traditional government an acceptance of a constitution. The constitutional regime that followed made a serious effort to bring to Iran Enlightenment
values, and constitutional government was not finally overthrown until the
last days of 1911. Furthermore its overthrow was the direct consequence of a
British-endorsed Russian ultimatum. The immediate cause of this intervention
was the too successful performance of an American financial advisor and his
largely American team of experts. Even though the U.S. government took no
responsibility for the activity of this American, Morgan Shuster, and his team
of experts, Iranians—both friends and foes of Shuster—refused to take seriously
this denial of responsibility.[2]

The second period of relative freedom in Iran extends from the final days
of World War I, after the Bolshevik Revolution in Russia, to 1921. Disorder and
confusion accompanied freedom of expression, and societal divisions were such
that democratic governments were doomed to weakness. Lord Curzon, the
British foreign minister and close student of Iran, advocated in 1919 a treaty,
the Anglo-Persian Agreement, by which Iran would accept and support financially a large number of British technical experts. In Curzon's mind the agreement
would constitute beneficent tutelage. To both Wilsonian Americans and Iranian
nationalists the proposal was one calculated to make of Iran a protectorate.
Support for the agreement was drawn almost exclusively from members of the
Iranian oligarchy known for their willingness to cooperate with the British. Of
the Iranian press, often exuberantly independent, support came mainly from the
newspaper *Raad*, which was and still is universally assumed to have been British
subsidized.

This was a symbolic moment for Iranian advocates of a liberal nationalism,
and, just as in the constitutional period, the Americans, this time officially,
sided with the tiny liberal nationalist elite. Secretary of State Lansing not only
expressed his abhorrence of the proposed agreement to the British government,
he ordered the American minister in Tehran, John Caldwell, to release to the
Tehran press a statement clearly indicating American displeasure with the agreement. He did this after the newspaper *Raad* reported that the United States was
giving tacit support to the agreement.[3]

In 1921, the British clearly abandoned the project of an institutionalized
British tutelage. But the instability in Iran, one of the strategically most vital
areas of British concern, remained a threat to British security as the British
government perceived it. There followed a coup which placed in power one
Sayyed Zia ad-din Tabatabai, the editor of *Raad*, and Colonel Reza Khan, soon

to be Reza Shah Pahlavi. Official documentation still does not confirm the British role in this coup. But testimony by participants, British and Iranian alike, is so detailed and so corroborative that there is no more doubt of the British role in 1921 than of the American role in 1953.[4] Quite clearly the American legation in Tehran was undismayed by this event. Minister Caldwell, though antagonistic to the British, regarded the anti-Bolshevism of Reza Khan with favor.[5] But for Iranian advocates of freedom this was the second and successful part of the British assault on their freedom and independence. American opposition to the coup was assumed; but that assumption cannot be supported empirically. The progression toward despotic control by Reza Khan, inaugurated by the coup and culminating in his accession to the Iranian throne in 1925, was not a subject of particular concern in the American diplomatic correspondence in this period.[6]

The final period in which freedom of expression suffered few curbs extended from 1946 until 1953. Reza Shah had been compelled to abdicate in 1941 after the Anglo-Soviet occupation of Iran. His son, Mohammed Reza Shah, did not become the dominant figure in the Iranian government until 1955. In the years between the departure of the occupation forces in 1946 and the dictatorship of General Fazlollah Zahedi in 1953, there began to crystallize in Iran the institutional base and societal support for liberal democracy. Political parties that were far more than the personal vehicles of ambitious politicians appeared. A press developed which reflected the transitional stage of Iranian development. Some newspapers were published primarily for the purpose of blackmail and extortion. Others shamelessly solicited and frequently received foreign subsidies. Still others were the self-serving organs of individuals who were variously motivated. But there were more than a few large-circulation newspapers that made a serious effort to deal with the major social, economic, and political questions of the day.

By 1951 the crystallizing process had progressed to the point that the observer could identify the kinds of men who would be acceptable leaders for this changed Iran. The range was broad. It included men who would meet anyone's definition of fascist. It included religious leaders who favored change only in one area: the elimination of foreign control. But it also included religious leaders who were social and political reformists. At its core was a group of intellectuals, many of them from aristrocratic families, who were basically social reformists and, as events would demonstrate, remarkably loyal to the liberal democratic process. There were many among them who claimed to be dedicated Socialists, but their influence was never manifested in regime policies. The dominance of the liberal center was the consequence of another phenomenon— the emergence of a leader, Dr. Mohammed Mossadeq, whose appeal to the politically aware 10 percent of the population was charismatic. Mossadeq was liberal and centrist and the power his charisma granted enabled him to impose his own political personality on the national movement.[7]

There was basically two competing elite elements and the elections of 1952 spelled out very clearly their relative strength. Those elections can be described as free, especially since the outcome was unfavorable to the government. And they reflected Iran. One of the competing elites was Communist. The 20 percent vote the Communist candidates received in Tehran is probably a reasonably accurate measure of their support. But a great many people who voted in Tehran surely had no idea of the meaning of the election. They were literally trucked to the polls by religious and bazaari supporters of the Mossadeq government. The votes of the substantial middle class, however, were not purchased and the overwhelming Mossadeq victory in Tehran was in part a reflection of genuine popularity.

Outside Tehran the story was different. Several provincial cities followed the Tehran pattern. The election was staggered over several weeks and a pattern in rural voting soon emerged. The peasantry overwhelmingly did not vote and was surely unaware of the fact of an election. But the section that did vote was transported to the polls by and voted for the candidate of the dominant landowner coalition in the district. Their votes easily smothered the votes of the small, pro-Mossadeq modernized element found in the larger towns. The third competing elite was, therefore, the landowning elite. Its strength, like that of some of Mossadeq's religio-political allies, lay in its ability to manipulate an uncomprehending mass. It was overwhelmingly opposed to reform and not really uncomfortable with a system in which foreign intervention, now almost exclusively British, was a characteristic feature.

When it became clear that the election would ultimately produce a substantial landowning majority, the Mossadeq government made a pragmatic decision. With the election of a bare quorum for parliament, the election was suspended. But Mossadeq did not have a majority, and in 1952, when the Shah first dismissed Mossadeq as prime minister, the parliament happily acquiesced until it saw the enormity of the sense of public outrage in Tehran. At no time, however, and in spite of his great popularity among the politically aware, was Mossadeq's control of Iran a stable one.

The overthrow of Mossadeq was one of four extraordinary Central Intelligence Agency political operations. In these cases and in all other major political operations, the CIA operated as part of an alliance system. Included among the allies were always groups of local elites and often other foreign intelligence services. The CIA's role in these alliances varied widely in terms of resource outlay, logistics support, and overall operational control. The evidence thus far suggests that in four cases, each involving an attempt to overthrow a regime, CIA monetary and logistics support was great and the control exercised over the operation was a dominant one. These included two unsuccessful and two successful operations. The unsuccessful were Cuba in 1961 and Syria in 1957. The successful were Iran in 1953 and Guatemala in 1954.

Why should the struggling and fragile liberal democratic regime of Dr. Mossadeq in Iran have deserved such attention? Needless to say those responsible for American participation in the ouster of Dr. Mossadeq would not agree with the description. The psychological balancing process necessitated the construction of a picture of the Mossadeq regime that would make the act of ousting him congruent with American norms. Thus he and his supporters had to be wrapped in symbolically negative garb: a group of self-serving fanatics, dupes of communism, who wittingly or unwittingly, were destroying their country and preparing the ground work for its absorption with the Soviet bloc. In the context of the Cold War, Iran was strategically vital—both because of its geography and because of its enormous oil resources. Few American officials in the 1950s doubted that the incorporation of Iran within the Soviet block was a major Soviet objective. Furthermore, given the developing *modus operandi* of the Cold War, expectations were that the most likely means for bringing Iran into the fold was political subversion. Iran needed, therefore, an orderly, stable regime fully alive to the dangers of Communist subversions. What it had was a wild, irrational, and unstable regime which adamantly refused to deal seriously with the internal Communist threat. Those who advocated and planned the overthrow of the Mossadeq regime certainly saw this act as one that would save Iran from a totalitarian control that would deprive Iran of any form of freedom.[8]

Iran's last experiment with political freedom ended as a result of an American directed and controlled plot. But there was no debate on this point in the United States. Neither the American role in Mossadeq's overthrow nor the extent to which the Mossadeq phenomenon involved questions of political freedom was perceived in the United States. Even when a self-evidently authorized—and of course selectively fictitious—account of the operation was published in a mass circulation journal,[9] there was no conscious taking note of the affair by even the most attentive elements of the public. This typified American Cold War interventions. The American public, confronted with a Soviet Union perceived to be Hitler-like in aggressive intent, perceived policy responses selectively. The bizarre, irrational, dupe-of-communism image of Mossadeq was congruent with the wish for an orderly anticommunist regime in Iran. Blocked out was all cacophonous evidence for the image and all evidence of America imposing its will on Iran. Only as the perception of threat from the Soviet Union began to atrophy did there develop an ability on the part of the highly attentive public in the United States to perceive the nature of the Mossadeq regime and of American actions against it.

Many Iranians, possibly most of the highly attentive, see in American policy toward Iran a diabolically clever and brilliantly executed plan. The facts argue otherwise. Having lucked out in the overthrow of Mossadeq—the CIA plot was badly bungled—the American government lucked out in the development of the royal dictatorship of Mohammed Reza Shah. American policy was virtually without either theory or political-social analysis. Jehangir Amuzegar's study of

American economic aid to Iran is a good case history of a chaotic and inco-
herent policy.[10] Yet it can be said that American policy, like British policy
before it, was pragmatically adaptable. It recognized the control promise of
the second Pahlavi dictatorship and gave it full support. At no time, including
the present, has American policy indulged in the luxury of a concern for lost
freedoms in Iran. Nor can it be said that the academic community was guilty
of any such indulgence. In the development/decay dichotomy popularized by
Samuel Huntington,[11] the Shah's Iran was clearly developing. There would
be time later as Iran grew and matured for institutional development in the
area of political parties, a free press, and a freely elected parliament.

In response to human rights criticisms directed against Iran, spokesmen
for the regime countered even before the changes in 1978 that the Iranian case
was a mixed and improving one.[12] There was something to be said for this
position. In the area of human freedom, Iran ranked well in one dimension.
There was substantial freedom in the economic area. For anyone who
thoroughly understood the system, including how to get around regulations
and how to get positive government support, Iran offered almost endless
opportunity.

The case can also be made that the old Mossadeq supporters, preoccupied
as they were with fighting foreign intervention, had a poor record in providing
improvements in the material basis for a dignified life. Even if the Shah's
regime followed a trickle-down economic policy, there was a great deal that
did trickle down in a period in which the rate of growth in Iran was often
comparable to that of Japan. Furthermore in the areas of health, education,
and welfare programs, Iran advanced a great distance, especially in the past
decade. Then there was indeed a land-reform program that resulted in an
improved life for some of the peasantry[13] —although not for others. The position of women improved, and this was a real, not paper, improvement. Wages
were high and rising and workers were given the right to buy into the owner-
ship of the companies they worked for.

There is of course another side to this picture. A heavy price is paid for
the decision, however consciously made, to base regime stability on an entre-
preneurial class. The free economy of Iran has surely had much to do with
the innovation and spectacular growth rates. But this sector of the society
also dictated developmental patterns generally. As a result it was a system in
which the wealthy were heavily favored. Inflation at rates sometimes as high
as 25 to 35 percent lowered the real income of workers and others living on
a fixed income to the point that real improvements in standard of living were
modest. Unrestrained speculation in real estate made fortunes for a few but
raised the price of housing to levels that middle-income families attempting to
live on salaries simply could not afford. Agriculture was generally neglected
and since the regime, to avoid the consequences of consumer anger, maintained
the price of many staples at an artificially low level, most peasants who received

land were in serious difficulty and tenant farmers were often compelled to migrate to the cities. Iran turned increasingly to imports of agricultural products. There was little entrepreneurship in agriculture, especially as compared with real estate, service, and consumer industries, because of pricing policies. But the controls were the stuff that corruption in Iran breeds on— fortunes were made in agriculture sometimes by manipulating bankruptcy laws. There was in fact deep resentment generally, even on the part of those profiting most extravagantly, at the pervasiveness of corruption. It was inefficient, expensive, and demeaning. But there was almost universal agreement in Iran that indulging in corrupt practices was an essential aspect of succeeding in the system.

Still there were improvements in material conditions in Iran in the past decade. In the area of political freedom the trend was an entirely negative one.

The great turning point for Iran was 1963. In January of that year the old pro-Mossadeq elite, sensing the end of the royal dictatorship, were preparing to return to power. Candidates for succession to Mossadeq's mantle were openly maneuvering for position. Communist leaders were waiting across the border in Iraq, prepared at any moment to return. Even the crippled landowning elite saw some hope for a larger voice in affairs. Six months later the Pahlavi dictatorship had survived its greatest test and was consolidating totalitarian political control. In January the Shah simply arrested the entire Mossadeqist National Front leadership; and its followers proved to be unable to make even a serious show of resistance. In April a plebiscite was held to endorse the Shah's White Revolution and the returns bear the unmistakable mark of totalitarian control— over 99 percent endorsed the program.[14] Then in June an inchoate, largely spontaneous protest occurred that quickly mushroomed into a major riot. Ten years after Mossadeq's overthrow a new opposition was developing—far more lower and lower middle class in focus and looking to the mullahs and religious bazaaris for leadership. They had in common only a revulsion toward the regime; but they revealed the shallowness of real support for the regime. After all, this was the very element the Shah hoped to make his base of support. Furthermore they were almost successful.[15] But the feared defection from the security forces did not develop and, amid great bloodshed,[16] the revolt was suppressed. Its primary leader, Ayatollah Ruhollah Khomeini, one of the most respected leaders of Shiah Islam, went into exile and became the central rallying point for the active opposition.

Since those critical days of 1963, Iranians overwhelmingly accommodated to the royal dictatorship. The Shah's success in suppressing a major if formless challenge to his authority destroyed for many years any belief that the regime could be overthrown through violence. Since that time SAVAK achieved the ultimate success for such an organization. It was assumed to be ubiquitous. Any individual courageous enough to express open opposition to the government was certain to be suspected of being an agent provocateur. The image of SAVAK thus became self-perpetuating. Even Iranians in opposition abroad were paralyzed by this sense of SAVAK omnipotence. The suspicion it generated reinforced the normal exile tendency to factionate. And naturally the competing factions each believed the others were SAVAK-dominated. All SAVAK needed to do was to provide occasional confirmation of suspicions.

How many political prisoners were there in Iran in 1977? Estimates run as high as 125,000.[17] But it follows from the fact of Iran's totalitarian control that the numbers could not be known. The government could hardly be expected to release the figures, and Iranian citizens were far too frightened to admit to any stranger who of his friends and relatives had disappeared. The statement one heard from Iranians, that everyone in Iran, no matter what the social stratum, knew individuals who had been jailed for political reasons, simply could not be verified. Since those who said that were likely to have been in at least quiet opposition to the regime, the statement was self-serving. At any time it was possible to identify several hundred reasonably prominent individuals who were political prisoners. But the others of necessity remained the subject of conjecture. There is little reason to doubt, however, the sincerity of those whose estimates were in the 100,000 range. The belief was entirely congruent with the police-state image SAVAK generated in Iran.[18]

The same point must be made for the extent of torture in Iran. Opposition groups operating abroad detailed hundreds of examples of unspeakable torture committed by the regime.[19] The case histories described do have the ring of truth. If they are fabrications, they are expertly done because the descriptions of those doing the torturing fit closely classical patterns. The Shah personally confirmed on a CBS interview with Mike Wallace that there has been torturing in Iran in the recent past. But eyewitness testimony, such as that of Reza Baraheny,[20] was challenged by the government of Iran and by officials of the U.S. government. Indeed a compaign was launched to discredit Baraheny by asserting that he too was a SAVAK agent.[21] By pure accident in 1971 I over- heard an unskilled worker in the city of Meshed telling a Moslem priest about his arrest and torture by SAVAK. He opened his shirt and revealed hideous cuts on his body. The episode reduced considerably my own skepticism; but the fact is that the extent to which torture was utilized in Iran could not be investigated by anyone whose report would be credible.

Still coercion was probably a less powerful control device in Iran than was purchase. Except for those highly conspicuous but numerically small number of Iranians who were manipulating the system with enormous profit, life was difficult in Iran. With rents for modest apartments running at well over $1,000 a month, the salaried white-collar class had to be unhappy. But there was employment and salaries were at a level that was inconceivable a decade ago. For most people there had been an overall improvement in life-style. So even though they may have believed that corruption, waste, and extravagance were at the obscene level, the middle class was not likely to take action that would involve risking what they had achieved.

Evidence of the shallowness of support for the regime in Iran was neverthe-less strong. Most obvious was the security apparatus itself. It was expensive and implicitly dangerous for the Shah. Having to rely on a terror instrument for control makes one personally vulnerable. If the terror instrument is to be effective, it must be well organized and efficiently run. But if it achieves a high level of effectiveness, its chiefs gain a dangerous degree of influence. Presum-ably, had it been possible to relax the control, the Shah would have done so.

Another major indicator of lack of support was found in opposition student activities. Inside Iran, where education was free, universities were frequently disrupted and closed. Outside Iran the Confederation of Iranian Students, though badly factionated and certainly SAVAK infiltrated, was in adamant opposition. To be sure, this represented only a fraction of Iranian students. The large majority was carefully nonpolitical and basically willing to accommodate to the regime. But conformity pressures among activist students were strongly antiregime. This was true in spite of the fact that this generation of Iranian students learned nothing about Iran's modern history while in Iran that was not highly favorable to the regime. A typical student would know very little about the Mossadeq phenomenon before leaving Iran, and the discovery of Mossadeq was a shock that pushed many students abroad toward antiregime activities.

Still, in spite of the historical rewrite in Iran, the Shah's primary problem with the most highly attentive and opinion-formulating section of his popula-tion lay with his nationalist legitimacy. His father's rise to power and his rise to power both owed much to foreign intervention. In the case of Mohammed Reza Shah, that foreign intervention ousted a man who for many had become the symbolic figure in Iran's search for independence and national dignity. Opposition newspapers published abroad spoke of that event as if it had just occurred.

The Shah's efforts to overcome this problem involved some imaginative efforts to invoke counter symbols. "Positive nationalism" was an early failure. More enduring was the "white revolution." In the 1970s it was the Shah-people revolution, but its success was greater abroad than in Iran. Evidence for this came with the failure of the extravaganza of 1971—the celebration of 2,500 years of Iranian kings. Despite an expenditure of at least $100 million—mainly on monuments and urban beautification projects for the occasion—the Shah personally admitted bitter disappointment with the results.[22] Anger at this symbolic effort to tie the Shah to the history of Iran's great dynasties and thus to erase the foreign-imposed image was surprisingly pervasive and intense. University life was disrupted for days or weeks by hostile demonstrations.

More subtle was the treatment of Iran's one major foreign adventure of contemporary times: the military intervention in the Dhofar province of Oman. The intervention was made at the formal request of the Oman govern-ment to help suppress a local rebellion with international leftist backing including that of the Soviet Union. The Iranian force of probably 3,500 men was entirely self-supporting, supplied from Iran, and played a major role in defeating the rebels.[23] Its performance may not have been consistently glorious, but the lack of publicity it received in Iran was surely not for that reason. The operation was generally successful and one would think a government hungry for nationalist credibility would have publicized and glorified it. But in fact the operation received minimal publicity. Why? An answer can easily be inferred. Iran's partners in Oman, a country long under British control, were subject to the same charge of Western imperial control as was the Iranian government.[24] The image of an Anglo-American operation executed by regional puppets was too obvious to risk activating. Raising oil prices against the wishes of the Western governments would be a safer policy to publicize. The seizing of several islands in the Straits of Hormoz was at the expense of Sheikdoms long under British protection and that adventure did receive maximal publicity.

This control picture points to a real dilemma which faced Americans who in 1977 sought to pressure the Shah to move in the direction of granting increased political freedom. The Shah's regime was a reasonably stable one. But it was based on a combination of coercion and utilitarian satisfaction. Support for the regime lacked depth, and the basis for dissatisfaction was substantial. Granting increased freedom to the press, for example, would surely result in scathing attacks on waste, corruption, extravagance, and grotesquely unfair income distribution patterns. Such attacks could force the regime to move in directions that might improve its stability even though stirring dissatisfaction among the parvenu element. But a free press would also give voice to the persisting anger at the American imposition of the royal dictatorship on Iran. Attacks of this order could only add to the Shah's image-difficulties and thus could weaken his control to a point that regime change could occur. Were American advocates of increased human rights for Iran prepared to accept responsibility for change in Iran on that order?

Arms Sales in the Iranian Context

1963 was also a major turning point in United States-Iranian relations. In the decade following Mossadeq's overthrow, the primary American task concerning Iran was regime preservation. Iran was in this sense an American dependency. The regime's survival was dependent on American support; and, since the maintenance of the Shah in power was a primary U.S. objective, the regime's very weakness was its primary source of bargaining strength. The American government could not afford to appear as anything but totally supportive of the Iranian government. Military aid given in this decade was primarily for the purpose of internal security.

However, once the Shah appeared to be internally secure, the purpose behind American military support for Iran began to change. By the time of the

Nixon-Kissinger era, Iran was already playing a deterrent and a surrogate role for the United States. As Iran's military force became increasingly respectable, the price the Soviets must pay to overrun Iran or to disrupt Persian Gulf sea lanes rose steadily. Obviously Iran could not long stand against a determined Soviet military move across its borders. But, so the theory goes, the price exacted would be sufficient to preclude any casual Soviet move and thus would reduce substantially Soviet options.

The surrogate role was well illustrated by the Dhofar intervention. Iran had the capability to counter the subversive potential of the Soviet Union or of any Soviet surrogates in the region. Indeed, Iran's was prototypical of the kind of regime that should be supported under the Nixon Doctrine. Even before that doctrine was articulated, Iran was following the desired course of action.

Arms sales to Iran must be seen in this context. American policy in Iran has had a great deal to do with the reduction of Iranian freedom of expression. But there is little direct relationship between the sale of arms to Iran and the suppression of human rights in Iran. The sales of arms to Iran has been in the security interests of the United States as those who make American policy perceive those interests. The effort to approach the subject of denial of human rights in Iran through a restriction of sale of arms to Iran amounts to an evasion of the real issue between proponents and opponents of arms sales—that is, a difference in assessments of the security interests of the United States.

Iran was an original Cold War battleground. For whatever reasons, the Soviet Union did make the effort to establish an autonomous people's democratic republic in Iranian Azerbaijan and in Iranian Kurdistan.[25] The Soviet Union also engaged heavily in the internal politics of Iran by a direct involvement with the Iranian Tudeh party—the political arm of Iranian communism.[26] These activities were part of a pattern especially in countries on the Soviet littoral. Fresh from their experience of underestimating Hitler's aggressive intent, the American people and their leaders came to the natural conclusion that the Soviet government was Hitler-like in the extent of its ambitions. Containing the Soviet Union's aggressions in Iran, as in much of the third world, required an American counter-involvement. The objective in Iran and elsewhere in the strategically vital Third World was a regime sensitive to, capable of resisting, and willing to resist Soviet subversive efforts.

In 1953, the primary American decision-makers concluded that the goal of a stable, noncommunist Iran could only be achieved by replacing the regime. A similar conclusion was drawn over the years regarding many other Third World regimes. Frequently the regime to be overthrown was one that was uncharacteristically concerned with human rights and political freedom—as was true in the Iranian case. But in periods of rapid change such regimes are almost certain to be unstable, even chaotic, and hence are easily perceived to be vulnerable to external subversion. The American choice for more reliable leadership in Iran was also typical of American Cold War interventions—a leader drawn from among the outspokenly anticommunist traditional elite. But functionally there was also a recognition by American policymakers that this traditional leadership must modernize in order to maintain stable control. The dangers involved in the phenomenon of "rising expectations" were explicitly recognized, and a strategy for meeting those expectations, at least at a minimal level, did evolve for Iran and elsewhere. Thus the pattern was one of opposing, even ousting from power, a liberal, modernizing elite, replacing it with a segment of the old, traditional elite but pressuring that elite to move in a modernizing direction.

In Iran, in Jordan, and in Syria this process involved replacing regimes with a real concern for human rights and political freedom with ones with little concern for human rights and in outright opposition to political freedom. But in those cases as elsewhere, the absence of any significant direct American role on behalf of human rights did not produce a significant opposition from any element of the American public except the far left. The others preferred not to see the American role. Even disciples of John F. Kennedy, who favored American cooperation with liberal modernizing elements, did so on pragmatic grounds. They argued that the United States must ally itself with local nationalist movements or run the risk of throwing those nationalists into Soviet arms.[27]

The conclusion of this for me is inescapable. Among those individuals for whom human rights and political freedom are intensely held values, a concern for those values as an objective of American foreign policy varies in inverse proportion to perception of threat from the Soviet Untion. In Iran during the 1953-1963 decade, when American policy was directly involved in the suppression of political freedom, the threat perception was great and the American role was not perceived. On the contrary, there was a general acceptance of the symbolically favorable garb in which the media wrapped the Iranian regime. "The progressive, young monarch" phrase came most easily to mind when the Shah was referred to, as it does today when Hussein is referred to. Later, when the Iranian regime needed no help in suppressing political dissent but the perception of threat was declining in intensity, the brutality of the regime was perceived and the American role in its creation was, among the highly attentive, a generally accepted fact. Coupling of arms sales and human rights in Iran was an understandable response to the frustration that followed the discovery of past American policy. We wanted to punish this regime that was in part our own creation.

Foreign policy debates are notorious as examples of two sides talking past each other. This tendency can usually be accounted for by the fact that the two sides operate from fundamentally different assumptional bases. But it is not the assumptional differences that are the subject of debate. Rather it is specific policy preferences that follow from the assumptions.

The debate over arms sales to Iran was a case in point. There had been an atrophy of perception of threat from the Soviet Union among Americans. But the atrophying process occurred among the public at rates that varied sharply.

For some Americans in fact the monolithic enemy stereotype of the Soviet Union remained essentially unchanged from that held by most Americans in the 1950s. Individuals in or close to this category were likely to see a very strong case indeed for the sale of arms to Iran. The two roles—deterrent and surrogate, as mentioned earlier—that Iran played were seen as essential for American security. Typically, individuals in this category—as did most Americans in the 1950s—had a favorable image of the Iranian regime and were inclined to accept the regime's contention that it was moving at an optimal rate for a developing country in advancing human rights in Iran. As the populace matured further, political freedoms would gradually be established.

Individuals who accepted this view had great difficulty understanding either the opposition to arms sales or the obsession with human rights. "Everyone favors human rights," they are inclined to say. But the effort to deny Iran the arms it seeks to purchase and to do so in the name of a concern with human rights is, they believe, both dangerous to American security and likely to impede the development of human rights in Iran. Given the assumptions, the case for arms sales was a strong one. The tendency to see a favorable picture of human rights in Iran was a natural one.

But the case was entirely different for those who saw a Soviet Union that was in its foreign policy essentially status quo. They were likely to accept a picture of a large Soviet bureaucracy which incorporated a wide diversity of foreign policy-related vested interests. This Soviet Union was at most sluggishly aggressive and hence easily deterred or at best willing to move rapidly in the direction of real détente with the United States. Even earlier, in the immediate post-World War II period, the interventions in Iran and elsewhere in the Middle East were probably motivated primarily by security concerns. But now Soviet interventions have declined to the point that no state in the Middle East can any longer be characterized as a Soviet dependency.

For those who accepted this view, there was not much of a case that could be made for the sale of arms to Iran. Iran already had a security force far in excess of any real security needs. The suspicion was natural therefore that Iran entertained expansionist notions concerning the region. Already there was evidence of this. Iran had seized several islands in the Persian Gulf and had intervened in the affairs of Yemen and Oman, both politically and militarily. Scenarios in which Iran intervened to suppress a rebellion in Saudi Arabia occurred both to analysts and to novelists. On the eastern border, Iran had made full use of its great wealth to influence Afghanistan, and had warned India against any further efforts to partition Pakistan. Also easily imagined were scenarios in which India and Iraq, often close to the Soviet Union, become involved in open conflict with Iran, thus threatening a Soviet-American confrontation—a serious accidental-war situation. The vagueness of the Shah's responses to the question of whom he was arming against and the utterly unpersuasive nature of the scenarios Iranians offered[28] were evidence for the conclusion that

Iran did not have serious defense motivations and was concealing its real motives.

Individuals in this category were most likely to look closely at the nature of Iranian suppression of political freedom. They found only cant in the Iranian government's case that it was advancing human rights and would, when the country was ready, add the dimension of political freedom as well. The idea of a cutoff in arms sales to Iran because of the suppression of freedom there found its appeal with individuals in this category.

Most interested Americans could be mapped at various points between these polar views. In general, though, the attractiveness of the policy alternatives would vary according to the relative proximity to one or the other pole.

President Carter, Human Rights, and Iran

There is a profound innocence in President Carter's pronouncements on human rights. Both he and those in his administration responsible for formulating a human rights program fail to understand the impact of presidential statements on the multitude of unfree societies in the world. Iran is a case in point. Foreign intervention in Iranian affairs is in this era habitual. American intervention specifically has in fact been substantial and is perceived by Iranians as a basic element of their political process. Thus a statement from an American president in support of human rights will not be perceived in Iran as most Americans perceive it—that is, a vague, almost platitudinous admonition. Iran has had a regime that owed its very existence to American intervention and that regime stood in flagrant violation of political rights and many human rights. To Iranians, regime supporters and regime opponents alike, the Carter statement was a diplomatic signal of potentially momentous importance. Could it be, they wondered, that the United States is considering once again precipitating a leadership change in Iran?

The Shah's initial response was to take some concrete measures to reduce his vulnerability to charges of violations of political and human rights. He released from jail some prominent political prisoners, improved the prison conditions, and ceased torturing others. He allowed Red Cross officials to inspect selected prisons. A human rights commission was activated, some improvements were made, and more were promised in legal procedures. Even opposition spokesmen conceded that the changes were more than cosmetic. But they insisted that conditions had not changed for the vast majority of political prisoners whose fate was known only to a small circle of family and friends.

There were indeed strong grounds for skepticism about the government's intent. Selective repression was intensifying, not diminishing. Of significance was the fact that in the summer of 1977 the regime was arresting and giving harsh sentences to opponents with strong ties in religious and bazaari circles.

Ayatollah Mahmud Taleqani, for example, one of Iran's most respected progressive theologians, was, in the middle of this liberalization period, sentenced to ten years in prison. This act reflected the regime's sense of vulnerability from religious-based opposition. But there was not yet an across-the-board crackdown on opposition activities.

Inside Iran response to the Carter pronouncements was slow in surfacing, but by the summer of 1977 it was rapidly gaining momentum. One group, calling itself the Radical Movement of Iran, began circulating mimeographed statements that were far more moderate than radical in their criticisms of the regime. Then an associated group of artists, composers, and literati called for the right of free association and an end to government censorship. The government's response was encouraging. In addition a number of individuals wrote letters, given wide but private circulation, critizing the government. One such individual, Ali Asghar Haj Sayyid Javadi, was gaining in Iran a stature comparable to that of Sakharov in the Soviet Union. Most of the others were men with histories of association with Dr. Mossadeq and the national movement.

The rhythm of this activity was revealing. In the early stages there was a call for a return to the rule of law and an end to corruption and the extravagant waste of Iran's precious oil wealth. But, as competition for leadership of a genuine opposition grew, the charges and demands escalated and became more concrete. Now demands for free elections, a free press, and the release of all political prisoners were made by those seeking to lead the opposition. A clear indication of the direction toward which opposition statements were tending was given by the opposition press published outside Iran. That press included regular denunciations of the regime in absolute terms on religious grounds by Ayatollah Khomeini, the most prominent of Iran's political priests, who at the time resided in Iraq. By both religious-oriented and secular opponents, there was a portrait of the Shah as a product of the CIA and the dutiful agent of American imperialism. Arms sales to Iran were treated as the most obvious of Iranian payoffs to the American defense industry from a grateful Shah; and the strategic purpose those arms were intended to serve was American, not Iranian.

In an earlier draft of this chapter, written before the dramatic events of 1978 in Iran, I stated, "There is no reason to believe that the Shah will tolerate opposition activities that move much further in this direction. Nor is there much reason to doubt the continued, even accelerating, movement of opposition criticism in this direction. . . . There is motion toward confrontation and just how severe the government response will be depends very much on how Carter's purpose is perceived." In fact by the end of 1977 it had become difficult to believe that the Iranian government felt any real pressure from Carter to move in a liberalizing direction. Signals from Carter favorable to Iranians seeking change were always in the form of abstract expressions of concern. Unfavorable signals were generally concrete. There was first the selection of William Sullivan as American ambassador. Sullivan was widely known as a Vietnam hard-liner who was entirely comfortable in Southeast Asia in dealing with regimes that were perceived to be quite comparable to the Iranian royal dictatorship. Then the administration strongly endorsed the sale of a $1.2 billion advanced warning system, AWACS, to Iran. This was fully in tune with the image of arms sales for the dual purpose of giving orders to America's defense industry for weapons of no use to Iran but of significant use for Iran's American patron. Following this, President Carter chose to make a symbolic stop in Iran on a rapid foreign tour, thus signaling support and favor. Finally there was the signal of nonaction with regard to opposition activities in Iran. The opposition had used many channels to make sure that the Carter adminis-tration was aware of their activities and of the fact that they had been greatly encouraged by his statements. Yet there was no public taking note of this activity within the Carter administration. There was indeed no sign that Ameri-can responsibility was recognized or even understood for dissident activity that resulted in incarceration, torture, and even death.

The case is a strong one that Iranian responses to Carter's advocacy of human rights abroad did in fact generate a momentum for basic change in Iran. Both government and those in opposition appeared to be testing Carter's intent. In the process of doing so the fragility of the base of the Shah's support became increasingly apparent and the argument from the Shah's point of view for suppressing the newly assertive opposition should have been compelling. Fur-thermore, overt American policy suggested that a decision to suppress those who had had the temerity to surface in opposition would not be opposed by the American government. Yet the Shah confounded my prediction and surely that of most of his countrymen that he would act decisively to reverse the opposition momentum.

On February 18, 1978, rioting broke out in Tabriz in northwest Iran which changed fundamentally Iran's internal security picture. Public participation was very great, especially among lower middle and working class elements. The opposition activities reflected an organization and discipline the regime had not anticipated. And for the first time it became clear that Ayatollah Ruhollah Khomeini was not just a popular religious leader. He had become a symbolic figure for much of the religious population—a man personifying both national and Islamic dignity. Local police and SAVAK efforts to break up the demon-stration only served to enrage the crowd, which proceeded to destroy a number of banks, cinemas, and hotels. The army had to be brought in to restore order. Rumors spread that elements of the police had joined the rioters and, in any case, SAVAK's mystique was badly damaged. Instead of a ubiquitous and omni-scient organization capable of orchestrating the most elaborate conspiracies, SAVAK was revealed as badly informed, inefficient, and, at critical moments, paralyzed. The Shah summarily removed the regional officers of SAVAK, and this act simply underlined the growing public sense that the Shah's internal security was in fact vulnerable.

Tabriz was of course infectious. Rioting occurred in cities across the country and, even more significantly, in rather small provincial centers. The forty-day Moslem mourning period predicted the timing of rioting, and evidence that the elements of the population most attracted to the Moslem leadership were the major force in the demonstrations multiplied. The Shah in January 1963 jailed the entire National Front leadership and in July 1963 sent into exile the Moslem leaders of the June rioting. But in the winter and spring of 1978 his response was indecisive and inconsistent to an extreme. Instead of arresting the opposition coalition *en masse,* the government permitted para-military attacks on opposition leaders by groups pretending to be vigilantes. In so doing, the Shah demonstrated simultaneous weakness and brutality—a recipe that could not fail to result in escalating resistance.

In late summer 1978 a theater in the oil refining center of Abadan burned and 400 to 700 customers were killed. The government charged that this was the act of fanatical Moslems who opposed the showing of films. But the opposition charged the fire was the Shah's Reichstag and the belief spread that indeed SAVAK, acting under the Shah's direct orders, had burned the theater to kill some Islamic oppositionists who had taken refuge in the theater. This event, and probably more the interpretation, seems to have further demoralized the Shah. He responded by removing his highly competent technocratic premier Jamshid Amuzegar and replaced him with the ineffectual Jafar Sherif-Emami. The latter was expected to make contact with both religious and secular opponents of the regime, but he was not given the independence necessary to carry out such a task.

The new government then proceeded to carry out policies that could only produce further deterioration. The Shah was now heavily reliant on his security force and his bureaucracy for survival. But he chose to prepare for trial on grounds of corruption several of his most prominent and loyal sup-porters. The list included his prime minister for twelve years and the former chief of SAVAK. Virtually everyone on fixed income in Iran chose this time to strike for wage increases large enough to compensate for some of their inflation-induced losses. The government granted a great many of these demands and in the process made a shambles of economic planning. These government policies, adversely affecting the economy, naturally were alarming to the Shah's newly rich base of support and many people who had profited most from the regime left Iran.

Having offended his supporters, the Shah continued with his inconsistent responses to the open opposition. On September 5 over 3 million Iranians demonstrated against the regime. The demonstrators were orderly and in Tehran they gave flowers to watching security forces. There was that day almost an atmosphere of brotherhood. Three days later, martial law was imposed and a large group of demonstrators in Jaleh Square in Tehran was fired on by the troops. Estimates of the number killed range from the government figure of seventy-eight to a widely accepted opposition figure of 4,500. A short time later the government granted freedom to the press greater than Iran had seen since Mossadeq's days. Naturally, a preoccupation of the newly free press was governmental brutality. Thus the formula of a show of weakness followed by brutality was repeated.

Finally on November 6, following a day of restrained rioting which the opposition argues was encouraged by the government, the Shah appointed General Gholam Reza Azhari to head a military government. Even then suppression was more episodic than general. Momentum had only been slowed.

The critical variable in the rapid deterioration of regime stability in Iran was almost incontestably the Shah's own behavior. But the case is nevertheless strong that Carter's pronouncements on human rights served to set in motion a force which the Shah, strangely, did not control. As such the Iranian case stands as an illustration of the potential force of a general human rights policy advocated by an American president. Because of a history of interference in Irano-American relations, the very proclamation of human rights as a central concern of American policy set into motion forces of change. It is idle to speculate whether Iran would have faced this crisis had there been no Carter policy on human rights. Situational receptivity for rapid change was high in Iran in 1977. The Shah's base of societal support was both thin and fragile. Because of the economic distress induced for most Iranians by prolonged inflation there developed a predisposition among much of the public to join in direct action for basic policy change. Thus the stage was set; and we know now that regime vulnerability was far greater than imagined because the Shah, one of the most absolute rulers in the world at the beginning of this period, was personality-predisposed toward paralysis in dealing with a severe crisis and would not use his loyal security forces effectively. A regime-threatening crisis was therefore possible; but the fact is that Carter's human rights stance played a precipitating role.

The case of Iran should indeed create skepticism concerning the advisability of an official American foreign policy advocacy of human rights. Such an advocacy constitutes intervention in the affairs of other states and it is an intervention with the bluntest and least controllable of instruments. The first question to be asked is how will that instrument be perceived? The Iran case argues that perception of the policy will be in tune with American historical relations with the target state. However, since American officials dealing with that state are likely to have no more than a shallow understanding of historical relationships, there will be little official understanding of how the human rights policy is perceived and therefore of the challenge this response poses for American policy. That Soviet and East European leaders would see human rights advocacy by the United States as a manifestation of roll-back policy, for example, is understandable. In historical context the Carter policy can be interpreted easily as resembling closely that of Dulles; but that interpretation is not likely to be taken seriously by Carter and American advisors of a generation later.

Second, what will be the impact of an advocacy of human rights on the internal political process of a target state? As the Iranian case illustrates, for the category of states which have had a dependency relationship with the United States, the impact can be profound and again will not be anticipated by American officials. Similarly with respect to the Soviet Union, human rights advocacy might well result in a shift among Soviet policymakers in a hard-line direction, given the natural rollback interpretation given that policy.

Third, can a human rights advocacy be manifested consistently throughout the world? The Iranian case loudly argues "no" to that question. Especially for those officials who continue to hold a Cold War view, Iran was a vital ally for a policy of containing and deterring an aggressive Soviet Union. When this view is held, human rights violations are either not seen or are explained away— thus no pressure need be applied. But for those, especially in the Third World, who do not have these particular blinders, an American refusal to criticize Iran on human rights grounds is seen as consciously and blatantly hypocritical. Administration criticism of Soviet human rights violations and failure to criticize Chinese human rights violations similarly are noted throughout the world as evidence that the advocacy of human rights is a consciously manipulated instrument of American political power.

The irony is that Carter's human rights advocacy has had a major impact on the history of Iran and that that impact was entirely unintended. And if, partly as a result of Carter's policy, a regime appears in Iran that is sharply sensitive to human rights, it will regard the American administration as having been the primary obstacle to its achieving power.

The Iranian case, and quite likely the Soviet case as well, suggest that presidential advocacy of human rights as a central objective of American foreign policy has been and is likely always to be a mistake. Any government's foreign policy is a compound of responses to pressures placed upon it. A basic contention here is that even with optimal conditions, including presidential receptivity, pressures working for human rights abroad can never be strong enough to give anything approaching a primary coloring to American foreign policy. Thus when, as under President Carter, human rights advocacy is presented as a central aspect of American policy, that policy will be inconsistent, will be interpreted as hypocritical, and will produce unintended effects possibly of momentous importance. On the other hand, an American foreign policy that is compelled to take into account strong and highly visible domestic pressure from human rights advocates is far less likely to be misinterpreted and may well be productive of results in the form of human rights achievements. For example, a policy that is clearly responding to an insistence by Congress that the observation of human rights be taken seriously into account in determining arms sales, is not likely to be misinterpreted by affected governments. If such a government badly neeeded American arms, the human rights proviso could strengthen the hands of those in government who argued for a policy of greater sensitivity to human rights without stirring suspicions of some other devious American interest.

At the very least, the case of Iran suggests that human rights advocates must address far more seriously than they have questions of strategy.

Notes

1. The Freedom House survey for 1976 placed Iran in the next-to-least-free category.

2. See Shuster's own account of this. Morgan Shuster, *The Strangling of Persia* (New York: The Century Co., 1920).

3. Abraham Yeselson, *United States-Persian Diplomatic Relations, 1883-1921* (New Brunswick: Rutgers University Press, 1956), p. 161.

4. Gerard de Villiers, *The Imperial Shah: An Informal Biography* (Boston: Little Brown and Co., 1976). This journalist account summarizes the explanations.

5. Yeselson, p. 173.

6. Having read most of the diplomatic correspondence for those years, I have yet to find one that comments seriously on the question of the loss of freedom in Iran. What appears instead is an intense distrust of the British and willingness to counter their perceived machinations. See for example in document 819.51 the dispatch from Copley Amory, Jr., to the Department of State, dated December 16, 1923.

7. For a discussion of the Mossadeq period see Richard Cottam, *Nationalism in Iran* (Pittsburgh: The University of Pittsburgh Press, 1964).

8. An easy way to recapture the imagery of the period is to look at two accounts in *Time* magazine, one August 24, 1953, when the coup appeared to have failed, p. 19, and the other August 31, 1953, written after the success of the coup, pp. 14-15.

9. Richard and Gladys Harkness, "The Mysterious Doings of CIA," *Saturday Evening Post,* November 6, 1954, pp. 66-68.

10. Jehangir Amuzegar, *Technical Assistance in Theory and Practice: The Case of Iran* (New York: Praeger, 1966).

11. Samuel Huntington, "Political Development and Political Decay," *World Politics,* 17 (April 1965), 386-430.

12. See Fereydoun Hoveyda, "Not All Clocks for Human Rights Are the Same," *New York Times,* op ed, May 18, 1977.

13. Ann K.S. Lambton, *The Persian Land Reform, 1962-1966* (Oxford: Clarendon Press, 1969). Miss Lambton looks at a number of villages and describes improvements in individual households.

14. *New York Times,* June 10, 1963.

15. For a brief account of this episode see Marvin Zonis, *The Political Elite of Iran* (Princeton: Princeton University Press, 1971), pp. 44-47.

16. Cottam, p. 308.

17. The 125,000 figure is a mysterious and surely arbitrary one. An article in *Le Monde* I have yet to see is referred to as a source but with "international organizations" as the ultimate source for Iranian oppositionists. *Resistance,* an opposition publication, uses the more restrained figure of 40,000. See *Resistance,* Vol. 5, No. 4, p. 12. *Payam* in 1974 referred to 25,000 political prisoners.

18. See the report of William J. Butler of the International Commission of Jurists. "Human Rights and the Legal System in Iran," Geneva, 1976.

19. There are numerous publications on this subject. See for example *Resistance,* Special Issue, Vol. 2, No. 5.

20. Reza Baraheny, Excerpts from testimony on torture in Iran, *New York Times,* April 21, 1976, 37:2.

21. Ambassador Ardeshir Zahedi and State Department spokesmen both told the CBS "Sixty Minutes" staff that Baraheny had been a SAVAK agent. This was communicated to me personally.

22. The Shah made this clear in interviews held after the celebration which were reported in the Iranian press.

23. Shahram Chubin and Sepehr Zabih, *The Foreign Relations of Iran* (Berkeley: University of California Press, 1974). This book has an account of the Dhofar intervention from an Iranian perspective.

24. For an account that describes this picture of Western imperialist-Iranian collusion, see Fred Halliday, *Arabia Without Sultans* (New York: Vintage Books, 1975), chapters 10 and 11.

25. For a strongly anti-Soviet description, see George Leczowski, *Russia and the West in Iran:: 1918-1948* (Ithaca: Cornell University Press, 1949).

26. Sepehr Zabih, *The Communist Movement in Iran* (Berkeley: University of California Press, 1966).

27. The lumping of all so-called cold warriors together has concealed the very real differences between Kennedy and both his predecessors and successors. See for example Richard J. Walton, *Cold War and Counter Revolution: The Foreign Policy of John F. Kennedy* (New York: Viking Press, 1972). A quick comparison of Kennedy's policies in Peru, Dominican Republic, Congo, Yemen, and Laos with that of both Eisenhower and Johnson points to the difference in emphasis on the role of local nationalists that is desirable from a U.S. security point of view.

28. See the Shah's interview with Orianna Fallaci, *New Republic,* December 1, 1972, pp. 16-21, for the Shah's answer to such questions. See also *Kayhan International,* July 6, 1974.

Index

Index

About the Contributors

Hugo Adam Bedau has written or edited many books and articles on moral and political philosophy, including *The Courts, the Constitution, and Capital Punishment* and *Justice and Equality.* He is Austin Fletcher Professor of Philosophy at Tufts University.

Charles R. Beitz is assistant professor of political science at Swarthmore College. His publications include "Justice and International Relations," *Philosophy and Public Affairs* 4 (1975); and *Political Theory and International Relations* (Princeton University Press, forthcoming, 1979).

Thomas Buergenthal is professor of international law at the School of Law of the University of Texas at Austin. His books include *International Protection of Human Rights* (with L.B. Sohn), *International Human Rights and International Education* (with J.V. Torney), and *Human Rights, International Law and the Helsinki Accord.* He is chairman of the Human Rights Committee of the U.S. National Commission for UNESCO, and he has represented the U.S. government at various intergovernmental conferences relating to international human rights.

Richard P. Claude is professor of government and politics at the University of Maryland. He is the author of *The Supreme Court and the Electoral Process* and editor and principal author of *Comparative Human Rights.* Currently he is editor-in-chief of *Universal Human Rights,* a quarterly journal of the social sciences, philosophy, and law.

Jerome A. Cohen is professor of law, director of East Asian legal studies, and associate dean at the Harvard Law School. His books include *The Criminal Process in the People's Republic of China: 1949-1963; People's China and International Law* (with Hungdah Chiu); and *China Today* (with Joan Lebold Cohen).

Richard W. Cottam is the author of *Foreign Policy Motivation, Nationalism in Iran,* and *Competitive Interference and 20th Century Diplomacy.* He is professor of political science at the University of Pittsburgh.

Howard M. Fish is a lieutenant-general in the United States Air Force. From 1974 to 1978 he was director of the Defense Security Assistance Agency and deputy assistant secretary of defense (international security affairs) for security assistance. He is the assistant vice chief of staff, United States Air Force.

Tom Harkin is a U.S. Congressman from Iowa. He has been one of the most outspoken defenders of human rights in the Congress and is the author of two of the most important human rights laws.

J. Bryan Hehir is associate secretary, Office of International Justice and Peace, U.S. Catholic Conference, and, concurrently, a lecturer in social ethics at St. John's Seminary in Brighton, Massachusetts. He is on the editorial board of *Worldview* magazine and is a member of the Council on Foreign Relations. He has published a number of articles on Catholic perspectives on issues of public policy.

John Salzberg is staff consultant on human rights to the U.S. House of Representatives Committee on Foreign Affairs. He was formerly representative to the United Nations for the International Committee of Jurists. He received the Ph.D. in political science and has published "The Parliamentary Role in Implementing International Human Rights" (with Donald Young), *Texas International Law Journal* 12 (1977).

Thomas M. Scanlon is professor of philosophy at Princeton University, where he teaches moral and political philosophy. He is the author of numerous publications and is an associate editor of *Philosophy & Public Affairs.*

Mark L. Schneider is currently a deputy assistant secretary of state for human rights in the Office of Human Rights and Humanitarian Affairs. He was a Peace Corps volunteer in El Salvador and later served seven years as a legislative assistant to Senator Edward M. Kennedy and as a professional staff member of the Senate Refugee Subcommittee. He was a recipient of a Fulbright Special Fellowship. His chapter in this book was prepared in part prior to his entrance to the Department of State.

Henry Shue is the author of several articles in moral philosophy, including "Liberty and Self-Respect," *Ethics* 85 (1975), and "Torture," *Philosophy and Public Affairs,* Vol. 7 (1978), as well as the forthcoming book *Basic Rights: A Philosophical Perspective on Some Foreign Policy Choices.* He is a senior research associate at the Center for Philosophy and Public Policy.

Abraham M. Sirkin, a former member of the Policy Planning Staff of the U.S. Department of State, is a Washington consultant on international affairs. He served as counselor for public affairs at the American Embassy in Athens from 1967 to 1972 and has held U.S. government information posts in London, Tokyo, and South India.

Mark R. Wicclair received the Ph.D. in philosophy from Columbia University. He taught at Lafayette College for three years, and is currently an assistant professor of philosophy at West Virginia University.

William L. Wipfler, Ph.D., is presently director of the Human Rights Office, National Council of Churches, and was Latin American director from 1967 to 1977. He has traveled extensively through Latin America, where he lived for many years in the Dominican Republic and Costa Rica.

About the Editors

Peter G. Brown is director of the Center for Philosophy and Public Policy at the University of Maryland, where he also teaches courses in applied ethics. He received the Ph.D. in philosophy from Columbia University. He is co-editor of *Food Policy: The Responsibility of the United States in the Life and Death Choices* and of *Markets and Morals,* and is the author of monographs and a number of articles on public policy. Prior to founding the Center in 1976, Dr. Brown was a fellow in law and ethics at the Academy for Contemporary Problems, served as assistant vice president for research operations at the Urban Institute, and taught at St. John's College.

Douglas MacLean is a research associate at the Center for Philosophy and Public Policy at the University of Maryland, where he also teaches courses in applied ethics. He received the Ph.D. in philosophy from Yale University and has taught philosophy at Yale and Livingston College, Rutgers.